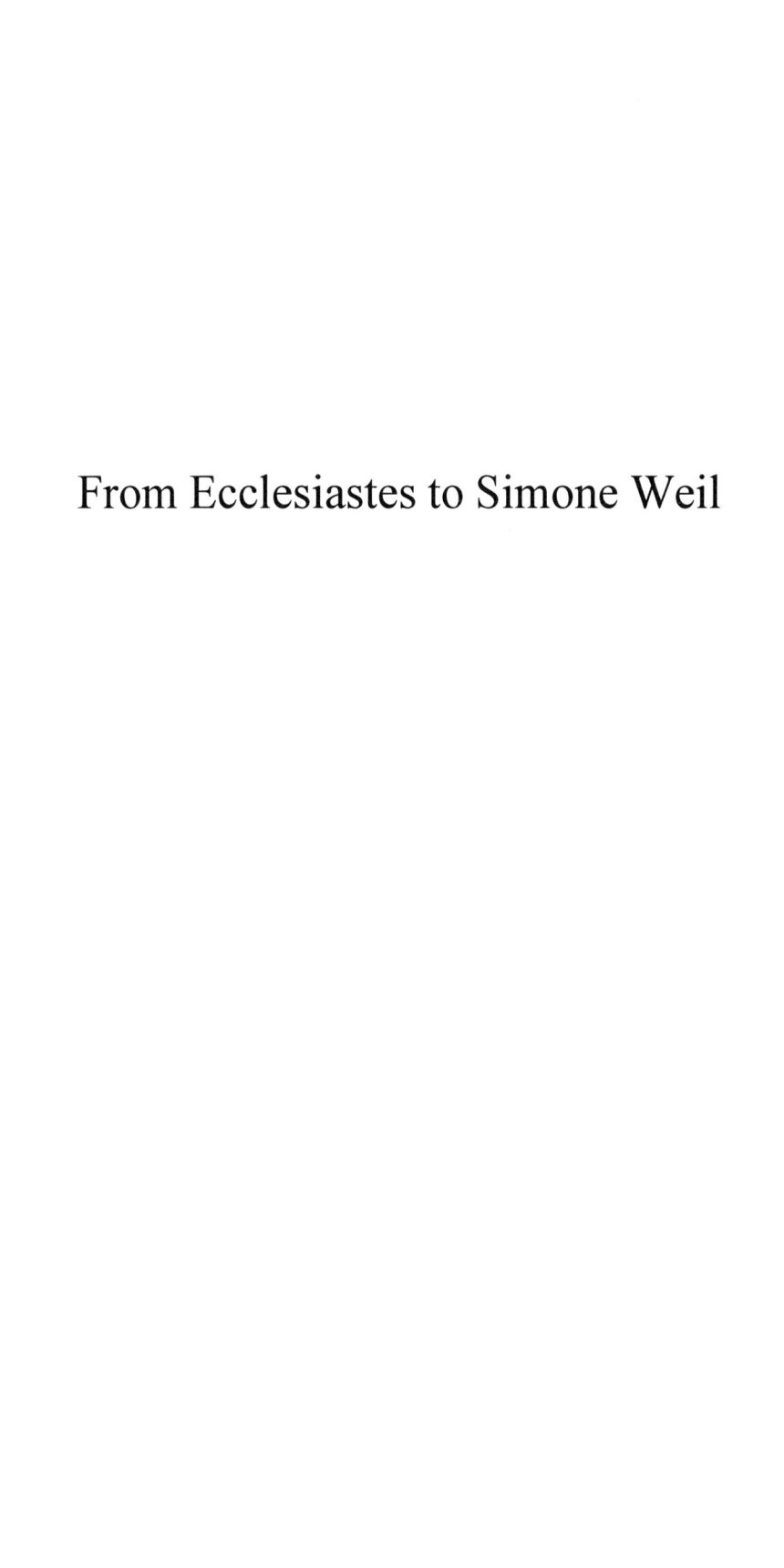

From Ecclesiastes to Simone Weil

From Ecclesiastes to Simone Weil

Varieties of Philosophical Spirituality

Ernest Rubinstein

FAIRLEIGH DICKINSON UNIVERSITY PRESS
Madison • Teaneck

Revised Standard Version of the Bible, copyright 1952 [second edition, 1971] by the Division of Christian Education of the National Council of Churches of Christ in the United States of America. Used by permission. All rights reserved.

Published by Fairleigh Dickinson University Press
Copublished by Rowman & Littlefield
4501 Forbes Boulevard, Suite 200, Lanham, Maryland 20706
www.rowman.com

16 Carlisle Street, London W1D 3BT, United Kingdom

Copyright © 2014 by Ernest Rubinstein

Cover image courtesy of Drew University. The image shows personifications of Philosophy and History, part of a stained glass window designed by English artist Henry Holiday in 1890, and installed over the entrance to the Drew University Library.

All rights reserved. No part of this book may be reproduced in any form or by any electronic or mechanical means, including information storage and retrieval systems, without written permission from the publisher, except by a reviewer who may quote passages in a review.

British Library Cataloguing in Publication Information Available

Library of Congress Cataloging-in-Publication Data

Rubinstein, Ernest.
From Ecclesiastes to Simone Weil : varieties of philosophical spirituality / Ernest Rubinstein.
pages cm.
Includes bibliographical references and index.
ISBN 978-1-61147-724-5 (cloth) -- ISBN 978-1-61147-725-2 (electronic)
1. Philosophical theology. 2. Philosophy. 3. Spirituality. I. Title.
BT40.R83 2014
141--dc23
                                                                                                   2014016964

∞™ The paper used in this publication meets the minimum requirements of American National Standard for Information Sciences Permanence of Paper for Printed Library Materials, ANSI/NISO Z39.48-1992.

Printed in the United States of America

In memory of Géza von Molnár, *z"l*, (1932-2001)
scholar, teacher, mentor

Itaque ubi in eam deduxi oculos intuitumque defixi, respicio nutricem meam, cuius ab adulescentia laribus obuersatus fueram, Philosophiam.
—Boethius, *Consolatio Philosophiae*

[Accordingly, when I had lifted my eyes and fixed my gaze upon her, I beheld my nurse, Philosophy, whose halls I had frequented from my youth up. —H. R. James, translator, 1874]

Contents

Acknowledgments		xi
Abbreviations		xiii
Preface		xv
1	Philosophy as Religion	1
2	Ecclesiastes	13
3	Plato	25
4	Lucretius and Marcus Aurelius	41
5	Descartes	59
6	Spinoza	75
7	Kant	91
8	Novalis	105
9	Hegel: *The Phenomenology of Spirit*	127
10	Kierkegaard	145
11	Emerson	163
12	William James	181
13	Bertrand Russell	205
14	Simone Weil	227
15	Conclusion: Philosophical Sensibility as Philosophical Spirituality	251
Bibliography		263
Index		271
About the Author		283

Acknowledgments

This book began as lecture notes for a class entitled, "Philosophical Spirituality," which I taught several times at the New York University School of Continuing and Professional Studies and at the New School University. I would like to thank the administrators of those schools for admitting the class to their curricula, and the students who enrolled and participated in the sessions. I would also like to thank my former library colleagues at Drew University, who together fashion an ideal work environment I cherished while I worked there, and who, with the endorsement of then Dean of Libraries, Dr. Andrew Scrimgeour, granted me a summer sabbatical in 2012 from my post there as Theological Librarian, to complete this book. I am grateful to Paul Baumann and his colleagues at *Commonweal* magazine for publishing my preliminary sketch of this book in the February 24, 2006 issue of their much esteemed periodical, and to Dr. Robin N. Lathangue of Sacred Heart of Peterborough College (Ontario, Canada) for his thorough reading and warm review of the book in manuscript. I thank Dr. Catherine Keller of Drew University's Theological School for the invitation she extended me to lead tours for Drew graduate students of philosophical iconography in the Morningside Heights neighborhood of New York City, and Dr. Virginia Burrus, of the Religion Department of Syracuse University, for her friendly inquiries into my progress in writing this book. Finally, I thank once again Dr. Andrew Scrimgeour, for the special interest he took in the book's publication, and Dr. Harry Keyishian, director of Fairleigh Dickinson University Press, for guiding the book through publication.

Abbreviations

1 Apol.	*First Apology*, by Justin Martyr
B. Shab.	Babylonian Talmud, Tractate Shabbat
1 Cor.	First Letter to the Corinthians (biblical text)
Col.	Letter to the Colossians (biblical text)
Deut.	Deuteronomy (biblical text)
Dial.	*Dialogue with Trypho*, by Justin Martyr
DM	*Discourse on Method*, by Descartes
E2p47s	*Ethics*, by Spinoza (part 2, proposition 47, scholium)
Ecc.	Ecclesiastes (biblical text)
EO	*Either/Or*, by Kierkegaard
Ex.	Exodus (biblical text)
Ez.	Ezekiel (biblical text)
FT	*Fear and Trembling*, by Kierkegaard
Gen.	Genesis (biblical text)
Isa.	Isaiah (biblical text)
Jer.	Jeremiah (biblical text)
Josh.	Joshua (biblical text)
JPS	Jewish Publication Society
Mal.	Malachi (biblical text)
Matt.	Gospel of Matthew (biblical text)
Med.	*Meditations*, by Descartes
Num.	Numbers (biblical text)
Phaed.	*Phaedrus*, by Plato
Ps.	Psalms (biblical text)
Rep.	*Republic*, by Plato
RN	*Rerum Natura* [*On the Nature of Things*], by Lucretius
RSV	Revised Standard Version of the Bible
TEI	*Treatise on the Emendation of the Intellect*, by Spinoza
TP	*Treatise on the Passions*, by Descartes

Preface

Philosophical therapy is undergoing a revival. It is a revival only because philosophy already functioned therapeutically in the ancient world, among the Stoics, Epicureans, Cynics and Platonists. For the medieval world, personified philosophy descended from on high to console sufferers, as it did Boethius, whose *Consolation of Philosophy* was popular reading in the Middle Ages. But now we have the American Philosophical Practitioners Association, and the International Society for Philosophy Practice, which serve as professional associations for philosophical counselors. These practitioners take Plato, Spinoza, and Kant out of the classroom and into the struggling lives of workaday people, where their philosophical writings were intended to have their most important effects, rather than in academic journals.

With the book classification system named for it, the Library of Congress acknowledges the emergence of therapy from philosophy by assigning psychology a place within the classification scheme in the midst of the section devoted to philosophy. In that way, the Library of Congress affirms a key part of philosophy's own self-conception, that it have practical implications. Indeed, book classification systems may themselves be seen as practical applications of a subfield within philosophy: epistemology. And librarianship itself has been cast as one line of work, among many others, that realize philosophical abstractions in some concrete way.[1]

The notion that philosophy is a kind of potential that needs to be realized is itself quite old within philosophical reflection. For some philosophers, like Spinoza, ideas were animated with a power to realize themselves. But for others, some agency outside ideas was understood to concretize them. This agency might be divine or human, and if human, might take the form of, for example, social activists, engineers, technologists, or artists—if not philosophers themselves.

Art is one of the more improbable contexts within which philosophy has become most literally sensible. Most of us recognize the philosophical references in Raphael's famous *School of Athens*, a picture that adorns some introductory philosophy textbooks. But philosophical iconography can take a variety of forms: pictures of historical philosophers; portraits or sculptures of what is understood to be the philosophical type; representations of philosophy personified.[2]

Within the history of western philosophy, certain philosophers seemed especially to draw the attention of portraitists. An example is Spinoza, who enjoys a whole book devoted to pictures of him. When we are told of this philosopher's "large, almond-shaped eyes, dark and of a lustrous shimmering softness," we long to see them, and are happy to learn that "representations of Spinoza bearing some resemblance to his original portraits but made by artists who relied chiefly on their imagination, are legion."[3] The philosophical type for its part has appeared throughout the history of art. Ancient Hellenistic philosophers wore a simple cloak that publicly identified them, so they were easy to represent in sculpture, some of which can be seen at New York's Metropolitan Museum of Art. The cloak implied poverty and detachment, much as a religious habit did in the medieval world. We have a modern transposition of the image in Edouard Manet's pair of paintings both entitled *The Philosopher*, and subtitled respectively *Beggar in a Cloak* and *Beggar with Oysters*—a far cry from the elegantly attired European philosopher, posing as Aristotle, Rembrandt portrayed in his *Aristotle Contemplating a Bust of Homer*—an intriguing image indeed, given the philosophical inheritance from Plato of distrust of Homer. Finally, we have from Boethius the self-contradictory portrait of Lady Philosophy, simultaneously tall and short, old and young, who inspired many a medieval artisan to try to fix her image in ink, paint, or glass. Lady Philosophy is a personification in line with earlier imaging of the liberal arts, dating back to Martianus Capella, of the early fifth century, whose *Marriage of Philology and Mercury*[4] was an allegorical narrative on all seven of the medieval liberal arts. In later pictorial renderings, Philosophy was sometimes portrayed as subsuming, culminating or by implication overseeing these arts.[5]

Perhaps unexpectedly, the iconography of philosophy draws us to yet another realization of philosophy that, thanks in many ways to Christianity, links intimately to art, namely spirituality, and the topic of this book: philosophical spirituality. For if we are seeking depictions of philosophy, either as an historic individual, a type, or a personification, the most likely place to find them is in churches. Given two hours of free time, anyone interested in these depictions would find many to ponder on a guided stroll through the Morningside Heights neighborhood of New York City. That does not surprise, given the dominating presence of Columbia University in that neighborhood. And the campus does indeed yield up to the curious seeker several inscribed namings of Plato on buildings, for example, Butler Library and Teachers College; a lovely building named for Philosophy itself, that a student critic of it praised for its "modulated . . . balance of brick and stone," its "unusually fine" wrought iron entrance and other marks of the "secure and delicate touch" that designed it;[6] in the courtyard fronting Philosophy Hall, a cast of one of the best-known depictions of the philosophic type, Rodin's *The Thinker*, whose energized posture at seeming rest recalls the contradictory nature of Lady Philosophy; and in the stunning chapel named for Saint Paul, a stained glass triptych at the altar showing the philosophers Paul addressed at Athens, some of them attired in the characteristically simple robe that identified them, and arrayed in elegant poses that suggest sinuosity of thought.

But it is the neighborhood churches, unaffiliated with the university, that offer up so much more, especially the two that mark the borders of the area: The Cathedral of Saint John the Divine to the southeast, Riverside Church to the northwest. Either on or within these churches we find images of Ecclesiastes, Plato, Descartes, Spinoza, Kant, Hegel, Emerson, and even Marcus Aurelius, the least probable, given his persecutions of the ancient church—all of whom are discussed in the following pages. We even find what the Columbia campus appears to withhold from us, a reference to philosophy personified, in the upper reaches of the Cathedral clerestories, where we see high above the bay devoted to education references to the seven liberal arts associated with a single amalgam of three images: a book, a scepter, and a ladder[7] —the traditional iconographic markers of Lady Philosophy, drawn from Boethius' classic text.[8]

A modest apartment building just north of Riverside Church supplies our last image here, which evokes the philosopher who also closes this book, Simone Weil. A plaque affixed to 549 Riverside Drive identifies that building as the home of French philosopher Simone Weil from July 6 to November 10, 1942. It quotes from her: "Attention is the rarest and purest form of generosity." That is the generosity we hope to bring here towards the fourteen philosophers discussed in this book, for an aspect of their work that is not always highlighted, but which makes of them a community over time, the spirituality implicit in their metaphysics, epistemology, logic, ethics, or aesthetics.

NOTES

1. For example, see Joan B. Fiscella, "Embedded Philosophy: A Case for Librarianship as Philosophy in Practice," *The International Journal of Applied Philosophy* 4 (Spring 1989): 61–66.

2. See Lucien Braun, *Iconographie et Philosophie: Essai de Definition d'un Champ de Recherche* (Strasbourg: Presses Universitaires de Strasbourg, 1994).

3. Samuel L. Millner, *The Face of Benedictus Spinoza* (New York: Machmadim Art Editions, 1946), 8, 49.

4. Martianus Capella, *The Marriage of Philology and Mercury*, tr. William Harris Stahl and Richard Johnson (New York: Columbia University Press, 1977).

5. Braun, *Iconographie et Philosophie*.

6. Robert Bowman Stewart, "Some Aspects of Campus Architecture," *The Columbia Varsity* (Dec. 12?, 1924), 10. Philosophy Hall, from 1910, was designed, as most of the older campus buildings, by McKim, Mead and White.

7. In the upper windows of the Education Bay, the cusps surrounding the figure of Christ show "the time-honored symbols of philosophy . . . a book and scepter, and a ladder." Edward Hagaman Hall, *A Guide to the Cathedral Church of Saint John the Divine*

in the City of New York, 17th ed. (New York: the Dean and Chapter of the Cathedral Church, 1965), 53.

8. According to Boethius, Lady Philosophy holds books and a scepter, and a ladder is depicted rising from the Greek letter Pi (standing for practical philosophy) embroidered on the bottom of her garment, up to the letter Theta (standing for theoretical philosophy), embroidered on the top. Boethius, *The Consolation of Philosophy*, tr. V. E. Watts (New York: Penguin, 1969), 36.

ONE
Philosophy as Religion

Philosophy, we have all but forgotten, is a type of love. It is the love of wisdom. Some may say that such a love is too abstract to count for love. But they are wrong. We can fall in love with a philosophy as much as with a person. Philosophies extend their worldviews as lovers do their arms, to embrace and shelter. We inhabit them as we do the touch, and smiles, and brightened eyes, of our particular friend.

Judaism and Christianity must resign themselves to the fact that, for all their claims to channel love, it is philosophy that incorporates the word into its very name. But they are right to suspect philosophy's love. The love of wisdom rests, as Plato showed in the Symposium (202–204), on lack of wisdom; whereas the love that the monotheisms preach overflows from its source in God towards human beings. The categorical distinction between the divine and the human which the mono- of monotheism partially implies sets the stage for love's remarkable triumph over that very separation, as the Song of Songs so startlingly proclaims: "Love is strong as death" (Song 8:6 RSV[1]). At just this juncture, western philosophy and religion part ways. For neither reason nor common experience, philosophy's stock in trade, find much evidence in reality of monotheism's love. And the God philosophy would take us to does not necessarily reside at the other end of a categorical distinction from us; or if it does, philosophy will explore avenues of approach to it that do not presume that scandal of particularity: historic revelation.

Western philosophy and religion unfold from different presuppositions of interest. On at least one account of its origins, religion begins in story. The rereading (or retelling) implied by one etymology of the very word religion (from *relegere*, to reread) is centrally of stories. Stories enacted are rituals; rituals repeated shape community and personal religious experience; interpretations of story yield doctrine and ethics. But philosophy, Aristotle tells us, begins in wonder. And for all the defined subdisciplines into which philosophy resolves—metaphysics, epistemology, ethics, logic, aesthetics—the persistence within it of wonder continually undermines the declarative voice in which individual philosophies are written. The famous portrait of Lady Philosophy that Boethius paints, simultaneously old and young, tall and short, theoretical and practical,[2] does indeed inspire wonder and elicits a response more interrogative than indicative, more contemplative than narrative, more fluid than set. A religion's stories, by contrast, hold its practitioners to an identity predefined for them, and attach to them a past beyond their own, personal beginnings. An identity so prescribed simultaneously fulfills and confines. When the confinement has become too burdensome, philosophy holds out the prospect of other-storied or even un-storied freedom.

In the respective unfoldings of religion and philosophy, points of intersection occur. God is the signal actor of biblical history, and also an object of philosophical reflection, even demonstration. Ethics is simultaneously a religious extraction from story and a subdiscipline within philosophy. The experience of the sacred may be shaped by religious ritual or by philosophic contemplation. These three points of intersection—God, ethics, experience—mark the sites of some of the most enduring stress between philosophy and religion. And they fashion between them an organic nexus of questions that religion and philosophy differently answer. Ethics poses the question which is perhaps the most troubling of all for monotheistic religion, the one on which it most often founders in the eyes of prospective or former believers, namely, how an all powerful, good God can countenance pointless suffering. This question opens naturally onto the neighboring one at issue between religion and philosophy: what is the nature of God? And this question, in turn, invites the last, which asks to understand the role of experience and reason in fostering relation with the Divine, however that nature is understood.

The drama of the diverging interplay between philosophy and religion, as they answer these questions, shows up most dramatically when philosophy, like religion, presented itself most publicly as a life-guide, as it did in the ancient world, rather than a purely intellectual engagement. As two scholars in particular, Pierre Hadot and Martha Nussbaum,[3] have emphasized in their research, the Hellenistic schools of Stoicism, Epicureanism, and Platonism competed with each other, as well as with the religions, for life adherents (in a way that our modern schools of empiricism and rationalism, for example, do not). Ancient Judaism and Christianity took themselves to either refute or supersede philosophy. And through the philosophical and religious texts that survive from the ancient world we can recover some of the intensity of the contest between them, especially as it shows not only in the different ways they answer our three questions, but in the awareness each evinces of the other's opposing response.

A rich context for observing ancient rabbinic Judaism's response to philosophy is the Midrash, which contains many stories of encounter between rabbis and Hellenistic philosophers. Like the more famous stories of encounter between Jesus and Pharisees in the New Testament, these are contest stories in which the superior reasoning or wit of the one party defeats the inimical intentions of the other. For ancient Judaism, philosophy was more than an intellectual challenge; it was a life-threat, as appears from one story of contest between rabbi and philosopher in which the philosopher admits to wishing to destroy Judaism.[4] And to the extent that worldviews undermine each other's presuppositions, they are indeed enemies. In process of denying that the divine goodness could be responsible for anything evil, Plato initiated a stream of thought that detached the world from origins in God, in direct counter to biblical thought. In one of the contest stories, Judaism reads onto philosophy a challenge to its own creation doctrine: a philosopher dismisses creation on grounds that the God of Genesis 1 had ready at hand the materials with which he fashioned the world, to which the rabbi replies that God created, or perhaps pre-created, these too.[5] But Judaism acknowledges the weight of the challenge to creation that evil is in the story it preserves of one of its own great, apostatizing teachers, the infamous Elisha ben Abuyya, who so "othered" himself from Judaism that he goes by the epithet, *Aher*, or Other. According to one of the stories about him, he lost his faith in the God of Israel when he witnessed an observance of ritual law that brought death to its pious practitioner, and, conversely, a defiance of ritual law from which its rebellious practitioner emerged unscathed.[6] Judaism would develop responses to this challenge; but to its great credit, it was capable of presenting the challenge of this story without resolution, as though to allow its audience to experience the force of it in their depths, where it could, and did, open onto paths leading out of Judaism entirely.

A philosophical response to evil was to deny that God intervened significantly in daily human affairs. This view, too, has origins in Plato, whose idea of the Good was beyond debasing contact with the material world, whose best hope was to copy or behold it. Though creation doctrine is one of the most blatant claims of the monotheisms that God directly connects with the world, it serves as prelude to their even bolder claims of historic revelation. One of the first Platonists on record to directly challenge Christian creation doctrine was Celsus, who believed that Genesis 1 reduced God to the status of "a common workman."[7] Celsus heaps scorn on the biblical anthropomorphisms, which, in the intimate match they make of form to content, image God in worldly ways, not so much to identify God with the world, which would be idolatry, but to underscore how much God does indeed act on and in the world. Jewish and Christian doctrines of revelation are even more scandalous: "they say that God has form, namely the form of the Logos, who became flesh in Jesus Christ. But we know that God is without shape . . . [and] one wonders why he sent this spirit of his only to some little backwater village of the Jews."[8] By contrast, "the God of the philosophers . . . cannot be comprehended in terms of attributes or human experience, contrary to what the Christians teach."[9]

Part of the dispute between ancient philosophy and the monotheisms was on the knowability of God. Celsus knows the Christian critique of the Platonic Goodness, that it is "unnamable . . . [and] cannot be comprehended in terms of attributes or human experience,"[10] and so is fundamentally unknowable. His rendition of the critique echoes Paul's speech to the Athenians, as told in the book of Acts, where the apostle assesses the deficiency of a Greek god precisely on grounds that it is unknown (Acts 17:23–31). The Platonic answer to that charge, as Celsus presents it, is that the philosopher, under Plato's guidance, is "led out of this darkness into the light,"[11] where he does indeed behold God in a vision, which may indeed transcend human knowledge, a claim common enough even among later distinctly Christian mystics. When Celsus adds, disparagingly, that the Christian God by contrast is known through his having "cast his spirit into a human body and journeyed down to earth,"[12] he is not far off from a central claim of the Nicene Creed, though he misses the importance nuance of the creedal view that Christ was not simply inspirited, but begotten, by God.

This debate on the knowability of God introduces the last and chief point of dispute between the philosophers and the monotheists we will consider here, namely *how* God is known. As the distinction Pascal later neatly framed between the God of the philosophers and the God of Abraham, Isaac, and Jacob[13] suggests, we may expect the manner of knowing these Gods to differ markedly. Celsus insists "one ought first to follow reason as a guide before accepting any belief."[14] And the problem with the Christians is that they do not, nor do they entertain reasoned questions about their belief. "Their favorite expressions are 'Do not ask questions, just believe!' and 'Your faith will save you!'"[15] And this time, the Christian who Celsus appears to have been reading is Tertullian, whose famous battle cry against the philosophers was, "It is by all means to be believed, because it is absurd."[16] The Midrash offers a window onto a parallel debate between Judaism and philosophy, when it tells a story of Rabbi Gamaliel, who got the better of a philosopher on the curious debate of the gestation period of snakes. The philosopher knew the answer, from having studied snakes in their natural state for seven years; whereas Gamaliel was able in a matter of minutes to deduce it from sacred scripture.[17] The absurdity of the answer, that it takes seven years, ought not detract from an implication of this midrash, that if all knowledge of the natural world is inferable from divine revelation, then all the more so is all knowledge of God; whereas the implication of the philosopher's point is that, alongside the reason that Celsus esteems, natural (as opposed to supernatural) human experience also provides an avenue of approach to knowledge, whether of snakes or deity. Such independence from revelation and the bonds of tradition it forges over time becomes a point of pride for philosophy in the debate that unfolds between it and monotheism. But this is a point on which St. Paul already challenged it, very early on, when he suggested that philosophers were as bound by tradition as Christians are (Col. 2:8). And Tertullian would add that, to the extent that the pride the philosophers feel in reason and experience turns on the presumed universality of the inferences that can be drawn from them, it is a false pride, on account of the "many sharp disagreements" that exist among the philosophers themselves.[18]

Part of Tertullian's complaint against philosophy is that its conflicts are with more than itself, but also with medicine, which shares with it a curative role. His implicit pairing of the two under the larger rubric of therapy points up for us moderns how much, for the ancients, philosophy presumed to cure humans of unhappiness, a rarity among its claims for itself today. Many of the philosophical spiritualities treated here subsume a therapy, a recipe for happiness or at least a means of coping with misery, but they do not necessarily presume to eliminate unhappiness or even deem that desirable. An ancient book called simply *Problems*, and falsely attributed to Aristotle asks: "Why is it that all those who have become eminent in philosophy or politics or poetry or the arts are clearly of an atrabilious [melancholic] temperament?"[19] The question is a problem because melancholy was presumed to enervate, but here it actually seems to stimulate creative activity. The association between philosophy and melancholy remains, as Rodin seemed to teach with his famous statue, *The Thinker*; but neither is melancholy necessarily divorced from spirituality (philosophical or otherwise). Melancholy was either a reality or theme (or both) for Kierkegaard, William James, Bertrand Russell, and Simone Weil. Philosophical proximity to the sacred does not necessarily eliminate all pain. But our philosophers do not agree on this.

Tertullian's complaint about philosophy, that there was too much disagreement in it, has been voiced by many others, including Justin Martyr, Boethius, and Simone Weil. If Lady Philosophy's garment is torn, according to Boethius, that is because of all the infighting among her practitioners. And yet she remains enough of a whole to appear before the prisoner Boethius a single figure bearing her balms of Platonic-Stoic comfort. Much of the purpose of this book is to answer Tertullian, who lacked the retrospective vantage point of 2,000 years of history, from which to look back upon philosophy, its practitioners, and what may indeed be, as St. Paul might have called it, a philosophical tradition of spirituality, but treated here appreciatively, as Paul would not have. This book is an exercise in the articulation of what comparative religionist Wilfred Cantwell Smith called, "*philosophia* as one of the religious traditions of humankind,"[20] constructed here from a sampling of philosophical systems from the West (with occasional references to the East, where philosophy and religion are much more in sync). In contrast to the connotation of the Latin word, the attempt here is to uncover a common spirituality among philosophies that are distinctly exoteric, and that lie open to the scrutiny of anyone who chooses to study them in, for example, academic course work. Indeed, the hope here is precisely to uncover in some of the standard fare of philosophy survey classes a spirituality, or lived orientation towards the divine, that, as philosophy has increasingly professionalized, has all but disappeared from view in the academy.

The concept of spirituality has surely become what Descartes might have called one of the most unclear and indistinct ideas of our time. Its original meaning, within the modern Catholic Church where it first arose, connoted the different foci of prayerful attention within the religious orders. But in recent years the term has exploded into a range of meanings. Pierre Hadot suggests that what spirituality most generally connotes is "the individual's entire psychism . . . within the perspective of the Whole."[21] Its opposite is an inconsequential intellectualism. But in the context of this book, spirituality means more than just entirety and wholes; it presupposes a concept of the divine, or sacred. In these chapters, a spiritual life is understood to be one lived in proximity to or in orientation towards the divine, taken most broadly (so as to subsume a diversity of philosophical specifications of it) as the source of all being. Spirituality presupposes that proximity to the divine is maximally desirable for human beings, a condition of our *soteria*[22] or wellbeing. But spirituality, here, also incorporates from the ancient concept of the sacred — which implies, from its Hebrew roots, separation from the ordinary — a measure of difficulty to realizing that proximity. Emile Durkheim famously postulated that there was no greater separation between opposites than that between the sacred and profane.[23] This separation need not manifest metaphysically; the sacred, or divine, may be so much in our midst as to subsume us in it; but then the separation must manifest epistemologically, as a distance from our knowing the divine — otherwise the philosophy that would take us there has no work to do. Experientially, there may not be much difference between the approach of the sacred across an ontological or epistemological distance. The thesis of this book is that there is a western philosophical tradition of spirituality that incorporates both these views of the sacred and a range of understandings on how it is available to and through exoteric human experience and thought. In terms of a typology proposed by Charles Taylor, this book adumbrates a "non-exclusive humanism," that is, a humanism that acknowledges from a realm of either ontological or epistemological transcendence "the solicitations of the spiritual — be they in nature, in art, in some contact with religious faith, or in a sense of God which may break through."[24]

Fourteen philosophers supply our evidence. They come from antiquity and the modern age. If we do not include Boethius, whose *Consolation of Philosophy* gave us Lady Philosophy, a beloved icon of the Middle Ages, it is because her comforts for Boethius amalgamate teachings we will already have explored in Plato and Marcus Aurelius. Indeed the whole Neo-Platonic tradition, fruitful for a thorough treatment of philosophical spirituality as it is, does not figure here, if only because its aspiring (and, to some, inspiring) spirituality, which its daunting metaphysics channels, is already implicit—to adopt the self-conception of the Neo-Platonists themselves—in Plato himself. The European Middle Ages does indeed offer up instances of philosophy aspiring to spiritual self-sufficiency—the followers of Averroes among Jews and Christians illustrate this—but their work, admirable as it is within the context of its day and within the larger framework of the history of ideas, is so indebted to the philosophy of antiquity and, beyond that, so constrained in its expression by the dogmatic and communal environments of monotheism, that it does not, apart from its historical interest, and the stimulant it provides to Jewish and Christian theologians revisioning their respective faiths today, readily proffer itself for recovery to a twenty-first century philosophical spirituality. And so, beyond antiquity, the philosophers on view here come from the modern west and chiefly the four national traditions of French, German, English, and American philosophy—the traditions that supply most of the names encountered in an introductory class in the history of western philosophy. Some students of that history have attempted broad characterizations of differences within those traditions. William James, for example, who helped found the American tradition characterizes the other three: "The English mind and the French mind, thank heaven . . . show fewer obvious falsities and monstrosities than that of Germany."[25] The *Oxford Companion to Philosophy* supports in separate articles devoted to each, the common impression that among these nationalities of philosophy, the German is distinctive for its idealism, the English for its empiricism, the French for its rationalism, the American for its pragmatism.[26] Insofar as James was right that, within the philosophical traditions, idealism is closest to religion,[27] then the German tradition, much as James maligned it, allies the most naturally with spirituality as understood in these chapters, and so figures the largest in them.[28] Simone Weil exhibits within the French tradition a methodical, if anguished, variation on Descartes, while pantheistic Emerson, thinking towards pluralistic William James, foretells a humanistic pragmatism in American philosophy. Bertrand Russell is our sole representative of English philosophy—the Church of England having so peaceably accommodated the philosophic temper that it did not, for the most part, need to define a separate space from religion of its own.

The choice of the particular fourteen philosophers examined here is not definitive but neither is it arbitrary. Even agnostic Bertrand Russell concedes that Plato is an originating point for western spirituality. And by philosophical consensus, the Stoics and Epicureans, represented here by Marcus Aurelius and Lucretius, contributed especially through their therapies to that evolving spirituality and remain, for some, highly relevant today. Among the moderns, Descartes is indispensable for shifting the context of philosophical spirituality away from metaphysics towards epistemology; and Spinoza, for restating the metaphysical in a thoroughgoing monism that is, for some, a paradigm of philosophical spirituality. Kant reasserts the epistemological bias in ways that shape much succeeding philosophy. Novalis and Hegel are alternatively romantic and idealist responses to lacunae in Kant. Kierkegaard is our first full stop to German idealism and introduction of a non-rationalist spirituality. The same movement from idealism to non-rationalism appears in the American philosophical sequence from Emerson to William James. Bertrand Russell supplies an example of English spirituality and an instance of the fracture the horrors of the twentieth century introduce to the concept itself, which must now accommodate frightful realities of suffering and fragmentation. Simone Weil's spirituality of affliction registers most especially the traumas of mid-twentieth century Europe, and illustrates how remnants of the rationalist-idealist tradition can survive in their wake. She also provides an occasion to review the whole sweep of the philosophical history under consideration here.

What the philosophers explicitly say about God or the sacred is certainly important, especially among the metaphysicians, like Plato and Spinoza. But where epistemology reigns, the claims for God may be less interesting or helpful for spirituality and in those cases, of Descartes, Kant, and Hegel, for example, we are especially interested in spiritualities extractable from between the lines. The philosophers do not necessarily themselves draw attention to the most spiritually fruitful areas of their thought. Spirituality may hide in the crevices of a metaphysics (as in the case of Lucretius), an epistemology or ethics (as in the case of Kant), or an aesthetics (as in the case of two who help us interpret William James and Bertrand Russell—Henry James and Vincent Van Gogh, respectively).

Though religion—whether biblical, Greco-Roman, Christian, or Jewish—is the significant other to all our philosophers here, the relation is not always tense. Some philosophers, such as Plato, Lucretius, and Spinoza, define themselves enough against it that their relation to it must figure in our account. Others, such as Ecclesiastes, Kierkegaard, Emerson, and Weil, have a more dialectically complex relation with it that will need some teasing out of their thought. Religion, for Emerson, William James, and Simone Weil is a positive resource for aspects of their philosophical spirituality. For still others, such as Marcus Aurelius, Descartes, and Novalis, it is not engagingly confrontational enough to need much comment; while for Bertrand Russell, the interest of his philosophy for spirituality really excludes all that he wrote specifically (and negatively) about religion.

Bertrand Russell is rather an extreme instance of tension between philosophy and religion. In the modern west, between Europe and the United States, both philosophy and religion experience marginalizations that naturally conjoin them, as indeed many academic departments of American colleges do. Christianity is notably diminished in Europe today, where philosophy still enjoys some public prestige. Conversely, while Christianity still thrives in the United States, Alexis de Tocqueville observed of America that "in no country in the civilized world is less attention paid to philosophy."[29] What verifies his claim still today is the paucity of public references to philosophy in the civic life of the United States and its relative absence in the iconography of public buildings. So slight a role for it puts it in unexpectedly friendly relation with its religious Other which can condescend to accommodate it in its own public spaces. As already noted, it is striking how many philosophers, some of them markedly hostile to Christianity, are represented in two of the great and neighboring churches of New York City—Riverside Church and the Cathedral of Saint John the Divine—including, within the clerestories of the Cathedral, a reference to Lady Philosophy and the liberal arts associated with her.[30] Medieval Christianity took philosophy for its handmaid, which, far from diminishing it, identified it with no less a figure than the Virgin Mary (handmaid to the Lord, according to Luke 1:38), which in turn may help to explain associations of the Virgin with wisdom. But for us the Cathedral image, recalling as it does the medieval trivium of language arts and quadrivium of mathematical arts, both flourishing under philosophy's aegis, also points up the contrasting methods of procedure within philosophy itself, inclining in some hands towards science, in others towards literature, and still others towards both, in uneasy balance. In the first group fall Descartes, Spinoza, Kant, Hegel, and Russell; in the second, Novalis, Kierkegaard, and Emerson; in the third, Plato (the poetic geometer), Ecclesiastes (the literary empiricist), Lucretius (the scientific poet), Weil (playwright, poet, and philosopher of science), and William James when interpreted in conversation with his brother Henry (master novelist).

All these philosophers are deceased. That is to our advantage at least insofar as we are seeking guidance towards the sacred from beyond ourselves. As Hubert Dreyfus and Sean Dorrance Kelly suggest in their book, *All Things Shining*, about meaning generally, it seems to need to come in some sense from outside us, for what we ourselves construct or adapt to ourselves has "no authority over the maker."[31] What the dead supply is already *ipso facto* from another world, even if it does not exist. Philosophy, of course, did not end with the date of the last work under consideration here, Bertrand Russell's *History of Western Philosophy*, from 1945. But World War II does make a convenient termination date for this study, whose concluding figures, Russell and Weil, would insist that preoccupation with the sacred, philosophically considered in our own times, draws significant nurture from the sanctifying Past. Many other available works by living philosophers and scholars of philosophy continue the story and creatively shape it towards the future.[32]

NOTES

1. All Bible translations to follow are from the Revised Standard Version (RSV).
2. Boethius, *Consolation of Philosophy*, trans. V. E. Watts (New York: Penguin, 1969), 35–36 [1:1].
3. See for example, Pierre Hadot, *Philosophy as a Way of Life*, trans. Michael Chase (Malden, MA: Blackwell, 1995) and Martha Nussbaum, *The Therapy of Desire: Theory and Practice in Hellenistic Ethics* (Princeton, NJ: Princeton University Press, 1994).
4. Yalkut, Mal. 587. Find all the midrashic texts cited here in The *Book of Legends: Sefer Ha-Aggadah*, ed. H. N. Bialik and Y. H. Ravnitzky, trans. William Braude (New York: Schocken Books, 1992). Find this excerpt from Yalkut on p. 383 of *Book of Legends*.
5. Genesis Rabbah 1:9. Find this on p. 6 of *Book of Legends*.
6. Ecclesiastes Rabbah 7:8. Find this on p. 244 of *Book of Legends*.
7. Celsus, *On the True Doctrine: A Discourse against the Christians*, tr. R. Joseph Hoffmann (New York: Oxford University Press, 1987), 103. "Celsus' *True Doctrine* was the first systematic critique by an opponent who was both well-educated and well informed concerning Christianity." Robert Hauck, "Omnes Contra Celsum?" *The Second Century* 5:4 (1985/1986): 211. For another interpretation of Celsus' critique of Christianity, see Peter van Nuffelen, "Celsus and Christian Superstition," in *Rethinking the Gods: Philosophical Readings of Religion in the Post-Hellenistic Period* (New York: Cambridge University Press, 2011).
8. Celsus, *On the True Doctrine*, 103, 105.
9. Ibid., 103–104.
10. Ibid.
11. Ibid., 104
12. Ibid.
13. Blaise Pascal, "The Memorial," in *Pensées and Other Writings*, tr. Honor Levi (New York: Oxford University Press, 1995), 178.
14. Celsus, *On the True Doctrine*, 54.
15. Ibid.
16. Tertullian, *On the Flesh of Christ*, trans. Dr. Holmes, The Ante-Nicene Fathers, 3 (Grand Rapids, MI: Eerdmans, 1951), ch. 57. In fact, though nothing is known for certain on this point, it was probably Tertullian who responded to Celsus. A puzzle of early Christian apologetics is that it appears to have taken so long—until Origen's time—for a Christian response to Celsus to appear. Hauck, "Omnes Contra Celsum," 213.
17. Genesis Rabbah 20:4. Find this on p. 774 of the *Book of Legends*.
18. Tertullian, *On the Soul*, trans. Edwin Quain, in *Tertullian, Apologetical Works and Minucius Felix, Octavius* (New York: Fathers of the Church, 1950), ch. 2, para. 6.
19. Problemata 30.1 in *The Works of Aristotle*, vol. 7, trans. E. S. Forster (Oxford, England: Clarendon, 1927)), 953a.
20. See Wilfred Cantwell Smith, "Philosophia as one of the Religious Traditions of Humankind," in *Modern Culture from a Comparative Perspective*, ed. John Burbidge (Albany: State University of New York Press, 1997). Smith suggests that what chiefly characterizes philosophy so understood is idealism, humanism, and rationality.
21. Pierre Hadot, *Philosophy as a Way of Life*, 82.
22. With appreciations to Rabbi Alvin Reines, z"l, for preferring this Greek term to "happiness" in his lectures at Hebrew Union College on Spinoza and Freud in the fall

of 1982. My notes record his definition of soteria: "intrinsically meaningful existence, in which all moods that annihilate the meaningfulness of existence are overcome." The value of this term over "happiness" is the greater breadth and depth its Greek context gives it, accommodating as it does a presence of pain.

23. Emile Durkheim, *Elementary Forms of the Religious Life*, trans. Joseph Ward Swain (New York: Free Press, 1915), 53.

24. Charles Taylor, *A Secular Age* (Cambridge, MA: Harvard University Press, 2007), 254, 360.

25. William James, *A Pluralistic Universe* (Rockville, MD: Arc Manor, 2008), 13. Originally published: (New York: Longmans Green, 1909). http://www.googlebooks.com.

26. *Oxford Companion to Philosophy*, 2nd ed., ed. Ted Honderich (New York: Oxford University Press, 2005).

27. William James, *Pragmatism* (New York: Longmans Green, 1907), 12.

28. And in lieu of the German figures here treated many others might have been included, for instance, Karl Jaspers, who developed what was explicitly a "philosophical faith." See his *Philosophy of Existence*, trans. Richard Grabay (Philadelphia: University of Pennsylvania Press, 1971).

29. Tocqueville, *Democracy in America*, vol. 2, ed. Phillips Bradley (New York: Vintage, 1945), [3].

30. See Preface.

31. Hubert Dreyfus and Sean Dorrance Kelly, *All Things Shining: Reading the Western Classics to Find Meaning in a Secular Age* (New York: Free Press, 2011), 142.

32. For instance, the work of Robert Solomon on skeptical spirituality in his *Spirituality for the Skeptic: The Thoughtful Love of Life* (New York: Oxford, 2002); Charles Taylor on non-exclusive humanism in his *A Secular Age* (Cambridge, MA: Harvard University Press, 2007); Robert Corrington on ecstatic naturalism in his *Nature's Sublime: An Essay in Aesthetic Naturalism* (Lanham, MD: Lexington Books, 2013); and John Caputo on Derrida in *The Prayers and Tears of Jacques Derrida: Religion without Religion* (Bloomington IN: Indiana University Press, 1997), among many others. For a look at how philosophers' lives have been informed by their thought, see James Miller, *Examined Lives: From Socrates to Nietzsche* (New York: Farrar, Straus and Giroux, 2011).

TWO
Ecclesiastes

An endearing feature of Judaism is that it preserves within it stories and rituals that undermine its own self-conception. An actual existence of such a rabbi as Elisha ben Abuyya is less interesting than the memorialization of him in the Midrash. His presence is not singular, but translates into the religion at the point of its broadest base: its liturgy. For at Passover, a holiday that continues to draw observance from even the most secular Jews, one of the children ritually positioned at the Seder table is "evil," in the sense that Elisha was, by distancing himself from the tradition. The tradition acknowledges its distanced members and carves out spaces for them, even despite themselves. But it does so even earlier than the Midrash, in its foundational scripture, by including there a text as radically different and distancing from its companions as Ecclesiastes.

But the tradition is not content merely to include Ecclesiastes in its canon: it presses it forward into its ritual at a crucial point in the liturgical year, at Sukkot, when the cycle of Torah readings, extending over the first five books of Hebrew scripture, the Torah, from Genesis to Deuteronomy, is about to conclude. Ecclesiastes is ritually chanted in the synagogue during Sukkot, in anticipation of Simchat Torah, when the cycle of Torah readings ends and re-begins, by concluding the ritual reading of Deuteronomy and re-beginning that of Genesis. Sandwiched between those two framing pillars of Torah, Ecclesiastes cannot but appear as a corrosive commentary on them. For Deuteronomy, which ends the cycle of readings, has throughout the summer been proclaiming its sunny self-certainties over the role of God in our lives, that God's actions follow a reliable pattern of promise and fulfillment. This is the pattern that infuses Jewish history with meaning, explains the suffering there, and offers hope of redemption. Moses acts in this book to personify its confidence, which stands out all the more in him for the striking contrast it makes to the self-doubt he showed in Exodus, at his call. His charge to the people, poised before the Promised Land, is bold and purposive: "Behold, I have set the land before you; go in and take possession" (Deut 1:8 RSV), and his assurances, unfaltering, that God is sufficient to guide their lives: "And now, O Israel, give heed to the statutes and the ordinances, which I teach you, and do them; that you may live" (Deut. 4:1). The claim that rewards follow on obedience, punishments on disobedience, occurs many times in the ensuing chapters. The rewards promised for obedience include: possession of land, abundant harvests, long life, physical health, progeny, and power over enemies and other nations. Nature itself, by God's agency, rewards obedience with life-giving rain. The punishments for disobedience include: dispossession, exile, enslavement, disease, and destruction. Nature withholds its blessings. Natural expectations based on ordinary reliable causal links, like those between planting and harvesting, marrying and loving, begetting and rearing, are frustrated.

The tone of the first two chapters of Ecclesiastes suggests a longing after just such certainties as Deuteronomy offers. Ecclesiastes lacks all reference to the sanctity of Israel's calling, or of its land, and shows very little interest in its law. But it does hold within its worldview a desideratum that is as important to it as those more ethno-centered values are to Torah, namely: wisdom. The difference is that this value does not offer itself as an assured consequence of purposeful behavior or striving. It does not necessarily come in response to the quest for it. Ecclesiastes has purposefully sought wisdom, as well as many material things. And the activist stance of Deuteronomy appears in the references Ecclesiastes makes to doing (Ecc. 2:1) and seizing (2:3), and perhaps the often repeated word for profit, *yitron*, echoes some of Deuteronomy's confidence in rewards. But it is as though Ecclesiastes echoes just enough of Deuteronomy to establish the older book as its target, upon which it brings down the full force of its negating judgment when, in refrains and paraphrase as relatively frequent within it as the doctrine of promise and fulfillment is in its tradition-making predecessor, it pronounces: "Vanity of vanities, all is vanity" (Ecc. 1:2). By the end of his life, the average human will have "spent all his days in darkness and grief, in much vexation and sickness and resentment" (Ecc. 5:16). These evils do not follow any pattern that allows us to control or avoid them. In the ubiquity of pain, both oppressor and oppressed suffer. There is no option for perfect righteousness. Even the seeming innocence of hard work is tainted by the wish to surpass a neighbor (Ecc 4:4), as though flatly to violate the last of the Deuteronomic Ten Commandments (5:18). There is no connection between the moral evils of the heart and the natural evils of life. The one does not punish the other (as Deuteronomy would have it). The fate of the righteous and the wicked is the same. This is so much true that we should hardly wonder if the wicked flourish and the righteous suffer. Material prosperity does not reward goodness, nor does suffering or oppression purify the soul (Ecc 7:7). Where the wise suffer, their wisdom occurs despite, not because of, their suffering.

Deuteronomy's promise of progeny to the obedient man opens a way for his children's good fortune to compensate for the lack of his own. But in Ecclesiastes' world, chance blocks this path too. The upsets and interferences in relations between parents and children that, according to Deuteronomy, punish wickedness, are in Ecclesiastes' world arbitrary occurrences. A rich man's wealth perishes before his son can inherit it, or falls to a stranger, or to a fool. Ecclesiastes finds no hopeful continuities stretching through time. Death is the stark end of our own lives and we do not know what will succeed us. Wisdom does not pass from one generation to another. No memories link the present to the past, nor will any link the future to what is now present. In general, our expectations are confounded. The break in natural and reliable causal chains, which only arises in Deuteronomy as punishment, is ordinary experience in Ecclesiastes, and defines the world as we know it.

And now, to complete this picture of rejection of one of the tradition's dearest teachings, that God providentially oversees the world towards human good, the cycle of Torah readings positions the very idea of creation itself, as presented in Genesis 1, to suffer the same merciless scrutiny at Ecclesiastes' hand. For it is difficult not to read the opening verses of Ecclesiastes as a judgmental commentary on the doctrine of creation as we have it from Genesis. Genesis recounts the origins of wind, earth, seas, and sun. The wind is God's spirit hovering over the face of the waters; the earth supplies the ground on which life begins; the sea, the home for fish; the sun, the divisions between day and night and between the seasons. And now Ecclesiastes comments: If the earth is created to support life, its continual abiding now merely underscores how fragile and non-abiding all that lives upon it is. If the sun was created to establish the seasons, its principal functions now are to mark one of the several limits on human endeavor, which all occur under it, and to endlessly rise and set. If the seas were to be emblems of fullness, teeming with life, they are now metaphors of insatiable longing, by receiving waters that never fill them. And the wind, linked to the primal spirit of God by the same Hebrew word, *ruach*, is as inscrutable now as God has always been. It turns endlessly in circuits, but can never be caught or harnessed. Ecclesiastes draws from nature one of our most enduring metaphors of pointlessness: striving after wind. Genesis 1 pronounces a resounding good on all that it recounts. But the endless cycles of Ecclesiastes 1 accomplish little else than confirm that "all things are full of weariness" (Ecc 1:8). If Deuteronomy loves to recall the past—"For ask now of the days that are past" (Deut 4:32)—Ecclesiastes is simply bored by it. Events in time repeat endlessly, obviating any need to ask about the past: "Say not, 'Why were the former days better than these?' For it is not from wisdom that you ask this" (Ecc 7:10). Not even the days of creation are worth remembering, if indeed they occurred at all.

But then, what can the tradition have in mind by featuring this exercise in self-rejection at a critical juncture of its annual liturgical cycle? The tradition is indeed troubled by the book, and remembers that its founding rabbinical figures debated whether to include it in its canon of sacred scripture. What pressed its claim for inclusion was its seeming self-presentation as the work of King Solomon. What counted against it, according to the rabbis, were its self-contradictions, its inscrutability, and its obvious heresy.[1] But then, these very objections to it were themselves self-contradictory, for how could a book that obscured its meaning in inscrutabilities say anything definitely and clearly enough to count for heresy? and, if it could, how could its self-contradictoriness not undermine whatever heresy it uttered? And so the book was included, on grounds the rabbis found that would persuade no critical scholar of the Bible today, that King Solomon wrote it.

The rabbis were right about the self-contradictions of the book. These are easily proof-texted. But the book masks them by couching them in a pattern of speech very common to its kindred books in the Wisdom tradition of the Bible: x is better than y. The more conventionally wise book of Proverbs is filled with such statements. Ecclesiastes adopts that pattern of speech even within the context of his much less conventional wisdom, which questions the very integrity and applicability of pattern as such. The result is an appearance of confusion and self-contradiction over what things really are better than other things. Each of these things is, according to Ecclesiastes, both good and bad; pleasure (Ecc 2:2 and 8:15); laughter (Ecc 2:2 and 3:4); toil (Ecc 5:18 and 6:7); death (4:2 and 9:4–5); and wisdom (1:18 and 2:13). Its attitude towards memory is also contradictory. For, how can we be aware that there is nothing new, unless we remember enough of the past (as Ecclesiastes insists we do not) to see the repetition? The book is not scholastic enough to resolve these contradictions through refinements of distinction. But these very contradictions are the first hint that it carries a worldview alternative to both Deuteronomy and Genesis that is more philosophical than religious. For the contradictions can be read as question marks punctuating the themes the book raises. And that interrogative sound (as opposed to the persistent declaratives of Deuteronomy and Genesis 1) is the first speech of philosophy.

The rabbis were also right about the heresies of the book. For Ecclesiastes stands in opposition to much more of the Bible than just Deuteronomy and Genesis 1. As though to mock the proclamations of the prophets, it employs their language to undermine their intent, as when we read, in echo of Isaiah's comforting hope that God will "make the crooked places straight" (Isa 45:2, KJV), "what is crooked cannot be made straight" (Ecc 1:15); or, alternatively, when we read, in what appears as a troubling gloss on Jeremiah's "I will put my law within them, I will write it upon their hearts" (Jer. 31:33), that God "has put eternity into man's mind, yet so that he cannot find out what God has done from the beginning to the end" (Ecc 3:10). Ecclesiastes performs the same inversions on the more orthodox teachings of its neighboring book, and companion among the Wisdom books, Proverbs. The conventional wisdom teachings of Proverbs, and some of the Psalms, promote righteousness and moderation; Ecclesiastes counsels moderation in the one place where Proverbs does not commend it, namely righteousness itself, when he admonishes: "Be not righteous overmuch, and do not make yourself overwise" (Ecc. 7:16). The wisdom of Ecclesiastes is a crooked wisdom, designed to help its practitioners negotiate a hopelessly crooked world. Or, it is an inversive wisdom, that follows the mirror-image reflection of the adages it receives, which invert them, rather than the adages themselves, like the creatures of Lewis Carroll's looking-glass world. In a world where those who dig ditches fall into them (10:8), the way to any desired goal is through behaviors *prima facie* counter to it: to attain bread, cast it away (Ecc. 11:1); to acquire wisdom, do not study (Ecc. 12:12); to prepare for a peaceful old age, indulge in youthful pleasures now (Ecc. 11: 9–10). That the last of these cited verses introduces a poem that, as we shall see, also works to therapeutic effect, by mirroring death in captivating metaphors, invites the thought that Ecclesiastes' inversive wisdom and his poetry accomplish their healings by the same means: reflection.

And the rabbis were right that the book is obscure. It was the "parables," or metaphors, of the book, that the rabbis found obscure. Modern readers may indeed find several of the metaphors baffling. What does this succession of verses teach: "the fool folds his hands, and eats his own flesh" (Ecc. 4:5), and then: "Better is a handful of quietness than two hands full of toil and striving after wind" (Ecc. 4:6). One modern interpretation is that 4:5 is a bit of conventional wisdom, on which Ecclesiastes caustically comments in 4:6.[2] The tradition counsels us to busy ourselves with productive work, else we will starve (eat our own flesh); but, says Ecclesiastes, because reality does not obey sensible causal laws of action and consequence, it is better to sit in quiet self-containment and abjure a pointless labor. But as the manuscript text of scripture itself did not contain such punctuation as quotation marks, we cannot be sure if this is what the writer meant. Ecclesiastes does more than illustrate obscurity, he also describes it, for he finds it in a place where the rest of the Bible would largely not locate it, in God's plan for the world. For as the Torah and prophets make abundantly clear, this plan is straightforward, to harmonize good behavior with material flourishing and peace. And this is just the plan for which Ecclesiastes finds so little evidence. On the contrary, God's work in the world is something "you do not know" (Ecc. 11:5), nor can we have any hope to "find it out" (Ecc. 8:17), a point obliquely confirmed by the famous poem of the seasons, which promises a time to lose and a time to seek, but not a time to find (Ecc. 3:6).

Ecclesiastes does not lack a sense of the divine. But his concept of God is not the rest of the Bible's. Unlike in the biblical book that is perhaps its closest logical neighbor, Job, God does not speak, nor is any divine word recorded. Ecclesiastes does not address God, who carries what, according to later tradition, was the most impersonal name of the divine—Elohim, based as it is on the generic name for God or gods. But then, the writer does not personally name himself either, since the term "Ecclesiastes," the Greek translation of the Hebrew, "Kohelet," connotes more an office than a name, of one who gathers a community to hear him (hence, "The Preacher," as he is sometimes called). The doubled impersonality of the author and his God is a far cry from the multiple genealogies, and many names of God, that course through the Torah and make it so personal. God appears to have created the world (Ecc. 11:5), but not in such a way as to elicit heartfelt thanks or praise from us. The temple sacrifice of Ecclesiastes' day, which anticipated what the rabbis would later warmly call the "sacrifice of praise and thanksgiving," is, for Ecclesiastes, more of a temptation to promise what cannot be delivered (Ecc. 5:1–2), than a communicative bridge between human and divine. Neither the Temple nor what may have been the nascent synagogue of Ecclesiastes' time is cited as a location of affective linkage between our life and God's. Assuming the vantage point of tradition, whose revelatory pronouncements supply the rationale for the whole sacrificial system, Ecclesiastes can only imply that there is no reason to believe they ever divinely occurred: "God is heaven and you upon earth" (5:2), and no supernatural revelation bridges the gap.

It is the distance of this God that has prompted some to subsume Ecclesiastes under the larger, Hellenistic rubric of Epicureanism. For a cardinal teaching of that philosophy, which was in effect a rival religion to Judaism, was that, while the divine existed, it took no interest in us and so prayers to it were pointless. The Epicureans were more inclined to take their succor from nature, which they observed with attentive appreciation, as the work of Lucretius, from later on, attests. In the famous poem of chapter 3, Ecclesiastes does also. The unifying structure of the verses that the Hebrew establishes, in its characteristic simplicity, by repeatedly juxtaposing nothing more than two words, the noun, 'eth, for time, and the variable verbal infinitive, lulls the reader with the reassuring comfort of the cycles it describes. Scarcely any significant human activity escapes the embrace of the cycles. Even the absence of finding among the alternatives seemingly exhausted by losing and seeking, fails to trouble, since finding characterizes the whole of the poem, in the peace that is found there. The cycles explain the joys and sorrows that befall us in terms alternative to the paradigm of reward and punishment that informs so much of the rest of scripture. They invert the relation between actor and activity that the paradigm of reward and punishment presumes, namely, that if we are giving birth, embracing, loving, or laughing it is because of good deeds we antecedently performed; the cycles tell us, instead, that the activities they alternate demand their own existence, prior to our performance of them, which merely realizes the potential they will actualize with or without our cooperation. As instruments of their self-expression, our agency is no longer causative, but consequential. Killing, casting away, and hating are separated from the motives that appear to occasion them, and rendered comprehensible, instead, by the cycles that ask for them, in much the way that the prophets divorced the significance, for Israel, of the oncoming conquests of the Assyrians or Babylonians from the greed or pride that humanly motivated them. Such a view may disempower us, but it also frees our flourishings and sufferings of the burden they carry, on the conventional biblical view, of rewarding or punishing our prior behavior; a burden that would, according to Ecclesiastes, on account of its utter unconformity to any rational pattern, otherwise overwhelm us with meaninglessness.

If this had been Ecclesiastes' final answer to our sufferings, he might have been an Epicurean. For like them, he would then have comforted us by exhorting us to take the larger view of nature's activity. The cycles of nature, like the Epicurean atoms, would carry all the burden of explaining why things happen as they do. But, in Ecclesiastes' case, this would not be a spirituality; for nature is not for him as, taken as a whole, it may indeed have been for the Epicureans, a location of the divine. He would have offered a philosophical therapy, but not a philosophical spirituality. But the cycles of chapter 3 are not the last word of Ecclesiastes' counsel to us. There is the repeating idea that each of us "should eat and drink, and find enjoyment in his toil" (Ecc. 2:24). This too might seem Epicurean counsel, except for this singular addendum, occurring only once, and all the more absorbing for that, that "this also I saw is from the hand of God" (Ecc. 2:24). By that addendum, Ecclesiastes brings into play an image from the larger biblical and extra-biblical world that so transforms the import of eating, drinking, and toiling as to render them vehicles of a new, distinctively worldly spirituality.

In the context of other biblical books, it is momentous things that happen by the hand of God, chiefly the Exodus from Egypt (Ex. 6:1), but also the miraculous chastisements visited upon the Egyptians and other foreign powers, and the calling and ecstasy of prophets (Ez. 1:3). In the extra-biblical world, the expression occurs with more consistently negative connotations, of disaster and madness.[3] By associating this expression with the commonest of everyday experiences, Ecclesiastes implies that it is these very experiences by which God is most strikingly and transformingly known. Whatever connotations of negating power the term carries are transformed into the opposite, a sustaining power for enjoyment of elemental pleasure. Like the cycles of nature, this attribution of our pleasure in eating, drinking, and working directly to God also opens a way for us to understand what happens to us independently of larger patterns of cause and effect, reward and punishment, whose explanatory power Ecclesiastes has shown to be so deficient. For what the pleasures of eating and drinking share is the momentariness of them. Even toiling, as Ecclesiastes first presents it, shows the pleasure it affords to lie not in what it accomplishes, not in the presumed effects of it as cause, but in the moment-to-moment process of it, whether goal-accomplishing or not. The reward for toil is itself (Ecc. 2:10), just as the "reward" of eating and drinking is in the very acts themselves. By constraining the pleasures he commends to us to the passing moment, he frees them from dependence on causal chains outside them, and renders them, over their admittedly brief duration, self-sufficient. Such moments are ripe for what Henry James calls, "the quality that fortune distills in a single drop at a time."[4] The cycles of chapter 3 already point this way; when the radius of the circle that images the cycle reduces to zero, it becomes the point of the passing moment.

If these moments of self-contained pleasure that come to us by the hand of God are any reflection of their origin, then part of what they teach is that the divine activity, too, must be understood in terms of discrete, self-contained acts that do not, in sum, necessarily form a pattern discernible to us. If any geometric figure can image this for us, as the circle does the natural cycles of chapter 3, it is the point, which, mathematically speaking, occupies no space at all. The two figures are not unrelated. A point is a circle whose radius has reduced to zero. And it is just at this occurrence of nothing, that the divine hand shows.

If such occurrences of nothing are also vanity, then Ecclesiastes' claim that all is vanity takes on another meaning. But "vanity" is, in its English meaning, too limited in scope to embrace the full range of connotations that the Hebrew word it translates, *hevel*, carries. A dictionary of biblical Hebrew reveals that the word can mean, in a tone free of value judgment, simply breath, vapor, the vanishing or evanescent.[5] The fact that the word supplies one of the positively judged, but indeed evanescent, characters of the Bible with his name, Abel, who offered up sacrifices pleasing to God, shows that the connotations of the word are far from wholly negative. Abel and his murderous brother, Cain, suggest between them a contrast of value structures that positions *hevel*/Abel in a very positive light. Cain is the grounded brother, who tills the soil; after he has slain Abel, the curse upon him calls up from the ground and holds him. But this has been the problem with him from the start. Neither he nor his offerings are lifted up, or rise heavenward (Gen 4:7). Cain is in homonymous agreement with a Hebrew verbal root that connotes heaviness, in the sense of the fixed, firm, and established, namely *kwn*. Abel, the brother whose sacrifices rise to heaven, allies with what is precisely not fixed or firm but breathy, airy, spiritual, or, to use a modern Hebrew word that descends from the Bible, *ruchani*. In another biblical use of *hevel*, it does indeed mean to rise up. In part, this is a contest between metaphors to be the most apt evocation of the spiritual life: earth or air? To the extent that burnt animal offerings become aromas, that ride up on the winds to the nostrils of God, they transform to air. While the vegetable offerings that Cain brought must draw divine attention down to them, like still-life paintings of fruit that hold the gaze of an art connoisseur.

To the extent that the application of God's hand to a human being (as to Job) connotes suffering, we could say that God's hand was upon Cain after he murdered Abel; but, more importantly, that the vehicle of that hand's appearance was, indeed, *hevel* (Abel), precisely Ecclesiastes' point about *hevel* in relation to the passing pleasures of life. These pleasures are pleasures despite their passing, or evanescence, to the extent that the expectation upon them to endure is lifted; or, to the extent that they are freed from the obligation to conform to predictable and so controllable patterns of any kind. This spirituality of *hevel*, for all its lightness, is not necessarily easy, as Milan Kundera taught by naming a novel, *The Unbearable Lightness of Being*. The moment freed from the status of causal or consequential relation to other moments becomes light, in contrast to all the implications of bondage and weight that causality draws down upon it when it *anchors* things in *chains* of cause and effect. And yet, insofar as meaning devolves onto a moment only insofar as it is precisely so located, a moment of lightness, in all its lightness, is difficult to bear; so much so, that the book has been said to illustrate a spirituality of asceticism.[6] But then, the point of such a lightness is not to bear it, but be borne by it. The image of the hand of God plays perfectly to this picture; it is what bears us in the vanishing of the moment into nothing.

To appreciate a biblical spirituality of the moment, especially at a time such as ours when such spiritualities are far from unusual, we must register the extent to which it bucks the grain of its biblical context. We must not imagine that such canonical verses from the New Testament as enjoin us to live like the lilies of the field represent a kindred spirituality, for all the attention they draw to the idea of momentariness. For those verses, moving as they do within the pervasive eschatology of the gospels, whether understood as realized in the here-and-now, or hovering, apocalyptically, just over the horizon, are foreign to Ecclesiastes' worldly restraint. As to the rest of Hebrew scripture, the opposing spirituality of *kwn* carries the day, to the extent of supplying the very word of affirmation itself: *ken* (yes)! The spirituality of *hevel* must appeal to its conceptually kindred, but etymologically remote cousin, *ruach*, to receive a hearing among the diverse spiritualities of the Bible.

What makes Ecclesiastes' spirituality philosophical is that its foundation is in reasoned, natural experience, rather than revelation. Eating and drinking are among the commonest experiences of everyday, necessities of nature that draw us so close to the animals, and Ecclesiastes doubts there is much difference between us (3:21). But they do not become spiritual pleasures except as strained through a transforming, rationalist, almost mathematical sieve. These moments of animal pleasure must not be understood to endure. We must envision them on the model of a very short, horizontally placed cone, realizing itself in movement from its wide to narrow end. At the wide, or open end of each moment its duration has hardly begun before it has ended, funneling to the point where it has vanished into nothing at all. Such a view of momentary pleasure asks to be imaged through no less a picture of narrowing to nothing than death. For as much as each moment constitutes a new beginning, it also stages its own end. But it is just by ending so abruptly that it ensures the freedom of its successor, which is unbound to anything that precedes. Ecclesiastes does indeed lament the unbearableness of such a succession of lightened moments, showing as each does, in lightning succession, the face of death. Death is the seal on broken ties that gradually unhinges the whole spirituality of *kwn* that continues to attract him in the other biblical books, but that he gradually forswears; so much so, that by the final chapter, he can hymn the onset of death in a sequence of startling metaphors that constitute "a brilliant and moving poem that does not resemble anything else in the book."[7] At least one verse of it, 12:4—"and one rises up at the voice of a bird"—does resemble another verse from a wholly different book of Hebrew Scripture, namely Leviticus 26:36—"the sound of a driven leaf shall put them to flight." Both verses describe a vulnerable frame of mind, easily alarmed. The Leviticus verse is part of a catalogue of punishments that Torah warns will befall the Israelites if they defy the law. Ecclesiastes naturalizes the consequence that in Leviticus is a moral one: the fragile state he describes is the inevitable result of aging. It is not a punishment at all, but the one predictable pattern of life to which we can expect to conform. But then, the wholesale rejection of the reward and punishment model, in Ecclesiastes, lifts off of the sufferings we endure the additional burden they carry in much of the rest of the Bible, of punishing sin. This is already to lighten them. The punishment that death itself was, according to Gen 2, is neutralized in Ecclesiastes. But Ecclesiastes' poem to death does more than neutralize, it beautifies death. Part of the import of that for the rest of the poem is to shift death into a positive role, in contrast to the despairing lines of 4:2 ("I thought the dead . . . more fortunate than the living"), simultaneously ending every moment and allowing whatever inhabits that moment to be "beautiful in its time" (3:11). In opposition to much of the rest of the Bible, and millennia before what became Romantic *de rigueur*, Ecclesiastes poeticized death, and in so doing uncovered another therapeutic office of reason, to, by mirroring terrors, tame them.

That is indeed the role of wisdom in the book. The wisdom that accumulates objects, people, or ideas (even of wisdom itself), in relentless pursuit of them, is the folly he derides (1:16–18). The wisdom he commends only dawns on him at the first moment of his self-awareness. In another echo of Genesis 1, but this time an affirming one, Ecclesiastes "turned to consider wisdom" itself (2:12), as God turns towards completed creation, to contemplate it, and pronounces, now in imitation of God's affirming words towards the sun and moon, "I saw that wisdom exceeds folly as light excels darkness" (2:13). What differentiates wisdom contemplated from wisdom pursued as an object? A similar dividing line separates all that God has done in Genesis 1, on the first six days, which are good, from the seventh day of rest, which is holy. In both cases, the activity has obscured the distinction of the subject from the object it shapes. In the moment of reflection (on the wisdom pursued, or the creation fashioned), the subject recovers its separation from what it shaped. That separation is part of what supplies God with holiness in the first place; but is also what separates Ecclesiastes from the burdens of that very same creation, whose ultimately unpromising and unfulfillable enticements have troubled him for so long. An astute self-awareness deprives the debilitating of its power to harm, and may even convert it to its opposite. This offers another avenue of interpreting the many superficial contradictions in the book. Ecclesiastes is a lamentation converted to a paean, and all the stages of the process show. Even single verses invite precisely opposite interpretations, depending upon the stage of the process through which they are read. For example, the seeming lament, in reference to the living and the dead, that "better than both is he who has not yet been" (4:3), may be read either as a wish to have never been born, or as an invitation to enter that part of any passing moment that borders on nonbeing, where the hand of God shows through.

The self-awareness Ecclesiastes attains by differentiating himself so markedly from the world has import, too, for his understanding of his separation from God. For the curious words of 3:15—*ha-elohim yevakesh eth-nirdaph*—that, according to a standard lexicon of Biblical Hebrew, translate to "God seeketh the pursued,"[8] may register the wisdom Ecclesiastes has acquired, that all matters of deliberate pursuit, in expectation of attaining ends, must, if they have reference at all, refer to God's agency alone. Only God, not humans, realizes intentions.

The self-awareness of the author who wrote Ecclesiastes shows in the multiple references to "I" in the book, which exceed the references to God. Self-awareness may have become the torment of modern subjectivity, which seeks a way back to the objectivity it has lost, but in the ancient context of the Bible, self-awareness was liberative. By means of it, Ecclesiastes uncovers within himself an assumption inherited from the rest of scripture and responsible for much of his sufferings, that fulfillments follow on promises. The assumption once uncovered is disarmed, as modern proponents of philosophical counseling might teach; and the vacant space it now leaves in consciousness allows other, more health-promoting assertions about reality to supersede, such as that it is cyclic, rather than linear (as the model of promise-fulfillment presupposes), or momentary, rather than continuous (as the model of promise-fulfillment also presupposes). The very act of self-awareness enacts the spirituality of the moment, by enwrapping itself in a self-contained whole of its own beginning and end. When Ecclesiastes' knowing turns towards his own pursuit of knowing, he is freed of the pursuit entirely, a blessing of self-awareness upon which later philosophical therapies will elaborate. And independently of Plato, and perhaps of Greek philosophy generally, he has helped to initiate what will become the variegated theme in the history of philosophy of the therapeutic and spiritual import of reason.

NOTES

1. B. Shab. 13b and 30b; Abot de Rabbi Nathan 1; Leviticus Rabbah 28:1. See Bialik and Ravnitzky, *Book of Legends*, 446.
2. R.B.Y. Scott, *Proverbs, Ecclesiastes*, Anchor Bible (Garden City, NY: Doubleday, 1965), 225.
3. See J. J. M. Roberts, "The Hand of Yahweh," *Vetus Testamentum* (1971): 244–251.
4. Henry James, "The Lesson of the Master," in *Selected Tales*, ed. John Lyon (New York: Penguin Books, 2001), 145.
5. F. Brown, S. Driver, and C. Briggs, *A Hebrew and English Lexicon of the Old Testament* (New York: Clarendon Press, 1907, 1977), 210.
6. Jerome Walsh, "Despair as a Theological Virtue in the Spirituality of Ecclesiastes," *Biblical Theology Bulletin* 12, no. 2 (1992): 48.
7. Scott, *Proverbs, Ecclesiastes*, 199.
8. Brown, Driver, Briggs, *A Hebrew and English Lexicon of the Old Testament*, 923.

THREE
Plato

Plato did not entirely reject the religion of his culture. He is less out of sync with his Greek polytheistic context than Ecclesiastes is with his biblical one. For, unlike Ecclesiastes, who adopts the forms of biblical language only to undermine it, Plato adapts the forms of Greek religion to a new religion of his own making. Ancient Greek religion comprised at least three elements: the civic religion of the Greek city-states, the mystery cults, and the epic-poetic myths. At the beginning of The Republic, Socrates prepares to participate in the cultic worship of Artemis and he looks forward, with child-like pleasure, to a chariot race that will be part of the festival (Rep. 327–8); in the Phaedrus, another cultic procession of chariots appears, this time in heaven, as the gods proceed in orderly fashion behind the lead of Zeus, who guides their attention towards eternal ideas (Phaed. 246–7); in the Laws, Plato explicitly provides for civic worship of the gods. The mystery cults, which allowed worshipers an intimate relationship with one of the deities, are a vehicle by which Plato admits a select few to Hesiod's more violent tales, where they receive an edifying, allegorical interpretation (Rep. 378). But then, the whole of heavenly ascent to the idea of the Good, as Plato describes it in the Republic, has the feel of a mystery, especially when Socrates suggests that the willing but limited Glaucon will not be able to follow him on the upward path. Plato's concessions to the imagery and language of the civic and mystery cults of his time may be little more than further instances of what he called the noble lie: affirmations of false but fruitful stories that serve a greater good. But this is still more than Ecclesiastes allowed to the language of biblical religion.

What Plato forcefully rejects in the religion of his heritage is its poetry. Long passages of the Republic detail the offense of the stories Hesiod and Homer told about the gods. These are to be heavily purged of their violence or simply not told at all. The problem, for Plato, relates to the imitative nature of story as such. Story-telling is itself an imitative act, fashioning action, character and setting after what we perceive in real life. The problem is that the imitative force of a story communicates just as strongly when it is a poor and misrepresentative copy of true reality. Indeed, for Plato, because the best stories valorize the least attractive aspects of human nature, accomplished storytelling excites and strengthens the least attractive sides of its audience. The action the story performs, in imitating reality, reproduces itself, almost like a cancer, in the listener, who becomes an imitator, too, but this time of the story. The imitative form of a story is independent of the truth or falsity of its content, and traps its hearers inside of it; so ensnared, they copy the story — the behavior of its characters, the implicit message of its plot — towards their own good or ill. The force of stories is so powerful that it is indeed only by a mystery that their amoral coerciveness can be tamed. But Plato will not trust to the mysteries, whether the instated ones of his day, or any he might invent, to harness the potential ill of Homer and Hesiod; better simply to banish them and their ilk entirely, as he does at the end of the Republic, and tell new, edifying stories in their stead, as he does throughout the corpus of his dialogues.

Because of the role of stories in his thought, Plato, of all the philosophers, comes closer than most others to shaping an actual religion. His dialogues supply more than just the myths religions demand; there are also accounts of and prescriptions for spiritual experience; and there is ethics. In the hands of his interpretive successors, the Neo-Platonists, Plato becomes a religion that critiques and rivals Christianity, and that surfaces from time to time in the history of religious sensibility even after its official schools were closed, as a spiritual path of its own.

Part of the appeal of Plato is his clear-eyed, non-rationalizing assessment, akin to Buddha's, of the pervasiveness of human suffering. In its social dimension, suffering ranges from the common burdens of family life to the sophistry and oppressiveness of public opinion, to the madness of tyrannies. Plato's despair is that the condition for release from these evils — the rule of philosophers — is so unlikely as to be a dream. Though under these conditions the best life is the retired one of the philosopher, evils from within the soul threaten this too. Because the soul's largest parts desire material satisfaction and glory, the smallest part, which seeks the good, is easily overwhelmed. The "ordinary goods of life" (Rep. 491)[1] become destructive allurements away from the soul's best path. Conventional education and culture, by valorizing violence and pitying the just, obscure the path to goodness and happiness. Apart from all this, the soul's embodied state is a physical misery, "disfigured by ten thousand ills" (Rep. 611).

There is much here in common with Ecclesiastes' itemizations of human suffering, but also significant differences, chief of which is the implication that there is indeed a *path* to the good which lies concealed by the ordinary attractions of life. It was just in despair over such a path, paved by reliable relations between cause and effect, that Ecclesiastes turned precisely to those momentary, ephemeral goods that Plato so disparaged. What allows human beings a healing handle on their sufferings is that, contra Ecclesiastes, they do indeed follow a predictable pattern. But to see the pattern requires renunciation of a distinction so fundamental to biblical thought that not even Ecclesiastes could escape it: the distinction between natural and moral evil. Natural evils are the ones that befall us as nature runs its course, understood according to the famous cycles of Ecclesiastes, or the laws of science, or—as Ecclesiastes also insists—bereft of any explicability at all. Moral evils are the ones we inflict on each other through deliberate, harmful intent. But one of the signal marks of the Platonic worldview is that there is no such thing as moral evil in that sense. There can be no deliberate will to harm because a soul willing harm is disordered; a disordered soul is unhappy; no one deliberately wills his own unhappiness; and therefore no one can deliberately will to harm. The argument finds more protracted articulation in the Republic in the context of a question that Ecclesiastes, too, had put, namely, how is it that the wicked prosper? Ecclesiastes had no answer; Plato undermines the question itself by arguing that the wicked do not prosper, outward appearances to the contrary. In an exquisite refinement of this proverbial question, anticipating many of the memorable villains of modern literature, Plato imagines what ordinary opinion might think the best possible scenario: to be actually wicked, but apparently good, so that one could reap all the fruits of wickedness under the protective, public guise of seeming goodness (Rep. 364–365). This picture of wickedness derives in part from Hesiod, whom Plato quotes, to the effect that wickedness is easy and goodness hard. But even before Socrates can respond to this assertion, which the interlocutor Adeimantus defends, Plato begins to undermine it. For as Adeimantus paints his portrait of false goodness, it appears that "the concealment of wickedness is often difficult" after all (Rep. 365); and that the difficulty of goodness, too, converts to its opposite, since, by its very resistance to human effort, it can only occur in human action at the inspiration of the gods, and so, effortlessly (Rep. 366). In the end, it is goodness that is easy and wickedness hard.

By planting this refutation of false goodness' ease within the very argument made for it, Plato suggests three things at once: that the reality of things is the opposite of appearance; that the passage from appearance to reality occurs naturally, by following out the implications of ideas; and that goodness allies with happiness (or ease). From the interlocking character of these multiple suggestions, two central pillars of the Platonic worldview rise up: the importance of what is natural; the pervasiveness of analogy. Indeed, the natural, together with its opposite, the unnatural, erect an analogy that finds correspondences across the fields of philosophy: metaphysics, epistemology, ethics and psychology. For as the natural is to the unnatural, so is reality to appearance, truth to falseness, goodness to wickedness, and happiness to misery. Like an organism, the whole of the Platonic system shows itself in its smallest parts, as here, in the argument that false goodness is not profitable after all. But then, philosophies that turn on analogy are naturally organic.

It is because nature, goodness and happiness ally in a united front of analogy against unnaturalness, wickedness and misery, that the wicked can never be happy. The concept of the natural is approbatory in Plato. Another form of its disparaged opposite is the artificial (Rep. 498), which subsumes most poetry. Things that are or can be natural include a very broad range: numbers (Rep. 531), words (Rep. 498), laws (Rep. 327), pleasures (Rep. 586–7), reason (Rep. 530), and most especially philosophers, whose "naturally well-proportioned and gracious minds will move spontaneously toward the true being of everything" (Rep. 486). The link philosophers make between the natural and the well-proportioned is significant. For part of what makes a complex entity natural is that its component parts are in proportional or harmonious order with each other, a view Plato undergirds with an additional analogy to disease: the naturally ordered soul is healthy, and the disordered one diseased (Rep. 444; Timaeus 82). Nature itself plays the role that God does in the Bible of assuring that the good prosper and wicked suffer. It is able to do so because it subsumes the orders of ethics within itself. There is no distinction between natural and moral evil. Justice and injustice are attributes of nature in different orderings: justice occurs where the naturally ruling rule, and injustice where they do not. To extend the analogy with disease, injustice is a kind of cancer that rises up from within an organism, as opposed to the viral or infectious evil of epic poetry, which affects souls from without. But both are natural evils, in which a part of nature disturbs the order that should properly contain it. This gives Plato more in common than he would like to admit with a character of his we are clearly primed to dislike, Thrasymachus, who famously insists at the opening of the Republic that justice is the power of the stronger. Plato accepts the deeper assumption of Thrasymachus' claim that justice occurs in a hierarchical ordering of power between contending parties. The reason an entity as vexed by politics as the state can image the soul, as it does do in the Republic, is that the soul, too, is political, divided by regions of desire—for material things, for *amour-propre*, and for wisdom—that compete for rule of the whole. Justice occurs in the soul when the desire there for wisdom is the strongest. But this is also the natural order of the soul; for only when the desire for wisdom (i.e., philosophy) rules is the whole of the soul harmonious and happy. Consequently, any unnatural order in the soul, or disorder there, is multiply productive: it yields both injustice and unhappiness, simultaneously, and without the need of such a supervening agent as the biblical God to link the two together.

Plato appears to have purchased the justice of the happy soul at the price of our ordinary concept of justice. Of course, if a certain order within the soul constitutes both its happiness and justice, then all and only just souls are happy. But Plato knew the conventional view of evil. In one itemization of it (Rep. 443), which includes theft and murder, it sounds very much like what the Ten Commandments prohibit. Might the Platonically just soul be unjust in that conventional sense? Plato blocks that possibility through this apparently empirical line of reasoning: to behave unjustly in the conventional sense, by willfully harming others, requires anger, resentment, or hatred in the soul (the very qualities so exploited by poets). But these qualities disturb the order of the soul, and so deprive it of justice in Plato's technical sense, as well as in the conventional sense. Properly ordered souls always act to preserve their harmonious condition (Rep. 443–444) and so never behave unjustly in the conventional sense.

Like Ecclesiastes, Plato offers a therapy that precedes his spirituality. The therapy of the soul, that the desire for wisdom rule there, does not yet directly implicate the divine. And the concept of divinity does indeed hover on the margins of Plato's thought, as though unnecessary. The gods of the Greek pantheon, though trappings of the dialogues, are neither a serious object of Platonic inquiry nor a significant source of benefit to humankind. The god closest to Socrates, through his pronouncement at Delphi on his wisdom, namely Apollo, goes unnamed in the passage from the Apology that credits him with that utterance, as though to discourage undue, and perhaps diverting, interest in him. But if the proper location of the sacred in any philosophical system is at the source of all being and well-being, then the Greek gods, in Plato, fail by both counts, for they are not significant creators. Where an agency going under the name of God does create is in the Timaeus. But here, the recalcitrance of the material of creation necessitates a final product that in many ways disappoints, and that in any case fails to inspire devotion to, or any expectation of happiness from, its maker.

Plato is one among the many philosophers who so alter the understanding of the sacred, taught by the inherited religion of their day, as to name it other than God. What holds the place of the sacred in Plato's system is the idea of Goodness. It does so because it comes closer than any other part of his system to being both an origin of the world and the ultimate guarantor of human well-being. The Good does not create the whole world, but is "the universal author of all things beautiful and right," (Rep. 517) which fail by a great deal to exhaust the whole. Even the creator God, insofar as he is good, can author no more than that (Rep. 379). But the idea of Goodness goes much farther than the creator God to enable human happiness. And it does so without willing, thinking, or exhibiting any marks of personality at all. For the ideas, which are more helpfully translated, *forms*, are simply those abstractions that account for the types of things there are in the world, a formal and impersonal function of them that Aristotle clarifies when he brings them down from heaven and locates them, within things, as their *formal* (as opposed to material) cause. But for Plato, the form or idea of the Good occupies a pinnacle far above this world, beyond even the reach of reasoned language, which it nonetheless inspires. It is "seen only with an effort" (Rep. 517), and once seen, scarcely submits to description. While in one sense it is the "highest knowledge" (Rep. 505), in another, it surpasses anything that can be formulated as truth (Rep. 509). We might think, on analogy with the just state and soul, that the Good is a natural ordering of parts. But it does not appear to admit of parts. Like the apophatic theology Plato would inspire, his descriptions of the Good are more negative than positive: invariable, unchanging, incorruptible, too much of being ever to become (Rep. 381, 485, 521, 526, 585).

Ideas are an epistemological category for which Plato finds a metaphysical use. They explain how diverse things can instance a single kind of thing, or how the many can be one. They also explain how a succession of different states over time can constitute a single object. This is already a unifying function for them that allies them with at least one etymological reading of the word, "religion": to bind back and, by extension, make whole. But they are even more unifying than that, for by the epistemological and metaphysical status they simultaneously hold, they transcend the distance between knowing and being. They are both enablers and objects of knowing. By Plato's metaphysical understanding of them, they do not require the habitat of a mind and are free to define a "space" of their own. Apart from their unifying function, what additionally recommends them to Plato is that in a world of painful change, they are sublimely static. Independence from change is a mark of higher reality for Plato. By their simultaneous independence from and attraction to mind, they imply both self-containment and desirability. If, by their abstractness, they are difficult to access (as Aristotle implied when he denied them any existence at all apart from the concrete particulars that instance them), they play all the more to the role of the sacred, which cannot define itself except over a separation from our ordinary life.

If the Good is the most sacred of the ideas, that is because it is the most self-contained of all, underlying all but itself requiring none of the other ideas; and also because, of all ideas, its import for the soul is most profound. It is just here that Platonic therapy links up with Platonic spirituality. The Good is the perfect counterpart of poetry in its effect upon the soul. As poetry excites and strengthens the lowest parts of the soul, where desires for material things reign, the Good, once present to the soul, excites the highest part, which longs for wisdom. And so, in knowing the Good, the soul becomes naturally ordered, which means, by the string of traits in analogy with the natural, it becomes happy, healthy, wise and just. It is not that the soul could not right itself without the Good. Plato does not consider the possibility of a purely secular therapy. It is that the Good, in its effects upon the human soul, is naturally, ineluctably, therapeutic. But as most sacred idea, it is also most remote: "In the world of knowledge, the idea of the good appears last of all" (Rep. 517). In addition, by the wrenchings required to prompt even the most philosophical denizens of the cave, in Plato's allegory, to ascend up out of it, Plato implies that we ourselves resist the upward ascent, fearing, perhaps, the revolutions in our worldview it implies.

But the Good does eventually appear, at least to some who seek it. By the almost reproductive urgency of analogy within Plato's system, the Good is approachable from different quarters and along different paths. Arrayed in analogy with the other analogies we have already encountered, the Good, expectedly, illuminates. For, by its very transcendence of language it, unlike truth or happiness, lacks a strict opposite. There is no Idea of Evil in Plato. Its opposite can only be its absence. But if the Good is to the absence of Good, what truth is to falsity, and happiness to misery, then these second terms within the analogies must also be species of absence, which casts doubt on their reality. They are seeming realities, or appearances. Through this suggestive door of the opposite to Goodness, Plato admits a concept that will later flourish at the hands of the medieval thinkers, that reality admits of degrees; which in turn implies degrees of veracity in the knowledge that takes reality, in its various degrees, for object. And this positions us to view what might go by the name of the Great Analogy in Plato, not only because it so expressly presents itself as an analogy, but also because it accentuates for us how much analogy, for Plato, implies a vertical ascent, rather than a horizontal succession, namely the divided line.

The divided line, which is a geometric concept and best conceived vertically, appears in the Republic just before the famous myth of the cave more engagingly dramatizes its message. Like the disordered soul that produces with a single stroke its psychic unhappiness and its moral wickedness, the divided line, too, is coincidence of content from different philosophic subdisciplines, in this case, metaphysics and epistemology. For it simultaneously divides the upper reaches of being and knowing from their lower regions. The line is constructed on an analogy of proportions: the first division, which unequally halves the line, is proportionally reproduced in each of the halves themselves. And the four unequal quarters that result provide spaces for the four degrees of reality, and the four degrees of knowing, to show themselves, in ascending order: reflections and perception, physical objects and conviction, hypotheses and understanding, self-substantiating principles and reason. The subsuming analogy, between the two original halves of the line, is of reality to appearance, and of knowledge to opinion. The divided line is the perfect form to illustrate analogy. For in one standard way of representing them, analogies take the form of fractions, which are already vertical structures. The significance of the divided line for Platonic spirituality is that, in an unexpected move, it doubles the verticality of that representation, by superimposing the fraction within itself. In this way, the analogies involved in the divided line abandon the horizontal structure in which they would more expectedly array themselves, for a vertical one. And the verticality of the line becomes, like the proverbial beanstalk, an avenue of approach to heaven.

It is difficult to ascend a vertical line. There is no slope to scale. And Plato does want the line to be navigable. And so the line leans a bit, to acquire slope. The ascent it suggests is by way of knowledge of being. For, by the analogy between being and knowledge, a rise in the one is simultaneously a rise in the other. If the Idea of the Good resides at the pinnacle of being, then knowing, at its peak, should bring us there. The Republic charts this way. But from the Platonic oeuvre, another dialogue offers up an alternative and analogous path of ascent, namely the Phaedrus, whose upward path goes by way of love of beauty. Knowledge is to being as love is to beauty. Knowledge and love intensified culminate in being and beauty, respectively, whose own origins are in Goodness. If the two sloping lines are brought to meet, they form the steep sides of a very thin isosceles triangle, whose foundations are different, but whose climactic peak is the same. If the circle, constricting to a point, was the geometric image for Ecclesiastes' spirituality, then an isosceles triangle, narrowing just short of collapse into a single vertical line, is the image for Plato's.

The Republic and the Phaedrus are natural partners in analogy.[2] They are both about desire, in the first case for wisdom and in the second, for beauty but ultimately in both cases, for the Good. The satisfaction of desire is in both cases an ascent, for example, in the Republic, where Socrates invites Glaucon to "come up hither" (Rep. 445) to the "height" their discussion has reached, in the vicinity of justice; or, in the Phaedrus, in the dramatic depiction of souls sprouting wings (Phaed. 251) in the face of beauty. But the moods of the two dialogues contrast markedly. The Republic is ostensibly an exercise in Platonic dialectic. We have already encountered an instance in the argument that, from its initial assignment of ease to vice and difficulty to virtue, by the end reverses that distribution. From its root in the Greek, dialectic is most simply reasoning through speaking, by question and answer. At its most philosophically refined, it is the process of identifying the essence or nature of a thing, from which its most important qualities can be inferred (Rep. 533). Dialectic so understood fuels the Platonic fascination with definition. But the process is difficult. When practiced in the question and answer form so characteristic of Plato, it is combative. The successful dialectician is like a warrior (Rep. 521, 543), ready to "run the gauntlet of all objections and ... disprove them" (Rep. 534). Scrapes, raids, battles, and overthrows are the metaphors for Socrates' exchanges with his interlocutors (Rep. 357, 472, 474, 487). The interlocutors themselves are combative, Glaucon explicitly so (Rep. 357, 549) and Adeimantus, at least once, implicitly, by the role of devil's advocate he assumes (Rep. 367), to say nothing of Thrasymachus. The Phaedrus, by contrast, is pastoral, playful, and prayerful. Images of rural tranquility dot the dialogue from start to finish. Socrates' relation to Phaedrus, the interlocutor, is teasingly playful (Phaed. 228). The playfulness informs Socrates' speech in praise of love (Phaed. 265) and tempers his harsh attitude evident in other dialogues towards pretenders to knowledge (Phaed. 268–269). Uncharacteristically, in this dialogue, Socrates allows himself to completely reverse himself, here on the issue of love, and, more uncharacteristically still, he prays (Phaed. 279). In the Phaedrus, philosophers are inspired lovers (Phaed. 249), not conquerors, and Socrates himself the model philosopher not through reasoning cogently, but through speaking ecstatically (Phaed. 249). The muses provide the mythological frame for what the Phaedrus values in analogy with the Republic's dialectic, namely inspiration. When Socrates asserts that "that which is moved from within has a soul" (Phaed. 245), he could be defining inspiration as such, whether the moving agent actually resides in his soul, like his inner voice (Phaed. 242), or touches it from without, like a muse. Knowledge-disclosing dialectic and beauty-infatuated love map quite different paths of upward ascent. But that Plato offers both is another mark of his proximity to religion, which, not only in Greek polytheism but also in the monotheisms of Judaism and Christianity offers up diverse paths to its stated goals of communion with the divine.

Dialectic is so important to spiritual ascent, in Plato, that it receives not simply discussion but what Socrates designates a hymn (Rep. 532). But this very designation must raise our suspicions. In an ideal world from which poetry has been banished and conventional religion appropriately constrained, how apt a metaphor is "hymn" for that very endeavor that has exiled poetry in the first place, namely philosophy? Plato presents dialectic as the culmination of philosophical method. It has such elevating powers that it can lift us up a line so vertical it has scarcely any slope. "Dialectic, and dialectic alone, goes directly to the first principle," (Rep. 533) pronounces Socrates some centuries ahead of Jesus laying claim to an analogous exclusivity in John 14:6. But unlike Jesus, dialectic does not appear to ascend directly to "the father". Dialectic can only function on objects of inquiry that have a nature or essence. It functions precisely by articulating that essence, from which everything important about the object can be inferred. But the Good transcends not only knowledge, but essence (Rep. 509). And so it appears to exceed the reach of dialectic. But then, dialectic is not the only means to knowledge, even if Socrates leads us to believe that it is the preferred one.

At the point where Glaucon and Socrates are on the cusp of understanding what makes a soul just, a curious exchange occurs between them. They have concluded that justice occurs in society when each of the several classes within it fulfills its own designated function. The reasoning process that led them there was, in its conversational refinements and corrections of various candidates offered to define justice, a model of dialectic. Now they are on the verge of applying this definition to the soul, which admits of parts analogous to social classes. But suddenly Socrates disparages the method of reasoning behind that application, which is not "at all adequate to the accurate solution of this question; the true method is another and a longer one" (Rep. 435). Socrates is about to reason by analogy and this is presumably what he means by the inadequate method; though the other and longer method goes unnamed here, we may surmise that he refers to dialectic, which only receives its "hymn" much later on, after the Divided Line and the Allegory of the Cave have made their propaedeutic appearance, at the point where Socrates evidently believes Glaucon may finally have been sufficiently prepared to understand it. Analogy and dialectic are themselves different but analogous modes of reasoning. As conversation is to dialectic, so is vision to analogy. Analogies are a type of metaphor. Like artworks, or poems, the impression they make is in the synthesis, not the analysis, of their parts. To understand the analogy is to "see" the similarity between the unlike things being compared. Analysis may be necessary to awaken that vision in some viewers, but once the metaphor has come into focus, analysis compromises rather than enhances its effectiveness. Otherwise, literalism and analysis would obviate the need of metaphor and analogy. And Socrates insists that these are surely needed (Rep. 487, Phaed. 257). As though to underscore how much understanding an analogy is like an act of vision, the metaphors that center the Republic, beginning with the divided line and proceeding to the cave, situate the sun at their culmination: The Good is to being what the sun is to perception.

Of these two modes of knowing, dialectic and analogy, Socrates explicitly prefers the first. Where the sun allows sight to encompass "the end of the visible world" (Rep. 532), dialectic allows reason to encompass the end of the intellectual world, which according to the divided line, surpasses the visible one. But the analogy is imperfect. The sun, as the most prominent of the heavenly bodies, and indeed, as a god, can function as both means and end of the knowledge it enables, as the allegory of the cave, which makes of it a climax, suggests; while dialectic is only a means. But the very fact that analogy itself serves to connect dialectic and analogy as means of knowing suggests that analogy is the greater and more encompassing avenue of knowledge. And for all Socrates' praise of dialectic, and implicit judgment on analogy, it is analogy that supplies the culminating access to the Good. Philosophers are "lovers of the vision of truth" (Rep. 475). What they aspire to is vision of the idea of Goodness

(Rep. 526), a beholding (Rep. 540) by the eye of the soul. Dialectic may go towards the first principle but it never quite arrives there. In precise reversal of what we would expect, it plays a preparatory rather than concluding role in the Republic's reasoning. It is what leads Socrates and his friends to clarify their idea of justice. But this is hardly the goal of their inquiry; the homelier and more accessible concept of justice (Socrates compares it to carpentry and shoemaking, Rep. 443) is a way station on the ascent to the Good, since, though justice is not goodness, "of all the things in a man's soul which he has within him, it is the greatest good" (Rep. 366). Socrates implies that intellectual vision takes up where dialectic ends. The Good which transcends knowledge and essence is nonetheless susceptible to vision. If vision is the medium of analogy, as conversation is of dialectic, then we should expect it to be analogy, and not dialectic, that carries us up to what Socrates calls "our final rest" (Rep. 532) in the vision of the Good. To the extent that the allegory of the cave, and the metaphor of the sun, position us to see, rather than analyze the Good, they are indeed the analogies that complete the Platonic ascent. Why, then, is not Plato's hymn to analogy? Perhaps because analogy, as a type of metaphor, is too close to poetry. And Plato, who excels at poetry, is loath to praise it, lest that admit back into his ideal state the disordering epic poems of his religious and cultural inheritance.

Perhaps the Platonic ascent is more poetic than Plato will admit. To realize or even merely to articulate an ideal state is not the true goal of the Republic. As Socrates observes, insofar as we can behold the pattern of the ideal state, and model our souls after its order, it hardly matters whether it exists or not (Rep. 592). But insofar as the ideal state is the reigning metaphor of the Republic, Socrates is constrained by it. If poetry disturbs the order that the Republic models, then he cannot praise it in this dialogue. But it is not as though poetry is in any case any more indulgent a tutor than philosophy. For however happy the soul made just by contemplation of the Good may be, it is still wed to a body that remains prey to ten thousand ills. Apart from the diseases that threaten, it may be unjustly imprisoned and condemned to death, as Socrates' was. The insurance of the embodied soul's happiness comes at the high price of the body itself. For the soul whose gaze is set as continuously as possible on the Good scarcely registers bodily sensations at all (Rep. 485). By the analogous ties between metaphysics and epistemology, there is a correspondence between the hierarchy of faculties in the soul and the rank of objects in being. "The several faculties have clearness to the same degree that their objects have truth" (Rep. 514). Opinion, a lesser faculty of the soul, can only be of objects in the world, a lesser form of being. Knowledge, the highest faculty of the soul, can only be of the highest forms of being, the ideas, and especially the Good (Rep. 477–478). At their highest upward reaches, the soul and its objects of knowledge comingle (Rep 490). Indeed the heights of being and of knowing have more in common with each other than the highest and lowliest forms of being have with each other, or the highest and lowliest forms of knowing. It is as though a highly developed reason, nourished on visions of the Good, attaches itself more to the Good than to its own body; and so freed of the body, even before its death, the soul maintains its self-contained happiness independently of the body whatever might befall it. This self-containment of the soul apart from the body also assures its immortality. For, as Socrates argues, a thing is only prey to the evils appropriate to it; the evils of the body, which are its susceptibility to physical suffering and death, do not touch the soul, whose own evils—the disorders of inner injustice—do not destroy it. And therefore nothing can destroy it. A soul that has failed to attain wisdom in this life has the opportunity to reach it in another, as the myth of Er, which closes the Republic, aims to show.

The Phaedrus, which like the Republic, pictures our afterlife, imagines philosophers and lovers to occupy, uniquely, the highest status there, of souls most primed to enjoy eternal visions of the Good (Phaed. 249). How lovers can come to hold that position is one of Phaedrus' themes. But this dialogue, as though under a burden to free itself of the spell cast by the Republic, can only begin by disparaging love for the disorders it occasions in the soul. Only after Socrates' inner voice prompts him to reverse himself on that position, do we get a view up the other side of the isosceles triangle, whose slope we scale, not on the propulsions of intellect, but on the wings of love. In counterpoint to the Republic, the hymn that this dialogue sings is to Love (Phaed. 265); nor does it rationalize love, or, to the extent that it does, in the first two speeches in praise of the non-lover, or mere friend, it renounces that view. On the contrary, love is allowed here to be a kind of madness, along with prophecy, healing power, and poetic inspiration. But the disorder of madness is here a recommendation in love's favor (Phaed. 265). For madness oriented towards the world of ideas, which is Plato's sacred world, can transport there more easily and readily than dialectic can.

The abstract beauty that enables erotic love is an object of vision in its own right. The soul saw it in the world of true being before embodiment muddied its perception. Once we "saw beauty shining in brightness . . . and then we beheld the beatific vision and were initiated into a mystery which may truly be called most blessed" (Phaed. 250). Perhaps the beatific vision, which appears to succeed the sight of beauty, is of Goodness itself. The two are in any case very close, for the "divine is beauty, wisdom, goodness and the like" (Phaed. 246). Plato defines beauty's relation to the good much less precisely than knowledge's, perhaps because beauty, more than knowledge, resists encapsulation, but the visions of the two do go together. At the level of the soul, too, the relation is close but loosely articulated. Thus the beautiful youth who excites love also draws good will from his lover (Phaed. 255), and, insofar as the soul resembles a horse-drawn chariot, the good horse of the soul, which, next to the bad, pulls the chariot is itself beautiful (Phaed. 254). Socrates' closing prayer for beauty of soul, allying it as he does with wisdom and temperance, is probably for goodness, too (Phaed. 279).

As knowledge draws the soul close to what it knows, so does beauty bind its perceivers to itself. Beauty is an effluence of particles which reach the soul from without, transforming it (Phaed. 251), and a stream which pours out of the soul to others' perception and back again, like an echo (Phaed. 255). That power of beauty to communicate over distance, imparting something of itself to those who see it, helps explain how it functions as a way to the good. Beauty, unlike wisdom, is literally visible to sight, as well as in its celestial form, to the eye of the soul. It is the only important celestial form of which this is true. By that double visibility, it uniquely links the world of sense to the world of forms. The preborn soul saw the form of beauty. One who now "sees the beauty of earth, is transported with the recollection of the true beauty" (Phaed. 249). And, if ideal beauty and goodness are celestial neighbors, the soul beholding one, sees the other too.

The earthly beauty that especially transports belongs to human beings. It inevitably sparks love in its beholders. Love is the fuel which propels the beauty-intoxicated soul heavenward, as desire for truth propels the philosopher. In Socrates' tale of pre-born life, each soul's character is patterned after a god's. Through love, a celestial character becomes human in the lover, so far as this is possible, and linked to other humans, prospective beloveds, in whom the same character is potential. Two such loving souls who discipline the physical pull of their love horizontally towards each other, divert the energy of it vertically, which, so redirected, elevates them towards the world of ideas. All that love needs to transform itself into a heavenly path is self-control, not the rigorous regimen of dialectic training. The lover need not be a philosopher, merely "not devoid of philosophy" (Phaed. 249).

Beauty's way to the good passes through love. Platonic love is erotic but unphysical in its most powerfully transporting form. The transporting is to visions of ideal beauty, whose place among the celestial forms allies it with the good. Beauty's way, unlike knowledge's, does not wholly sacrifice the world of sense, or imply a sharp division from the body. Its springboard to the other world is human beauty in this one. And though the love of that beauty must be disciplined, it need never be renounced, but bears the soul through to death, and beyond. For like the Republic, the Phaedrus too affirms the immortality of the soul.

But then the two dialogues have more in common than at first appears and by their commonalities suggest that knowledge and love do not define two such different paths of ascent after all. We might expect as much from the isosceles triangle that symbolizes their relation, since, by way of accentuating the verticality of the ascent, the two ascending sides of it come as close to merging into a single line as they can without losing their triangularity. The Phaedrus theorizes on knowledge, just as the Republic does on beauty and love. To some extent, the two dialogues may be set in dialectical relation with each other, each by its amplification and critique of the other distinguishing more clearly the helpful forms of knowledge, beauty and love from the unhelpful.

The Phaedrus is as capable of the Republic, if not more so, of defining just what dialectic is: "to divide all things into classes and to comprehend them under single ideas" (Phaed. 266, 274). Its tributes to knowledge are as enthusiastic as the Republic's and in places highlight more effectively the appropriateness of privative characterizations of the highest objects of knowledge: "colorless, formless, intangible" (Phaed. 247). To be sure, the Phaedrus clothes its praise of knowledge in its own distinctive, more bodily oriented imagery. It cannot resist transforming the transcendent *gazing* upon supernal ideas into *grazing* upon them (Phaed. 248). Feeding, an activity which the Republic confines to the lowest parts of the soul, becomes a metaphor in the Phaedrus for how reason incorporates ideas. The Socrates of the Phaedrus favors bodily imagery of pasturage, nourishment, nurture, and food. He moves beyond these images of taste to still deeper ones of touch when, in one of his loveliest metaphors for knowledge, he praises the "intelligent word graven in the soul of the learner" (Phaed. 276). The passage suggests a union of sexual intensity between word and soul; it is not just that the soul has received knowledge, but that knowledge has become ensouled, a living word that has a soul.

The Republic, for its part, understands the limits on the path of knowledge it commends. Dialectic can produce noxious weeds (Rep. 492). The Phaedrus' Socrates helps clarify that deviance when he criticizes the non-lover of Lysias' speech for his "worldly prudence" and "niggardly ways" (Phaed. 257). The non-lover of Lysias' speech bore a superficial resemblance to the Republic's philosopher, since "non-lovers desire the beautiful and good" (Phaed. 237). The Phaedrus' tribute to love serves the Republic's to knowledge by showing how philosophers differ from all types of non-lover. Philosophers are too close to what fills their souls with happiness to be prudent about how they "dole out benefits" (Phaed. 257). Knowledge which is calculatingly self-interested and not impassioned towards the most intimate union with the soul belongs to that deviant type the Republic deplores. From a blending of the Phaedrus' stance on love and the Republic's on knowledge emerges the view that only evils come of loveless knowing.

The Republic, for its part, in deference to the world of the Phaedrus, recognizes several levels of bond between beauty and goodness. Graceful rhythms and harmonies are taught the guardians very early on, when they first learn music, since "grace and harmony are the twin sisters of goodness and virtue and bear their likeness" (Rep. 401). Later, the growing guardian learns to appreciate the more abstract beauty of measure and number (Rep. 602), The soul which ascends from reasoning about numbers to astronomy (Rep. 530) takes the heavens as figures for an absolute beauty (Rep. 476), for "visions of inconceivable beauty" (Rep. 615), and itself grows in beauty all the while (Rep. 444, 588). Socrates, having completed his portrait of the guardians' souls, has in Glaucon's view revealed himself an artist: "You are a sculptor, Socrates, and have made statues of our governors faultless in beauty" (Rep. 540).

Like the Republic, the Phaedrus too critiques its own most cherished values. It is aware that not all love is good. Some of it is mad and furious. The Phaedrus' Socrates calls his second speech, in praise of love, a recantation of his first, which condemned it (Phaed. 244); but later, taking the two speeches as examples of rhetoric, he relates them dialectically, distinguishing between them two kinds of love, one "evil or left-handed" and the other divine (Phaed. 266). Left-handed love is a selfish, truth-denying madness that culminates in self-destruction (Phaed. 237–242). This is the very love, which the Republic assigns to the tyrant, that commands reckless deeds, frenzy and madness (Rep .573, 574). It is the same love from which old age has freed Cephalus, who quotes Sophocles on the peace of old age (Rep. 329). The Republic helps to reinforce what the sensuality of the Phaedrus may obscure, but on which both dialogues nonetheless agree, that the ultimate object of all divine love is ideas. The Republic also clarifies an issue in the Phaedrus that hovers beneath the surface there, that the problem of rhetoric is, in part, a problem of false or destructive beauty. The opening problem of the dialogue is that Phaedrus himself has so recklessly succumbed to the artificial appeal of Lysias' speech. Socrates must shear rhetoric of its seeming beauty, so that Phaedrus can behold the only commendable form its language can take, namely that of truth-seeking dialectic; he must convert the seeming beauty of rhetoric into philosophy. But Socrates had already developed this critique of a sister art to rhetoric, namely poetry, in the Republic. The Republic's critique of poetry juxtaposed to the Phaedrus' of rhetoric, points up how much the latter is an issue of beauty, which, like love, is divisible into lefthanded and divine expressions. The Socrates of the Phaedrus might borrow words from his namesake in the Republic, who warned against "sounds and sights" that hold us so irrevocably to this world, that we become "incapable of seeing or loving absolute beauty" (Rep. 476). And so the Republic serves the Phaedrus as a dialectical enhancement of what distinguishes the useful from the harmful in our attraction to beauty.

Socrates is the paradigmatic hero of Platonic spirituality, which finds more of a kinship with Hinduism than with Christianity. For though Socrates' story includes the account of his own death, as Jesus' does, the triumph of his ending is less over death than over life. The Bhagavad Gita, too, models a philosophy that incorporates rather than defeats death. For the hero of that poem, Arjuna, allows himself to become an instrument of death only on condition that he perform the acts of a warrior without desiring the results of them. A poem on the execution of war thereby becomes a tribute to peace, through this teaching it implicitly makes: that if actions that appear to require such focused attention on results, as those that warriors perform, can be executed with utter detachment from desire for results, then there are no acts in life that cannot be detachedly performed. Under the influence of such detachment, motivations towards acts that culminate in death evaporate; at the same time, death is no longer the evil it appeared to be, but actually incorporates into life, at least to the extent that desirelessness, from the standpoint of desire's ubiquity, appears to be a kind of death. Platonic spirituality is aflame with desire, but for objects—supernal ideas—so removed from our ordinary lives (to the point, for Aristotle, of not existing at all) that the effect on our lives of desiring them is to become universally detached. And so Plato takes us to the threshold of the Stoics, and to the syntheses that would evolve of his thought with theirs.

NOTES

1. All translations of Plato to follow are from *The Dialogues of Plato*, tr. Benjamin Jowett (New York: Random House, 1937).

2. Interestingly, they are sometimes treated together in the secondary literature. See, for example, David Ross, *Plato's Theory of Ideas* (Oxford: Clarendon, 1951); Martha Nussbaum, *The Therapy of Desire*. For an overview of religious sensibility in Plato, see Michael Morgan, *Platonic Piety: Philosophy and Ritual in Fourth Century Athens* (New Haven, CT: Yale University Press, 1990), which includes chapters specifically on the Republic and the Phaedrus. For a recent, popular appreciation of Plato, especially in contrast with Aristotle, see Arthur Herman, *The Cave and the Light: Plato versus Aristotle and the Struggle for the Soul of Western Civilization* (New York: Random House, 2013).

FOUR
Lucretius and Marcus Aurelius

The jump from Plato to the Stoics and the complementary philosophy of the Epicureans is a movement across opposites, from idealism to materialism. That passage becomes easier to make if it charts its course through Aristotle. Aristotle himself does not bid for inclusion in a book such as this. Whether because he inherited, and so took for granted, Plato's own rejection of the Greek myths, or because he was more receptive to metaphorical interpretations of them, he did not protest against them with the same harsh animus as his teacher did. On the contrary, the myths were a narrative form of science, intuiting supernal intelligence in the heavenly bodies which, according to his own science, they did indeed have. The personifications of those intelligences in human form were a dismissible anthropomorphism, designed for a popular audience. But they remain, to the philosophically discerning "relics of the ancient treasure"[1] of Greek wisdom. Perhaps Aristotle's astronomy of intelligent planets visible to the naked eye allowed him to be more generous to the myths, opening up paths of allegorical correspondence between them and science that Plato's austerely transcendent ideas blocked off. And some scholars suggest that Aristotle may actually have believed in the Greek gods.[2] But the chief reason his thought does not qualify for a philosophical spirituality is that he seems so relatively uninterested in the import of the sacred. At least his thought does not culminate in that or provide an apex from which to understand the rest of it. Much of Aristotle's thought on the sacred is confined to a single book, number 12, of the Metaphysics. Here we find a version of what would later be called the cosmological argument for God's existence, that from the necessity of causation, and the impossibility of an infinite string of causes, there follows an uncaused cause, or unmoved mover: "a self-dependent actuality most good and eternal."[3]

Aristotle's God is an activated version of Plato's serenely static idea of the Good. The Aristotelian God is the activity, not the stasis, of thought thinking what ranks highest in the world of thought, namely itself (as Plato would have it do). By activating the sacred, Aristotle fills a gap left by Plato of how to enlist the ideal world to explain change within the material world. All change or movement in the cosmos derives from love for the unmoved mover, whose perfection of self-containment draws all things, in their longing love of the independence they lack, towards it. But God takes no interest in us. This fact weighs more heavily in Aristotle's theology than Plato's only because, to the extent that an activated God is already a more personal one, we might hope for attention from it. But its indifference to us is not what accounts for the lack of spirituality in Aristotle; this owes, rather, to the fact that we ourselves need give over so little of our own minds to God. The way we become most like the unmoved mover, which is thought at its best, is by maximally activating our intellect. And this we do simply by exercising our mind. Our finite minds cannot grasp all that God's does (namely, God's self). And we should not even aspire to do so. But insofar as we actualize all that we are capable of thinking, we are as much like the unmoved mover as we can be. We will then think about the unmoved mover, in our limited way, but of much else besides. Indeed, the unmoved mover may, over the course of our thinking, occupy a relatively small portion of our thought, as it does in Aristotle's own corpus. Aristotle himself tips the balance of his philosophy away from spirituality and towards therapy when he remarks about happiness that, "if there is any gift of the gods to men, it is . . . happiness"; and to this speculation that already doubts the grounding of happiness in the sacred, Aristotle adds, "happiness seems, however, even if it is not god-sent, but comes as a result of virtue and some process of learning or training, to be among the most god-like things."[4] It is as though, on consideration, Aristotle identifies the grantor of happiness as ourselves, and implies that it is we who thereby become godlike, on attaining it, rather than gods who show their significance to us, by granting it.

But Aristotle is still a stepping stone to the more overt spirituality of Hellenistic materialism through his concept of the soul. The soul was an independent entity for Plato, imprisoned in the body. But for Aristotle, the soul is, famously, the *form* of the body. This would be as though to say, from Plato's perspective, that the soul is the supernal idea in which the body participates; a puzzling claim, to the extent that, if the body copies any idea, it must be simply the idea of the body. But Aristotle has secularized the supernal ideas. They are now simply one of four causes, the forms of material things, shaping them as a sculptor does his clay into the things they are. This is what the soul does for the body: musters a material complex of flesh and bone that might not otherwise be significantly distinguishable from any other inanimate matter, into the organic whole we know as a person. But the forms, as Aristotle understands them, lack the eternal home they had in Plato's world, and do not exist apart from the material things they cause. The Aristotelian soul which now animates the body in turn depends on it for its own being. The two are inseparable.

The consequence of this for the Platonic immortality of the soul is ambiguous. For the soul, as Aristotelian form of the body, cannot survive it. But, on the other hand, as bearer of the mind, it may enjoy a measure of immortality. For the mind is the one part of the Aristotelian soul that is recognizably Platonic. It "seems to be an independent substance implanted within the soul and . . . incapable of being destroyed."[5] "This alone is immortal and eternal."[6] But it is not clear that the identity of the ensouled body, which is our personal identity, persists in the mind that survives it. For Aristotle suggests that the mind comes into an identity of its own once freed of the soul that bears it, much like the Platonic soul does once freed of the body. What is clear is that Aristotle has opened up a possibility, inconceivable to Plato, of materializing the soul, which his successors, the Stoics and Epicureans, fully realized. The surprising result, for those who identify materialism with worldliness, is a revival of spirituality at the hands of these most materialistic of ancient ethicists.

In his great poem, *On the Nature of Things*,[7] Lucretius follows the spirit (if not the letter) of Aristotle when he says that body and mind are inseparable (3:584–594) (for Aristotle, it was body and soul that could not be parted). But he exceeds Aristotle, in his materialism, when he links mind to spirit so intimately the two cannot be parted (3:421–424). In this usage, spirit clings to its etymological origins in breath, referring as it does to the sheer life of the body, whereas mind connotes the workings of our intellect and emotions (the two together make up the soul). For Aristotle, the intellect enjoys a measure of independence from the body, which Lucretius has eliminated. By its union with spirit, and spirit's with body, mind, too, depends on body. Lucretius' materialism is not arbitrary. He simply builds on a common intuition that the epistemological court of last appeal for judging an object real is our sense of touch (2:434–441). (It is to this sense that Jesus appeals when he demonstrates his resurrected reality to Thomas [John 20:24–29], or, for that matter, to which Samuel Johnson appeals when he kicks a stone in an effort to refute George Berkeley's idealism.)[8] Touch is so thoroughly the dominant sense that all others reduce to it, even the one that served Plato as metaphor for wholly immaterial intellection—sight. For the way we see is by registering the impact on our eyes of diaphanous films that all objects emit, carrying images of themselves (4:26ff) abroad to whomever has organs to receive them.

In consequence, there is no refuge from physical suffering in a sanctuary of Platonic ideas. We are never so independent of the body as not to feel its pains. Lucretius finds the very idea of eternal Platonic soul consorting with mortal body absurd (3:800–805). With characteristically entertaining sarcasm, he demotes disembodied souls to the station of squabbling contestants for possession of newly born bodies (3:776–783). But he shares with Plato the intuition that many of our sufferings come through the body (3:731–734). And so by the confluence of his inheritance from Aristotle, that no soul escapes the body, and from Plato, that the body subjects us to some of our worst ills, he primes us for a philosophy that raises the volume of suffering even above what we heard in Ecclesiastes.

In some places, Lucretius sounds remarkably like Ecclesiastes, as when he notes both the orderliness of nature (3:789, 5:656ff) and its burdensome repetitiveness (2:294ff, 3:944–951); its indifference to the enduring satisfaction of human need (2:177–181) or to whether the sufferings it generates are merited or not (6:387ff; 6:1243–1246); the voraciousness of desire (2:10–14), which is never satisfied (3:1003–1016, 3:1080–1086, 6:20–21); the evil of politics (1:39–40); and, overall, the purposelessness of being (4:823ff) and the inevitability of decay and pain (1:1039–1041, 2:1131–1132, 2:1173–1174, 5:222–227, 6:29–32).[9] The closing verses of both authors' works are haunting depictions of the onset of death, as though the conclusion of the words foretells the conclusion of life. But the elements within the spectrum of suffering the two writers emphasize are different. The lament Ecclesiastes repeats, writing within a tradition for which genealogy was key, is that lines of inheritance are continuously foiled—itself an instance of the failure of nature to follow predictable moral laws of cause and effect; whereas part of Lucretius' whole point in writing is to elucidate the laws or principles governing the nature of things. If a single origin of suffering is discernible in Lucretius, it does not lie in the absence of laws binding effect to cause, but in a domain that receives only passing, dismissive reference in Ecclesiastes, namely religious ritual. For according to Lucretius, the rituals Rome practiced to appease the wrath of the gods were the single greatest obstacle to the one effective therapy for all human suffering. Religious ritual is much more intimately bound up with the problem of suffering than it was for either Plato or Ecclesiastes.

Lucretius' rejection of religion therefore carries a more venomous barb than Ecclesiastes' or even Plato's. It is "dead weight" under which we are "crushed" (1:63); it is "tight knots" that bind our reason (1:932). But chiefly, it is fear (1:62–65, 6:50–52). In locating the origin of religion in fear, Lucretius inaugurates a reading of it that has found many elaborators. But this is a different critique of it than Plato advanced. For Plato, the problem with religion was the stories it told, for these were largely false and corrupting of good, human behavior (insofar as they modeled, in the gods, bad behavior). For Lucretius, the problem with religion is the rituals it practices, for these presuppose a theology of vindictive deities that bind humans who believe in them to fear. Lucretius is not indifferent to the myths that so exercised Plato. He critiques them, too, but more for their falsity than for any corrupting influence he suspects they have. For example, when he explains that it is on account of lightning that humans possess the good of fire, it is difficult not to sense him implicitly rejecting Prometheus as the cause (5:1091–1093). But his one sustained critique of myth proceeds very differently from Plato's many criticisms. At the beginning of his book, Lucretius instances the evil of religion in a story of child sacrifice, Agamemnon's of Iphigenia. On a Platonic reading, this narrative, interpreted as story, would be rejected for modeling unacceptable behavior. But Lucretius reads it as history. For his critique is of what he takes Agamemnon to have actually done. And what he did was simply an extreme case of observing a religious rite. Agamemnon's act, on this reading, is a kind of *reductio ad absurdum* of religious ritual itself. Child sacrifice, he seems to say, is the practice at the bottom of the slippery slope of all religious rites, and the measure of the lengths to which the fear of gods they inculcate can go. It is this fear of the gods that troubles Lucretius, as their bad behavior did Plato, and the rites sustaining it that thereby draw his wrath, as the myths of their evil deeds did Plato's. And it is no small thing. It "abases our spirits" to the point of "cringing on the ground" with fear (6:51–53); it infantilizes us with terrors of the kind children experience in the dark but that we, to our shame, know in broad daylight (2:55–58); and, for all our obedience to it, it leaves us lacking in the end any true succor (6:1271–1277).

Part of Lucretius' persuasiveness as a philosopher depends on his having, like the Buddha, heightened our awareness of suffering. The vivid punishments of the afterlife, as recounted by the Greek myths (for example, the myth of Sisyphus), in which Lucretius does not believe, become metaphors of suffering in this life (3:978ff). The mere cessation of suffering thereby becomes happiness in itself, without any additional need (2:16–21). And that allows for the happiness-inducing enhancements of life to be simple indeed, as they in fact are for Lucretius and Epicureans generally, turning as they do on the contemplation of nature,[10] and on friendship (2:29–33).[11] These simple pleasures are less prey to disruptive sufferings. But Lucretius' persuasiveness also depends on the particular account of suffering he gives. For religion only counts for the evil it does because of the cure it occludes for suffering. It is the wrong answer to the right question: how can we cease to fear death? For, according to Lucretius, this fear is the deeper fount, than religion, of our woes, and his tone towards it, like for a foe we admire for his strength or skill, is more respectful. Once religion has been cleared from our path we can attend seriously to this respectable fear and advance so far in understanding as to eliminate it.

Anti-religious readers of Lucretius must not be lulled by his arguments against religion, with which they may agree, into thinking that they count equally to defend the importance of the question religion wrongly answers, of how to overcome the fear of death. Lucretius needs to additionally argue that this is our greatest fear. For it is not obvious that it is. Of the major world religions, only Christianity, especially in its Pauline expression, seems to stake its claim to our attentions on the fear or horror of death. Lucretius' arguments for the centrality of this fear bear some resemblance to the transcendental reasoning of Kantian philosophy: to the detriment of our peace of mind we pursue the vain goods of wealth, power and complex pleasure, involve ourselves in war, and blind ourselves with religion. More of our sufferings than is superficially obvious derive from our entanglements with these pursuits. What can explain this self-destructive behavior but the fear of death, which goads us unthinkingly into these excesses by way of concealing itself from our reasoned attention. We might think that any concealed fear would work to the same effect. But the fact that these self-destructive behaviors ultimately culminate in death suggests to even some modern therapeutic ways of thinking that Lucretius may have rightly pinpointed the originating source of these behaviors in the fear itself of death. In his autobiographical *Confession*, Tolstoy observed that his own profound fear of death provoked in him, paradoxically, thoughts of suicide,[12] a possible consequence that Lucretius himself acknowledges (3:79–82), and which suggests, as Sophocles also did in Oedipus, that the objects we most irrationally fear are the very ones we unknowingly pursue. Conversely, if we can be shown that our behavior is irrational, the ultimate object of it may reveal itself to us as our deepest fear; and so revealed, cease to bind us. If irrational fear is the ultimate ground of our suffering, reason, which exposes the irrational, is its cure (2:47–53).

Only Epicurus himself receives more enthusiastic tributes from Lucretius than reason does for evincing the power to heal. But this is not Plato's visionary reason. Lucretius' comparison of reason to an army, whose power to defend us it exceeds, shows how far his reason is from Plato's, whose image, explicitly rejected by Lucretius (2:60), for this highest faculty of human knowing was the sun. Lucretius' reason attends precisely to those muddled aspects of our experience, such as our emotions, that Plato disdained and allowed to sink to the bottom of our souls. Reason trained on our fear of death dispels it, not through the promise of immortality, which it withholds from us, but from undermining a rational condition of that (and any) fear, that, in the actual presence of its object, we are under genuine threat. But if, in the presence of our own death, we have died, then we no longer constitute a subject under threat, since we are no more. And so the fear of death, in anticipation of it, is irrational (3:862–869).

Whatever the therapeutic power of this argument, Lucretius must acknowledge that its beneficent effects extend only to our minds. But he has committed us, as well, to the life of the body, whose non-psychosomatic sufferings persist even for the fear-cured mind. And he has linked mind and body so closely that the sufferings of the one produce sympathetic reactions in the other. Diseases of body effect disturbances of mind (3:152–160, 3:463–469). But the direction and quality of interaction are reversible: tranquility of mind can ease disturbances of body. Apart from his arguments against the fear of death, much of Lucretius' metaphysics works in the service of tranquility, even in the midst of bodily pain. This is true even of the form of its presentation: the epic poem, which, as Lucretius tells us, he employs to ease the internalization of his possibly difficult teachings (1:936–950). But the bitterness of the teachings, which mandates the poetic coating, is superficial. Much like the ancient Hindu philosophical systems, which paired a metaphysics with a therapy, for example, Samkhya with Yoga, suggesting that what we believe about reality affects our emotional wellbeing, Epicureanism joined a discipline of therapy with the atomistic materialism inherited from Democritus. The atomism, which reduces everything, including soul and deity, to configurations of tiny, insentient particles, has salutary effects on our emotional life. For the exclusion of intent from them means they can never intend the suffering they occasion. Our bodily pain results from disturbance of the atoms that constitute our being; our wellbeing returns when the disturbance dissipates (2:963–966). That the whole of the disturbance is explicable in physical terms comes as a balm, at least to psyches that were accustomed to think of physical suffering as divine punishment. But Lucretius' evident pleasure in the sheer act of understanding—"divine delight and shuddering awe" (3:28–29)—suggests that the insights of the mind over the sufferings of the body afford some counteractive relief. If bodily suffering is simply a temporary rearrangement of atoms, then perhaps the suffering it occasions must be understood in terms of what Pierre Hadot calls, "the view from above."[13] The sum of the two fundamental laws of cause and effect that Lucretius discerns, that "nothing is ever created by divine power out of nothing" (1:150), and that "nature . . . never reduces anything to nothing" (1:216), is an equilibrium in the totality of nature that contrasts with the ceaseless change in its parts. This becomes another argument against the fear of death, by recasting decomposition as a mere reordering of indestructible parts (2:1002–1004). But, in addition, the observer of nature who perceives that equilibrium from "the view from above" participates in the peace of it (2:1–21). By way of making this point, Lucretius suggests a sophisticated perspectivism. He pictures an army on maneuvers on a hillside, seen from a distance so great that the real motion there is imperceptible. That perception of stasis is illusion; but Lucretius takes it for the truer view of reality since, for all the movement there the atoms undergo, there is no change in the whole of them (2:320–332). If we can view our own bodily sufferings from above, in the same way, we may enjoy some relief from them.[14]

The more difficult question for Lucretius is whether his therapy also constitutes a spirituality. For all his hostility to organized religion, Lucretius does communicate to some readers a religious sensibility (as outwardly unreligious scientists, such as Darwin and Einstein, sometimes do).[15] But where does his sense of the sacred point? To constitute a spirituality, Lucretian Epicureanism must identify a location of the sacred, i.e., a place from which all reality springs, removed from us either metaphysically or epistemologically, but nonetheless accessible to us and, above that, necessary to and sufficient for our wellbeing. At first sight, the gods might seem to fill this role. They are not, for Lucretius, the arbitrarily vindictive beings of Greco-Roman mythology, but sublime, diaphanous entities that exist between the boundaries of worlds. So positioned, they enjoy self-contained contentment, removed from and indifferent to all the anxieties that plague human life. But in their removal from the world, this or any other, they fail to serve as source for it, and so lack a prime mark of the sacred. But two features of the gods suggest they may not even be significantly real to Lucretius himself. The first of these is that they are intangible by nature (5:150). If the sense of touch is our test of reality, then the gods must fail the test. It is surely no accident that Lucretius never proves what he promises to do, that the divine world differs radically from ours (5:155),[16] since worldliness at all, as he has presented it, is inseparable from tangibility—even if a tangibility so refined that senses more acute than ours would be needed to feel it. The confirmation of the unreality of the gods comes when Lucretius, illustrating the three different kinds of "everlasting objects" (5:351ff), where some reference to gods would surely be appropriate, fails to mention them at all. It is as though Lucretius' genealogy of the divine (5:1161ff), which precedes Nietzsche's of morals by many centuries, and which grounds our sense of the divine in delusive dreams, applies not just to the purported gods of human imagination, but to the very idea of gods as such.

Still, the idea of the gods is propaedeutic. The gods hold the place of the happiness Lucretius would inspire in us. Why else would Lucretius begin his poem as he does with such high praise for Venus? The usefulness of the idea of gods is, in a faint echo of Plato, that it models the practice of contemplation. Lucretius tells us what true piety is: "the power to contemplate the universe with a quiet mind" (5:1203). It is not so much the gods themselves who do this, as we who do, in the presence of their godly statues (6:71–78), which provoke a reflective stance.[17] And what do we contemplate in our attention to the universe? It is the point of Lucretius' whole book to tell us: "the ultimate realities . . . those atoms from which nature creates all things" (1:55–56). The atoms, then, fulfill that function of the sacred the gods fail to fill, as source of all reality. They are also at an epistemological distance from us. Lucretius must argue for their existence (e.g., 1:623–626). But once established, they show themselves to have further qualities traditionally associated with the divine: eternal, infinite (in number), self-moving (2:133), resistant to descriptions in language (3:258–260). A comparison with the concept of soul in Hindu Samkhya philosophy heightens the suggestive aura of the sacred that hovers over them: for both entities, the soul in Samkhya, and the atom in Epicureanism, are small beyond our powers to conceive; both systems evoke the concept of these infinitesimals by placing them at the end, or limit, of a series of progressive diminutions, stopping just short of nothingness (cf. 4:110 and Svetasvatara Upanishad 5:8).[18]

The atoms are insentient and indifferent to our wellbeing. Their frenetic movement is hardly contemplative. But, as Lucretius has suggested, by his ancient equivalent of our modern laws of thermodynamics, the totality of them enjoys perfect rest. Lucretius' word for the totality of atoms in their interrelationships, by which the specifics of reality arise, is nature. And it is this totality, poetically personified as Venus, and taken for an object of contemplation, that supplies our greatest happiness. Nature is: "all-creating," "free and uncontrolled," "the clever inventor" (1:629, 2:1090–1092, 5:234). Like the wisdom figure of Proverbs 8, she counsels us (3:931ff). But it is as though this personification is the true coating of Lucretius' teaching, and not his Muse-inspired poetry. Insofar as Greco-Roman polytheism is already a kind of nature religion, as his tribute to Venus suggests, Lucretius has ready at hand a familiar image in which to clothe his own, atomic understanding of nature; perhaps even the rival stoic view of nature, as cosmic reason, dresses his own nature more appealingly, simply by sharing the same name. But then, Lucretius has already suggested that his true vision of the whole comes by way of an illusion of rest in the moving parts of the whole, beheld at great distances. Venus and the cosmic reason of the Stoics are simply variations on that truth-disclosing illusion.

If the atoms hold the place of the sacred in Lucretius' philosophy, all that remains to show is that knowledge of them is accessible to us even across our epistemological distance from them. It is true that their existence is the great, hidden mystery of nature, because they are so small. But that hiddenness supplies the epistemological distance that allows them to qualify for sacred in the first place. Like love in the Judeo-Christian systems, which spans a metaphysical distance as great as that between life and death (Song of Songs 8:6), so reason in Epicureanism is strong enough to span the epistemological distance between the atoms and our knowledge of them. We need not rehearse Lucretius' arguments for them, which turn on the reality reason already accords other imperceptibles, such as change so gradual it is unnoticeable between any two contiguous points along a continuum of it (1:322–328). From the standpoint of philosophical spirituality, what matters is that Lucretius' arguments are based on reasoned inference from experience (rather than on revelation). Lucretius is sure, as Hegel would later be, that thought running its natural course leads its followers to what they need to know. On the one hand, Lucretius' antiquated science compromises his persuasiveness for modern readers. For example, his theory of perception—images conveyed by diaphanous films that touch the eye—works to precisely the opposite effect he intends, as a tribute less to the salvific powers of reason than to the seductive charms of the imagination. But then, the imagination is just another word for what Lucretius calls the coating—the poetry—of his substantive teaching. If, for modern readers, the relation between substance and coating is reversed—a seeming of science is the coating, while the substance is the poetry—then, for all his belonging to classical antiquity, he is more romantic and modern in his philosophical spirituality than he would have been able to imagine.[19]

Most of us would not say the same of Marcus Aurelius, who lacks the lightness of touch to be interpreted, as Lucretius can be, in ironical terms. Perhaps the very form of meditations, which came to supply the name of his work,[20] as opposed to poetry, discourages the detachment from his own words that irony demands (much as detachment was for him and Stoics generally one of the highest values). The mood of Marcus' meditations is pathos. The pathos derives from the impossible situation in which Marcus finds himself, adhering to a Platonic therapy of withdrawal from this world, without the metaphysical sanctuary of another world. Marcus must create his sanctuary within himself—must fashion, as Hadot puts it, quoting Marcus, an "inner citadel"[21]—in an internal space of the soul, that is doomed soon, in any case, to vanish. It is as though Plato were confined to a purely material world, or allowed to languish at the bottom of the cave, from which there was no recourse, except perhaps to close his eyes so as at least not to be deceived by the false images he was forced to see. The reasonings by which Marcus manages not to despair in this situation must wrench the heart of attentive readers.

Marcus is in the unique situation among philosophers of having been worshipped, himself, as a god. In the complex hierarchy of the Roman civic rites, what was understood as the *genius* of the emperor—a personification of his energy, simultaneously identical with and distinct from his actual person, in the same way that the gods themselves, in accord with the ambiguity of which polytheism is so tolerant, both identified with and transcended elements of nature—received veneration akin to god-directed worship.[22] (After Marcus died, his son Commodus took the further step of deifying Marcus himself, in accord with precedents of emperor-worship already established, but not consistently followed, in Roman religion.) If Marcus himself does not register this fact in his book, Ittai Gradel, in his *Emperor Worship and Roman Religion* may supply a plausible explanation: emperor worship, according to Gradel, was a purely ritual practice marking a maximal power differential between ruler and subject; it operated in an intellectual and philosophical vacuum, and implied nothing about the internal nature of the emperor himself.[23] Consequently, Marcus' book, which is directly solely to his inner nature, appropriately ignores so purely outward a status, a perfect indifferent. Marcus has his own understanding of the sacred, but it does not include himself in any way that does not also potentially include everyone else.

Certainly there is no record of his insisting on worship of himself or his genius. The one passage of his book that may acknowledge his quasi-divine status, according to Roman religion, simultaneously dismisses it, when he admonishes himself not to become "Caesarized" (6:30), as though to block an outward taint from becoming inward. When once asked about the appropriate form a statue of him should take, he advised that the material be bronze, rather than the more precious gold or silver, precisely to discourage worship.[24] And so there is no contradiction, that might have been exploited to ironic effect, between the outward veneration that fell to Marcus, and his own internal judgments of personal inadequacy; which leaves the pathos, alone, to set the tone.

In the spirit of Aristotle, Marcus is tolerant enough of traditional religious vocabulary to use it. He names Zeus (5:7) and alludes to Apollo (11:18). He frames his book, as the final redactor of Ecclesiastes did, with pious affirmations of traditional religion. The prefatory expressions of gratitude that open the book conclude with a long list of goods in his life for which he thanks the gods; and, in the last book, he confesses quite openly his faith in the gods, and on grounds reminiscent of Lucretius' arguments for atoms, that imperceptibility is no argument against reality (12:28). But he is not consistently faithful. It may be that the gods do not exist (2:11). They are, in any case, transformed in his hands beyond recognition into paragons of reasonableness. And so transformed, they resolve back into their polytheistic origins in nature, the presumed subject and possessor of the reason that guides the whole of reality. As personifications, apart from their identity with nature, they do not hold the place of the sacred in his thought, as he credits them neither with creation of the world nor with an indispensable role in our own wellbeing. Even when he thanks them for their gifts to him, almost everything listed is what, in Stoic terms, is indifferent, subject to forces beyond human control; and the one true good he lists, to have had "a clear picture in mind of what it means to live in accord with nature," (1:17) comes from the gods to an only relative degree, "insofar as it lay with the gods" to grant it; which cannot be to any very great degree, insofar as that clear picture is a function of reason, which renders those who exercise it actively self-determining, rather than passively receptive of gifts from without.

But the frame of piety, bounding a body of impious text, or text that radically reinterprets the nature of piety away from traditional religious views, is not all that Marcus shares with Ecclesiastes. Both speak from a persona of aristocratic rulership. And both sound the note of world weariness that comes naturally to reflective natures that have known a surfeit of comfort and opportunity. "The things much honored in life are vain" (5:33); "All is ephemeral" (4:35); "you are always seeing the same things and the monotony makes the spectacle tiresome" (6:46); "nothing is new" (7:1). These are English translations of Marcus' words, from the Greek, not Ecclesiastes', from the Hebrew. Marcus matches Ecclesiastes' image of dead flies in perfume (Ecc 10:1) with a corresponding image of his own, for much of life: bath water soiled with sweat and grime (8:24). He darkly inverts Ecclesiastes' lament over the failure of continuities across the generations; what continues from one generation to the next is death. As though to underscore this reliable repetition, Marcus repeats his statement of it, cast in the form of chains of death—one who has buried another, will soon himself be buried—to suggest that this is all that the dead bequeath to the living (8:25, 8:31, 8:37, 9:33, 10:34). Marcus also acknowledges a fact that disturbed Ecclesiastes, that the good appear to suffer and the bad flourish (2:11, 9:1), but he is less vexed by this than Ecclesiastes was. When itemizing the evils of life, he dwells more, as Plato did, on the sheer existence of inner disturbances of soul: anger, hatred, deceitfulness, insolence, guile, pride (2:1, 9:2). But he is also aware of physical pain—cuts and burns (4:39), disease and lameness (5:8), fever (7:71), plague (9:2), loss of limb (7:68)—as commentators suggest is natural for one writing in the thick of military campaigns.[25]

If the sufferings Marcus notes are not even more varied than this, it is probably because of the urgency with which he applies his therapy to them. The sufferings can barely speak before they have been transformed into their own cure. This is especially true of that suffering which, for the sheer bulk of space it consumes within the meditations, surpasses all the others: fear of death. Marcus, like Lucretius, marshals against death a cadre of fear-banishing argument. We need not fear death because: it is a mere redistribution of parts (5:13); it is the intention of nature (8:19); it either ends the awareness that enables fear at all or transforms it into new life (8:58); it is the release from our shell (9:3). Lucretius resonates in the first and third of these arguments. The second, with its presupposition of a teleology lacking in Epicureanism generally, is distinctly Stoic (and Aristotelian). But the fourth is most striking for its Platonism. The Stoic pathos shows most forcefully here in the absence of a destination for our shell-released soul, which, according to Stoic theory, simply dies with the death of the body. Death itself becomes his redoubt when Marcus beseeches it to come quickly (9:3).

Marcus has another therapy for the fear of death, more characteristically philosophical for the movement it follows, of subsuming a problematic specific, in this case death, under a resolving universal: change. Death is a species of change (10:7). And change more easily converts itself, than death does, from problem to solution. Many of Marcus' comments on change themselves instance the very reality they describe. They are mobile conversions of evil to good. We hear at first about the melancholy of change, which takes from us even the things closest to us (5:23). But then, out of that, Marcus extracts the happy lesson: that none of our troubles are lasting (5:23). But soon it appears that all the processes of nature, itself governed by an all-wise reason, depend on change, whose former overtones of sadness, for us, now utterly vanish: "Do you not see then that for you too to be changed is precisely similar, and similarly necessary to the universal nature?" (7:18). What began as a source of grief ends as a link to the sacred.

But then all the sadnesses of life that Marcus cites undergo instant conversions to their opposite. Some of these transitions have precedent in Plato, who craved them almost as much as Marcus did. Marcus subscribes to the Platonic view that evil in the soul is simultaneously a suffering there; and conversely, goodness of soul an immunity to suffering. By the identification of moral with natural evil, so characteristic of Plato, Marcus too obtains for us a bulwark against pain: only what depraves us harms us (4:8); whether we are depraved depends entirely on us; therefore, we need never suffer harm. But then, Plato offered us an outside aid to the resistance of evil: the world of ideas, which sustained us in goodness through our sheer act of contemplating it. As our contemplation of the Good intensified, our sense of connection to the body and its many ills lessened. That world is lacking in Marcus, who must muster from within himself whatever self-defensive powers he can; which is all the harder since the body and its sufferings are inescapable. Here is where the pathos sounds most movingly. For Marcus borrows Plato's vocabulary for and attitude towards the body—it is this "paltry flesh" (7:66), "this doughlike matter which has grown up around you" (7:68), an encasement (12:3), an envelope (12:2), a shell (9:3), a corpse (10:33)—without granting us sanctuary from it; for, contra Plato, we and our body are "organically one" (5:26). And so Marcus' therapy for the ills of the body comes at the high price of self-division. The sufferings of the body are its own concern (7:64, 8:40, 12:1). Who Marcus really is is his mind (12:3). The mind distances the body by withholding judgment on its ills, which (again, contra Plato) cannot but register with it. Like the Buddhist who observes his sensations of pleasure or pain, but withholds affirmation or negation of them, and so escapes karma formations, Marcus fashions a measure of self-detachment. "The mind preserves its own calm by withdrawal" (7:33), and "sets itself apart" (7:55) from the body. It dwells in solitude from the body, as though on a mountaintop (10:15), even while wed to it.

And now it is this picture of the self-divided human person—a body prey to suffering, a self-contained mind—that is converted to a whole. For bodily suffering becomes, from a vantage point the mind can adopt, a register of the workings of a larger nature. For nature is a body, too. If the sufferings of our body can be reconceived as changes in nature's, necessary to its well-being, like the deaths of cells in our own body needed for our ongoing health, then the burden of them becomes a blessing. They are bridge to a view of oneself from the vantage point of nature's whole. And from that perspective, there is no pain, as there is nothing outside of nature that could cause it (8:50, 10:6). Pressing further the analogy to our own organism, Marcus can say that nothing that is good for the whole of nature can truly harm a part of it (10:6). But nothing happens that is not for the good of the whole. And so none of its parts ever really suffer.

Marcus can sustain such a view only on the assumption that nature, writ large, is an organism. Perhaps the urgency of the social, in Marcus, and sense of obligation to the common good, which characterizes Stoicism generally, in contrast to the Epicureans, is partly motivated by the part it can play in a suggestive analogy with nature. If nature does indeed constitute a kind of city (4:4), whose parts are as intimately complementary as those of Plato's ideal state, then we can view our part in it from the vantage point of reasoning mind—the philosopher king—that rules it. Marcus' word for this process of converting a seeming harm to a true good, is adaptation. It is the availability of this perspective to us, joined to his conviction that we are free to initiate only good acts, that underlie the binary form of advice Marcus often gives himself, to maintain: "imperturbability in the face of what comes upon you through an external cause; righteousness in activities caused from within you" (9:31). Nor do this imperturbability and this righteousness any longer belong to unrelated parts of the human person. For it is just the part of righteousness to withhold judgment on the uncontrollable ills that befall the body. To judge those ills bad is to become bad, by the rebellion it constitutes against nature (2:16). In the consummate conversion of Marcus' Stoicism, the seeming passivity of withholding judgment becomes the paradigmatic instance of moral action.

Therapy and spirituality are much more intimately related in Stoicism than in Epicureanism. We had to tease the spirituality out of Lucretius; but in Marcus it is irrepressible; his therapy is barely presentable without recourse to his understanding of the sacred: the whole of nature and the reason that governs it. Plato too taught, in the Timaeus, that nature was an organism, but a flawed one governed by an imperfect reason. This allowed for him to acknowledge genuine defects in the world. Marcus perfects Plato's imperfect world and its governing reason; and thereby deprives himself of any cause for complaint against the world. For the Stoics generally, nature was famously both passive body and active mind. The mind of nature, which governed its body, was the perfection of reason. It holds the place of the sacred in the Stoic worldview by virtue of the source it is of nature's processes (it is "creative Reason" (4:14), and the indispensability of it for human wellbeing. The homologous relation between human nature and the whole of nature—both are passive bodies governed by active reason—opens a way to apply to nature's reason what Marcus has already attributed to humanity's, namely that separation from the rest of reality (7:55) that constitutes a characteristic mark of the sacred. Lest we miss the divinity of nature's governing reason, Marcus also sometimes equates or implies the equation of it with god, the gods, or Zeus (3:11, 5:8, 5:27, 6:35, 7:53, 8:27, 9:28, 10:1, 12:31).

The homology of the divine and human natures, at the macro- and microcosmic levels, invites a very obvious spirituality into Marcus' meditations, to which he repeatedly alludes. Our own reason is the same as nature's, assigned to oversee the small part we are of nature's whole. We are more than connected to the divine; we are part of it, if only we could see it (2:1, 2:15, 7:67). It is the effort of seeing that allows such wide scope for us to be out of sync with our essential homology with nature. Our separation from the sacred is here, as in Lucretius' case, wholly epistemological and rests on our mistaken predilection to judge reality rather than simply see it. Following Plato, Marcus ascribes serious moral consequences to our errors of judgment. These both sadden and deprave us. And they are temptations to the soul at every turn. (In one passage, Marcus itemizes four species of error to which we may succumb: contingency, antisociability, falsity, and disproportion [11:118]). Marcus' deconstructions of our images of the realities that give us pleasure—food as corpses (6:13), clothes as hairs (9:36), precious metals as sediments (9:36)—and his injunctions to "erase imaginings" (7:29) and to "observe the causes stripped of their coverings" (12:8)—are more than exercises in self-denial. They are efforts at clarity of vision. The difficulty of this is part of what motivates the meditations themselves, which provide a vehicle for internalizing what his mind has seen without digesting. The results of his "theoretical contemplation" (3:1) are more than merely intellectual; they are also experiential (3:1), and constitute what Marcus in some places calls worship (6:10). In consequence of this worship, we become more like nature's governing mind: more reasonable and more immune to false perceptions of suffering. We perceive and act upon the fact that my path and nature's are identical (5:3).

Paradoxically, given the significance of the social to Marcus and Stoicism generally, we also become more solitary, and more accustomed to live out of the inner retreat of detachment that is ever available to us (4:3). Marcus' faith in reason to see the truths of Stoicism—that nature is an organic whole governed by an all-wise reason with which our own is identical—is unbounded: "Intellect and reason . . . can overcome any obstacle in their way" (10:33); they are "powers sufficient unto themselves and to their works" (5:14); so much so that they are all we ever need to consult (1:8). However, Marcus himself does not supply the lines of argument that culminate in those Stoic truths. Indeed, at the level of his therapy he is content to allow on several occasions that Epicureanism may be true. In that case, Marcus' spirituality becomes the very thing he warns himself against, an imagining or covering. That he clings to it all the same is a further confirmation of the pathos that sets the tone of his writing. Then too, should he fail to follow his own advice, he denies himself the excuse that he marshals for others, that the unhappy and demoralizing consequences of his errors of judgment may in fact be part of nature's larger plan. If Lucretius' perspectivism shows in a willingness to read the false as true, Marcus' shows in the radical distinction he keeps between that which he can control, namely his own soul, and everything else, including nature and other human beings. No judgment appropriately falls on the things he cannot control; all judgment appropriately falls on himself.[26] That distribution of judgment corresponds to Marcus' measure of the extent of his own freedom, which is absolute over his own soul, and extinguished everywhere else—a striking judgment, indeed, coming from an emperor. If Plato sacrificed the body to secure his happiness, Marcus, in effect, sacrificed the world.[27]

Their respective moods of irony and pathos make of Lucretius and Marcus the perfect complements. But the two philosophers also have much in common: quite apart from their distinct philosophies of nature, both delight in the unexpected beauties of nature (*Rerum Natura* 2:22–36 and *Meditations* 3:2); they both believe in the essential equilibrium of being (RN 1:216 and Med. 4:4); they both savor what Hadot calls, the view from above (RN 2:1–21 and Med. 9:30); they are both materialists. Between the similarities and complementarities, unexpected reversals occur. Consider, for example, a metaphor they share, of waves beating against a stone on the shore (RN 1:326, Med. 4:49). The stone appears to resist the waves, but in fact is slowly eroded by them, a diminishment imperceptible to the naked eye that can only be measured over great stretches of time. We might think that the long-suffering Marcus would adopt the long-term view of the stone, and comment on its slow demise; and Lucretius, who allows falsity to figure truth, to capitalize on the illusion of the stone's stasis. In fact, just the opposite happens. It is Lucretius who accepts the demise of the stone, and Marcus who holds to the illusion of its permanence, yet another pointer to the fragility of the foundation of his spirituality, which is itself, perhaps, prey to the encroachment of undermining arguments. Pathos and irony are alternative responses to suffering. Pierre Hadot suggests that we take Epicureanism and Stoicism in concert, for they "correspond to two opposite but inseparable poles of our inner life;"[28] which is to suggest that they remain live options of choice for practitioners of spiritual life today.[29] We shall have occasion to remember them as we move closer to the philosophies of our own time.

NOTES

1. Metaphysics 1074b (tr. W. D. Ross) in *The Basic Works of Aristotle*, ed. Richard McKeon (New York: Random House, 1941).
2. See Richard Bodeus, *Aristotle and the Theology of the Living Immortals*, tr. Jan Edward Garrett (Albany: State University of New York Press, 2000).
3. Metaphysics 1072b (tr. W. D. Ross).
4. Nicomachean Ethics 1099b (tr. W. D. Ross) in *The Basic Works of Aristotle*.
5. On the Soul (tr. J. A. Smith) 408b in *The Basic Works of Aristotle*.
6. On the Soul (tr. J. A. Smith) 430a.

Lucretius and Marcus Aurelius 57

7. The edition followed and quoted from here is: *On the Nature of the Universe*, tr. R. E. Latham (New York: Penguin, 1951).

8. James Boswell, *The Life of Samuel Johnson*, edited by Arnold Glover (London: Dent, 1901), 1:313.

9. Ecclesiastes and Lucretius make a natural comparison, and some take Ecclesiastes precisely for an early Epicurean.

10. E. J. Kenney notes the "rapturous" quality to Lucretius' appreciations of nature. E. J. Kenney, *Lucretius* (New York: Oxford University Press, 1977), 5.

11. Pierre Hadot, *Philosophy as a Way of Life*, tr. by Michael Chase. (Malden, MA: Blackwell, 1995), 88–89.

12. Leo Tolstoy, *Confession and other Religious Writings*, tr. Louise and Alymer Maude ([n.p.]: Digireads.com, 2010), 13–14.

13. Hadot, *Philosophy as a Way of Life*, 238–250, and especially p. 243 for its Epicurean expression.

14. Martha Nussbaum suggests that Epicurus himself found the more effective antidote to bodily pain in friendship. Martha Nussbaum, *The Therapy of Desire* (Princeton, NJ: Princeton University Press, 1994), 111.

15. For example: "Lucretius' nature was essentially a religious one." E. J. Kenney, *Lucretius*, 5; "His motives are religious in the deepest sense." Anthony M. Esolen, introduction to *On the Nature of Things* (Baltimore, MD: Johns Hopkins University Press, 1995), 5.

16. As observed by John Godwin in Lucretius, *On the Nature of the Universe*, tr. R. E. Latham, notes by John Godwin (New York: Penguin, 1994), 230–231.

17. "The Epicurean religion was essentially contemplative." E. E. Sikes, *Lucretius, Poet & Philosopher* (Cambridge: Cambridge University Press, 1936), 116.

18. Svetasvatara Upanishad in *The Thirteen Principal Upanishads*, tr. Robert Ernest Hume (London: H. Milford, 1934).

19. For a look at Lucretius' impact on and affinities with modernity, see Stephen Greenblatt, *The Swerve: How the World Became Modern* (New York: Norton, 2011).

20. The edition used here: *The Meditations of Marcus Aurelius*, tr. G. M. A. Grube (Indianapolis, IN: Hackett, 1983).

21. Pierre Hadot, *The Inner Citadel: The Meditations of Marcus Aurelius*, tr. Michael Chase (Cambridge, MA.: Harvard University Press, 1998).

22. What follows draws from Ittai Gradel, *Emperor Worship and Roman Religion* (New York: Clarendon, 2002).

23. Ibid., 26.

24. Cornelius Motschmann, *Die Religionspolitik Marc Aurels* (Stuttgart: F. Steiner Verlag, 2002), 81.

25. Anthony Birley, *Marcus Aurelius* (Boston: Little Brown, 1966), 291, 293.

26. In his zeal for self-judgment, Marcus even allows that his own inner, self-caused disturbances of soul may harm the whole of nature, which magnifies their import beyond the bounds of his own soul (5:8). But other passages remedy this excess, by ascribing to nature the power to adapt all that happens to its own good ends (8:35) — another instance of Marcan conversion.

27. This is a negative way to capture the extremity of Stoicism's longing for sanctuary. But it can also be stated more positively: the Stoics "were the only Greek philosophers who tried to find a rationale for everything within their concept of a perfect, all-embracing nature." A. A. Long, *Hellenistic Philosophy: Stoics, Epicureans, Sceptics* (London: Duckworth, 1974), 170.

28. Hadot, *Philosophy as a Way of Life*, 273.

29. Martha Nussbaum adds that the modern academic disciplines of psychology, economics, and political theory, to say nothing of ethics, could profit from revisiting ancient Hellenistic philosophy. Nussbaum, *The Therapy of Desire*, 484–510. For a sympathetic look at Stoicism as a still livable philosophy, see William Irvine, *A Guide to the Good Life: The Ancient Art of Stoic Joy* (New York: Oxford University Press, 2009).

FIVE

Descartes

One of the ways in which Descartes departs markedly from Marcus is in his evaluation of philosophy itself. Marcus loved and esteemed philosophy. It was his repose and his guardian (Meditations 6:12, 2:17). His language towards it anticipates Boethius' later personification of it, Lady Philosophy. But Descartes adopts a skeptical tone towards philosophy. Reviewing the subjects he had been taught in school, he reserves for philosophy his most dismissive judgment, that it dealt in plausibility merely and bestowed on its practitioners little more than a fatuous admiration (DM 6) from those less learned.[1] Because everything it claims can be successfully disputed, it attracts arrogant adepts at mere argumentation (Med. 5). The problem with philosophy was that it was self-divided among its many schools and teachings. This was an ancient, Christian critique of philosophy.[2] Though Boethius acknowledged these self-divisions, picturing them as tears in the robe of Lady Philosophy, he implied these were due not to any failing in philosophy itself but to false philosophers who plundered her teachings, which were in fact unified. For Descartes, philosophy bore the responsibility for its self-divisions, which rendered it an ineffective teacher, and on attaining maturity he abandoned it, according to his own account, as simply one among many inadequate, book-bound instructors (DM 9).

But then, the philosophy Descartes inherited was vastly different from the one that Marcus had. Between Marcus' time and Descartes', philosophy acquired the epithet with which its medieval expression is still largely identified: the handmaid of theology.[3] To the extent that it was, it no longer served as a self-contained, religion-independent spiritual way. The philosophy that Descartes inherited came to him by way of the then recently founded Jesuit order, who in turn received it from the Middle Ages, some traditions of which it was their mission to defend against the assaults of the Reformation. Chief among those traditions was Aristotelian philosophy as interpreted by Thomas Aquinas who, though a radical in his own day for championing Aristotle, had by the time of the Reformation himself become traditional, school-bound, scholastic. It is not that philosophy at Thomas' hand was not vibrant. Étienne Gilson suggests that the signal achievement of medieval philosophy was to uncover previously concealed rational solutions to philosophical problems by shining on them the light of faith,[4] in somewhat the same way many of us learn the grammar of our own language, which was always incipient in our speech, only by first being taught that of another. This reverses the direction of the handmaid relation, except that the philosophy so aided would never presume to constitute a self-sufficient spirituality. Certainly Thomas never intended Aristotle to be understood that way. The trouble was that, after Thomas, Aristotle had become so wedded to the distinctly Christian spiritual way, as a philosophical foundation for it, critiques of him sounded to official ears like attacks on the church.

This put Descartes in a bind with respect to philosophy. For, on the hand, he inherited the ancient Christian critique of it, that it was too self-divided to offer substantive human guidance. In the modern, epistemological inflection of this critique, the problem of philosophy was that its multiple, mutually negating views provoked skepticism. And part of Descartes' self-appointed charge was to refute skepticism, in defense of Christianity. But on the other hand, from the stream of Christianity that was friendly to philosophy—insofar as it could be subordinated—he also inherited the Aristotelian tradition, which he largely rejected. As a result, he sided with Christianity where it rejected philosophy, and contested it where it defended philosophy. From the standpoint of philosophical spirituality, this infects his thought with a profound ambiguity: for, insofar as he defends Christianity, does he reject philosophy as an independent spiritual way? or, insofar as he contests Christianity, does he offer in its stead a philosophy that constitutes, as over against Aristotle, a self-sufficient spiritual way?

Descartes falls victim to his own critique of philosophy here, for his accounts of his philosophical project can be read in defense of either view. On the one hand, he implicitly ranks himself with the wider band of Christian philosophers (Med. 3)—those thinkers who, as Gilson suggests, uncover new rational truth within the provinces of faith—and confesses to hold most dear those truths unique to faith (DM 28); but on the other, he also acknowledges that his discoveries cannot but disturb some of his readers: "I do not know whether I ought to tell you about the first meditation" (DM 31), he coyly confides for, as it transpires, this involved a radical doubt that momentarily undermined belief in the very existence of God. If we were to base our resolution of this ambiguity on the evidence of history, we would have to deny that Descartes was in any obvious way a Christian philosopher. For his thinking outraged both the

Dutch Calvinist and French Catholic expressions of the church of his day. And no wonder. What Amelie Rorty has called Descartes' "breathtaking presumption"[5] in the area of natural theology—offering as a defense of faith newly nuanced proofs that, by implication, all previous "Christian philosophers" must have overlooked, for what is scarcely the Christian god—cannot please Calvinists of any stripe. And Catholics rightly suspected in this new anti-Aristotelianism a loss of philosophical foundation for their interpretation of a central rite, the Eucharist,[6] which mediated, according to them, a transformation of inner, (Aristotelian) matter from wine to blood, while leaving the outward form of the wine untouched; to say nothing of the judgment the intensely Catholic and spiritual Pascal pronounced on Descartes, that his subordination of God's existence to guarantor of the external world, was unforgivable.[7] In 1663, Descartes was added to the Index Librorum Prohibitorum, and in 1671 his teachings were banned at the University of Paris.[8]

But this direction, in which history leads us, away from Descartes the Christian philosopher, does not necessarily uncover for us, within Descartes, a philosophical spirituality. For, as Pascal implied, the problem of Descartes may be that he is not spiritual at all—not overly interested, that is, as Aristotle seems not to have been, in the realm of the sacred or its presumed importance to us. There is already a hint of this in the transformation the ancient and medieval concept of soul underwent at the hands of Descartes, who subsumed it under mind—a subsumption so thoroughly bequeathed to posterity that the language of soul, unless it is a genre of song, has become archaic—and, in the process subordinated and attenuated the emotional life that, together with mind, used to constitute the soul. And so another ambiguity surfaces, between Descartes' aim, as stated in the Dedication of his *Meditations*, to defend the faith against skepticism (Med. 1–2), and his aim, implied at the beginning of the first meditation, to lay a foundation for the sciences (Med. 17). This ambiguity will trail us throughout this chapter and confront us repeatedly. But if Descartes himself fails to offer a philosophical spirituality, he lays the foundation for one who does, and whose work is scarcely comprehensible apart from Descartes,' namely Spinoza.

Descartes is the first of our philosophers to relieve philosophy of the task of palliating by mental means our physical ills. Although his characterization of physical pain as a confused idea suggests that clarity of understanding brought to bodily suffering can ease it, he does not rest content with such Stoic measures. He enthusiastically entrusts the care of our body to medicine, for which he has unbounded, almost messianic hopes (DM 62). But ambiguity clouds his choice of which of the two remaining category of ills, the moral or epistemological, is more philosophically pressing for him. For one of the marks of the modernity of Descartes' thinking, distinguishing it from the ancients,' which he alternatively appreciates and disparages, is the primacy in it of epistemology.

So pushed to the fore, it leaves the ethics with which Plato and the Hellenistic philosophers linked it so closely in the background. On the one hand, a greater urgency attaches to theoretical beliefs when they are understood to have practical consequences (DM 10); but on the other, it is a virtue of theory to proceed without regard for "beliefs which belong to the conduct of life" (Med. 15). Descartes lived during the Thirty Years War. And he echoes the sorrows and disappointments with the world that all our previous philosophers voiced. He speaks with Ecclesiastes when he says that "looking with a philosopher's eye at the various actions and enterprises of all men, there is hardly one of them that does not seem to me vain and useless" (DM 3); with Plato, when he worries that "few would prefer what is right to what is useful" (Med. 2); and with the Hellenistic philosophers when he laments the "infinity of maladies" (DM 62) that plague us, of both body and mind, and longs, in the face of these for "tranquility . . . above all things" (DM 74).

But these ills pale in the face of the one that most preoccupies Descartes, the ill of error. "We are prone to error" (DM 3) and "confounded" by it (DM 4). Error is so much our chief problem that it defines our imperfection (Med. 56), and a rule for avoiding it would ground "the greatest and chief perfection of man" (Med. 62). Lest we think Descartes has practical errors in mind, he informs us that, at least within the confines of the *Meditations,* his concern is solely with errors of truth, not of goodness (Med. 15). It would never have occurred to Lucretius or Marcus or perhaps even to Plato, at least in some of his dialogues, to distinguish between these, either because theoretical truth so clearly bore on the conduct of life or because, where it did not, it was not significant. That Descartes does distinguish between them raises the question of how they are related. The connection is not Platonic: it is not ignorance that underlies and occasions evil, but rather will. It is when our will to affirm or negate exceeds our knowledge of what is true or false that we both err and—Descartes adds startlingly (given his just cited disclaimer about moral error)—sin (Med. 58). Does the sin reside in epistemological error itself, or in the consequences that error has for our behavior, corrupting it? If the first, then Descartes has transformed ethics into epistemology, a move that coheres with a relative lack of interest in spirituality and raises doubts about the ethics of God. For it is by virtue of our greatest commonality with God that we sin at all. The only activity we can perform to an infinite degree, and hence to the degree that God does, is to will. This, for Descartes, is what makes us in the image of God; which raises doubts about the goodness of that image.

On the assumption of a distinction between practical and theoretical ills, Descartes proposes a different therapy for each: a method of reasoning for the theoretical ills, and maxims of life for the practical ones. If error is the evil that the method of reasoning excludes, then hesitancy of act is the evil that the maxims exclude. Indeed, part of the reason two kinds of therapy are necessary in the first place is that the method of reasoning may take years to apply—as, according to Descartes, it did in his own case—while daily activity demands a ready decisiveness. A deep suspicion of hesitancy to act is part of the Western (Latin) Catholic inheritance—it was Dante who consigned the indecisive to a kind of prefatory realm of hell. In *The Passions of the Soul,* Descartes devotes a section to the ill of irresoluteness, which he characterizes as a species of anxiety that as often as not imagines a necessity of paralyzing choice where none actually exists.[9] Within the context of the *Meditations,* it may be understood as the analog in practice to the theoretical doubt and skepticism Descartes is at pains to overcome. In any case, the tenors of the two therapies differ. The therapy for error—to begin with clear and distinct ideas, resolve all complex ideas into their parts, build assuredly from the simple to the complex, and review work along the way—is extreme, simple, certain, and unreligious. The extremity is in the scope of what must be doubted before clear and distinct ideas are attained; the simplicity, in the clarity and distinctness of the few ideas that pass the test of radical doubt; the certainty, in the assurance of the steps that bridge the simple to the complex; and the unreligiousness in the fact that all this is possible by the sheer exercise of reason, without recourse to religion. The maxims, by contrast—to follow religion's lead, to be firm in decisions made, to subordinate desire to reality, and to exercise, as far as possible, the method for avoiding theoretical error—is moderate, tolerant of given complexity and uncertainty, and religious. For though, like the Four Noble Truths of Buddhism, the four Cartesian maxims include as their fourth the way to overcome the ills explicit or implicit in the preceding three—they allow the ills to stand and even indirectly affirm them. That the maxims of life may rest on theoretical error does not disturb Descartes; which, given the grave imperfection that error constitutes, implies either that imperfection of practice is unimportant, or that the criteria for evaluating practice are radically different from those for evaluating theory. If the second, then Descartes has driven deeper the wedge between the two kinds of therapy. This appears most noticeably in the second maxim which, from the standpoint of theory, sounds like a prescription for sin: to extend the deciding will beyond the reach of reason's light.

But then, the methodical life and the maximed life part ways at the very beginning over the issue of clear and distinct ideas, which, for the sake of the exigencies of daily action, which the maxims are intended to address, are foresworn in their case. But the divisive consequence of these ideas does not stop there, for they are founded on an ideal of reflexivity, which, in turn, presupposes self-division. For what makes an idea clear—as opposed to distinct—is that it carries its truthfulness within itself; which it can only do if its very occurrence in the mind is its verification. Such ideas, which produce their truth through their sheer existence, are rarer than the onomatopoeic words within the realm of language that they resemble. In fact, Descartes discovers only two, the idea of himself, and of God. They both presuppose reflexivity. For the assurance of his own existence only comes from his observation of himself having an idea (any idea); and this self-observational stance is inescapably self-divisive. The consequences of it, in Descartes, are perhaps the most radical dualism of body and mind that western philosophy conceived. Where Plato denied the body for the sake of happiness, Descartes denies it for the sake of truth. The body is not part of the self-affirming idea, whose truth is guaranteed, with which Descartes identifies himself—and so it is not part of Descartes or, by extension, of any of us.

The theoretic therapy which yields so disembodied a mind seems useless for any kind of practical therapy, which must take into account the body and its ills. This explains why Descartes supplies both kinds of therapy. But from the standpoint of practical therapy, Descartes offers something we have not encountered before: an incipient spirituality that does not emerge from a practical therapy. For, entirely independent of the practical therapy, which, attending faithfully to inherited religious teachings, continues to operate while Descartes undergoes his cure from epistemic error, the theoretic therapy leaps to God and the possibility of one of the most intense spiritualities imaginable. For by another, but different, version of an argument from reflexivity, the idea of God that Descartes finds within himself guarantees the reality of its referent. It is an idea of such perfection that only a being as perfect as its object could account for its existence at all. It is as though we are a mirror in which God has reflected an image of himself, which we could never, ourselves, have devised. Wakening to that fact would be a little like a creature within Lewis Carroll's looking glass coming to the realization that it is the reflection of something realer than it, to which it owes its existence, across the divide of the glass. The division on which Cartesian knowledge rests is not simply within ourselves, but in God too. Perhaps that is the deeper sense in which the Cartesian self is made in the image of God.

Much as Descartes may have relished an imaginative literary vehicle for expressing a philosophical idea—he was fascinated by dream narratives not only for theory but also in practice[10]—he would not have rested content with it for purposes of argument. And his arguments for God draw deeply from just the kinds of distinction he disdained in "the schools". If we, who know at first only the image of himself God has cast in us, can infer from it the God who cast it, that is because of the peculiarly dual reality that ideas carry. Part of their reality owes to the fact that they are, indeed, ideas, or occurrences in mind.[11] This is their formal and material reality. But, "because ideas can only be, as it were, of things" (Med. 44), they derive another degree of reality from the objects they purportedly represent. And this is their objective reality. The degree of objective reality an idea has correlates with the degree of formal reality its object has. And the degree of formal reality entities possess is a function of their independence of other entities: the more independence, the more formal reality. Ideas themselves, dependent as they are on mind, enjoy, pace Plato, only a modest formal reality. But they can bear immense objective reality. Typically, there is no sound inference from a mere idea to the reality of its object. But as the objective reality of an idea rises, in direct proportion to the independence of what it purportedly represents, a point comes that its formal and objective reality merge. An utterly independent entity would lack for nothing, no perfection, not even existence, and so must exist. The very idea of such an entity constitutes its own secure bridge to the reality it represents.

Like the sacred Idea of the Good in Plato's system, Descartes' God is at least in part ideational. It is an idea that guarantees its own objectivity. Descartes' God differs from Plato's in that it is the metaphysical realization of all perfections, not just goodness. Metaphysical perfection rests on the concept of degrees of reality, whose criterion is independence of other things: the more independent, the more real and perfect. God is the perfection of independence from all other things. Descartes has reasoned to this God from the assumed vantage point of disembodied mind. And in so doing, he has arrayed before us the simple ingredients of heaven, as previously conceived by some of the medieval thinkers: disembodied thought in perennial contemplation of God. And so it is no wonder that Descartes pauses momentarily, at the end of his Third Meditation, before the God to which pure reason has taken him, "to gaze upon, to admire, to adore the beauty of this immense light," for here is "the greatest pleasure of which we are capable in this life" (Med. 52).

On what basis does this God hold Descartes' attention? Part of the appeal of the Cartesian God is that he is indeed a creator God, who fashioned Descartes himself, and on whose being Descartes continually depends. In so believing, we might suspect that Descartes has resorted to the maxims of his inherited religion. In fact, he has subsumed under the concept of perfection itself creation of all that exists. We can tease out the tie between perfection and creation. If perfection is measured by independence, then nothing in the world is perfect. But in the dependence from which all worldly things suffer, they must depend on something else; what could fill the role of sustaining them but the one absolutely independent entity, namely God? The dependence of all on God is not the same as the creation of all by God. Aristotle too subordinated all of matter to God without attributing its creation to the divine. But from the standpoint of philosophical spirituality, it is enough if the sacred conditions, even if it does not create, all the rest of reality. It is this summation of perfections that Descartes momentarily pauses to contemplate at the end of Meditation Three.

But only pauses. Descartes does not linger too long in the presence of it. His sights are soon directed toward the world, whose reality is guaranteed by the perfect God he has just proved. For a perfect God would not deceive us with only seemingly veridical sense impressions into accepting as real a world that was not. This argument turns on what we might characterize either as an ambiguity or a breadth in the concept of perfection. For the divine being is not only metaphysically perfect, it is also morally so. In fact, we can construct a chain of logic on Descartes' behalf connecting the two kinds of perfection. All reality apart from God depends on God for existence. Goodness is the moral characterization of a divine subject that sustains the rest of reality.[12] But the soundness of the move from metaphysical to moral perfection, and the divine guarantee thereby attained for external reality, is less significant for our purposes than the fact of the move at all. A Platonist, or Platonically inspired mystic would linger lovingly in the relation Descartes just proved, between a disembodied mind and the sacred; the relation would flower out of its epistemic confines into a full blown vision of heaven, for it was in such terms that some of the medieval thinkers conceived it. But Descartes quickly descends from this height to the world of the senses. As he wrote to the Princess of Bohemia, "It is necessary to have properly understood once in a lifetime the principles of metaphysics, because they are what give us knowledge of God and our soul but it would be very harmful to occupy one's intellect frequently in meditating upon them because it would impede it from attending to the functions of the senses."[13] And here is where Descartes lost Pascal.

The *Meditations* climax not in the vision of the philosophical God, but, by the time of Meditation Six, in the reinforced assertion of the mind's independence of the body. If independence is the measure of reality, then Descartes has positioned the mind to enjoy a higher reality of its own. Readers of Descartes who side with Pascal would suspect that the argument for God was an unnecessary diversion from Descartes' true aim, voiced at the beginning of the *Meditations*, to lay groundwork for science. And they could summon the critique of that argument, sounding out ever since Descartes made it, that it is circular, since, pushed to the extreme of corrosive doubt, Descartes has God both guarantee and be guaranteed by the truth of clear and distinct ideas. A Pascalian reading would be: the argument for God is an affectation. The clear and distinct ideas are self-guaranteeing. The mind that has them is absolutely independent, and so itself occupies the place of a now redundant God. The proof of the external world need not go by way of God, since the coherence of our current perceptions "with the whole rest of my life" (Med. 90) argues, by contrast with its absence in deceiving dreams, for an ordered world we genuinely perceive. Like the red slippers to Dorothy, orderliness has been available all along to us as a criterion of truth, since it constitutes the third rule of Cartesian method, and it is a frequent reference point in Descartes' writing. But in consequence, Descartes fails in both philosophical and religious spirituality. He is a secularist in the literal sense: one whose focus is the world. The, to modern ears, chilling confirmation of that and final proof of his indifference to God is the aspiration Descartes holds out for us, once we know the world truly exists, to become "masters and possessors of nature" (DM 62).[14]

Whether we pronounce this judgment on Descartes depends in part on how moved we are by the contemplative interlude that interrupts the flow of argument at the end of the Third Meditation. Descartes can have had little to gain from the Catholic authorities by inserting it there. It is too recessed to draw attention and its implication, that a God proved by philosophical reason can also sustain a spiritual life, would not have pleased religious authorities of any kind. And so, like a clear and distinct idea, it seems to verify its own authenticity. But the very title of the book invites a spiritual reading of it, for *Meditations* would raise in readers expectations of a devotional work as much in the seventeenth century as now. Like Marcus' meditations, Descartes' ostensibly serve to internalize superficially simple ideas that either human nature or common sense resist. This was necessary for Descartes, as it was for Marcus, insofar as he adopts the authorial persona of an undistinguished intelligence (DM 2). Readings of the *Meditations* have appeared that explicitly analogize it to the *Spiritual Exercises* of Ignatius Loyola, and the prayerful practices in which Descartes' Jesuit education would have tutored him.[15] Both writers commend a rigorously reasoned discipline of alternating purgation and illumination which works best in solitude, on retreat. Both temporarily withdraw us from the world for the sake of a more productive return to work within it. But then, the Jesuits would withdraw us again from the world, on successive retreats, whereas, having brought us back to a world that was temporarily in doubt, Descartes is content to leave us there. This itself should trouble us, given how purely mechanical, colorless, and reducible to mathematical formulae that world turns out to be.

There is other cause for doubt that Descartes' thought constitutes a philosophical spirituality. Towards the end of his life, in response to questions from the Princess of Bohemia, he wrote another book of therapeutic import in which spiritual sensibility is virtually absent, the *Treatise on the Passions*. It is as though the *Meditations*, having briefly scaled the heights of a philosophical spirituality, prepare the way for a return, not simply to the world, but to a secular therapy. At the same time, the *Passions* is a test case for the application of Cartesian method. For at least one feature of the passions is clear and distinct, and provides the opening for further reflection about them, that insofar as they occur, they do so unmistakably. For, in contrast to the ordinary representative idea, which may or may not correspond to the reality it purportedly represents, "we cannot be misled in the same way regarding the passions, in that they are so close and so internal to our soul that it cannot possibly feel them unless they are truly as it feels them to be" (TP 26). Descartes here expresses what would later find articulation in the therapeutic principle that no one presume to tell another what they are feeling; but he also fails to account for the fact that we can misname, misidentify or wholly fail to see an emotion of our own. There is, in any case, in the analysis of emotion, ample room for obscurity and confusion, features which Descartes believes especially characterize the treatment they received from ancient philosophers (such as Marcus) and which require them to be studied afresh, from the standpoint of "a natural philosopher" (TP, Pref.). There is, further, a distinct reason for their obscurity: because they depend on the body for their cause and existence, and as no clear and distinct idea bridges its way to the obstructive body, its secrets are only disclosed through experiment and observation. Accordingly, the passions, as ideas or occurrences in our mind, are "confused and obscure" (TP 28). Part of what accounts for their obscurity is that they are indeed, from the standpoint of our minds, passive: occurrences that happen to us, rather than ones we (that is, our minds) initiate. Descartes' explanations of their origin in the body are surprisingly confident for one who insists on their confusion and obscurity. The explanations have, for modern readers, the same appeal of quaintness that Lucretius' account of perceptions does, and read more as story than as science: a rarefied form of blood, called animal spirits, moves an organ in the brain (the pineal gland), which converts its own physical motion into mental impressions of emotion. But the reduction of something as immeasurably qualitative as passion to something as measurably quantitative as blood (its volume and speed) is a hallmark of Cartesianism, which also gave us analytic geometry and a mechanism for reducing the elegance of curves to algebraic equations.

Passions can be pleasant or painful. Even the pleasant ones, insofar as they are passive, provoke therapeutic concern, but it is the painful ones that most urgently ask for therapy.

Following his epistemic method, Descartes isolates six simple passions from which all the others are compounded: wonder, love, hatred, desire, joy, and sadness. This treatise provides more scope than the *Discourse* or *Meditations* did to itemize kinds of human suffering. Hatred and sadness in various combinations with each other and the other passions yield vanity, jealousy, fear, anxiety, and despair. These emotions are not necessarily bad in themselves. Like pain of any kind, they can warn us away from things or actions that are ultimately harmful to us (TP 137). But our therapeutic tools need not be so merely reactive. The mind comes equipped with a counter to the passivity of the passions through its capacity to will. For the pineal gland can take its direction as much from the willing mind as from the moving body. Emotions that are caused by our own acts of will have more the quality of actions than passions. It is, once again, self-reflection that enables the possibility of pleasure that we ourselves cause, when we become self-consciously aware that we are willing well. But this is a pleasure over which we have absolute control. Insofar as we locate our chief pleasure in this, we are less dependent on causes of pleasure or pain outside us, including our own body. Descartes might say (though he does not explicitly) that, according as the most independent things are the most real, we become more real. But we also become more moral in the expected religious sense. For, insofar as we can assure our own happiness, we are freed of fears that others could take it from us, and empowered to believe that others are capable of the same self-determined happiness as ourselves; which makes us behave more generously towards our neighbor. And a generosity grounded in our own self-esteem, through the willing well we perceive in ourselves, and over which we have complete control, is the chief remedy against all the painful passions.

Though, in this treatise, Descartes does not define or deduce what it means to will well, we can infer his meaning from the *Discourse on Method*. Keeping in mind that our theoretical and practical lives ask for different therapies, we could say that to will well in our thinking is to affirm only what we know clearly and distinctly to be true; and to will well in our practical lives is to behave religiously, singlemindedly, stoically, and reasonably. We may indeed recognize a religious maxim in Descartes' admiration for those who "esteem nothing more highly than doing good to others" (TP 156). But, in showing his admiration for these good folk, he neither cites the Golden Rule of the New Testament, nor deduces their principle of acting from any stance they may have towards the sacred. The reason is evident: what Descartes has just admired is generosity, and this quality he believes he has deduced from sheer human self-esteem. God is not necessary for it either as a ground or a bulwark, any more than he may have been necessary to prove the external world. Descartes already hints this way when he suggests that as we locate our pleasures more exclusively in what we control, namely our own volitions, we become more independent and so "in a certain way like God by making us masters of ourselves" (TP 152).

But becoming like God is quite different from coming into relation with God, may indeed supersede it. The *Treatise on the Passions* has nothing in it like the contemplative interlude, pointing to a philosophical spirituality, at the end of the Third Meditation. Where the book refers to God, it withholds sustained attention from that idea, or even, as though to confirm Pascal's suspicions, subordinates it to therapeutic aims. For example, in a Stoic moment, Descartes suggests a dual therapy for the painful passions: to focus our desires on what we control, namely willing well, and to accept all that merely happens to us as divine providence (TP 146)—a subordination, once again, of God to human need, this time for consolation rather than knowledge. One way to read the *Treatise on the Passions* is for how it would interpret the contemplative interlude that closes the Third Meditation. What Descartes describes there—"a being having all those perfections that I cannot comprehend, but can somehow touch with my thought" (Med. 52)—appears to provoke wonder in him. But wonder receives a very mixed review in his study of the passions because it impedes understanding, and so we should "attempt to free ourselves from this inclination as much as possible" (TP 76). In extreme expressions of it (into which the contemplation of God would presumably draw us) "it can never be other than bad" (TP 73). Under the heading of love Descartes does acknowledge devotion, whose "principal object is undoubtedly the supreme Deity" (TP 83). But he does not encourage us to exercise devotion, or locate our highest happiness there, as he appeared to do in the Third Meditation. Rather, when he defines and illustrates joy he does so in terms of what the soul can attain for itself: "the purely intellectual joy that arises in the soul through an action of the soul alone" (TP 91). For Spinoza, such joy found its highest expression in the contemplation of God. For Descartes, this joy might show more in the self-esteem he felt on willing well, or in the pleasure he had in the successful application of epistemic method, which yielded a contentment greater than any other he claimed to know and which "so filled my mind that nothing else was of any consequence to me" (DM 27). But then, insofar as the proof of God itself was a successful application of epistemic method, the happiness Descartes felt in it may have owed more to the power of his own it demonstrated, than God's.

If Alan Bloom was right about Descartes, that the choice between him and Pascal, which every French person faces, was between "reason and revelation, science and piety"[16] then we should never have devoted a chapter to him at all but for his anticipation of Spinoza. Others have read him differently. Karl Jaspers wrote that Catholicism "was essential to the meaning of his entire philosophy and to the practical grounding of his life."[17] His spirituality may in that case have been more religious than philosophical. But perhaps the evaluation of him that must give us most pause is Simone Weil's. That intensely spiritual compatriot of his, who lay outside the bounds of both Christianity and Judaism, and exhibited so much in common with Pascal[18] that we would expect her to share his evaluation of Descartes, did not. She admired him greatly and referred to him more often in her writings than to Pascal. A reading of Descartes through Weil, who aspired to an ideal of self-abnegation, would attend, in Descartes, to its logical analog, namely contradiction. A complexity of contradiction[19] weaves through Descartes, not only between science and spirituality, but between theory and practice, innovation and tradition, nature and reason, self-sufficiency and interdependence, conjecture and certainty, dream and reality, even French and Latin. Consider Descartes' long apology for withholding from the public the fullness of his thought, which occurs in the sixth part of the *Discourse*. On the one hand, he was simply afraid of the censure that might fall to him, as it had to Galileo only a few years before. But on the other, for all his democratic welcome of coworkers in the fields of science, "joining together the lives and labors of many" (DM 63), he expects no insight from sharing his thought with others, and resigns himself to the fact that his task "could not be accomplished so well by anyone else but the same person who began it" (DM 72). Contradiction can communicate more than impasse. In Hegelian dialectic, it is the raw material which the dialectic resolves. In Ecclesiastes, it accentuates an interrogative mood. Where philosophy indulges poetry, the contradictions that beset it may become metaphors, as they sometimes do in theology, where the human mediates the divine, and earthly love, heavenly love. Contradictions that have become metaphors may serve as bridges to the sacred. One way to read the contradictions in Descartes is as unrealized metaphors, denied their overt expression for fear of the blockage they would be to clearness and distinctness. The spirituality of Descartes shows in the blank places where the metaphors would be, and where he has carved spaces for them, but where they do not actually occur. Such a spirituality of absence, of promise unfulfilled, would appeal to ascetics like Simone Weil: Cartesian spirituality as exercise in self-denial.

Let us take, for example, the contrast between Descartes' choice of French for the *Discourse* and Latin for the *Meditations*. We can read this divergence as, if not a strict contradiction within Descartes, at least a tension. To the extent that languages define worlds, and a contrast between two of them two different worlds, a juxtaposition of them can be read metaphorically. Seventeenth century French was, of course, a vernacular, and European Latin the language of scholarship and the Catholic Church. Descartes himself explains the choice of French in terms of his hope to reach a fresh and receptive audience, beyond the censorious readings he expects from the bookishly learned (DM 77). A typical explanation of the subsequent choice for Latin is that, under the chastening of the chilly reception the French book received, he was wise to at least attempt to win the approval of the learned, i.e., the theologians, after all. But the juxtaposition of the two languages in two books which are often bound together in English translations suggests a metaphorical reading of the pair they make. The two languages bound together invite explication by a theory propounded centuries after Descartes, who would not have likely conceived it himself, by the German philosopher Walter Benjamin, that in the space between two languages, there appears a third, otherwise invisible, which is primal, pure, and heavenly, enabling what would otherwise be impossible, namely translation between them.[20] Read through such a theory, the tension in Descartes between French and Latin becomes symbolic of a transcendent language that connects its speakers to the sacred.

At first, Descartes' literalistic reductionism and his denigrations of the imagination count against such readings of him. How much more literalistic could a theory of perception be than Descartes', which insists that the dual image our two eyes must generate of each thing we perceive can only be united into one by passing through the further medium of a single, nondual organ (the pineal gland) (TP 32). When he criticizes fables for misleading their readers he rehearses the old Platonic critique of literature. And when he cites, in particular, those misled by "the extravagances of the knights of our romances," (DM7) it is tempting to imagine he had Don Quixote in mind, whose story Cervantes published in Descartes' lifetime. And yet, Descartes expressed appreciation for literature. As against philosophy, whose study in school he remembers so critically, he fondly recalls the "ravishing delicacy and sweetness" (DM 6) of poetry. And it is possible to read the *Meditations* as itself a kind of fabulous narrative.[21]

Descartes was a poor metaphor-maker. His most extended metaphor in the *Discourse* (DM 42) is clumsy. There, he compares the painted light in which an artist shows the objects he represents, to the actual phenomenon of light within nature. The metaphor labors under the fact that the painted light is intended to resemble actual light. Then, midway, the metaphor switches gears and moves in the direction we might have expected it to go: just as the light the artist paints leaves some of his objects in shadow, so must Descartes conceal some of what he means to say. And then comes an imaginative leap, almost the opposite in procedure from the radical doubt of the *Meditations*, whereby Descartes proposes to deduce the truths of this world by imagining how an utterly new world, suddenly created by God, would naturally unfold. This, also, is too literalistic for metaphor, since the imagined world turns out to be, in accord with Descartes' stated aim, virtually the same as ours. He laid the foundation for a metaphor which he did not realize.

Outside the context of his philosophical writing, Descartes approached metaphorical thinking more nearly. The dreams which in the *Meditations* serve the self-undermining purpose of establishing the reality opposed to them, were, in his personal life, a source for navigating that very reality. For, according to Descartes himself, part of what launched him on his quest for truth was a series of dreams he had that pointed him in that direction. The dreams were filled with images that could only have life-directing import if interpreted as metaphors. For example, one of the dreams showed a melon, whose spherical shape suggested the wide world Descartes was meant to study.[22] It is not difficult to imagine a poetic writer completing or improving the metaphors that Descartes either poorly or only half executes in his philosophical texts. An example surfaces in the work of Descartes' compatriot of centuries later, Marcel Proust. In a passage of the *Treatise on Passions*, Descartes explains how the brain can effect movement in the extremities of the body through the mediation of the animal spirits, "as we make one end of a cord move by pulling the other end" (TP 12). It is a homely but effective metaphor, of cord and animal spirits, though both are bodily entities. The same metaphor is transformed, in Proust, into a vehicle for capturing the startling impact of involuntary memory, when the strangeness of his environment recalls to the narrator an estranging scene from his past, "as if an invisible chain had managed to connect an organ to the pictures of my memory."[23] Though both metaphors turn on the image of a chain or cord, allowing for action at a distance, Descartes' languishes in the world of the body (brain and extremities), while Proust's more successfully negotiates the space between body and mind, through the sharp juxtapositions of images from both realms: chain and invisibility, organ (of the eye) and memory. The Cartesian mind-body dualism would have left a less troubling legacy if it had been interpreted through a poetic eye.

The comparison of Descartes' *Meditations* to Ignatius' *Spiritual Exercises* reads differently if, instead of constituting an assimilation of Descartes to Ignatius, it is taken for a metaphor. The two works really are very different. The word "meditation" functions as a homonym across the two works. Descartes' choice of that word to title his work is then an invitation to the reader, not to pray with his book but to consider the charged space between it and Ignatius,' which only comes about by their juxtaposition. The metaphor is in the juxtaposition, not the assimilation of one to the other. But even this metaphor is not explicit and must be constructed. Spirituality cannot show in the extremes of Cartesian dualism where bodies are mechanisms manipulated by self-guaranteeing minds. But it can show in spaces outside the dualism, in contradictions turned metaphor, which Descartes—having supplied the contradictions—leaves his readers to construct.

NOTES

1. Descartes, *Discourse on Method and Meditations on First Philosophy*, 4th ed., tr. Donald A. Cress (Indianapolis, IN: Hackett, 1998). Further citations to the *Discourse* are noted parenthetically in the text, with the abbreviation DM; citations to the *Meditations* are noted parenthetically with abbreviation Med. Quotations are from the translation by Donald Cress.
2. Étienne Gilson, *The Spirit of Medieval Philosophy*, tr. A. H. C. Downes (Notre Dame, IN: University of Notre Dame Press, 1936, 1991), 30–31.
3. Peter Damian is credited with conceiving the image. Peter Damian, *De Divina Omnipotentia* in *Patrologia Latina*, ed. J. P. Migne (Paris: 1844–1855), v. 145, p. 603.
4. Gilson, *The Spirit of Medieval Philosophy*, 20–41.
5. Amelie Oksenberg Rorty, "The Structure of Descartes' *Meditations*," in *Essays on Descartes' Meditations*, ed. Amelie Oksenberg Rorty (Berkeley: University of California Press, 1986), 18.
6. See Nicholas Jolley, "The Reception of Descartes' Philosophy," in *The Cambridge Companion to Descartes*, ed. John Cottingham (New York: Cambridge University Press, 1992), 397–8.
7. James Byrne, *Religion and the Enlightenment* (Philadelphia, PA: Westminster, 1997), 83.
8. Jolley, "The Reception of Descartes' Philosophy," 398.
9. Descartes, *The Passions of the Soul* in *The Philosophical Writings of Descartes*, tr. John Cottingham, Robert Stoothoff and Dugald Murdoch (New York: Cambridge University Press, 1985), para 170. Succeeding references are given parenthetically, by paragraph number, in the text, with the abbreviation TP.

10. See Kyoo Lee, *Reading Descartes Otherwise: Blind, Mad, Dreamy, and Bad* (New York: Fordham University Press, 2013).

11. See especially, Vere Chappell, "The Theory of Ideas," in *Essays on Descartes' Meditations*, ed. Amelie Oksenberg Rorty (Berkeley: University of California Press, 1986), 177–198.

12. An ancient line of theological reasoning links divine goodness to creation. See Plato, Timaeus 29–30; Philo, De Opificio Mundi 21 [On the Creation 21]. Interestingly, the biblical account of creation pronounces only the world (not God) good.

13. Descartes and Elisabeth, of Bohemia, *The Correspondence between Princess Elisabeth of Bohemia and Rene Descartes*, ed. and tr. Lisa Shapiro (Chicago: University of Chicago Press, 2007), 71.

14. The Bible may invite us to master nature, but never to possess it in any ultimate sense, since it is God's.

15. See for example: Gary Hatfield, "The Senses and the Fleshless Eye: The *Meditations* as Cognitive Exercises," in *Essays on Descartes' Meditations*, 45–79; Bradley Rubidge, "Descartes *Meditations* and Devotional Meditations," *Journal of the History of Ideas* (1990): 27–49.

16. Alan Bloom, *The Closing of the American Mind* (New York: Simon and Schuster, 1987), 52.

17. Karl Jaspers, *The Great Philosophers: The Disturbers* (New York: Harcourt Brace, 1995), 8.

18. See John Hellman, *Simone Weil: An Introduction to Her Thought* (Waterloo, ON: Wilfrid Laurier University Press, 1982), 96–97; and David Tracy, "Simone Weil: The Impossible," in *The Christian Platonism of Simone Weil*, ed. E. Jane Doering and Eric O. Springsted (Notre Dame, IN: University of Notre Dame Press, 2004), 229–241.

19. See Andre A. DeVaux, "On the Right Use of Contradiction according to Simone Weil," tr. J. P. Little, in *Simone Weil's Philosophy of Culture*, ed. by Richard Bell (New York: Cambridge University Press, 1993), 150–157. Also, Simone Weil, "Science and Perception in Descartes," in *Formative Writings*, ed. Dorothy Tuck McFarland and Wilhelmina Van Ness (Amherst, MA: University of Massachusetts Press, 1987).

20. Walter Benjamin, "The Task of the Translator," in *Illuminations*, ed. Hannah Arendt (New York: Schocken Books, 1968), 69–82.

21. See L. Aryeh Kosman, "The Naïve Narrator: Meditation in Descartes' *Meditations*," in *Essays on Descartes' Meditations*, 21–43.

22. Hatfield, *Descartes and the Meditations*, 11.

23. Marcel Proust, *Sodom and Gomorrah*, tr. John Sturrock (New York: Penguin, 2004), 268. Proust might well have appreciated this prediction of himself in Descartes' words on love: "Having stranger effects than the passion, this inclination or desire provides writers of romances and poets with their principal subject matter" (TP 90).

SIX

Spinoza

If the anti-Semitic Baron Le Charlus, from Proust's *Remembrance of Things Past*, observes—after having commented, indignantly, on a propensity he detects among Jews to inhabit Parisian streets with Christian names, evocative of an ecclesiastical past, as though to supersede them—that he "can't condemn en bloc . . . a nation that numbers Spinoza among its illustrious sons,"[1] this expresses only a fraction of the ambiguity and transgression that characterize the life, work, and reception of Amsterdam's famous, seventeenth century Jewish philosopher. The disputes over the significance of Spinoza continue to this day, as witnessed by a judgment on the *Ethics* that appeared in a letter to the *New York Times Book Review*, in response to critic Harold Bloom's commendation to us there of that "superbly cryptic masterwork,"[2] that it is simply a "crushing bore."[3] Such polar differences in the evaluations of Spinoza lend him and his memory a drama that has not been lost on writers, who have fictionalized his life, or take-offs on it, in stories and novels.[4] This inconclusive and open-ended diversity of interpretations stands in marked contrast to the monistic singularity of Spinoza's own work, which aspires to the crystalline fixity of a snowflake, whose intricate patterns have been geometrically deduced from the laws of nature and frozen for all time.

Like the Christianity for which he expressed a qualified sympathy, Spinoza descends from two different strains, one Jewish, one Greek. He is, alternatively, the culmination of medieval Jewish philosophy, especially Maimonides,[5] or, closer to his own self-presentation, the modern student of and commentator on Descartes (who himself succeeded Aristotle). No reader of the *Tractatus Theologico Politicus* can fail to be impressed by Spinoza's knowledge of biblical tradition—which figures there much more overtly than Catholicism does in Descartes' philosophical work—startling as it may be (though, on reflection, utopian) to see Jesus and

Paul cited so casually next to Moses and Isaiah in a seventeenth century text redolent of deep (however much rejected) Jewish sensibility and nurture. The story of Spinoza's excommunication from the Jewish community of his time and place is well-known and need not be rehearsed here. Unlike Descartes, who invites us to read his *Discourse on Method* "as a story or, if you prefer, as a fable,"[6] Spinoza openly disdained story as such, as though, from his own life narrative he sought a liberative release. But this is already a break with story-laden Judaism. A brief look at Spinoza's account of the Divine Law, in chapter IV of the *Tractatus* underscores his stark departure from Jewish teaching. Divine Law, as Spinoza sees it, is ineluctably universal, applying to all humanity, never particular or addressed to a single people. It is so because it is deducible from universal human nature. To suppose it revealed in a miraculous act of divine condescension undermines the very notion of divinity and attributes to narrative a truth value it largely lacks. The ritual that constitutes so much of Jewish law is, from the standpoint of Divine Law, irrelevant. It once had a political purpose, to shape a Temple-centered Jewish monarchy, but which, having passed from history millennia ago, leaves the specifically Jewish law no continuing warrant. Elements of this view anticipate Moses Mendelssohn. Students of Jewish history will not be scandalized by it or at least not especially struck by it since it later became stock-in-trade of nineteenth century Reform Judaism and still finds a place in the minority redoubt of Classical Reform. But, as has been widely noted, views such as these threatened to undermine the communal identity of seventeenth century Amsterdam's Jews—most of them returnees to a Judaism they had never really known in the Spain and Portugal they had fled—that was already fragile not only in their own eyes but in those of the surrounding Calvinist community that had granted them sanctuary. Quite strikingly, Spinoza in the *Tractatus* never refers to the Jewish people as "we" but always as "they." This distancing of himself from Jewish ethnicity holds him, dialectically, all the closer to it, for the tradition acknowledges this reaction to itself among its bearers, and assigns them, as earlier noted, a place at the seder table under the rubric of the Wicked Child, who also speaks "they" to his fellow Jews. But the promise of return that designation carries (the wickedness is of a *child* after all) was not fulfilled in his case. The tradition holds him, in anticipation of the modern Jewish dilemma, to the ethnicity of Jewishness but not to Judaism, whose foundations he thoroughly rejected. The whole point of the *Tractatus* is "to separate faith from philosophy,"[7] and to so identify faith with action that the intellectual explorations of philosophers are completely uninhibited by its strictures. But the faith so separated from philosophy cannot but appear the loser in a philosophical tract, a second-rate accommodation of truth to the mass, as it verged on seeming in some medieval philosophy, and Judaism too readily fills the role of acts-based faith not to suffer from the contrast. In recent years, some scholars have suggested that Spinoza shared in a kind of Christianity, akin to that of the non-doctrinaire Collegiants of Amsterdam, or perhaps the radical Quakers, who had only recent appeared on the European religious scene, some of whose tracts he may have translated.[8] But, congenial as Spinoza might find the liberal wing of twenty-first century Quakerism, which inclines among some of its members to pantheism, it is hard to imagine his sober, geometric spirituality at home among the early Quaker enthusiasts.

Among his forbears in Jewish tradition, the one he cites most respectfully, almost lovingly, is King Solomon, whom he takes for the author of Ecclesiastes. The fact is filled with ironies. For while he cannot suppress his indignation over the rabbinic founders of the biblical canon, who nearly omitted Ecclesiastes from it—"I cannot pass over here in silence the audacity of the rabbis who wished to exclude from the sacred canon both the Proverbs and Ecclesiastes . . . it is indeed grievous to think that the settling of the sacred canon lay in the hands of such men"[9] —he nonetheless owes to those same rabbis the view that Solomon was indeed Ecclesiastes' author, a view that no scholar in the tradition of historical biblical criticism Spinoza virtually founded, and which he applied so assiduously and iconoclastically (for his day) to the rest of scripture, holds now. The value of Solomon is that, in contrast to the overly imaginative prophets, he is the Bible's one true paradigm of reason. For one as sensitive to the multiple forms of human suffering as Spinoza was it is striking how little ear he has for the sorrowful tone of Ecclesiastes, though he notes it once, in passing, within *The Ethics* (E4p17s). This particular deafness may owe as well to his either natural, cultivated, or ideological ascesis towards poetic language. (Poetry is after all a product of the *imagination,* which for Spinoza, as for Descartes, was too wed to the obscurities of the body not to generate more confusion than clarity.) Unlike Descartes, who banished the passions as focus of attention to the end of his writing life, Spinoza situates them center stage in his *Ethics,* where they occupy the third and fourth books. Perhaps nowhere more than here is Spinoza Descartes' student. Advancing his teacher's method one step further, he considers them not merely from the standpoint of natural philosophy, but *more geometrico.* But Spinoza's understanding of the problem of the passions, and his method of analyzing them, is very much Descartes': the problem of them is that they hold us passive, render us sufferers of fateful pleasure or pain, rather than actors and determiners of our own happiness. The method of analyzing them is to reduce them to their simplest parts, and to understand all the rest of them as compounds of these. Here too Spinoza surpasses Descartes in the application of his own method, by compressing all the passions into compounds of merely three (rather than the Cartesian six) elemental ones: pleasure, pain, and desire.

Though both Descartes and Spinoza exhibit the elitist condescension of the philosopher towards the untutored mass, the impediments each suffered at the hands of that mass, which, by their own analyses of the passions, must partly account for their tone towards it, do differ. Descartes voluntarily exiled himself from his home in France to Holland, so that he could think his thoughts uninterruptedly. Spinoza's exile in his home of Holland was imposed. If Spinoza could draw from Bertrand Russell a remark Russell would never have made of Descartes, that he was "the most lovable of the great philosophers,"[10] it is largely on account of the life he led, which found, as Plato said we could, a sustenance in ideas that the supposed ideals of community, family, social position and structure—the very things Spinoza explicitly distances at the start of his most moving and autobiographical work, the *Treatise on the Emendation of the Intellect*—withheld from him. Where Descartes meditatively assumes, in imitation of Ignatian retreats, a dark night of the soul in which he appears to lack all orientation—"it is as though I had suddenly fallen into a deep whirlpool"[11] —Spinoza's initial disorientation, like the pilgrim Dante's at the start of the *Divine Comedy*, is real. He finds himself in the position of a "sick man suffering from a fatal malady who, foreseeing certain death unless a remedy is forthcoming, is forced to seek it, however uncertain it be, with all his might."[12] Such expressions of existential angst are rare in the poetic spareness of Spinoza. But here again, in (unwitting and perhaps unwilling) imitation of at least some views of Jewish history, and so of Jewishness, it is as though the suffering is borne so fully by the life, the thought is freed of its telling marks (the opposite of Christianity).

If Spinoza can locate therapy so centrally in his thought, it may be because he underwent it in his life. At least this is the conceit of the opening paragraphs of the *Treatise on the Emendation of the Intellect*. His healing process begins with an admission that echoes Ecclesiastes: "After experience had taught me the hollowness and futility of everything that is ordinarily encountered in daily life" (TEI 1) and proceeds on a path partially paved with other philosophico-therapeutic antecedents: the Platonic "true good ... which ... could alone affect the mind to the exclusion of all else" (TEI 1); the Hellenistic freedom from "emotional agitation" (TEI 9); and the "persistent meditation" (TEI 7) of Descartes, "directed to the true knowledge of things" (this is the subtitle of the treatise). The autobiographical opening is a précis of a philosophical spirituality. At the beginning of the therapy is an uncertain rejection of such available but potentially disappointing goods as pleasure, honor and wealth. At the end is an assured acceptance of an alternative good, much less obviously available but much more reliably mediating our happiness, of "love towards a thing eternal and infinite" (TEI 10). In the advance from the unpromising goods at the beginning to the eternal and infinite one at the end Spinoza rehearses a line of argument that Plato had followed in his critique of injustice. Just as the initial, seeming ease of injustice proves to be difficult, and the initial difficulty of justice, easy, so pleasure, honor, and wealth, which at first seem available and promising prove not to be, while the infinite and eternal object of love is readily so. For pleasure, it turns out, culminates in regret; and honor and wealth, in the ongoing deferral of the satisfaction they promise, since the desire for them feeds, infernally, on itself (a ready image for Dante); while the infinite and eternal object of love unfolds from the very idea of itself its readiness to hand. Because this available object which secures our happiness turns out to be God, the therapy that Spinoza has offered issues in a spirituality, and so restores the ancient link between the two that Descartes, the great divider, had sundered.

But logic is not the sole or even primary propeller of this therapeutic and spiritual passage. For Spinoza does not here adumbrate how the reality of God unfolds from the sheer idea of God. Instead, it is as though, in anticipation of Kierkegaard, despair of the false goods, which leaves Spinoza in the predicament of imminent nothingness, catapults him into proximity with the previously remote good of the infinite and eternal object, which still remains unproved. In language that Spinoza would reject (and Kierkegaard affirm), what Spinoza has traced is passage by passion to the love of God. For Spinoza, such a means of reaching God may be religious—indeed, was, in part, the way in which the biblical prophets enjoyed a lesser knowledge of God, if knowledge it could be called—but does not qualify as philosophical. (We must leave to Kierkegaard the philosophical contextualization of passion as a legitimate spiritual way, which turns in part on deconstructing the whole rationalist enterprise that Spinoza helped erect.) Spinoza's *Ethics* translates this passionate précis of the spiritual life into a complete philosophical justification of it.

But to follow Spinoza we must begin not with ourselves, as Descartes did, but as the *Ethics* does, with God. The problem with the passionate account of spiritual life is that it implies God is the object of our longing. But God is never mere object. God is always, as Hegel would later teach, the subject. It is we who are the objects of the divine self-knowing. And it is with the deep internalization of that knowledge that Spinoza's therapy culminates. For, once again unlike Descartes, Spinoza is not at all ambiguous about his aim in writing, which is consistently therapeutic and spiritual, to subordinate all human efforts of knowing, scientific or otherwise, to human blessedness, the meaning of Spinoza's given name in both its Hebrew and Latin versions, carrying all the richness of its religious connotation but shorn of specifically Jewish or Christian content. Lest we forget that this is his aim, he repeatedly anticipates the last and climactic book of his *Ethics*, devoted to that blessedness, with predictive signposts in the earlier ones (see, for example, the opening paragraph of part 2, E2p47s, E4p16s, E4p39s).

From one perspective, Spinoza's God is designed to resolve the paradigmatic division of Cartesianism between mind and body. If, to employ

Spinoza's terminology, thought and extension are attributes of God, they are simply different expressions of the same fundamental essence. No pineal gland is needed to connect them if they are already identical with each other through the single entity they qualify, much like two sentences in different languages that, by carrying the same meaning, translate each other. And, like two distinct languages, thought and extension are wholly self-contained within their own spheres and unlimited by each other. Spinoza embeds the Cartesian division between them, paradoxically, in their mutual identity, and marshals the division to therapeutic ends. For one means of easing a painful passion, especially those seemingly caused by other persons' speech, is to realize that no "extended" object, such as another person's speaking body, could have actually caused that experience of pain; by the radical self-containment of thought and extension, no event within the one can cause any event within the other. If I experience a passionate pain, its cause must lie in a preceding string of mental events, each member of which is in turn caused by its predecessor(s), which do not include anyone's speaking or acting body. Those bodily acts, were, for their part, caused by previous bodies extending backwards similarly in an infinite causal sequence of extended things and events. The worlds of events within the two sequences of mind and body are actually identical, as German and English translations from the Latin of Spinoza's Latin text are, but they no more cause each other than the English version causes the German. In the private sphere each of the languages makes from the other, they also provide a kind of sanctuary from each other. The release from emotional pain we experience when we locate its cause in the proper sequence of wholly mental events, after the location a barely resistible but still erring common sense would make of it in the external world proves impossible, is, in reverse, a little like the burden eased on a German-Jewish Holocaust survivor who now speaks only English. Part of what carried the pain to our minds no longer does. Or, to shape the analogy differently, insofar as we are body and mind, we are all naturally bilingual, and, in our self-understanding, mix the two languages only to our confused and incommunicable unhappiness.

But there is more to the therapy. For insofar as a passionate pain is located within its proper causal sequence, it is understood; insofar as we understand it, we are active with respect to it; and insofar as we are active with respect to it, its passivity becomes an occasion of our energetic self-determination (what Spinoza calls *conatus*) and a cause of heightened pleasure. It is a little like the pleasure we feel when, having learned a new language, we can read in their original tongues the works of our favorite foreign authors, and need no longer receive them, passively, at the hands of translators. And there is still more to the therapy: difficult as it may be to specify the causal antecedents to any given passion we may suffer—in psychoanalysis it may take years—there is one cause of it that is always available to our understanding: God. For the entire causal sequence of mental events in which our passion resides itself constitutes the attribute of thought within God. Like Marcus and Lucretius, Spinoza too commends to us a larger view of the human drama, but he connects us to it in a more logically articulate way: passions are modes of thought; thought is an attribute of God; therefore in every passion we experience is the potential awareness of God as cause. (Descartes raises this image—"my existence depends entirely upon God at each and every moment" [Med. 53]—but does not exploit it spiritually). And now, added to the pleasure we feel from our own exercise of intellect in understanding the passion, is the happiness into which we are initiated by the awareness awakened in us of the infinite and eternal good that "could alone effect the mind to the exclusion of all else." Because, according to Spinoza, love is simply "pleasure accompanied by the idea of an external cause"[13] (E3Def. of the Emotions 6), God, as the perceived cause of our happiness, becomes an object of love. Spinoza's therapy culminates in a quotable précis of his spirituality, from book V of the *Ethics*, which could grace the pages of any Jewish or Christian devotional work: "From this we clearly understand in what our salvation or blessedness or freedom consists, namely in the constant and eternal love towards God" (E5p35s).

But in our eagerness for Spinoza's spirituality, we have rushed to God's place at the end of the *Ethics* without an adequate understanding of God's foundational role at the beginning, before the therapy has even begun or we, as finite modes of God, have yet been sighted as therapy-needing existents of any kind at all. Descartes' God was the fulfillment of all perfections. By the ambiguities inherent to the concept of perfection, Descartes, by yet another of his many sleights of hand, was able to assimilate his philosophical God to its religious counterpart. God is the good and trustworthy agent of the creation that the divine power matched to the divine will. But no partaker of the ontological argument for God's existence, which both Descartes and Spinoza were, can fail to import into their concept of God something of the apophatic. For the ontological argument at its most austere is a stunning triumph of form over content. For, for the very reason that Kant and Bertrand Russell would later reject it, it makes of sheer existence a content (rather than, as those philosophers would respectively teach, an operator, either as a category within the understanding, or a symbol within predicate logic). But sheer existence is empty of content. And so the ontological argument is the natural partner and promoter of that ancient intellectual counterpart to mysticism: negative theology.

Appearances to the contrary, Spinoza is more faithful to the apophatic implications of the ontological argument than Descartes is. For while he appears to invest God with every possible content of nature (the famous identifier of Spinozistic pantheism is: "God or Nature"), he recesses the essence of God far behind or beneath what turn out to be its mere sensible modes. Policing the path to knowledge of God, which in the wrong hands is claimed to come too easily and effortlessly, are the, for Spinoza scholarship, much disputed "attributes" of God. These are "that which the intellect perceives of substance [i.e., God] as constituting its essence" (E1d4). The very wording is redolent of apophatic attitudes, as though the essence of God cannot be perceived in itself, but only *as* constituted by something else. Even the attributes themselves are a challenge to intellect, since the infinite number of them (E1d6) vastly surpasses what intellect can register. But even the attributes we do know, which are only two, thought and extension, do not easily lend themselves to comprehension. The scholarly dispute over whether they are subjective or objective realities is a sign of that. Spinoza's wording suggests they may be lenses the intellect fashions for itself to get a better look at God; but this subsumes them both under the single attribute of thought and so undermines the distinction they are supposed to make between the mental and the physical. The features of extension are a particular challenge, as these include quantity, which we imagine to be finite and divisible, but "if we consider it intellectually and conceive it insofar as it is substance—*which is very difficult to do* [italics ours]—then it will be found to be infinite, one and indivisible" (E1p15s). Our misconceptions of extension arise from two misleading propensities of mind: to abstract and to imagine. Abstraction is a means of grouping particulars by ignoring the distinctions between them. By ignoring what makes a thing uniquely what it is abstraction misses the essence of that thing. This makes abstraction a practiced kind of ignorance. Spinoza, for all the abstractions he seems to advance, is not being ironic when he chides us for "conceiving things in too abstract a way" (TEI 75). Extension is not an abstract universal that subsumes concrete particulars. It is, itself, a concrete particular, but an infinite and indivisible one. The other misleading propensity of mind, imagination, rebels at this. For it insists on corporeal images for anything it takes for real; and an infinite, indivisible, and concrete particular resists bodily form, in the same way the geometric concept of an infinite line, figure though it may in a particular mathematical proof, resists encapsulation in any physical line drawn on paper or blackboard. And so while extension provides the context for understanding finite bodily things, it is itself neither finite nor body, and so exceeds the grasp of imagination.

But the resistance of extension is not simply to the imagination; it is also to language. For "words are a part of the imagination" (TEI 88). They "owe their formation to the whim and understanding of the common people so that they are merely symbols of things as they are in the imagination, not in the intellect" (TEI 89). But insofar as extension and thought, as attributes of God, show themselves truthfully only to a medium of human knowing that exceeds language, they occupy a place in the apophatic tradition, alongside Plato's Idea of the Good. How much more must the God of which they are attributes belong to that tradition. In simpler and more obvious ways, Spinoza speaks the language of negative theology when he calls God infinite (E1d6) and indivisible (E1p13), and denies, as against Descartes, that human intellect and will could resemble God's (E1p17s),

The significance of the apophatic tradition to Spinoza' philosophical spirituality is that it provides the distance the sacred needs from the commonplace to begin to qualify as sacred at all. The charge against Spinoza that he was atheistic rests on the assumption that he completely conflated God with the natural objects of our world. And if the sacred only arises on a separation from that world, then the conflation between them precludes spirituality. It is precisely the epistemic distance that separates human knowing from the sacred that allows pantheism, as a form of spirituality, to exist at all. But since pantheism is not an option in monotheistic eyes, the identification of God with nature must seem atheistic to them.

But Spinoza takes many fewer pains than Descartes to assimilate his God to the teachings of monotheistic religion. He even adds a version of the ontological argument beyond Descartes'—which had argued to God from the (perhaps overly) contentful concept of perfection—that proceeds, as apophatic theology would prefer, from sheer negation. Most everything around us is conditioned by something else. We encounter nothing purely unconditioned. But whatever answers to pure unconditionality must exist. For anything that impeded its existence would compromise its unconditionality. So insofar as we can conceive unconditionality, something answering to it must exist. And that is God.

Unconditionality is a contentless negation. Spinoza would say that this concept is intelligible only to our intellect, not our imagination. The intelligibility it has belongs to a God surpassingly austere. This God presents itself to us through the medium of another purely intelligible, that is, unimaginable and language-transcending concept, that of substance. That this concept functions as an antechamber to God makes of it another means of preserving the epistemic distance between us and the sacred. Spinozan substance is the hypostasis of self-containment, that ancient ideal of both Platonic and Stoic spirituality. It is "that which is in itself and is conceived through itself" (E1d3). This dual formulation of self-sufficiency—in itself and conceived through itself—reflects Spinoza's Cartesian inheritance of ideas, which carry both formal and objective reality. If we are thinking of a substance, our idea of it must be independent of all other ideas; but, in addition, its object in reality must be similarly independent of all other objective realities. It is another formulation of unconditionality, with consequences identical to those we have already encountered: so self-contained a being must exist. Infinity and eternity quickly unfold as features of substance: infinity, because substance, through its unconditionality, is incapable of being limited by anything; and eternity, according to Spinoza's understanding of that concept, because the reality of it follows from the idea of it. If incapable of being limited, substance must be one and unique; there could not be two, or each would limit the other, and both would cease to be substance. As we look around, we do not immediately recognize such a substance in being. What we perceive are multitudes of finite things and thoughts. If these are indeed real, they can only be conditioned by substance. And now Spinoza's tripartite structure of substance-attribute-mode arises to meet the need of understanding the relationship between finite things and substance. A finite thing is an expression in finitude of infinite attributes, which in turn express the infinity, eternity, and self-sufficiency of substance. If all finite things are conditioned by substance, which by its transcendence of imagination and language, is stationed at some remove from us, Spinoza has the makings of a concept of the sacred, which he does indeed name God.

But this God differs stunningly from the God of monotheism. Though it conditions reality, it does not create it, insofar as creation connotes willed action towards a goal, as it does so expressly in Genesis 1. God acts but not by willing. Its actions are unfoldings of consequences from its self-sufficiency, which proceed with the same logical necessity that infinity and eternity do. Though our own finite minds cannot follow it, it is by the same logical necessity that finite objects exist and act, each determined by its predecessors in the chains of mental and physical events that express the infinite attributes of thought and extension. God's acts are no more towards a goal than are the steps of a geometric proof, which stop where they do not because they have reached the goal they sought but because the implications of their premises have been fully realized. Most strikingly, this is the God that, notoriously among those most appalled by Spinoza, cannot even be wished to love us (E5p19). And so the second challenge to Spinozan spirituality, after distinguishing God from nature, is to show its relevance to our wellbeing.

Our origin lies in the ineluctable necessity of God to express itself. That necessity derives from a pervasive principle within Spinoza that reverses a standard premise of science, that everything has a cause, namely: everything has an effect (E1p36). Spinoza inherits Descartes' distinction between the formal and objective reality of ideas. But ideas now acquire, through their objective reality, an animation they lacked in Descartes. They assume the role that will played in the philosophy of Descartes, for whom the affirmation or negation of ideas was a function of our will. For Spinoza, ideas bear within them the affirmation or negation of themselves. And their self-affirmation comes so naturally to them that any idea that occurs to us will press itself upon us as objectively true, unless another idea cancels it out (1Ep49s). One idea, that of unconditionality, or God, affirms itself into existence, and out of it unfold, like steps in a proof of a theorem in geometry, an infinite string of other ideas, each bearing likewise its own objective reality. It is as though, in harmony with Plato, and in defiance of empirical common sense, ideas precede the realities they are of. In this sense, for all the reality Spinoza attributes to the body, and for all his regard for physicality—"I do not know why matter should be unworthy of the divine nature," (E1p15s)—he is fundamentally an idealist, and continues the ancient tradition of idealism. The physical body that I am is simply the objective reality of an idea that has unfolded out of God as the mind that I am. The logical, though not temporal, precedence of the idea of me (my mind) over the body of me will bear fruit for Spinoza's theory of immortality, for it will allow the idea of me to remain after the body of me has ceased.

But the reality of unconditionality and of the conditioned realities that unfold from out of it enjoy different grades of being. The notion that reality is graded comes to Spinoza from medieval philosophy, by way of Descartes: utter self-sufficiency resides at the top of the scale, and utter dependence at the bottom. This vision supplies the framework for understanding the all-important relationship of *expression* in Spinoza. But an additional assumption is needed to bring expression into focus: part of what a greater reality does in causing a lesser one is to communicate some of its own reality, downward, across a grade of being, without losing any of its own being in the process; in just the way, according to a favorite image among Neo-Platonists (to whom this vision is indebted), the sun loses none of its heat by casting its rays abroad. We who observe the effects of this process can tell where expression has occurred: when a quality is shared across a grade of being. It is just these junctures of sharing that Spinoza sights for us when he tells us, for example, that attributes express the essence of God. They do so by sharing with God the qualities of infinity and conceptual self-containment. But the attributes define a lesser state of being than God itself, since their existence does not follow from the idea of them. The finite modes within the attributes define a lesser state of being than the attributes since each is indeed finite. But, en masse, they express the attributes by constituting an infinite series. An anti-nihilistic attitude is implicit in Spinoza. The modes would cease to express the attributes if their sequence ever ended. Hence finitude is unceasing. This consequence is already implied by the assumption that everything has an effect.

And yet, apart from our participation in infinite series, finite things, such as ourselves, have a way of expressing the attributes of which we are modes through our own distinctive and unique individuality. And this is by our endeavor to persist in being as individuals. Spinoza identifies the essence of any finite individual with its endeavor to persist in its finitude. On the one hand, this is a resistance of its portion in the infinity of God; but on other, it constitutes the meaning of finitude itself, which would otherwise have no handle on being, and would lose itself in the infinity of God. What marks off one location in the infinite unfolding of God from another is its consciousness of itself as distinct from the rest, and part of what constitutes that very consciousness is the endeavor to persist in it. My intent to persist in finitude manifests the affirmation that the idea I am, along with the objective reality of the body I am, makes of itself. For all ideas that have unfolded from God affirm themselves by the very fact of that unfolding, in the same way the steps leading to the conclusion of a theorem in geometry affirm the conclusion. But this intent is also an opaque expression of infinity.[14] It is one ground for comparison of Spinoza with Nietzsche; except that, in Spinoza's case, this "will to power" is less a cause to celebrate than a necessary consequence of the expressing relation as it manifests across grades of being.[15] For Spinoza, it establishes an inescapable predicament for all finitude, since finite things, by their very finitude, cannot persist in being forever. Finite things are necessarily dependent on other things beyond their control (E4p2, E4p4, E4p18s). Humans in particular are weak (E4p32s) and unstable (TEI 45). They "do not exist from the necessity of their own natures" and "they are indefinitely surpassed by the power of external causes" (E4p32s). Their actions are "full of uncertainty and hazard."[16] This is the ground of finitude's suffering and of its urgent need for therapy. The dependence of finitude is inescapable; but its suffering over it is not. Here begins the therapy we have already begun to adumbrate. But now we have the skeleton of Spinoza's metaphysics in which to embed it.

The therapy begins with the realization that neither we nor any finitude is *wholly* dependent. This is already a consequence of the pervasive assumption that everything has an effect. But that further dimension of our activity, from which we drew therapeutic comfort several paragraphs back, that we can locate our passions as effects of prior causes, has its limits. Insofar as the causes of our passions lie outside our own mind, as most of them do, we cannot fully understand them. And though we can locate the whole sequence of mental events, of which our passions are a part, in a divine attribute derived from God, this provides only a general understanding of our passions as such rather than of the particular one from which we suffer. The release from that suffering comes only with a complete reformulation of who we are: a finite, self-perpetuating location of a portion of divine thought from whose sufferings we can be as detached as we are from a cell in our own body undergoing its death. Spinoza promotes this difficult self-understanding to his readers in a subtle way: by casting many of his proofs of propositions about us as proofs about God. For example, E2p34—"every idea which in us is absolute, that is, adequate and perfect, is true"—receives as part of its proof the claim that an adequate idea in us is "only . . . an adequate and perfect idea in God insofar as he constitutes the essence of our mind." The "only" registers the diminution, to the point of extinction, of the independent "us" referenced in the proposition. The soundness or not of these proofs is less important than the means by which—to use a favorite term from Simone Weil—they "decreate" us in the implied subsumption of ourselves under God. The movement of argument reverses Descartes, who established God on the foundation of our own consciousness. Spinoza disestablishes that consciousness on a foundation of God. But the net effect of these arguments is Cartesian. In the repetition of this structure of argument, especially in part II of the *Ethics*, Spinoza effects in us an unconscious meditation on the undoing of ourselves and so of the passions predicated on a false sense of self. It is for this reason that Spinoza, unlike Descartes, never interrupts his arguments *about* deity with a contemplative reflection *on* deity. The Cartesian "I" who would perform the meditation does not exist. There is only God.

It is no wonder that Spinoza, throughout his writings, disparages language, whose grammar uncritically accommodates a plurality of subjects, when there is really only one. The geometric form of the *Ethics* is less a privileging of mathematics than a testament to the strain language must undergo if it is to approximate truth at all. In the end, it never reaches the truth, which is always beyond words and available only to wordless intuition. It is in Spinoza's brief reflections on immortality that the paradoxes inevitable in any attempt to linguistically encode the wordless most manifest. Descartes asserted that one use of the passions was to alert the mind to the body's needs. Spinoza inherits that view and attaches the self-preserving instincts of the finite mind to the body it identifies with. That instinct is important enough to us to constitute the very essence of our being as humans. But it is an instinct doomed to failure. Paradoxically, the fulfillment of the drive to self-preservation comes with the death of the body, when all that remains of it are the ideas it had identified with, but now frozen within the larger system of the attribute of thought, rather than unfolding sequentially in identification with the body over a course of time. At our death, the very possibility of regarding ourselves as self-perpetuating locations of finitude is no longer available; the only self-conception remaining to us is as ideas with a fixed and eternal location in the geometric logic of God's mind—an identity scarcely continuous with what I had been before, but continuous enough to still be me. At last, in eternity, I enjoy guaranteed being, but only after my efforts to preserve it, in attachment to a body now gone, have come to nothing. What constituted my essence is over, but that for which it aimed, and sustained its essential life—the hope of eternal life—is now realized. Proust, who opened our reflection on Spinoza, supplies now towards its close, an image for capturing this thought: of a sound that carries so much the content of a sight, that it could be a "transcription for the blind."[17] The image is also biblical, as we find it in the prophets, where sounds communicate as images, and images as sounds. With a switch of perspective, which becomes permanent at death, but is available now to philosophers, we convert from subject to object, from time to eternity, from motion to fixity, from finitude to infinity, from flesh and blood to geometry.

The soteric perspective from which we regard ourselves "under a form of eternity" (E5p36) is a perfection of stasis. The movement that characterized us as we sought to preserve our finitude is gone. With it, falsity and evil have also vanished. For evil registers only to finitude as it encounters obstacles to its efforts to preserve itself; falsity too falls to finitude only when it fails to limit its thoughts to what unfolds from the far-recessed unconditionality and self-sufficiency of God. Spinoza extends the scope of Cartesian determinism, which only applied to matter, and the comfort of it, to the whole of being, in which the only modal options are necessity and impossibility. Freedom, that false trapping of an illusory contingency, is simply a form of ignorance which occurs as a necessary consequence of finitude. Error is not, as Descartes thought, an extension of infinite will beyond finite reason, but the shadowy idea of an impossibility that holds the attention of self-perpetuating finitude when it forgets its location in infinity. The awareness of that location transports us to a place very like the one Yeats sought in his figurative trip to Byzantium, where our messy three dimensionality reduced to the pellucid two of a holy mosaic on the wall—only now, at Spinoza's hand, the reduction advances yet further to the absolute zero of a geometric point on an infinite line.

NOTES

1. Marcel Proust, *Sodom and Gomorrah*, trans. John Sturrock (New York: Penguin, 2004), 490–1.
2. Harold Bloom, review of *Betraying Spinoza: The Renegade Jew Who Gave Us Modernity*, by Rebecca Goldstein. *New York Times Book Review*, June 18, 2006.
3. P. G. Kafka, "Reading Spinoza," *New York Times Book Review*, July 2, 2006.
4. See Pierre-Francois Moreau, "Spinoza's Reception and Influence," in *The Cambridge Companion to Spinoza*, ed. Don Garrett (New York: Cambridge University Press, 1996). I would add to Moreau's itemization of novels and stories Isaac Bashevis Singer's "The Spinoza of Market Street."
5. According to the respected interpretation of Harry Austryn Wolfson, who dubbed him "the last of the mediaevals." Wolfson, *The Philosophy of Spinoza* (New York: World Publishing, 1934), vii.
6. Descartes, *Discourse on Method*, 4.
7. Spinoza, *Tractatus Theologico Politicus*, trans. R. H. M. Elwes. (London: George Bell, 1891), 183.
8. See Richard Popkin and Michael Signer, *Spinoza's Earliest Publication? The Hebrew Translation of Margaret Fell's* A Loving Salutation to the Seed of Abraham among the Jews . . . (Wolfeboro, NH: Van Gorcum, 1987), 1–15.
9. Spinoza, *Tractatus Theologico Politicus*, 147–8.
10. Bertrand Russell, *History of Western Philosophy* (New York: Simon and Schuster, 1945), 569.
11. Descartes, *Meditations*, 24.
12. Spinoza, *Treatise on the Emendation of the Intellect*, 7, in *Ethics, Treatise on the Emendation of the Intellect, and Selected Letters*, trans. Samuel Shirley, ed. Seymour Feldman (Indianapolis, IN: Hackett, 1992). Hereafter cited parenthetically with the abbreviation TEI.

13. Translations from *Ethics, Treatise on the Emendation of the Intellect, and Selected Letters*, tr. Samuel Shirley.

14. It would be tempting to analogize this understanding of Spinoza's modes to understandings within Lurianic kabbalah of sparks trapped in vessels, except that Spinoza himself is so utterly discouraging: "I have read and known certain Kabbalistic triflers, whose insanity provokes my unceasing astonishment." Spinoza, *Tractatus Theologico Politicus*, 140.

15. The unexultant character of Spinoza's understanding of the instinct to self-preservation allows it to cohere with more traditional understandings of humility, a quality Spinoza otherwise disparages as a species of pain (E3Def of emotion 26). If he had allowed it to apply to corporate identities (and if he had had a less troubled relation with Judaism), it could have supplied a humanistic, compassionate and affirming understanding of Jewish survival, one that completely circumvents the troubling doctrine of election, rather than the painfully embittered one Spinoza actually offers towards the end of chapter III of the *Theological Political Treatise*.

16. Spinoza, *Tractatus Theologico Politicus*, 197.

17. Marcel Proust, *The Captive and the Fugitive*, trans. C. K. Scott Moncrieff and Terence Kilmartin, revised by D. J. Enright (New York: Modern Library, 1992), 103.

SEVEN
Kant

It was the noted philosophy historian of an earlier generation, Harry Austryn Wolfson, who interpreted Spinoza as the last in a line of essentially medieval thinkers.[1] On a philosophical typology that assigns a focus on the world to the ancient period, on God, to the medieval, and on humanity, to the modern, Spinoza may well appear a reversion to the Middle Ages. What count for temptations in his *Treatise on the Emendation of the Intellect*—pleasure, wealth, and fame—link his philosophy back even further, to antiquity, whose philosophers critiqued just those attractions, especially when compared with the Kantian view of what most blocks our path to goodness, namely the propensity, denounced in prophetic tones within "What is Enlightenment,"[2] to surrender our self-determination to traditions and professions of self-proclaimed authority. Kant resumed the preoccupation with epistemology that Descartes began. But the determinative and knowledge-assuring powers Kant claimed for our own minds had implications beyond epistemology, beyond even the moral lives newly liberated from authoritarian traditions Kant hoped we would lead; they also had implications for spirituality. The Copernican revolution in Kantian epistemology challenges philosophy to uncover the bridges to the sacred in new, unaccustomed spaces, much closer to home, and released from bondage to all externalities, in the workings of the human mind itself.

So humanistic a turn to spirituality is not what Kant had in mind when he famously wrote of his philosophical purpose, to "deny knowledge in order to make room for faith."[3] His intent was to allow for faith to flourish in the mental space he freed from the pretensions of theoretical reason to know God. But Kant's professed friendship to faith did not convince the pietistic Frederick II, King of Prussia, who censored Kant's later work, *Religion within the Limits of Reason Alone*. That work turned on a virtual pun on the word, "ethics," which affected to bridge the two otherwise opposed worlds of autonomy and heteronomy. The statutory religion that Kant disparaged had always included an ethical component alongside its several other facets of experience, narrative, doctrine, rite, and community. But ethics there was a heteronomous extract from doctrine and story; while the ethics that Kant championed was autonomous, a self-generating product of human reason. More than that, it was also the foundation for a new understanding of natural religion, based not on the data of the senses, but on the new, imperative voice that reason, which formerly spoke only in the indicative voice, found under Kant's care. The new natural religion culminated in the permission theoretical reason received to believe in God, based on the workings of a reason functioning in what for the ancient world—whose predilections Kant here, too, reversed—was its lesser, practical capacity. Kant's much critiqued moral argument for God's existence allows to theoretical reason enough contemplative distance from practical reason to hope, reasonably, that the goodness founded in obedience to law will finally know the happiness to which practical reason, by its very nature, is indifferent. But that happy union, which Kant calls the supreme good, and which is either stipulated or anticipated by virtually every book of the Bible except Ecclesiastes and, possibly, the original Job, requires a being good enough to wish it, and powerful enough to effect it, namely God. Kant is careful to call the God that functions here so reasonably as an object of belief, a postulate (rather than a demonstratum). For a line of argument to culminate in a postulate is yet another Kantian reversal, this time of Spinoza, for whom postulates initiated, rather than culminated, demonstrations. A God who functions as a deduced postulate, at the end of a system, must awaken a very different response from one who, demonstrated at the start, opens and closes a system—a true Alpha and Omega—as Spinoza's does. Certainly the response it awakened in Frederick II, to the extent that he was aware of it, can only have been lukewarm at best.

But even a reader sympathetic to the religious overtones of philosophy must be disappointed in Kant's divine "postulate of pure practical reason."[4] Kant commends this postulate to us on grounds that it has more purchase on our belief than the mere hypotheses of pure speculative reason (149–150 [142–143]), which may indeed include a creator God. The problem is that neither the practical postulate nor the speculative hypothesis can advance beyond the weak epistemic status each has of being a "subjective necessity"[5] or a "subjective effect" (150 [143]) (rather than a logical consequence) of the workings of reason itself. The supreme good towards which practical reason obligates us, and The Ideal of Pure Reason—speculative reason's God hypothesis, towards which it inexorably moves—have both a purely subjective basis in what Kant sometimes calls Reason's needs (4 [5]). Why should the one need be any less potentially deluding than the other? The presumed superior status of practical reason's need for God turns on yet another pun, this time on the word, "good." For this word, functioning as an attribute of human wills, which is how Kant famously introduces it in the *Foundations of the Metaphysics of Morals*—"Nothing in the world—indeed nothing even beyond the world—can possibly be conceived which could be called good without qualification except a good will"[6] —does not equate with the same word designating the harmony of happiness and virtue, as in: "furthering of the highest good ... is an a priori necessary object of our will" (120 [114]). The will rendered good by obedience takes its motive from con*form*ity to law (form), rather than from any desired object (content); the purity of the will's goodness is compromised as soon as any object functions as a motive for it at all, much less one already so compromised by desire as happiness (even happiness joined to virtue).[7] Kant inconsistently allows to practical reason what he forbids to theoretical reason: energizing nurture in an idea of totality that surpasses what either kind of reason, each within its own province, can establish. He does indeed consider, in the *Critique of Judgment*, what it would be like for a good will to operate without succor in the idea of the supreme good, which, for Kant, is tantamount to operating atheistically.[8] He suggests that the will would lose its resolve to behave well if it were deprived of hope in the supreme good.[9] But this is once again an argument on subjective grounds. And if critique can forestall the deleterious consequences of theoretical reason's need to project beyond the limits of knowledge, why can it not sustain a practical reason in its principled refusal to project in that way?

We are navigating the treacherous terrain within Kant of reason's propensities to self-deception. Long before Kierkegaard became the great philosopher of temptation, Kant confronted in reason its temptations to deceive itself. The first two critiques can be read as resistances of philosophical temptations to demonstrate God and to naturalize ethics. And long before Nietzsche became the celebrated genealogist of morals, Kant exposed that a proper account of the proofs for the existence of God is much less logical than genealogical. Kant is much less interested in the logical refutation of those proofs than in the explanation of why they appeal so much to reason in the first place. It is when ever-totalizing reason makes a match between two great endings it thinks it sights—to causation, at the ground of being; to perfection, at the culmination of being—that it capitulates to the proof for God, the ground and perfection of being, it thinks it has found. Its sightings are illusions since they are too encompassing to manifest in sensual experience and must thereby fall, by a foundational Kantian dictum, hopelessly beyond knowing. The interest of this explanation is in the need it exposes in reason to transcend its own limits. Reason is like a car fascinated by speeds on its speedometer it can never safely reach but which thereby always tempt it. In a startling illustration of Ecclesiastes' deceptively comforting thought, that there is a time to seek and a time to lose (Ecc. 3:6), but none to find, speculative reason is constituted to seek what it can never find. Before Kierkegaard personified the different kinds of consciousness in pseudonymous writers, Kant cast reason as an actor in its own tragic drama of self-deception, fooling itself with illusions

> sprung from the very nature of reason. They are sophistications not of men but of pure reason itself. Even the wisest of men cannot free himself from them. After long effort he perhaps succeeds in guarding himself against actual error; but he will never be able to free himself from the illusion, which unceasingly mocks and torments him.[10]

But this is only the epistemological half of the darkness we are ever imposing on ourselves. The moral half is even more pervasive and irresistible, so much so that, according to the title of book one of *Religion Within the Limits of Reason Alone*, it can only be designated "radical evil in human nature." Kant may never have credited his upbringing in Lutheran pietism for such an expression. But he need not have, since he found ample ground for it in his own philosophical ethics. The neutral location between good and evil for which the second critique seemed to allow[11] —a space for acts that, resisting universalization of any kind, fall outside the bounds of ethics entirely—disappears in the later book on reasoned religion. There we learn that the moral law is so much sufficient to govern any act we might perform that all behavior whose incentive is anything other than it, for example, natural desire, is evil. Kant is right to cite, if only in passing, "the severity of the commandment which excludes the influence of all other incentives" than the moral law.[12] So stringent a criterion of moral goodness provides the fine tuning needed to expose hypocrisy, which manifests in the moral self-satisfactions of those whose behavior outwardly accords with the moral law, without taking its inward incentive primarily from it, though only psychics, novelists, and perhaps Kierkegaard writing as Johannes de Silentio could discern the difference in any given case. But it also convicts us all of evil, insofar as we have ever acted from the incentive a natural desire provided us. It is a puzzle to the Kantian system why we so consistently take our incentives from desire when we are as free as we are to act from obedience to moral law. The consistency of our choice asks for explanation in causal precedents of some kind which, however, the imputability to us of the wrong of that choice, which lies in our absolute freedom, forever excludes. Kant negotiates this difficult terrain with, once again, the hybrid concept of subjective necessity: a proneness, resistible only with conscious effort, to acts, whether intellectual or moral, arising from the formal structure of our minds. Subjective necessity provides for a correlation natural and obvious to Plato, but otherwise elusive in Kant, between error and evil. For it is a subjective necessity within us both, when reasoning practically, to take our incentive from desire, and, when reasoning theoretically, to hypostasize totality. Both are mistakes, the first moral, the second epistemological.

It is just the pervasiveness of these mistakes, and the blanketing ubiquity of the temptation to make them that opens a space for a heartier concept of the sacred to appear within human experience than we find in the postulate at the end of Kant's moral argument for God. For how foreign we are to our own selves: in our ignorance of the power and impact of our minds; in the epistemological and moral evils to which we are prey with a persistent continuity that eludes our awareness. This foreignness can, like an aggressive virus or cancer, so colonize ourselves as to pass for ourselves; in which context, the sacred becomes the clearing in the illness that opens up the prospect for self-recovery, that remakes our world, and establishes foundations for a true happiness.

But we must tread carefully. No pre-Freudian philosophy contains as much grounds for suspecting therapy as Kant's does. Despite the Platonic overtones of the moral argument for God, where an idea of supreme goodness serves as conduit to the idea of God, its fundamental tenor is anti-Platonic. The difference is in their dualisms, Plato's between body and soul, and Kant's between natural and moral human being. Goodness and happiness naturally unite in the good Platonic soul; but they naturally split between the natural and moral dimensions of Kantian human being. Happiness is a function of natural desire, and goodness, of moral will. Happiness and goodness are thereby two "extremely heterogeneous concepts" (118 [111]). One half of the Platonic dualism simply exits the other; but we, "belonging to two worlds" (90 [87]) inexorably straddle the two halves of the Kantian divide. What makes Kantian anthropology a dualism is that the two halves of it are largely opposed. Desires "secretly work against" duty (90 [86]). The ancient quarrel that Plato found between philosophy and poetry, Kant locates—in a suggestive analogy with that—between goodness and happiness: "The moral law as ground of determination of the will, by thwarting our inclinations, must produce a feeling which can be called pain" (76 [73]). If, under this pain, the good person nonetheless continues to live, it is "because of his duty, not because he has the least taste for living" (92 [88]).

It was in part to balance the burden of this dualism that Kant offered up, in answer to the third of the three questions that close the first *Critique*—"What can I know? What ought I to do? What may I hope"[13] —his philosophy of religion. We can indeed hope, in imitation of the Psalmist's picture of "righteousness and peace", which on the day of salvation will "have kissed each other" (Ps. 85:11, JPS), that goodness and happiness will unite. But insofar as Kantian spirituality is not at its strongest in Kant's explicit philosophy of religion, we must seek its traces elsewhere.

There is already a glimmer of therapy even in the ascesis of Kantian ethics. For it turns out that, for all of their error in equating virtue with happiness, the ancients were right about one thing: undisciplined desire defeats itself. Kant is positively Stoic in his judgment on desire, or inclinations, that "they are . . . always burdensome to a rational being" and "elicit from him the wish to be free of them" (124 [118]).[14] To the extent that we can resist and mitigate them, we do experience a kind of happiness which Kant calls, somewhat Spinozistically, "intellectual contentment" (124 [117–118]). But then, this modest happiness is less a function of desirelessness than a byproduct of obedience to the moral law, which is always indifferent to natural inclinations. And so what this concession to therapy ultimately opens onto is ethics, rather than religion.

Revealingly, it is not the concept of God at all that draws from Kant his most devotional language. To the extent that the idea of God conduces to good will, through the confidence it supplies that virtue and happiness will eventually unite, and so functions for Kant as a mere means, it fails to win, on Kant's own grounds, the regard that sheer ends merit.[15] Certainly the postulate of pure practical reason is not a devotional object; but neither is the Ideal of Reason, which is the appearance God makes in the first *Critique* as, after the paralogisms of self, and the antinomies of world, the third totality to which reason is driven in its search for wholes it can never secure. If anything, Kant's language about the Ideal of Reason presages the existentialism of later philosophers, whose searchlights for traces of the divine in the universe turn up, instead, an "abyss of nothingness."[16]

The passage in Kant that points most meaningfully and memorably to the devotional center of his philosophy commences the conclusion of *The Critique of Practical Reason*: "Two things fill the mind with ever new and increasing wonder and awe, the oftener and more steadily we reflect on them: the starry heavens above me and the moral law within me" (169 [161]). The appeal of the starry heavens is not in any God that, by way of association with the argument from design, they might disclose. Kant sympathized with the argument from design but, along with all the other traditional arguments for the existence of God, dismissed it. The appeal of the starry heavens was in the limitless expanse they suggested there was to the world of appearances, which draws from Kant some of the reverential language that in more overtly theistic systems would have applied to God. But the starry heavens cannot themselves harbor the sacred. They satisfy none of our posited criteria of the holy. They are not distinctly separate from our ordinary experience. On the contrary, they "begin at the place I occupy in the external world of sense" (169 [162]). Though they awaken awe, they offer no promise of wellbeing. On the contrary, their very magnitude "annihilates as it were my importance as an animal creature," who must soon surrender its life (169 [162]). But perhaps most importantly, though they metonymically constitute a world, that of appearance, they do not found it. On the contrary, as appearances, they are founded in an existence logically prior to them, which grounds them.

The fact that the world is an appearance plays a pivotal role in Kantian epistemology. It is just because the world is an apparent construction, partially of our own minds, that, to the extent that we shape it, we can claim knowledge of it. But appearances presuppose something prior to them that appears. And here we stand on the brink of a key limit concept in Kant: that of the noumenon. The noumenon supplies a restful opening to the idea of unconditionality. It thereby contrasts with the other face unconditionality shows in Kant, when, like a siren, as part of the proofs for the existence of God, it beckons to reason from across an unbridgeable divide. Committed by its categories to the universal application of causality, speculative reason seeks for each appearance it ponders a prior cause. Reason can fathom that for any particular condition there is a prior cause. But it cannot encompass the infinite string of receding causes that its quest for the ever-preceding presents to it. Reason following a limitless string of apparent causes back to their projected start is like a rushing stream whose advance guard of anticipatory spray always precedes it. It exhausts itself in its anxiety to keep pace with itself. Unconditionality hovers on a horizon it can never reach. Here is another location for the image of abyss, which is the shape the untraversable space between reason and unconditionality takes in the very anxiety of reason to traverse it.

But the noumenon generates no anxiety. Though the ground of appearance, it stands outside all the categories including causality that shape appearance. It does not present itself to speculative reason as the potentially knowable endpoint of a limitless regress. On the contrary, the whole point of it is to mark a limit—"of our sensible knowledge."[17] Unlike the unconditionality of speculative argument, which wears a deceiving veil of knowability, the noumenon is open-faced in its unknowability. It is, paradoxically, the concept implicated by the very notion of appearance, of that which appears. For the ground of appearance eludes, by definition, whatever takes appearances for its object, namely concepts. It is therefore, as Kant calls it, a problematic concept. But the problem of it entails a closure on it that ends all obsessive worry over it. And Kant's tone towards it is serene. The noumenon is timeless (107–108 [102–103]. Like the content of a Zen meditation, it is empty, and in its emptiness, a redoubt from the ever busy determinations and pseudo-determinations of our over active reason. The noumenon invites into dialogue with itself the ancient, apophatic conceptions of God, which, for mystics, house a sanctum of ultimate rest. Kant himself evokes the comparison when, having denied to the concept of the noumenon any actual object, he nonetheless allows to it, as he does not to the Ideal of Reason, a "transcendental object."[18]

If all of reason were merely speculative, we would rest content with the empty, problematic concept of the noumenon. But now, as though to underscore how untherapeutic Kantian thinking can be, practical reason introduces a content to the noumenon that disturbs our rest, namely, freedom. Here we link up, by way of the noumenon, with the other source of wonder and awe in Kant—the moral law. For as Kant famously puts it, in religiously redolent language, "freedom . . . is revealed by the moral law" (4 [4]). The choice of religious language is consonant with the impression Kant gives that our discovery of freedom, by way of an indubitable moral law, is "different and unexpected" (49 [47]) from what we had erringly sought: some kind of naturalistic deduction of ethics. What nature truthfully bears to us is a possible context for the sacred in the underlying noumenon. We uncover in ourselves, by our capacity for ethics, an underlying freedom. By the associative link of the underlay, we discover our freedom to inhabit the same mysterious, other-world as the noumenon. And indeed, freedom, too, is at first an empty concept for us that receives definition, just as the God of negative theology does, by what it is not: determination by natural causes (29 [30]). But then through practical reason, it receives the content of the moral law. For the two concepts, of freedom and the moral law, "are so inextricably bound together that practical freedom could be defined through the will's independence of everything except the moral law" (98 [93–94]).

Kant's reverence for the moral law derives in part from its imperious relation to desire. It enables a kind of self-transcendence in humans, who can opt to follow it against their own natural interests. "It is a very sublime thing in human nature to be determined to actions directly by a pure law of reason" (123 [117]). This sublimity inspires one of the other few passages in Kant that suggest a devotional stance—what John Silber calls Kant's "hymn of praise to duty,"[19] which begins: "Duty! Thou sublime and mighty name." (90 [86]). If, by a mere change of the vowels in English (which would not even show in Hebrew), duty becomes deity, Kant could only be pleased. And indeed, the moral law wears features worn otherwise by some philosophical and religious versions of God. It speaks in a "heavenly voice" (36 [35]). It is "firmly established of itself" (49 [47]), like Spinoza's God, which was "in itself." And yet it is uncanny: "the thing is strange enough" (31 [31]). It commands apodictically and universally, like the God of Judaism. It is the means by which humans acquire supernatural dignity, an office performed by the image of God in Kant's Christian heritage. That the third of Kant's "hymnal" passages that Silber identified, towards the end of *Religion Within the Limits of Reason Alone,* is in praise of sincerity[20] is further evidence of a new location for the sacred—in human morality—since sincerity marks the unique spot where unqualified goodness shows in the human will.

If the moral law is a location of the sacred in Kant, then it must be in some sense separate, world-founding, and a condition of human wellbeing. Insofar as we carry the law within us, its separateness would be compromised if Kant had not been willing to pay the price he does of splitting us in two over its presence in us. He obtains the mark of sacred separation for the law by assigning that part of us that carries it to a world wholly other to the natural world we otherwise inhabit. It is only as citizens of two worlds that we can exhibit the conditions under which the sacred appears, as other to the ordinary. At the very least, the world it founds is the moral one. But by the equation that virtually identifies moral law as the content of an otherwise contentless freedom, it appears to found the entire noumenal world as well. If, in discussing the relative derivations of the phenomena and the noumena, Kant can allow for God to be the ground of the noumena (but not the phenomena) (107 [102])[21], such language only serves to draw upon the moral law and the freedom it guarantees more religious resonance. For the other side of the ground to appearance that the noumena are is their independence from the causality that determines all appearance, which is to say, their freedom. It is freedom, not the arguments for God's existence, that "brings such a great extension in the field of the supersensible" (108 [103]).[22] No wonder Kant is so undisturbed by the medieval conundrum of seeming inconsistency between divine omnipotence and human freedom (105ff [101ff]): if the sacred itself simply is the intimate complex of freedom and law, the seeming opposition between them and God dissolves. But then, what kind of happiness does the moral law ground?

We already know that the moral law works so far against human inclination as to judge us all wicked, and that its envisioned harmony with happiness can only show in an infinitely far-seeing hope. Freedom may confer upon us a supernatural dignity, but its role in our life is far from therapeutic. Spinoza demonstrated this in reverse by founding a therapy at least partially precisely in our lack of freedom. At the same time, Kant allows for a modest intellectual contentment in our self-awareness of obedience to the moral law, and a Stoical ease in our release from what Spinoza would have called the bondage of inclination. But more of the peace that the moral law holds in store for us, even as finite creatures who persistently fail to realize it, becomes visible if we view it as a species of two larger genera within Kant's system, of limitation, and of purity.

Kant employs the concept of the limit, almost in its mathematical sense, in his own explicit philosophy of religion. For it is just the notion of a holy or divine will, marking the end of a continuum we never reach in finite time, that grounds his argument for immortality. The desires of a holy will are ever fully and freely in sync with the dictates of the moral law. Such a will beckons to us at the end of a series defined by ever-decreasing space between inclination and law. A holy will is something we ought to realize in ourselves. If so then, by a fundamental Kantian principle, it is something we *can* realize, if not now then at some future time; but if at the end of no finite stretch of time, then at the end of an infinite one, in the immortality that necessarily follows. Kant does not weigh the unattainability of the holy will with the same dismissive critique that saddles the Ideal of Reason, which, in its unconditionality, also limits an infinite series. The difference is that in reaching for that unconditionality, speculative reason comes no closer to it; while the will, taking its inspiration from a holiness unattainable to finitude, does actually increasingly approximate it.

But approached in an unknowing spirit, as the theologians of apophatic mysticism would have us do, with full awareness of the limit on human knowledge it marks, even the God of speculative reason, the Ideal of Reason, can speak to spiritual longings. For, insofar as it is uncoerced into falsely representing an unknown object, the Ideal of Reason "remains always true in itself,"[23] and able to generate an inspiration of its own. Kant understands this in a scientific way. For the Ideal of Reason, as both ground and fulfillment of all natural appearances, inspires anyone who seeks the cause of a particular phenomenon to find it in other phenomena, that is, to pursue the scientific method. For the implicit promise of the Ideal of Reason is that all phenomena are ultimately linked. But neo-Kantians of a more Platonic bent found in the Ideal of Reason, or something like it, quite apart from science, sufficient inspiration to be their God. We need only think of Hermann Cohen, who in response to the implicit question of how God, conceived as an idea, could be loved, wrote, "How is it possible to love anything but an idea? Does one not love, even in the case of sensual love, only an idealized person, only the idea of the person."[24]

That Kant intends us to take God and immortality as serious sustenance of spiritual life may appear from the unlikely linking he makes of them to the concept of freedom. For he groups the three of them as postulates of practical reason (139 [132]). Freedom as postulate is indispensable to Kant. After Spinoza finessed this concept, in any way similar to Kant's understanding of it, out of existence, Kant instates it as the "keystone" of his system in both its practical and speculative parts (3 [3]). And yet, as Lewis White Beck notes, next to freedom, "the other two postulates are quite different and . . . the argument for them is less coercive."[25] What could Kant have had in mind by linking so central a principle as freedom, to ones so marginal as God and immortality, if not to allow the importance of the one to somewhat infuse the other two? In fact, his intention may have been just the opposite, to draw the religious reverence that God and immortality would evoke in traditional religious readers, onto freedom. In any case, the indispensability of freedom does not save God and immortality from their weak epistemic status. And so, if we are seeking openings onto the sacred from the concept of limit, we must look elsewhere.

In fact, it is where the concept of limit appears in contexts Kant does not explicitly commend for their sacred potentials, that it works in more spiritually satisfying ways. The very term itself could not have titled a long-ceased science fiction cum horror series on television—*Outer Lim-*

its—unless it already connoted otherness in what occupies the other side of it, a feature of it that Kant's idealist successors would exploit to assimilate the other to the same. It is when we stand at the limits of appearance that we encounter the noumenon. But the concept of limitation in Kant bears a conceptual link to the therapeutic determinism of Spinoza through the idea of boundary. And from a therapeutic standpoint, the Kantian limits do function in a similar way. This is most evident in Kant's reason-personifying epistemology. It is precisely because of the limit-setting critique of speculative reason that it does not "run riot into the transcendent" (59 [57]) and all of the anxiety attendant on that. When, in its thirst for unattainable knowledge, Kant accuses speculative reason of "vain curiosity instead of acting from a sober desire for knowledge" (57 [55]), he calls down upon it a sin of medieval provenance, which slowed Dante's upward ascent through Paradise. Critique is the antidote to vain curiosity. If we can only accept that "human insight is at an end as soon as we arrive at fundamental powers or faculties" (48 [46–47]), then our encounter with those powers, whether within or outside ourselves, is less a temptation than a resting point. The starry heavens illustrate. For the fragility of the life they, by contrast, reveal in us, exists, even in all its ephemeral finitude, "we know not how" (169 [162]). Our life which, by durational contrast with the starry heavens is already passing into death, is one of those fundamentals that, like the God of Job in relation to Job, answers the craving to know by silencing it.

Pure practical reason, whose office is to issue the moral law, has the advantage over speculative reason that nothing tempts it beyond the fulfillment of its allotted task. It is naturally and undistressfully self-limiting. The critique of practical reason limits the moral law from impure suggestions that it has origins in anything other than pure reason itself, such as God, or in anything merely empirical, such as nature, and so preserves its godlike self-sufficiency. But the moral law serves itself to limit what had, under Descartes' analysis, infinite scope, namely the will, whose unlimited powers of extension accounted for all human error. However far from the moral law human beings stray, it remains, like the father of the prodigal son, ready to receive back its erring charges. It never withholds from humanity the orientation it provides even in its violation. And that is a permanent comfort of it.

Purity is another face of the concept of limitation. Reason, whether speculative or practical, is pure in its formal operations, insofar as they are considered apart from content that fills them. It is the universal legislative form of a law, not its material content, that makes of it an apodictic imperative. That bare, abstract, contentless, form of law is the final product of the driving impulse of reason, in its practical expression, to universalize—but in this case truthfully, rather than falsely, as in the case of theoretical reason, since its ultimate issue is the human action, not a supersensible being, that manifests it. It is just because reason is so complexly active that we can learn so much from observing it in its purity, enough to occupy not only Kant's three volumes of critique, but the succeeding philosophical movement of absolute idealism, whose obsessions with action only finally found rest in a countervailing appreciation of passivity (and passion) to be found in such writers as Ludwig Feuerbach. Critique is possible because although in reality the form and content of reason are inseparable—"thoughts without content are empty, intuitions without concepts are blind"[26]—it is possible, on the model of a chemistry experiment, to isolate out the constitutive elements of reason's behavior.[27] The connotations of purity shade from the epistemological to the moral when Kant associates it with such descriptives as "genuine" (38 [37]). Reason in its purity marshals all the fundamental concepts of Kantian critique in a summary statement of the Kantian project: universal reason in its pure rational form reveals noumenal freedom that grounds law and goodness. In contrast, particular nature presents impure, empirical content which constitutes the determined phenomena that include inclination and happiness. In an analogy with statutory religion that Kant would never accept, philosophical purity, like ritual purity, implies fitness to receive the sacred; while philosophical impurity, like ritual impurity, connotes what is necessarily profane. The happiness in purity is ascetic. It turns on a self-limitation that voluntarily restricts experience. In a muted foretelling of Hegelian dialectic, Kantian spirituality approaches happiness through the very denial of it. But in this, Kantian philosophy is not so different from the ascetic saints that people the history of Christianity and Judaism.

The relation between religion and ethics in Kant is less simple than it seems. By Kant's own equation, "religion is the recognition of all duties as divine commands" (136 [130]). This equation aims to connect the periphery of the divine postulate of practical reason to the centrality of ethics. It works to enlist God in more of a role than assuring at some far future time, or perhaps beyond time, that duty and happiness will reconcile. But it is not clear what this additional role is. God cannot author the demands of duty we recognize, or at least such presumed authorship cannot motivate our obedience to them, or our moral autonomy, and ethics itself, collapses. Indeed, reason's failure to conclusively establish the existence of God is an advantage from this point of view, as it effectively precludes the heteronomy of traditional religious ethics. But Kant himself limits the content of the divine postulate of practical reason to the bridge it effects between virtue and happiness. For if "there remains nothing more in the concepts by which we think a pure rational being [God] than what is directly required for thinking a moral law" (144 [137]), and if what is directly required for that is simply an agency that harmonizes virtue and happiness, but not a superhuman author of virtue itself, then the moral concept of God must stop short of significantly infusing the moral law itself, or the duty it inspires, with any additional meaning. What then can it mean to recognize duties as divine commands? Perhaps Kant means merely to acknowledge that it is possible, or not, in the performance of duty, to be aware of a larger future context in which all acts of duty are rewarded with happiness—aware of it, but not dependent on it for any incentive it might provide; and to behave that way is to behave religiously.

But such a deliberately and emphatically uninspiring religiosity must have left even Kant unmoved, so much so that, rather than derive from it any evident succor from it for himself, he could only observe, in an almost confessional moment that "what is to bring true lasting advantage to our whole existence is veiled in impenetrable obscurity" (38 [36]). It is just when Kant takes us to the limits of where reason can go, as Virgil does Dante (and even as Socrates does Glaucon), that he positions us to sense, if not see, what might sustain a religious life. Spirituality in Kant bursts from the literal seams of his thought, where rationality reaches its limits. It is understandable that against the backdrop of Spinoza, who troubled Kant so much that his reproofs of that already much vilified thinker extended beyond his ideas to the privileged station his thought accorded geometry[28], freedom would seem to Kant himself the keystone of his system. But as over against his idealist successors, whom Spinoza inspired as much as he disturbed Kant, the concept most pressing its claim to center Kant's system is limitation. It is just in terms of human failure to discern limits that Kant characterizes a quality that, by both Jewish and Christian standards, festers at the heart of sin, namely pride.[29] Limits by their nature separate and so constitute one of the conditions of the sacred. Worlds, both phenomenal and noumenal, are founded on this concept, knowledge is secured, and some measure of serenity allowed us even in the subjective necessity of our moral imperfection.

NOTES

1. Harry Austryn Wolfson, *The Philosophy of Spinoza* (New York: World Publishing, 1934). Elsewhere, Wolfson calls him "an old-fashioned philosopher . . . more old-fashioned than the religious philosophers to whom he was opposed." Wolfson, "Spinoza and Religion," *Menorah Journal* (Autumn 1950): 151.
2. Immanuel Kant, "What is Enlightenment," in *Critique of Practical Reason and other Writings in Moral Philosophy*, ed. Lewis White Beck (Chicago: University of Chicago Press, 1949), 286–292.
3. Immanuel Kant, *Critique of Pure Reason*, tr. Norman Kemp Smith (New York: St. Martin's, 1965), sec. B xxx.
4. Immanuel Kant, *Critique of Practical Reason*, trans. Lewis Beck White (Upper Saddle River, NJ: Prentice Hall, 1993), 130 [124]. Subsequent references are cited parenthetically in the text. The bracketed number refers to pagination in the 1912 edition edited by Paul Natorp and published by the Prussian Royal Academy of Sciences.
5. Kant, *Critique of Pure Reason*, sec. A 297.
6. Kant, *Foundation of the Metaphysics of Morals*, in *Critique of Practical Reason and Other Writings in Moral Philosophy*, trans. Lewis Beck White (Chicago: University of Chicago Press, 1949), 55 [IV, 393].

7. "Pure practical reason does not require that we should renounce the claims for happiness; it requires only that we take no account of them whenever duty is a question" (97 [93]).

8. Kant's example of this is from our point of view highly paradoxical: Spinoza. But then, Kant inherited the view of Spinoza, shortly to change in his German philosophical successors, as atheistic.

9. We can imagine Pascal's critique of such a defense for belief in God. As much as Descartes profaned the idea of God by subordinating it to the world, so did Kant profane it by subordinating it to human goodness of will.

10. *Critique of Pure Reason*, B 397.

11. For example, with the claim, "duty . . . [is] the supreme life principle of all human morality," (89 [86]), but then, not necessarily of all human behavior.

12. Immanuel Kant, *Reason within the Limits of Reason Alone*, trans. Theodore M. Greene (New York: Harper Torchbooks, 1960), 37.

13. Kant, *Critique of Pure Reason*, sec. A 805.

14. Kant, agreeing with Spinoza, differed from the Stoics by denying we really could ever be free of them.

15. We can imagine that Pascal would fault Kant for this on the same grounds he faults Descartes: philosophy should never subordinate God to a means.

16. Kant, *Critique of Pure Reason* A 622.

17. Ibid., A 289.

18. Ibid., A 288.

19. John Silber, introduction to *Religion with the Limits of Reason Alone*, lxxix.

20. Ibid., lxxix, 178.

21. Our own determinative reason, in the form of understanding, takes much of the credit for the phenomenal world we inhabit. But this does not tempt Kant to divinize reason. For so parted from God, the phenomena lose the religious resonance they carry in the monotheisms and become little more, in Kant, than objects of scientific investigation, the starry heavens notwithstanding. What becomes so pronounced here is Kant's turn from the monotheisms, for which it is just what he calls the phenomenal world that finds explanation in God's creative act. The idealists, having dispensed with the noumena, would return to the creative activity of reason for their understanding of the sacred, and invest it with unlimited powers.

22. Alternatively, or better, equivalently, it is the moral law that performs this office (49 [47]; 155 [147]).

23. Kant, *Critique of Pure Reason*, A 694.

24. Hermann Cohen, *Religion of Reason out of the Sources of Judaism*, tr. Simon Kaplan (New York: Frederick Unger, 1972), 160. Cohen's view of romantic love invites serious feminist critique.

25. Lewis White Beck, translator's introduction to Kant, *Critique of Practical Reason*, xviii.

26. Kant, *Critique of Pure Reason*, A51.

27. As over against geometry, which was the model science for Descartes and Spinoza, chemistry set the tone for Kantian critique (170 [163]).

28. It is difficult not to sense Spinoza behind the opening of Kant's remark on the "Fundamental Law of Pure Practical Reason," where he consigns all life use of geometry to hypothetical rather than apodictic law (30–31 [30–31]).

29. It is "self-conceit as well as . . . self-love [that so] . . . readily mistake their boundaries" (90 [86]).

EIGHT
Novalis

If epistemology and ethics, the two weightiest fields of philosophical inquiry for Kant, each offered scope for a spirituality of limitation, then a third context for just such a spirituality opens up in the delimited space between them; for freedom marked a line of demarcation between the natural world of the first Kantian critique and the moral world of the second. Nature rested on a bedrock of determination; ethics on an abyssal ground of freedom. In his third critique, on (aesthetic) judgment, Kant explored this interstitial domain between nature and ethics which, by its very location there, combined features of both. This was aesthetics, where the free and the necessary united in the artwork, simultaneously a product of nature and of the freely working human imagination, as artists themselves attest when they speak of a drivenness to (freely) create, or art-appreciators, when they note in an artwork a fitness that is both unnecessitated and unchangeable.

Like moral freedom, what aesthetic freedom escapes are the determinations of natural necessity. But instead of issuing in acts conforming to moral law, aesthetic freedom culminates in what Kant calls "another nature [created] out of the material that actual nature gives it."[1] This other nature, which "surpasses nature,"[2] is the world of artworks, which are indeed fashioned from actual nature's materials. These objects differ from nature's in that they exhibit "a completeness for which no example can be found in nature."[3] This is because artworks instantiate in nature those representations from our mental repertoire that are already encompassing wholes, namely, ideas. But the ideas Kant has in mind here are not reason's—the ideas of God, humanity, and world—but the imagination's. Imagination is both reason's counterpart and opposite: where reason extracts ideas from what Kant would call sensual intuition, imagination implants them there. Aesthetic ideas are like rational ideas in that they transcend the reach of knowledge-conferring concepts; but differ, in that they seek material expression. The agency that effects the materialization of these imaginative ideas is Spirit, employed here in the old Platonic sense of that which stimulates to action. Kant calls it "the animating principle in the mind."[4] Thus, part of what excites admiration in a commendable artwork is the spirit it shows, an objectified trace of the subjective Spirit that affected it.[5]

This is not the spirituality we have been seeking. But from the artwork paths open up to the spiritualities of limitation we have already found in Kant, whether through the objectivity of the noumena, or the subjectivity of ethics. For insofar as art is sensual, it is, like all participants in the objective world of our senses, noumenal; and insofar as it is free, it connotes our ability to conform to moral law. If Kant was not emphatic about this spirituality, it is partly because it was so indirect. The price the artwork pays for mediating between nature and ethics is the loss of the forceful sense of limit either of those domains in their purity offers up to us. Indeed, far from imposing a spiritually efficacious limit on us, the artwork itself suffers from an inherent lack of *gravitas*. The supernatural world of the artwork, constructed out of our imagination, is merely an entertainment,[6] a kind of play.[7] The power by which the imagination executes artworks (i.e., the Spirit) is "only a talent,"[8] that, Kant implies, may be mustered now and then to relieve our boredom. Talent here contrasts self-diminishingly with what mattered more for Kant, the good of conformity to moral law, or insights of Understanding into laws of nature.

What especially troubled Kant's philosophical successors in this picture was the noumena. There was not just the logical problem of how the noumena, which transcended all categories of the understanding, including that of cause and effect, could partner with our categories to cause phenomena—there was the larger issue of the ineluctable constraint the noumena were on human understanding. Kant too readily submitted to this constraint (spiritually fruitful as it may have been). And the same critique could be made of him that he himself had made of Hume, that an epistemology that issued in such disturbing consequences must itself be flawed. The epistemologies of Absolute idealism and early German Romanticism, or Frühromantik, both dispense with noumena, though in contrastive ways. Hegel will represent for us, in the next chapter, the absolute idealist succession to Kant; in this chapter, Novalis, penname for Friedrich von Hardenburg (1772–1801), illustrates the early Romantic succession.

Novalis presumably became better known to Anglophone readers when English writer Penelope Fitzgerald published her novel about him, *The Blue Flower*, which its jacket copy called, "the most admired novel of 1995."[9] By now, a wide range of critical appreciation of him has appeared in English. Though identified mostly as a poet, known especially for his

Hymns to the Night, Novalis fills at least half the charge addressed to all the subjects of this book by having been what one critic calls "this enigmatic young *philosopher*-poet"[10] (emphasis ours). For he falls firmly within the line of philosophical descent from Kant, howsoever much mediated, as Kant partly was for him, by the absolute idealism of Fichte.[11] Indeed, the complex interdependencies of literature and philosophy in German intellectual history are one of its hallmarks.[12] One way to understand German romanticism and idealism is as alternative continuations, the first literary and the second philosophical, of the definitive gesture of Kantian critique, namely self-consciousness or reflection. By the critical method, Kant located consciousness as the object of its own intentional gaze. It is as if consciousness as subject, viewing itself, is thereby raised to a height above itself, as though it were having the mental equivalent of an out-of-body experience. From this new location, as inspector of its own knowing activity, consciousness could direct its attention back "down" on itself and its own operations, and so issue in the Kantian critiques and their idealist extensions; or, it could turn its back on itself and look "out" at what its new height brought into view beyond it. Idealism would eventually subsume all such outward beyonds under consciousness' watchful eye, and identify them with itself. It was a Frühromantik understanding, and especially Novalis', that the beyond enjoyed an independence from the self to which it could relate as partner rather than subsumer. The genuine space between knowing consciousness and its beyond supplied the play in which literature could flourish. For the romantics, poetry, more than philosophy, was the bridge to the wholeness both poets and philosophers sought in the wake of the stark Kantian divide between nature and ethics.

Ethics was redefined within this new romantic landscape, less as conformity to law than as unity, especially between what had previously been divided. Novalis puts it succinctly: "The moral sense is the ... sense for unity."[13] Separation, whether between nature and ethics, life and death, or good and evil, was the dark side of Kantian limitation, and a source of varied suffering.[14] For Kant, unity was only a prospect. Lying somewhere in the indefinite future, unity was a reasonable hope of harmony between nature and ethics. For the romantics (and the idealists) the harmony was potentially present, only concealed. That concealment supplies the distance that assures the holiness of unity.[15] For Novalis, "nature is a whole—in which each part in itself can never be wholly understood."[16] "Everything is a link in a chain."[17] But not a causal chain, as Kant might have said. Novalis aspired rather to what he called divination: "To perceive something without cause or contact."[18] The notion that an individual piece of reality was to be understood less in terms of the causes that effected it than the part it played in the whole reframed the context for understanding what constituted knowledge in the first place. Novalis built on the Kantian epistemology of reflection: it is because of our capacity for self-consciousness that we can not only know, but know that we can know. Consciousness turned *self*-knowing is the foundation for our claims to know anything else, for both Kant and Novalis. What Novalis abandoned was the elaborate structure of categories that Kant claimed to find in consciousness, by which it ordered the phenomena presented to it and so claimed—rightly, for Kant—to know the world. Here, too, is where the noumena fall by the way. For the objective noumena and the subjective categories were the twin pillars on which Kantian knowledge rested. In their place, Novalis substituted a single operation of mind that on its own was both creative and revealing, or knowledge-founding, namely potentization.

Novalis, who knew the technology of mining,[19] took this term from mathematics. What intrigued him was the idea that a number could be magnified by a measure of itself. To square a number, or raise it to the second power, is simply to multiply it by itself. By squaring itself a number can, as it were, pull itself up by its own bootstraps. More, there is no limit to the degree to which a number can be raised this way, it can be multiplied twice, thrice or any number of times by itself, and so approach infinity. The image was suggestive to Novalis for its application to objects and qualities of the world.[20] Just as for mathematics squaring a number yields a new number, so for the idealist friends of the romantics, consciousness applied to consciousness issued in something new, the Self as such. For Novalis, potentization had much broader application and yielded a host of new things. Most broadly, potentization was simply the application of something to itself. This could happen in several ways. Something could enact its own definitive quality, as when red reddens, or, to take an example from Novalis, when acuity enacts acuteness: "The acuity of genius is the acute use of acuity"[21] ["Genialischer Scharfsinn ist scharfsinniger Gebrauch des Scharfsinns."[22]] Acuity potentized is genius. Or, something could double itself in another context or medium as Novalis' much-admired Spinoza taught Substance did when it manifested less really as attribute of thought or extension, or less really still as individual mode. A more naturalistic example that intrigued Novalis, as a supervisor of mines, accustomed to the idea of the earth's depths, was fossilization;[23] but this type of potentization found ready application in the arts, which Kant had already taught transposed nature into an alternative super-nature. Potentization could herald startling transformations, as when Novalis writes, "We are close to waking when we dream of dreaming."[24] A potentization of common interest to romantics and idealists occurs when the characteristic activity of a thing takes itself for object; or, more precisely phrased, when the verbal form of a noun takes the noun for object. This is what Kantian critical philosophy does when it subjects the faculty of Understanding to the processes of understanding. The philosophical interest of this kind of potentization was in the self-contained circle it produced. This in itself was rich in paradoxical potential, for insofar as potentization is potentially infinite and so uncontained, it appears to undermine self-enclosure as such. Perhaps Kant foretold as much by leaving his own system incomplete. Successful self-containment was a rarity within the Kantian system anyway. Nothing in nature enjoyed such a status, for causal dependence was always on another. Human goodness was indeed human-dependent, but so fragile, according to Kant's late work, *Religion within the Limits of Reason Alone*, as to fall prey to "the radical evil in human nature."[25] But whatever potentized contained itself and so positioned itself to relate freely, both un-dependently and uncoercively, to what lay outside it. Freed of both causal dependence and causal efficacy, the potentized entity could enjoy a little joke at the expense of the causal, by transposing two of its letters, as happens in a common typographical error, to yield: the *casual*, a cousin to the playful, that domain of unweightiness to which Kant had already consigned works of art.

At this juncture, a portal opens up to a family of terms that move Novalis beyond his inherited Kantian framework: chance, contiguity, miracle, magic, dream, poetry, fairy tale, love. As Kristin Pfefferkorn helpfully notes of fairy tales as they functioned for Novalis—but has broader implications for his worldview—"they depict man as having a casual relation to the extraordinary and miraculous."[26] The power of the casual shows in the force of unnecessitated contiguities or juxtapositions that illuminate both or either of the juxtaposed, as in metaphor. For Novalis, everything in reality is already interrelated, we simply fail to see it. What poetry, novels, and fairy tales do is reconfigure the juxtapositions we take for granted—which generally conform to the Kantian model of cause-and-effect, and which fail to reveal the intra-relatedness within the whole of things—so as to uncover that network of relations. In contrast to the causal world of the Kantian understanding, the casual world of poetic insight is indeed magical, miraculous and dream-like, by the unnecessitated (noncausal) fitness of the relationships between things that constitute it, as in a poem, magic-act, or dream. Potentization fuels poetry by its power of juxtaposing the causally unrelated, indeed causally opposed, in fit ways: death potentized is the death of death, or life; suffering potentized is the suffering, or diminishment, of suffering: healing.[27] A new space opens up for love, which figured so faintly in the Kantian system, and effectually disappears in the idealist successions, in the relation between potentized individuals, who neither swallow each other up, nor are swallowed up in a larger whole, since they are already self-sustainingly whole in themselves. Géza von Molnár uncovers a pervasive schema of love in Novalis' romantic thought that takes some of its force from the contrast it makes with the idealist Fichte. The contrast turns on opposed interpretations of what appears to resist consciousness' own acts, namely, the other. For Fichte, the other is a projection of the self that by the seeming resistance it supplies invites the self's own countering self-expansion. The self, in effect, deceives itself with a seeming other to itself for the sake of its own growth. For Novalis, the other, which is genuinely there in the network of relations, need only be acknowledged for its genuine otherness to be transformed into a mediator of that network—and, by virtue of that office, an object and instrument of love.[28] Or, as Novalis puts it: "We should transform everything into a 'you'—into a second ego—only in this manner do we raise ourselves to the Great Ego—that is both One and All."[29]

The phrasing of this fragment begins to uncover both the epistemological and the spiritual overtones of potentization. For Novalis implies that the *other*, taken as an object of intimate personal address, as the *Du* in the original German connotes, constitutes a potentization of ego, raised to the second power. Only in this case, the potentization occurs not so much by doubling a single thing, an ego, as by uncovering in another a duplication of that ego already at hand. My potentization is my discovery of the other as a subject that doubles my own subjectivity, just by being other. A further potentization, more startling than this, is implicit here, of solitude, which has suddenly become relationship. For the self-enclosure, which is always the consequence of potentization, that results from this potentization consists of the relationship between me and the other, now a second ego. But it is not just relationality that has now opened up from solitude; it is also knowledge of the world beyond the self. For the other, who is genuinely so, now appears to me for what she truly is, a subjectivity other to mine, rather than a provocative block to my own self-expansion. The paradox of the situation cannot be overstated: insofar as potentizing is also intensifying, my intensification of myself becomes my knowledge of a genuine other to myself. It is as though I am looking at myself in a mirror only to discover that my mirror image is a self of its own, which only agrees, by a kind of miracle, to mimic my movements in reverse. This is not knowledge in the Kantian sense, for there is no necessity to the miraculous mirroring. It simply occurs or, so Novalis would say, does for the poetically inclined. Perhaps this is partly what Novalis indicates when he writes, "We shall never entirely comprehend ourselves, but we will and can do much more than comprehend ourselves."[30] How useful Novalis would have found Lewis Carroll's *Through the Looking Glass*; but then, he constructed his own fairy tales.

But there is still more to our fragment. For the relationality effected by this transformation in my regard of or for the other (it is really a move from *of* to *for*) does not stop there—by way of it, I am raised to "the Great Ego" that somehow connects me with "one and all," the universe of everything that can be taken for a second ego, which is really everything *simpliciter*. A relationality so pervasive is already implicit in the potential infinity of potentization, which need not stop at the second power. Such thinking anticipates the early twentieth century thought of Martin Buber on the I-Thou relation, which is available as much with trees as persons, and which similarly entails a connection to the divine Thou, or God.[31] That comparison also underscores how much potentization, for Novalis, is a spiritual process, connecting us with the sacred.

But we must not press the analogy with Buber, whose thinking on the divine was recognizably Jewish (and amenable to Christians), too far. Novalis' understanding of the sacred is much closer to Spinoza's, as he himself would acknowledge. Novalis was raised a Moravian and knew the vocabulary of Christianity from the inside. But here, as elsewhere, he prefers other designations for the sacred—as indeed the idealists would—not so much from a biblical regard for the sacredness of the divine name, as from a wish to connote the new and decidedly non-Christian framework in which to understand the sacred. Alongside such seemingly conventional understandings of God as we find in his fragments as this: "God is love,"[32] we also find: "God is a mixed concept,"[33] a characterization we would not expect to find in orthodox theology. But Novalis' notion of God is indeed mixed. On the one hand, God is a plural notion that subsumes all the ideals for which the various sciences strive but never reach—"Every science has its God, that is also its goal. . . . Philosophy seeks a first and single principle. The mathematician, the squaring of the circle and a principal equation. The human being—God."[34] This fragment presupposes enough play in the concept of science to cover, as an instance of it, human being—the science of being human, just so as to confound us with the probable mismatch that occurs when we superimpose whatever notion of God we carry onto this philosophical (Kantian) placeholder for it. It is subtly a pun, in which the double meaning of "god" is concealed and easily missed, as though Novalis were trying to expand our notion of God without our knowing it; on which Novalis might comment, "Don't God and Nature also play?"[35] On the other hand, Novalis can locate himself deeply enough within the mystical tradition to write, "God is now $1 \cdot \infty$, now $1/\infty$, now 0."[36] Perhaps Novalis means to suggest that God is where potentization, in all its connotations of infinity—both in what it can apply to and in the degree it can attain—coheres into a single whole. God is where the otherwise oppositional infinite and whole coincide.

But another aspect of our already so richly provocative fragment brings us closer to what is really sacred to Novalis: the fact that I am raised to the Great Ego by way on my relation with an other. There is a mediator. Novalis goes so far as to say that "nothing is more indispensable for true religious feeling than an intermediary—which connects us to the godhead."[37] Kantian limitation gives way to mediation as the bearer of spirituality or, as Novalis puts it, "Limitation will have turned into penetration."[38] Students of Novalis readily point to the significance of his biography to his thought, especially his romantic relation with Sophie von Kühn. Novalis' experience of romantic love supplied him with a punning reinterpretation of philosophy, after his beloved's name: "My favorite study basically bears the same name as my fiancée: Philo-Sophie—it is the soul of my life and the key to my inner self."[39] It was partly through this relation that Novalis found his romantic alternative to Fichte's egoistic idealism. As Géza von Molnár explains,

> In Sophie . . . he experienced the transformation of the world of things from an obstacle that hides the human goal into a medium for its revelation. . . . Now he . . . *knows* . . . that the self need not become a thing in order to gain objective currency for its subjectivity, that the forbidding otherness out there may smile back, that the object can shed its rigid independence and grant the subject its reality . . . that the I must no longer be either conqueror or conquered because it is confronted by a relentless It, that the I can encounter a Thou and be transformed from a subject complemented by the ever-present antagonism of the object into a self for whom there is but one reality.[40]

The one reality so revealed is both the single beloved and the larger world of things transformed into a single reality of intersubjectivities. Philo-Sophie teaches that the other has a face that can, unexpectedly, startlingly, smile back at the self and in so doing, uncover a world that builds, not by Fichtean self-assertions against an illusory other, but by relations between subjectivities. As in Christianity, so in Philo-Sophie, the mediator plays the essential role of foregrounding, even incarnating relationship, which, renamed love, has little difficulty holding the place of the sacred all by itself. It is as though the means the mediator supplies to the seeming end, is itself the end. Not that Novalis would have us deify our love objects. "It is idolatry, in a broader sense, if I regard this mediator as in fact God himself."[41] Rather, it is the activity of mediation that draws the language of sanctity to it. And most anything can perform that office, though typically not just anything can for a given self. Novalis' name for so pantheistic an individualized religion of relationship is: entheism, which we practice when, receiving our vision of cosmic interconnection through our single beloved, we nonetheless acknowledge that others receive it otherwise. If the sacred must be somehow other then relationship is so by the very incorporation of otherness into itself; if it must be foundational, then relationship is by founding a world on intersubjectivity; if it must supply our happiness then relationship, renamed love does, or so romantics of all varieties will tell us.

Novalis was, in his own estimation, the lucky recipient of the revelation that Sophie was to him. But the luck of the case had philosophical import, if only to suggest that philosophy, at least as inherited from Kant, was not the optimal medium for expressing Philo-Sophie. For what Novalis had experienced was momentous in its unconformity to scientific expectation or moral law, and the only terms Kant had for such a case were the somewhat self-diminishing ones of his aesthetics. Still, Kantian aesthetics pointed in the right direction towards what it had called another nature, a super-nature—which sounds like a raising of nature above itself—its potentization. It is as though when nature naturalizes, it posits a priority to itself of the somehow un- or super-natural, in analogy with the political process of naturalization, whereby an "alien" becomes a citizen, except that in this case, for Novalis, the prior state, brought into relief by the naturalizing, is the elevated one—and where poetry finds its home. For poetry *is* potentization. It is the potentization of language: "language to the second power."[42] Poetry "elevates each single thing through a particular combination with the rest of the whole."[43] Poetry "is the sense for the particular, personal, unknown, mysterious, for that which is to be revealed, what necessarily happens by chance."[44] Poetry is both an accomplishment and a simple sense for otherness. Poetry is both a product of potentization—in language—and an agent of it in others, especially humans. Like metaphors in a single poem, the self-containments it yields enter casually with each other into just the kinds of mutually illuminating relations that Novalis understands to lie hidden behind the causal relations we mistakenly take for ultimate. This means that part of poetry's point is just to free us from our customary ways of interpreting the world (typified by the Kantian Understanding), "to estrange art in a pleasant way, to make an object strange and yet known and attractive, that is romantic poetics."[45] As an agent of estrangement poetry questions the status quo, and may actually awaken hatred,[46] as Plato understood to be the danger to philosophy and philosophers. In partial explanation, Marianne Thalmann, writing about German romanticism generally, provocatively avers, "the word *strange*... contains a heresy."[47]

As Frederick Beiser argues in connection with Novalis' friend Friedrich Schlegel, the concept of poetry functioning here is more than literary. "It should be clear that the concept of *romantische Poesie* does not apply only to literature . . . rather it also refers to any creative work whatsoever, whether literary, artistic, or scientific. . . . [and even to] the productive principle in nature itself."[48] As one of Novalis' creations, the poet Klingsohr pronounces, "It is too bad that poesy has a special name and that poets make up a special guild. It is not anything special at all. It is the peculiar mode of activity of the human mind."[49] If the productive principle in nature is nature's own capacity to potentize, then poetry in the broadest sense is simply potentization itself, applied to anything. Poetry most broadly construed may be either the act of potentizing itself or the appreciative awareness of its occurrence in the face of all that conceals it. We are all poets in that sense. We create poetry when we convert ideas to things, and so produce poems, or things to ideas, and so realize something already given as a poem. But in a narrower sense, poetry does express itself in language: "Language is a poetic invention."[50] More narrowly still, poetry can be the literary genus of its several species: "the epic, the lyric and dramatic."[51] The capacity of the term to alternatively dilate and focus mimics the same feature of mathematical potentization, which can reverse itself into an extraction of roots.

That potentization is poetic is already implied in the grammatical characterization of it: the verbalization of a noun that takes the noun for object. This is already the language of language, its potentization. More broadly, the language of language is what it speaks on its own terms, without reference to anything outside itself. And this, according to that tantalizing essay by Novalis, "Monologue," is just what poetry is. Now poetry falls into perfect analogy with the self that knows the other through its own doubling. For it is just when language aims referentially to reach its distinctive other, the world, that it fails in that quest and produces "the most capricious and confused stuff."[52] Mathematics is once again the model: it is just in faithfulness to its own unfolding, without regard to anything outside it, that mathematical formulae apply accurately to nature.[53] Intentions to mirror nature block the capacity to do so. The same is true of poetry.

The seeming self-expressions of the poet mirror the reality beyond her; or they do when, in tighter analogy with mathematical formulae, and now also with prophecy, there is some inner necessity to them, as "if I [the poet] had to speak"[54] in just such a way. Language as the agent of its own speaking either usurps the place of the creator-deity of Genesis 1, or reveals him to be the agency of language itself. It is poetry we speak when we align with the issue of that agent, which only he can do who, with regard to language, is "sensitive to its fingering, its rhythm, its musical spirit, who perceives within himself the delicate working of its inner nature, and moves his tongue or his hand accordingly."[55] The necessity is in conforming to what language already gives of itself, as the prophet does to divine speech. But now, in a curious display of potentization within the essay itself, "Monologue" applies its own theory to itself as an instance of language, and wakens to the realization that it has indeed been trying all along intentionally to capture something outside itself, namely poetry—and so, as Kristin Pfefferkorn observes, "does not heed its own advice."[56] In consequence, the essay admits to itself that "I have said something quite foolish because I wanted to say it," and that "no one can understand it."[57] But has this not been equally true of all the fragments already cited that have tried to deliver up to us an understanding of God, poetry, potentization itself? Simply by self-consciously setting himself the writing projects he does—"My main occupations now will be 1. Encyclopedistics. 2. a novel. 3. the letter to Schlegel,"[58] —does not Novalis *want* to say things and so necessarily fail to say them in the prophetic way he intends?

One way to read this impasse is as a demonstration of philosophy's dead end. For neither "Monolog" nor any of the fragments present themselves as poetry. If it is just in virtue of these works of Novalis that he counts as a philosopher, then the point of them may be to defeat themselves, and *eo ipso*, philosophy itself. The problem with philosophy was that, according to one of Novalis' best known epigrams, it "is really homesickness."[59] Philosophy aches for a home it does not itself supply. Its very intentionality, its preoccupation with understanding, or as the German captures so much more viscerally, with *greifen*—as though to strangle the obdurately other into comprehensibility—defeats itself. Perhaps the form of the fragment that the romantics favored for their philosophy, as opposed to the systems of their idealist counterparts, is itself testimony to how little they expected philosophy to provide a long-term, habitable home. But then, what form of writing could express what lies at the heart of Novalis' vision: potentization and the freely interrelating self-enclosures it generates? Lyric poetry, certainly, with its juxtapositions of metaphors that cohere without mutual causation; though even here, in his most famous poems, the *Hymns to the Night*, Novalis alternates poetry with prose, as though to enclose the different parts of the poem not only in self-contained metaphors, but in self-contained genres of writing. The greater challenge was to express the same juxtapositions in narrative, in the form of the novel which Goethe and Schlegel were advancing in Novalis' own time. By the events it strings together outside the historical reality of cause and effect, a novel can illustrate a sustained sequence of the casually interrelated. One way to understand the potentization of life, or life enlivened, would be a picture of it that uncovers the unnecessitated coherence of its parts—what Kant might have called the spirit of it, or the incarnation within it of a regulating idea. And it is in just these terms that Novalis characterizes the novel: "The novel is about life—represents life . . . but not the image or fact of a proposition. It is the visible execution—the realization of an idea."[60] And the novel does indeed draw to itself the language of potentization, insofar as it realizes within itself a "geometrical progression,"[61] as happens, for example, when a novel subsumes within it another novel or when a character from one novel continues into another.[62]

But then, the plot of the novel must not be realistic, at least insofar as that implies a mimicking of events in causal sequence. Rather, in romantic novels, "our relation to chance and our insight into its qualitative nature are presented in one imaginative tableau."[63] Tableaux, understood as frozen drama, from which action has been eliminated—static, atemporal action—capture the logic of the romantic plot line, and are all the more effective if, arranged in sequence, they defy our expectations of cause and effect. Each tableau is like a bit of potentized life, raised to a repose of self-enclosure. For Novalis, the narrative genre that most behaves this way is the fairy tale. "A fairy tale is really a dream picture—devoid of all coherence—an *ensemble* of wondrous things and happenings . . . the harmonious effects of an Aeolian harp—Nature herself. If a *story* is introduced into a fairy tale, this is already a foreign intrusion."[64] The fairy tale is a story that undermines its own story line in the interest of converting sequence to simultaneity. At the same time, it is natural at a deeper level than meets the comprehending eye, where nature's parts are perceived to cohere voluntarily, rather than from necessity, as in the harmonies of the proverbial Aeolian harp, which is, "in fact," a tree the wind stirs to music. Insofar as fairy tales are the communal product of a folk—which is how later German romantics conceived them—and so escape dependence on a single author, they appear to arise *de novo*, out of language itself, in illustration of the language theory of "Monolog." The fairy tale captures in narrative form so much what poetry does in lyric form that it is "the canon of poesy as it were—everything poetic must be like a fairy tale."[65]

Novalis' best-known novel, *Heinrich von Ofterdingen*, is a potentized fairy tale—a fairy tale that enacts within it further fairy tales that narrate in progressively encompassing terms the unifying office of poetry. It is a short, unfinished work in two chapters, intended to be much longer. It traces a poet's maturation into his art, over the course of a physical journey that culminates in both marriage and poetic insight. In Novalis' oeuvre, it relates inversely to a work of roughly a year prior, his *Christendom or Europa*, which affects to tell a factual story—a history of Europe—in the form of a fairy tale. Beginning with an idyllic Middle Ages, the tale takes the reader through the progressively divisive Reformation, Enlightenment, and French Revolution, whose destructive spirit was only then, at the time of the essay's writing, according to its story, yielding to the onset of a new peace. The essay concludes with warm words heralding a new golden age. The fairy tale constraining itself to story mirrors the history expanding into fairy tale. The two works together illustrate not only Novalis' poetics at play, but a defining feature of that play: the self-determining and at the same time accurately duplicating mirror image.

What both works most obviously share is a predilection for mixing literary genres. Insofar as a single work of literature expresses itself across a range of genres, it already potentizes, in the sense of duplicating itself across a variety of transformative contexts. *Heinrich von Ofterdingen* does this most obviously by alternating between prose and poetry; *Christendom or Europa*, by alternatively assuming the marks of so many different genres as to defy classification, whether as essay, speech, sermon, or manifesto. Its generic identity has long troubled interpreters.[66] Its title works in sync with the ambiguity of the genre, as though to underscore it, for it can also be taken in alternative and mutually conflicting ways. Novalis originally referred to it simply as, *Europa*. It was only at its posthumous publication in 1826, with other works of Novalis, under the editorial care of his friends, Friedrich Schlegel and Ludwig Tieck, that Christianity also appeared in the title, perhaps out of sensitivity to revivals of Catholic fervor in the European politics of the time.[67] But the ambiguity of the conjunction, "or," complicates the meaning. If the "or" is appositional, then Europe is just another designation for Christianity, in support of conservative readings of the text. But the "or" may also be oppositional, implying a mutual incompatibility, in support of radical readings of the text. In the latter case, the attempt to intensify a pro-Christian reading of the work actually backfires, at least insofar as Europe is the intended hero of the tale.

What both works unambiguously celebrate is the Middle Ages, as German romanticism in general tended to do, partly from reaction against Enlightenment idealizations of classical antiquity, and partly from attraction to ideals of organic wholeness, which the social, political and religious structures of the medieval period were understood to illustrate. Géza von Molnár suggests that an additional appeal of this era for Novalis lay in the very place of middle it occupied between antiquity and modernity.[68] For it is just such middles that are best positioned to mediate, that connective act we have already seen to be sacred for Novalis. As the narrator of *Heinrich* observes, "During every period of transition higher spiritual powers appear to want to break through."[69] Insofar as the Middle Ages can be read as an extended period of transition between antiquity and modernity—a common modern way to read them—then the attribution of middlingness to them, that its denoters meant disparagingly, becomes a point of pride for them. Certainly *Europa* is explicit in its praise: "There were once beautiful, splendid times when Europe was a Christian land, when *one* Christendom dwelt in this continent."[70] This opening sentence of the text, in which the word "one" [*eine*] is italicized,[71] and twice repeated, begins a happy tribute to unity that continues into succeeding paragraphs, and is inversely recuperated, in terms of sadness, later in the text ("one misfortune, one sorrow, one feeling" [150]). Though the Middle Ages are not explicitly named, we know from the references to "one supreme ruler" (137), "the wise supreme head of the church" (138), and many allusions to the Catholic priesthood and ritual that they are intended. Most important, in light of the homesickness philosophy never cures, is the assurance the church supplied its faithful of "landing on the shore of a world that was truly a fatherland" (137), a homecoming whose allusiveness invites interpretation of whether it is understood to occur only in the next life or in proleptic anticipations here.

Allusiveness pervades the essay. Though Bruce Haywood notes in Novalis generally, "a remarkable fondness for periphrasis, the avoidance of direct identification,"[72] which, he observes, serves the ends of metaphor, in this case the unnaming of time helps transpose the history to fairy tale, as the very opening words, "There once were," seem already to have accomplished. Critics observe that what Novalis says of the Middle Ages is "strikingly at odds with historical reality."[73] The happy unity he envisions omits whatever could disturb it (inquisition, war, persecution of dissidents, Jews, Muslims, and others). More, the whole picture deconstructs, from the standpoint of history, on the issue of celibacy. For the essay claims to find within the Middle Ages itself a symptom of its own undoing in "the abolition of marriage for priests," characterized here as a shallowly "clever" and "earthly" measure intended to hold "the corpse of the order together (140)," after it had already begun to fail, but itself a wrong that properly ended the era. Apart from the audacity of such an evaluation of celibacy, which shamelessly performs the very dissidence from the medieval church the essay otherwise ignores, the chronology implied is impossible. For priestly celibacy was instituted at the very start of the Middle Ages. If it is also a symptom of decline, then the Middle Ages was over before it began, or never really existed at all. But then we are indeed in fairy tale, one of whose marks is the recognizably familiar recontextualized by the unworldly outlandish, which is how the idealization of the Middle Ages presented here now begins to read.

The opposite movement, from fairy tale to history, comes into view within *Heinrich* only if the whole of the novel is indeed a fairy tale, as Kristin Pfefferkorn avers.[74] What counts against that reading is the received understanding of novels, today, as realistic narratives. And, in fact, the longest and first part of the novel, "Expectation," confines the fabulous to stories told within the framework of a perfectly reasonable, if largely uneventful, journey from one actual place to another, Eisenach to Augsburg. Indeed the supernatural appears to be invoked in this part purely for the sake of confining it to stories, dreams, or superstition. But then, the subsequent chapter, "Fulfillment," reverses that relationship. For the Heinrich character, established realistically in the first part of the novel now undergoes a mountain journey that is truly miraculous, in which he encounters the guiding spirit of his deceased beloved. It is Novalis' distribution of the two chapter headings—"Expectation" to the realistic part; "Fulfillment" to the miraculous part—that encourages a reading of the whole as fairy tale, whose ultimate reference is otherworldly. Within "Fulfillment," Heinrich displays in his fictive life what the fairy tale form should accomplish for the reader: a displacement from the ordinary towards the extraordinary.

Still, as part of the realism's preliminary anchor of the tale, Novalis set it in the Middle Ages. Unlike in *Europa*, the past tense of the tale comes clear only several pages into the text, when the narrator, in a rare moment of self-indicating intrusion, takes us metaphorically by the hand as "we immerse ourselves willingly in the years when Henry lived" (25). And that these are the Middle Ages we know only from Heinrich's encounter, later on, with a band of Crusaders and their hapless captive.[75] Our immersion is willing because the medieval stage Novalis sets is so attractive. "An idyllic poverty adorned those times with a peculiarly earnest and innocent simplicity" (25). An ideal of possessionlessness, or of only few possessions, animates both *Europa* and *Heinrich*. Acquisitions require "so much time . . . to acquire skills in them that there is no time left for quietly gathering . . . thoughts or for the attentive contemplation of the inner world" (*Europa*, 139). The few possessions truly needed take on in consequence a special significance for their owners. According to the narrator of *Heinrich*, people loved the tools that took them through their daily tasks (*Heinrich*, 24). This was especially so in light of the known origin of these "mute companions of life" (25) in "the mysteries of nature" (24)—woods and minerals—which lent them an aura of sanctity. *Europa* had acknowledged the soulful quality of objects, but only in saints' relics, which functioned so importantly in the medieval piety that essay celebrates. It is a stroke for the realism at which *Heinrich* aims that it discovers this same sanctity in the ordinary objects of daily life. So naturalistic a recasting of medieval spirituality now enlists the sympathy of anyone who has ever had a favorite knife, plate, or drinking glass.

As a coming-of-age story, *Heinrich* requires that its hero undergo an inevitably painful separation from his happy childhood. This is the journey—his "first separation"(26)—that takes him to Augsburg. This "sorrow" (26) finds its political analog, within *Europa*, in the divisions that followed the happy Middle Ages. And as though to tighten the analogy, Novalis characterizes the trust the medievals showed in their priests as "childlike" (137). At the same time, "humanity was not mature enough, not cultivated enough for this splendid kingdom" (139), as though childlikeness must be, itself, mature. But Heinrich too evidences something within himself that begins to end his childhood: a longing for poetic insight. Heinrich's ignorance of poetry marks his immaturity and uncultivation. Dreams work to move the action forward. The first of Heinrich's reported dreams features a blue flower that beckons him with newly raised but unspecified longings. These account for the appearance Heinrich makes to his mother of being too sadly self-preoccupied (24) and so for the plot-defining trip to Augsburg she proposes as cure. When Heinrich reports at the very start of the novel on the appearance of a mysterious stranger who told oddly disquieting tales, this too may be dream, since no one else appears to remember him. But it is just the character most skeptical of dreams, Heinrich's father, who makes the point most forcefully for their significance. The father, who deems dreams "spendthrift" (18) plays to Heinrich's poetic temperament the same role the Enlightenment does to the new age *Europa* heralds. The father and the Enlightenment are the earlier generation about to be superseded. And yet, like Descartes, for whom dreams both deceived and revealed, Heinrich's father too witnesses to the foretelling agency of dreams when, at Heinrich's request, he tells the dream that led him to his spouse, Heinrich's mother. What induces the dream is a "homesickness"—that epithet for philosophy—that leads him to wander towards a distant farmhouse inhabited by a wise old man who collects books, art, and poetry. And in this house full of "strange thoughts and feelings" (21) the father has his dream, which features mountain peaks commanding panoramic views,[76] mysterious old men in caves, and, again, blue flowers redolent of happiness. This dream foretells scenes to follow in the realistic story, for Heinrich does indeed navigate mountains and caves and finds in his beloved Mathilda's face a repetition of the blue flower he saw in his early dream.

Dreams are the perfect analog in human psychology to the fairy tale. Both juxtapose images according to a self-contained logic of their own, independent of laws of cause and effect. And that very defiance of causal law is their claim on what Novalis takes for a deeper truth of casually cohering relationships outside of them. Dreams are self-contained mirror images of those deeper relationships, or, in Heinrich's words, they effect "a significant rent in the mysterious curtain that hangs a thousandfold about our inner life" (19). If the fairy tale is the canon of poetry, then dreams are its teacher.

Their analog in *Europa* is history, which does not simply comprise Middle Ages, Reformation, Enlightenment, and Revolution, but explains them according to its own "essential" "alternation of opposite movements" (139). This seems at first in stark contrast to the foretelling and forward moving agency of dreams; except that there is progress here too in the cyclic returns: "that which does not achieve perfection now will achieve it at some future attempt" (140). More analogously, the logic of history like that of dreams (and poetry) is self-contained. The evolving cycles of history are not determined by forces beyond them but unfold out of history's own nature. "Is not history independent, self-reliant, as good as infinitely loveable and prophetic?" Dreams and history mimic language in their self-contained mirrorings of deeper realities outside them. *Heinrich* develops this view further over the course of a history lesson given by the wise Count of Hohenzollern, a cave-dwelling hermit who appears about mid-tale, but already foretold by Heinrich's father's dream. The count dismisses any history told according to "incomplete and burdensome formulas" (81) such as we may imagine the very idea of cause and effect to instance. Instead, the historian must uncover how much "events near at hand . . . *sympathize* all the more wonderfully with remote events." She must "notice the hidden interlinking of the past and the future, and learn how to piece history together out of hope and memories" (83). History so pictured is more simultaneity than sequence and, so the count avers, more likely to be accurately captured by poets than mere chroniclers.

> There is more truth in their [the poets'] fairy tales than in learned chronicles. Even though the characters and their fates are invented, the spirit in which they are invented is nevertheless true and natural. To a certain extent it is all one, as far as our enjoyment and instruction are concerned, whether the characters in whose fates we trace out our own ever really lived or not. (85)

The count's words recall Socrates' when, after having sketched the ideal state, he concludes, at the end of the *Republic* that "whether such an one exists, or ever will exist in fact, is no matter,"[77] since the good person will live after the pattern of it anyway. The association of enjoyment with instruction is a subtle rebuke of Kant. For Novalis, history is most instructive when it is least effortfully factual, but allows a tale of storied progress revealing deeper patterns to unfold from out of its surface sequences. In those deeper patterns we see our own lives mirrored. The narrative of *Heinrich* makes the point dramatically towards the end of Heinrich's visit with the count. While leafing through an untitled book in the subterranean library, Heinrich encounters pictures of himself, his family and friends, illustrating what the count says is a novel, much older presumably than Heinrich, "about the wondrous fortunes of a poet" (91). In this realistic part of the story Novalis is not prepared to admit overt fantasy, so he qualifies the experience by suggesting that what Heinrich experienced in the book was also a dream. But the message is clear: whether history, novel, or fairy tale, a proper narrative is an otherness in identity with the reader. By way of potentization, the magic book is Novalis' own, reproduced within itself; but the reader of Novalis' tale is encouraged to see herself, too, mirrored in the fictive events and characters on view there. By an even further potentization, all of life is invested with this mirroring potential. As a fragment illuminates, "It is only because of the weakness of our organs and of our contact with ourselves that we do not discover ourselves to be in a fairy world."[78]

History so understood holds surprises in store. Surprise, or wonder, is the expected response to the mirroring correspondences that, it now appears, are the stock-in-trade of poets, historians, and dreamers. The surprise turns not so much on discovery as recognition of the same in a foreign context. To estrange the familiar was poetry's office already in Novalis' fragments; but this was not just to uncover another previously unsuspected world but to find our own world there. This is what Heinrich discovers in the magical book, whose characters familiar to him, including himself, wear clothes belonging to "another age" (91). Strangeness potentized in this way is refamiliarization: to estrange estrangement is to familiarize. No wonder the word itself is so frequent in *Heinrich*; less so in *Europa*, but still present there as a feature of history—for example, the "history of modern unbelief is extremely strange" (145).

That particular strangeness of modern unbelief turns on the paradox of the intensely believing Reformation unfolding so naturally into the skeptical Enlightenment. The chief culprit in that transformation, according to *Europa*, was "the letter"—that ancient trope for literalism that St. Paul contrasted with spirit. Spirit understood in the Kantian sense, as the capacity for infusing objects with ideas, was precisely what was needed for reading the Bible, an object otherwise of "inadequate content" whose "abstract sketch of religion . . . was all the more noticeably oppressive" (141). Any literal reading of the Bible, which is what Novalis accused Luther of doing under the rubric of "philology" (141), immediately precludes potentization, which can only occur in textual readings that presume multiple levels of meaning. And so it precludes poetry, as Novalis quickly notes: "the understanding of art suffers in sympathy" (142). And now we stand, for *Europa*, at the very threshold of Enlightenment, which simply universalizes, beyond the Bible, literalistic proscriptions on multivalence. The Enlighteners "made heretics of imagination and feeling." They "were tirelessly engaged in cleansing nature, the earth, human souls, and the learning of poetry, rooting out every trace of the sacred" (144). Fundamentally, they flattened and compressed a richly layered reality. *Heinrich* makes the point pictorially in the long, self-standing fairy tale, known as Klingsohr's tale, after its teller, that closes the first part of the novel. Among the characters of that tale is a malevolent scribe, who assiduously writes a chronicle. When the miraculous water within a nearby bowl touches more favored characters of the story, it turns to "a blue mist which displayed a thousand strange images." When it touched the scribe, "a multitude of numbers and geometrical figures fell on the floor," and excited his greed to possess and control, as he gathered and strung them into a necklace for himself (124). As Géza von Molnár teaches, blue functioned symbolically for Novalis as a color of transition between dark and light, and so imaged the notion of mediation so important to him.[79] Its presence reflects well on whoever is associated with it. The very precision of the numbers and figures (not noticeably blue) that the scribe effects weigh them down (they drop to the floor) and subject them to the scribe's control and possessiveness—an intended judgment, no doubt, on Enlightenment sensibility. Indeed, light itself (by itself) is a term of opprobrium for Novalis, who after all authored *Hymns to the Night*. Speaking of the Enlighteners, Novalis writes that "because of its mathematical obedience and its boldness, light had become their darling" (145) at the expense of dark-infused colors. In Klingsohr's tale, the sun itself is apocalyptically destroyed to make way for the more overtly mediating light of moon and stars.

The lucidity of Enlightenment is more glare than illumination. It eliminates all mediating shade. It is indeed destructive and its natural consequence is revolution, as all that has been oppressed bubbles up explosively from beneath the enforced flatness. For *Europa* the French Revolution was less a product of social than aesthetic oppression. But both *Europa* and *Heinrich* imply theodicies according to which a period of wresting pain naturally separates an original childlike Eden from a more mature golden age. *Heinrich* communicates this more forcefully through Klingsohr's fairy tale, in which the paradigmatic Mother is burned to ashes just so that, dissolved in magic water, she can become for all "a drink of eternal life" (145). But the realistic story mirrors the same truth, as Heinrich grasps by way of his deceased beloved, Mathilda, that death potentized (the death of death), or poeticized, is "a higher revelation of life" (156).

Insofar as *Europa* is a religious text, and *Heinrich* a poetic one, the two cross disciplines as they approach their climactic ends. As *Europa* draws to a close, it pronounces that the estimable Christianity of the Middle Ages is gone for good (151). The Reformation had already sealed its fate (142). But the destruction was really a purification towards a subtler version of religion: Christianity as "the notion of mediation itself" (151).[80] We already know that mediation is the chief office of the sacred, for Novalis; but it is also the work of poetry, insofar as potentization mediates between opposites. It is no accident that the stated herald of the new church is Novalis' friend Friedrich Schleiermacher, the "veilmaker,"[81] a theologian noted already in his day for his efforts at mediating between religion and art. In the third age of the mediating church, poetry will stand forth "like a bejeweled India" (148), an apt metaphor for a Europe whose own potentization will uncover for it affinities with other continents. Similarly, as *Heinrich* draws to a close, in the hero's last conversation with the naturalist healer, Sylvester, we learn that "with the higher powers [of poetry] religion comes into being; and what had before appeared as incomprehensible necessity of our innermost nature, a universal law without definite content, now turns into a marvelous, native, infinitely varied, and whole satisfying world, into an incomprehensibly intimate communion of all the blessed with God" (168). Otherwise put, we learn that poetry, far from being the weightless entertainment that Kant opined, unveils a new world of post-Kantian religion, where richness of interrelationship—itself divine—succeeds emotionless obedience to formalized law.

A tripartite movement structures both texts, from simple, unselfconscious unity, through painful self-division, to mature wholeness. We do not cause the movement, it simply happens in that pattern, revealed to the poetically attuned. A spirituality inspired by Novalis resembles the Platonic feeding or grazing on ideas, except here the nourishment is, pace Plato, poetry, which is both fantasy and deeper mirror of reality, where the casual and magical interconnections of the sacred reside.

NOTES

1. Kant, *Critique of Judgment*, tr. Werner Pluhar (Indianapolis, IN: Hackett, 1987), 182 [314].
2. Ibid.
3. Ibid., 183 [314].
4. Ibid., 181 [313].
5. Novalis, following suit, refers to "art that is vivified by pure ideas." Novalis, "Logological Fragments II," in *Novalis: Philosophical Writings*, trans. and ed. Margaret Mahony Stoljar (Albany: State University of New York Press, 1997), 77.
6. Kant, *Critique of Judgment*, 195 [326].
7. Ibid., 186 [317].
8. Ibid., 183 [314].
9. Penelope Fitzgerald, *The Blue Flower* (New York: Houghton Mifflin, 1995).

10. David Wood, introduction to Novalis, *Notes for a Romantic Encyclopedia*, trans. and ed. David Wood (Albany: State University of New York Press, 2007), ix.
11. See Géza von Molnár, *Novalis' "Fichte Studies"* (The Hague: Mouton, 1970).
12. John Neubaurer commends "the unique symbiosis of poetry and philosophic reflection in early Romanticism" that "all but disappeared" in later German romanticism. John Neubaurer, *Novalis* (Boston: Twayne Publishers, 1980), 160.
13. Novalis, *Notes for a Romantic Encyclopedia*, 10.
14. "All affliction and evil is isolated and isolating—it is the principle of separation." Ibid., 121.
15. And motivates an interest in the image of veils, for which, see note 81 below.
16. Novalis, *Last Fragments* in *Philosophical Writings*, trans. and ed. Marjorie Mahony Stoljar (Albany: State University of New York Press, 1997), 157.
17. Ibid.
18. Novalis, *Notes for a Romantic Encyclopedia*, 10.
19. Novalis was by trade an administrator of salt mines.
20. "Potentization broadened and rendered *qualitative* becomes in Novalis' terminology 'romanticizing.'" Wood, introduction to *Notes for a Romantic Encyclopedia*, xv.
21. Novalis, "Miscellaneous Observations," in *Novalis: Philosophical Writings*, 32.
22. Novalis, "Blütenstaub," in *Briefe und Werke*, Bd. 3 (Berlin: Verlag Lambert, 1943), 68.
23. Kristin Pfefferkorn, *Novalis: A Romantic's Theory of Language and Poetry* (New Haven, CT: Yale University Press, 1988), 84.
24. Novalis, "Miscellaneous Observations," 25. Even more strikingly: "I destroy evil and affliction, etc. through philosophism—elevation—by directing evil and affliction back on themselves." Novalis, *Notes for a Romantic Encyclopedia*, 121.
25. An expression which partially titles book 1 of that work.
26. Kristin Pfefferkorn, *Novalis: A Romantic's Theory of Language and Poetry*, 158.
27. Virginia Burrus suggests in her book, *Saving Shame*, that to shame shame is to obtain release from it. Virginia Burrus, *Saving Shame* (Philadelphia: University of Pennsylvania Press, 2008), 151.
28. See Géza von Molnár, *Romantic Vision, Ethical Context: Novalis and Artistic Autonomy* (Minneapolis: University of Minnesota Press, 1987).
29. Novalis, *Notes for a Romantic Encyclopedia*, 61.
30. Novalis, "Miscellaneous Observations," 23.
31. Martin Buber, *I and Thou*, trans. Walter Kaufmann (New York: Scribner's, 1970).
32. Novalis, *Notes for a Romantic Encyclopedia*, 12.
33. Ibid., 166.
34. Ibid., 46. Elsewhere in the same book Novalis casts God as the goal of *nature*, p. 9.
35. Ibid., 65.
36. Ibid., 166. A propos this fragment, a delightful typographical error occurs in the Reform Jewish prayerbook, *Gates of Prayer for Shabbat and Weekdays*, ed. Chaim Stern (New York: CCAR, 1994). Quoting from Psalm 92, the prayerbook offers up for recitation: "Your deeds, O God, fill me with gladness, Your work moves me to song. How great are your works, 0 God! How profound your design" (p. 47). From the vocative affirmation, "O God," this version of the psalm moves to the startling negation of "0 [zero] God." A Kabbalist could not have phrased it better.
37. Novalis, "Miscellaneous Observations," 35.
38. Novalis, "Logological Fragments I," 57.
39. Novalis, *Novalis Schriften*, ed. Richard Samuel, Hans-Joachim Mähl and Gerhard Schulz (Stuttgart: Kohlhammer Verlag, 1965–2005), 4:188, quoted in Wood, Introduction to *Notes for a Romantic Encyclopedia*, xx.
40. Molnár, *Romantic Vision*, 62.
41. Novalis, "Miscellaneous Observations," 35.
42. Novalis, "Logological Fragments I," 78.
43. Ibid., 54.

44. Novalis, "Last Fragments," in *Novalis: Philosophical Writings*, 162.
45. Novalis, quoted in Marianne Thalmann, *The Literary Sign Language of German Romanticism* (Detroit, MI: Wayne State University Press, 1972), 6.
46. It does so by the resistance to control it shows when it operates faithfully to itself, as Novalis says of language generally in "Monolog." Novalis, "Monolog," in *Novalis: Philosophical Writings*, 83.
47. Marianne Thalmann, *The Literary Sign Language of German Romanticism*, 84.
48. Frederick C. Beiser, *The Romantic Imperative: The Concept of Early German Romanticism* (Cambridge, MA: Harvard University Press, 2003), 15.
49. Novalis, *Heinrich von Oftendingen*, trans. Palmer Hilty (Prospect Heights, IL.: Waveland Press, 1990), 116.
50. Novalis, *Notes for a Romantic Encyclopedia*, 144.
51. Ibid., 32.
52. Novalis, "Monologue," in *Novalis: Philosophical Writings*, 54.
53. Ibid. Novalis recalls Spinoza here.
54. Ibid., 84.
55. Ibid., 83.
56. Pfefferkorn, *Novalis*, 69.
57. Novalis, "Monolog," 84.
58. Novalis, *Notes for a Romantic Encyclopedia*, 32.
59. Ibid., 155.
60. Novalis, "Logological Fragments II," 70.
61. Novalis, "Logological Fragments I," 55. Margaret Mahony Stoljar comments: "The Romantic theory of the novel placed it at the pinnacle of all modern writing. Like the terms of a geometrical progression it is raised to the power of itself and is always open to new development." Stolfar, *Novalis: Philosophical Writings*, 172n.
62. Alison McCulloch notes the generic name for these: "borrowed-character novels," in her review of *Gregorius* by Bengt Ohlsson (Norton, 2008) in the *New York Times Book Review* (July 13, 2008). The notion plays to a central idea from Schlegel that literature is a "progressive universal Poesie." See Friedrich Schlegel, "Athenaeum Fragments," in *Philosophical Fragments*, trans. Peter Firchow (Minneapolis: University of Minnesota Press, 1991), 31.
63. Pfefferkorn, *Novalis*, 158. Pfefferkorn is talking about fairy tales here, but this is all the better to our purpose.
64. Novalis, *Notes for a Romantic Encyclopedia*, 171.
65. Ibid., 167.
66. Neubarer introduces the piece as an essay, in his commentary on it, but quickly recharacterizes it as a speech, concluding that it was a "rhetorical exercise," for Novalis, in which he toyed with a variety of tones. See Neubarer, *Novalis*, 91–99. Nicholas Saul deems it a sermon, or, more precisely, "not even simply a sermon, but the dramatic *illusion* of a sermon." See Nicholas Saul, *History and Poetry in Novalis and in the Tradition of the German Enlightenment* (London: Institute of Germanic Studies, University of London, 1984), 118. Richard Littlejohns writes of the work that "it is, in a word, myth." See Richard Littlejohns, "Everlasting Peace and Medieval Europe: Romantic Myth-Making in Novalis' *Europa*," in *Myths of Europe*, ed. Richard Littlejohns and Sara Soncini (New York: Rodopi, 2007), 177. William Arctander O'Brien classifies the piece as "Hardenburg's most dramatic work of propaganda." See William Arctander O'Brien, *Novalis: Signs of Revolution* (Durham, NC: Duke University Press, 1995), 227.
67. Richard Littlejohns, "Everlasting Peace," 179.
68. Molnár, *Romantic Vision*, 125–128.
69. Novalis, *Heinrich von Ofterdingen*, trans. Palmer Hilty (Prospect Heights, IL: Waveland Press, 1964), 25. Page numbers for subsequent quotations to this work are given parenthetically.
70. Novalis, "Christendom or Europa," in *Novalis: Philosophical Writings*, 137. Page numbers for subsequent quotations to this work are cited parenthetically.

71. It is also typographically emphatic in the German. Novalis, *Briefe und Werke*, Bd. 3 (Berlin: Verlag Lambert Schneider, 1943), 31.

72. Bruce Haywood, *Novalis: The Veil of Imagery* (Cambridge, MA.: Harvard University Press, 1959), 15.

73. See Littlejohns, "Everlasting Peace," 175–176 for an exhaustive itemization of the dissonances.

74. Pfefferkorn assigns the novel to the genus of *Kunstmärchen*, artfully constructed fairy tales, rather than folk tales. Pfefferkorn, *Novalis*, 168.

75. And even so, we are grateful to scholar of romanticism, Ernst Behler, for definitively assuring us that in this novel, "we are in the age of the Crusades." Ernst Behler, *German Romantic Literary Theory* (New York: Cambridge University Press, 1993), 213.

76. This image coheres nicely with the elevation that potentization connotes, and the picture of a self raised above itself in its self-awareness. For Novalis, what the self knows in its self-awareness mirrors the vista outside it.

77. Republic (tr. Jowett) 592.

78. Novalis, "Logological Fragments II," 67.

79. Molnár, *Romantic Vision*, 113–115. "Blue is the color that emerges when the darkness of self-estrangement begins to appear in the light of self identity." Molnár, 151.

80. Though the essay does not so identify it, this could be the Christianization of Christianity, its potentization. More orthodox interpreters of Christianity are not amused. For Karl Barth, Novalis' sanctifications of poetry and the creativity required for it brought humanity "menacingly" close to "an abyss of appalling loneliness," and to views of deity "which could not be more energetic or more dangerous." Karl Barth, *Protestant Theology in the Nineteenth Century: Its Background and History*, trans. B. Cozens and J. Bowden (London: S.C.M. Press, 1972), 357, 365.

81. This is the literal meaning of the name, which Novalis plays on in his essay. For Novalis, veils reveal by taking the shape of what they cover. They play perfectly to the ideas of estranged familiarity and familiarized strangeness. See, in *Heinrich*, pp. 40, 50, 63, 85, 104, 145.

NINE
Hegel: *The Phenomenology of Spirit*

Hegel's *Phenomenology of Spirit* appears by its very title to headline the kind of philosophical spirituality we are seeking. We might think we had here a philosophical text that chiefly explores the phenomenon of human proximity to the sacred. We do not. For the spirit that Hegel here investigates descends from that activity of mind that Kant associated with artistic creativity. For Kant, this was simply one activity of consciousness, and not the most important. For Hegel, it was all. Hegelian consciousness is wholly absorbed into spirit. This is the spirit of activity, so efficacious as to fashion objects from thoughts as artists do, according to Kant, and as God did, according to some philosophical interpretations of Genesis 1. But Hegel is not interested here primarily in either artists or God, though they figure in the story he has to tell. Rather, the hero of his tale is the whole of being, what Spinoza took for Substance, but now understood more productively according to a refrain of this work simultaneously as its own subject. The formula, Substance is Subject, which occurs most prominently at the beginning and end of the *Phenomenology* enfolds the work in its embrace, and lends itself as a précis of the whole, as one of the few Hegelian dicta that, cited out of context, still points truly towards Hegel's intent to vivify or, in the Hegelian sense of spirit, spiritualize Spinoza. ("All reality is solely spiritual"[1]). To subjectify substance is to understand it as the conscious agent of its own self-understanding. Hegel is exploring the philosophical productivity of self-reference, which turns out to be momentous indeed. For thought thinking itself generates objects; "its thinking is itself directly actuality" (139). Otherwise put, form out of its sheer formalism generates content. It would be as though the Aristotelian forms of logic, the syllogisms, entailed not just that Socrates, if human, is mortal but the reality of Socrates, humanity, and mortality themselves, which is just what Plato failed to show his eternal forms could do.

This ability falls to form by way of a concept Hegel shares with Novalis, but employs to different ends: mediation. For Novalis, mediation was the instrument of unity, which virtually defined the sacred for him. For Hegel, mediation is the means by which knowledge occurs. Insofar as Hegel was a monist, the unity Novalis sought was already given. Mediation is what enables Kantian knowledge, which requires two (a subject and object), to occur within monism. It names the process of self-reference by which a unity of consciousness self-divides into subject and object. Where for Novalis, mediation connoted unity, for Hegel it presupposed division, just the opposite of the multiplication that served Novalis so well when he potentized. In the Preface to the *Phenomenology*, Hegel explains mediation by way of two terms that would later figure centrally in his *Science of Logic*: positing and reflecting.

> Living Substance . . . is in truth actual only insofar as it is the movement of positing itself, or is the mediation of its self-othering with itself. . . . It is the doubling which sets up opposition, and then again, the negation of this indifferent diversity . . . . Only this self-restoring sameness of this reflection in otherness within itself—not an original or immediate unity as such—is the true. (10)

To posit is to position something subjective objectively, to make of it an object differentiated from all else and thereby emphatically known (through what it is not), as navy blue might be first recognized as not-black only in juxtaposition with black. To reflect is to realize that the posited object is indeed still subjective, which "restores" it to subjectivity. Essential to the process is a liminal moment of self-deception, which sandwiches between the positing and reflecting, when the object is taken for independent of the subject and monism implicitly denied. The entire process is mediation. Hegel explicitly denies that knowledge can occur immediately, outside this process. Any such location is abyssal in a sense that Hegel emphatically rejects.[2]

Positing is a semblance of self-negation. But consciousness is never really free of itself. Insofar as positing and reflecting are the forms of Hegelian knowing, as the syllogisms were for Aristotle, content is implicit in them. The forms transpose to content in this way: a posited object of consciousness is reflected back into consciousness just when consciousness becomes aware of itself being aware of that object. In that case, consciousness has become aware of one of its forms of knowing—positing—so that its per(form)ance of it becomes content for it. The new content—consciousness-being-aware-of-itself-positing-something—is already a new form: reflecting, which in turn will yield to another act of positing. "What first appeared as the object sinks for consciousness to the level of its way of knowing it" (56). Hegel is exploring how our self-reflective awareness that we know changes what we know. Mediation changes what is mediated. Not just the object of knowledge, but our criteria of knowing change. Positing and reflecting alternately yielding to each other transform what is only potentially knowledge of a merely immediate consciousness into actual knowledge of a mediated consciousness, where the "of" ambiguously makes both a subject and object of consciousness. For it is both. As soon as consciousness becomes self-aware, it is invested with objectivity, and its object with subjectivity. But knowledge is not the only product of mediation; what also results is a new appreciation of the definite, the particular, the differentiable object. For this is what positing always yields. Hegel's solution to the problem of knowledge within monism simultaneously solves an old idealist conundrum inherited from Plato, of how manifest particulars relate to abstract and hidden universals. The problem of abstractions, Hegel wittily wrote—as captured in A. V. Miller's translation—is that they "edify but raise no edifice" (234).[3] For Hegel, universals are only as real as they are self-knowing; and they are only as self-knowing as they are positively manifest. Hegel thereby rebukes Kant as well, who lingered too longingly in the purity of theoretical and practical reason, at the expense of the real. Hegel might counter Kant by suggesting that the sheer logic by which the particular—what Kant might have called, "the positive,"—emerges from the abstract preserves its purity. Kant could have the purity of his abstractions and eat them too, they were that pregnant with materiality, if only he had seen it. But then, this drive towards the manifest—this conviction that ultimately "truth as well as presence and actuality are united" (355)—also threatens the conditions of spirituality, insofar as the sacred requires some measure of distance and separation.

Hegelianism is from a purely Kantian point of view more properly hooliganism. It shows no respect for the limits that gave us the ascesis of Kantian spirituality. There are no borders that by the sheer boundary line of them limn an other side that remains resolutely other and, potentially, holy. On the contrary, Hegel repeatedly diminishes the very notion of the beyond. The beyond is a placeholder for whatever at any given stage in its self-development, consciousness does not understand, or rather, needs to understand itself as not understanding on its way to full self-knowledge. The beyond is a burden. Picture-thinking, for example—which is so characteristic of what Kant would have called positive religion, because its pictorial claims are simply posited, without exhibiting themselves as logical derivations—"remains burdened with the antithesis of a beyond" (478). It can also be a mark of insincerity within consciousness. The Kantian ethicist, for example, who postpones the completion of morality to an infinitely remote future displays a failure to be "earnest about the perfection of morality" (378). Significantly, and phenomenologically, what Hegel seriously names with regard to the beyond are the shapes of consciousness that posit it, which include the famous Unhappy Consciousness, an ancient way of thinking that overemphasizes transcendence, at the expense of immanence, and Faith, a modern way of thinking that fails to see how much of its own self is implicated in its presumed opposite, which is insight, or enlightenment—which, if it did see, would undermine its own standing. Hegel is more interested in these forms of consciousness than in what they posit, which go by an assortment of religiously and philosophically familiar names for the divine: God (12), the Holy of Holies (89), the Unconditioned Universal (79). But God "by itself is a meaningless sound" (12), "the vacuous Être supreme" (358). The Holy of Holies is a mere picture taken from the biblical image of the tabernacle; and the Unconditioned Universal is a Kantian abstraction devoid of content. Hegel would not be so dismissive of these names if they did not presume to name something beyond consciousness' own self. The best name for whatever these terms refer to would be one that could also double for consciousness itself. And Hegel's candidate for that office is: Spirit.

The *Phenomenology of Spirit* is an observational recounting of the logical activity by which an abstracted consciousness comes to know itself. Over the course of its progress in self-knowing, consciousness assumes many shapes. A shape is a configuration of subject and object within consciousness.[4] At the start of its pilgrimage, consciousness does not even realize that what it regards is itself. Towards the end, it not only understands that, but that the object of its knowing is itself self-consciously aware of returning the gaze, that is, is itself a subject that objectifies what otherwise takes itself for subject. "Spirit [is] realized in the plurality of existent consciousnesses" (267). Spirit is the name for this relationship within consciousness between two or more self-consciously aware subjects, each of which takes the other for an object whose subjectivity it knows to be identical with its own.[5] More precisely, Spirit names the process of mutual recognition between these locations of subjectivity within consciousness. Mutuality of recognition within consciousness is what spares it the infinite regress of self-referencing that would be its fate if its object were not its own consciousness. For then the consciousness-knowing-itself would have to become consciousness-knowing-itself-knowing-itself, and so on, in perpetual and ever frustrated pursuit of itself. The reciprocity of its knowing within itself allows its expansion of knowing to occur there too, and not forever beyond itself—an answer, also, to the ever out self-distancing of romantic potentization.

Insofar as Hegel's system is monistic, spirituality falls naturally within the realm of epistemology. Monism effaces holiness unless the separation that partially defines the sacred is secured by our ignorance of it, which philosophy comes to correct. What makes a project for Hegel is human complacency in the mire of that ignorance. The knowing stance will be an "unwonted posture" (15) for Hegel's readers, which constitutes an apology for the difficulty of the work. As though to wean us from our accustomed misconceptions, Hegel postpones until the end of the book the most sustained section on the two terms that, paired, supply us with our most familiar worldly coordinates: history and nature. Only there do we learn that, whatever we may have incorrectly thought of these before, nature is "externalized spirit" (492) and history "spirit emptied out into time" (492). So long a postponement of the most broadly orienting coordinates may provoke the reader at the end of the book to return to the beginning, to reread from there in light of the end, in imitation of observed consciousness itself, which ever repeats its own process.[6] *The Phenomenology of Spirit* can be read as therapy for ignorance, or better, deception, both consciousness' and our own—as "a play of individualities . . . in which each and all find themselves both deceiving and deceived" (250). Deception is error exposed, or shows itself to have been deception only retrospectively, through having been exposed. And that is much how the logic of the *Phenomenology* proceeds. Consciousness wakens at one moment to the realization that it was deceived in the previous one, which now positions it anew for further deception, which will likewise come undone. Hegel cues the reader many times over to the driving force of deception, part of the "tremendous power of the negative" (19). Deception is one of the motivators of all idealisms, which only turn to ideas for their promise of truthfulness after the senses have disappointed in that regard (as the *Phenomenology* itself tries to show). But every objective shape of consciousness comes in response to a falseness exposed in a previous one. Here is the repeating formula: z comes in response to a prior contradiction between x and y, where x, y, and z might be, respectively: the singularity of a thing, the plurality of its properties, and the dynamic of force; or, present moral goodness, projected human happiness, and self-realization in art; or, God the Father, God the Son, and Spirit. For a moment, consciousness thinks it has in the object of a qualified thing a resolution of tension it previously encountered between a plurality of disparate sensations and the singularity of its sensing self, only to uncover in the thing of many properties a tension between the unsensed substratum of the thing and its sensed qualities, which in turn resolves into the oscillation between poles of self-contained unity and manifested expression, or, force. The notion of expression, which consciousness first recognizes when force becomes its object is key for supplying the means within monism for reconciling itself with plurality, and also, consequently, for envaluing the particular. Hegel's system is an expanding sequence of analogies, in which universality is to particularity, as singularity is to plurality, as thinghood to qualities, as mind to body, as intention to action, as consciousness to a community of consciousnesses, as essence to expression.

The logic of self-reference and the drive towards expression reinforce each other. There would be too little play within the bounds of self-reference for movement of any kind—the quarters would be too close—if expression did not open up some space there. As it is, the space hosts a vast diversity of things. Hegel characterizes the analogous shapes that consciousness assumes for itself as a "gallery of images" (492).[7] The language is playful, but misleading. Though the *Phenomenology* has been compared to a novel,[8] and to a Bildungsroman for consciousness,[9] the very notion of an image and its agent of production, the imagination, are far from his organon of truth. And though he might appreciate the romantic gesture of potentization, which resembles in some ways dialectical self-reference,[10] he would reject any important role for the imagination either in epistemology or in philosophical spirituality. The term for the means by which the objects of consciousness assume their different shapes is not imagination but logic, with all its "cold" (5) connotations of necessary implication and determination. The logic is the famous Hegelian dialectic of "transition of one opposite into its opposite" (26), by which an implied proposition "starts afresh on its own account ... the first [which implied it] having moved itself on to the next ... a necessary connection arising through the nature of the thing itself" (26). Such self-initiated movement marks a proposition as "speculative" rather than logically static. A language so self-determinedly alive is another affinity with Novalis, though Hegel is less interested in the artistry of language and the poet who channels it, than the self-determinations of language and the philosopher who observes them. The logic plays out on its own, without any importation of "our own bright ideas" (54). Our part is simply to watch. But it is just in virtue of having a part that "we" are implicated in Hegel's project and an understanding of spirituality, in the sense of human proximity to the sacred, becomes feasible.

Hegel is the master analyst of ambiguity, of commonly received concepts that on his inspection are actually polar dyads, each pole of which presupposes the other in a challenge to logic that is ultimately self-undermining and dissolving. "Each contains within it these two opposed self-contradictory moments of individuality and universality" (259). These ambiguities play a propulsive role in Hegel's system insofar as their dissolution stimulates progress towards final univocity. But the memory of them remains in the antecedent logic still visible beneath the final resolution. Hegel's analysis of inherently ambiguous concepts, especially ethical ones, may stand even outside his system. In that case the concepts do not so much dissolve under scrutiny as clarify for what they really are: pulsations between poles. An analysis of ambiguity does not so much eliminate the concept it inhabits as unveil its mechanism of survival, its Hegelian "spirit". Ambiguity both lives and wants to be lived with. This analysis of latent ambiguity is an unexpectedly satisfying answer to any number of anxieties over concepts that resist unproblematic dictionary definition, such as potential, purpose, achievement, altruism; a potential that precedes the realization on which it nonetheless depends; a purpose prior to the end that conditions it; an achievement that both presupposes and underwrites a culminating progress; an other-regard that feeds on its own self-disregard. To the extent that the *Phenomenology* itself conforms to this logic it is almost impossible to read. Where the end conditions the beginning, we must simply plunge in darkly and hope for illumination as we go. But then, since *going* is the mark of spirit, the quandary Hegel sets us is at the same time his enrollment of us in the inspirited quest of spirit, his entanglement[11] of us.

Just as consciousness is ambiguously subject and object within Hegel's system, so are we. On the one hand, we are products of positing consciousness, a many opposed to the one of consciousness, in analogy with the diverse properties of a single thing, or the many acts that realize a universal moral law. The division of consciousness is already a multiplication of it. But it is just at the onset of reason that consciousness "bursts asunder into many completely independent beings" (212). Insofar as reason at this juncture is roughly equivalent to the Kantian understanding (*Verstand*), it identifies a category, or universal, with the idea of its multiple instances. And so, applied to itself, consciousness as category becomes multiple consciousnesses, two poles of yet another configuration of the many in identity with the one. Such a multiplicity of consciousnesses conditions the appearance of "customs and laws" (213), which constitute the nation, to which any of us might belong. But on the other hand, as observers with Hegel of consciousness' movement, which he retrospectively reconstructs for us, we are subjects, not objects, of consciousness. We appear in this capacity early on, as the "single individual" (16) to be led "from his uneducated standpoint to knowledge" (16). But no sooner are we cast in this distanced manner of the third person singular, squirming under what feels like Hegel's condescension, than we are partnered, several paragraph's later, with Hegel in the privileged "we": "We take up the movement of the whole from the point when the sublation of existence as such is no longer necessary" (17), that is, from the point when consciousness has attained full self-knowledge, having exhausted all the permutations of positing and reflecting.

Self-consciousness always labors under the burden of catching up with consciousness. For consciousness always has more on its plate than self-consciousness has discerned. Indeed, the very process of discernment postpones itself, since consciousness changes in the very act of seeking to know itself. What it was at the end of any act of self-knowing is always different from what it was at the start, so that what it has in fact found of itself is different from what it sought. ("We learn from experience that we meant something other than we meant to mean" (39).) This accounts for the perduring tension in the *Phenomenology* between the criterion of knowing and what is claimed to be known or, more simply and evocatively put, between essence and existence. In that gap lies all the suffering of self-division within consciousness. What concludes the *Phenomenology* is the point where "substance shows itself to be essentially subject" and "spirit has made its existence identical with its essence" (21). There we begin, when consciousness simultaneously discerns both itself and its act of discerning, whole, without any residue of outstanding unknown. We begin but do not end there. For, from that standpoint, knowledge is no mere intuition but a hard-won conclusion of a very long logical process that consciousness has undergone over time, indeed, over history as such, and we cannot claim to be at the endpoint, much less begin there, without ourselves discerning the process that culminated there. Otherwise put, insofar as a fully knowing self-consciousness is the conclusion of an argument, we must understand the argument before we can claim to know the conclusion. The argument is what the *Phenomenology* supplies. So we begin where consciousness "once" did, with sense-perception, where "once" indicates a priority either logical or temporal: a much recessed conceptual presupposition or a past hovering somewhere at the beginning of consciousness as such; in either case, something nearly forgotten that requires a philosophical jolt of effort to recover, that is, an exercise of spirit.

The project of rehearsing the logical course of consciousness from sense-perception to self-knowing substance is no mere academic exercise. "We must step into its [consciousness'] place" (80). In so doing, we partially sacrifice our observer role, as subject, and *become* the object of our observation. Hegel quite rightly likens what consciousness undergoes to a pilgrimage between "stations" (49). Identified with consciousness, we too become pilgrims. And, as on any pilgrimage, the stations on the way, however much traversed before, raise in us as we linger at each an anxiety of incompletion. Each station holds us, the reader-pilgrim, with a conviction of its own finality—it must do so to be fully experienced, as though we were consciousness there for the first time. And so, having stepped into consciousness, all the delusions, sunderings, sufferings, and indeed deaths that it underwent, we do too, or at least a vivified semblance of them.

These sufferings are endemic to the knowing process, and array themselves over at least three stages of it: positing, contradiction, and collapse. For positing belies itself in the negation it actually accomplishes: the self-sundered projection of consciousness outside itself. This is "a violence it [consciousness] is expected to do to itself" (15), though one of which, prior to reason, it is unaware. Reasoning consciousness, having come to understand that its objects are really self-projections suffers newly from a sense of self-division. Kant explored this in his own way through the distinction between natural and moral behavior. Hegel contextualizes that by way of a more fundamental split between nature and culture, where consciousness opines that it "has its being in something outside of and alien to it" (295). The components of a contradiction can at least provide a worldview, as they did for Kant. But spirited consciousness cannot rest in contradictions, as Kant's successors could not in his. They collapse into their own instability. For example, the categorical imperative, in conflict with nature, nonetheless draws on nature for a motive, to anticipate the final harmony of itself with nature when desire and law coincide. But insofar as morality only shows in distinction from nature it must then cease. The very fulfillment of itself is its annihilation. Morality "involves the contradiction of a task which is to remain a task and yet ought to be fulfilled" (369). With that realization, Kantian morality loses its claim on consciousness, which can no longer believe in it, and dies before the end it implicitly projected for itself. Consciousness as Kantian object has died, and the grief of that remains even as subjective consciousness begins to fashion from the ruins a new object for itself, in art. For Hegel, these are the terms that capture the emotional register of these varied sufferings: despair (49), fear (119) bewilderment (125), agony (131), torture (328). At points along its way, "consciousness . . . can only find as a present reality the grave of its life" (132).

The *Phenomenology* enacts these sufferings on its readers, or tries to. We are already implicated in the suffering of self-division, by finding ourselves assigned dual roles within the book, as both objects and subjects of consciousness. Here again, Hegel divides where in an analogous situation Novalis multiplied—the mystery book that Heinrich reads in the cave does indeed double himself as object of his own perusing subjectivity, but the effect of that on Heinrich, and by extension the reader, is magical. By contrast, within the *Phenomenology* we are indeed bewildered and possibly anxious. Hegel admits as much when he confides that his work is part of the "birth-time . . . to a new era," which leaves those of us yet unacclimated to it beset by "vague foreboding of something unknown" (7). We who linger with earlier manifestations of consciousness see "dissolving bit by bit the structure of its previous world, whose tottering state is only hinted at by isolated symptoms" (6). But Hegel encourages us to submit, with him, to the "suffering, the patience, and the labor of the negative" (10), that is, of the knowing process itself, from beginning to end, confident that we are ready for the transition into "absolute knowing."[12]

If the *Phenomenology* is a drama, then it is more comedy than tragedy. Hegel signals this when he locates comedy further along the road to self-knowing than tragedy. After all, the comic actor may remove his mask and address the audience out-of-character in-character, a playful "sublation" of theatrical deception that is not typical of tragedy. But we need not wait till the end of the book for the mask to fall. For Hegel periodically restores us to our station outside the consciousness we observe, and which is rightly ours by the projection outside of it we are. We are part of the many in identity with the unity of consciousness itself, a doubling of its own self-consciousness. From this station we are protected from the suffering consciousness undergoes by the privileged awareness we enjoy of just what it is doing. In Hegel's retrospective reconstruction of its path, we see before consciousness does the healings and resolutions of its self-divisions, contradictions, and collapses. Hegel reminds us that, as observers of consciousness, we are always one step ahead of its movements. Many times along the way we are told something to the effect that "it is only for us that this truth exists, not yet for consciousness" (102). Thus, already at the very first stage of the journey, at the station of sense certainty, "we" see before sense certainty does that neither vantage point available to it for understanding what it claims to know, its sensation or its subjectivity, is any more essential than the other. That is, we see before it does its inevitable demise as a reigning shape of consciousness. Nor, as observers of consciousness, rather than observed objects of it, do we grieve over this, though at more evolved stations on the way we may mourn the passing of our objects, if only from identifying with them more keenly, for example, family relationships which, in tension with the state, hold a place in the unfolding sequence of analogies: family is to state, as divine law to human law, as woman to man. The dependence of a child for its existence on its parents, who in turn find their essence in their child, when both this existence and this essence must in their lifetimes cease (274), may sadden us, whether regarded from within or outside the parent-child relation, though we have the enduringly balanced model of the brother-sister relation, which Hegel deems a triumph of purity in the protean mix of family life, to comfort us. But then, even as observers of advances already accomplished, we sometimes exhort consciousness on, like fans of a cult film moving the action along by anticipating aloud well-known lines. There are some points of particular challenge to consciousness along its way, critical to later developments, for example, the concept of change. Consciousness is already unselfconsciously observing change as it contemplates force. The contradiction within force is between the unobserved in-itself of force and its outward expression. As consciousness wakens to the identity of these two, it realizes that self-identity and difference can inhabit a single thing, or that change occurs. This demands of the "thoughtless thinker" (96) a coincidence of opposites that stresses him. But who is this thoughtless thinker? Presumably, not the reader, who has been incorporated into the highly acute Hegelian "we"; and surely not the uninterested bystander to the Hegelian project, who will not have opened the book. A likely candidate for this uncomplimentary descriptive is consciousness itself at just this point along its way, when it struggles to conceive "pure change" (95). It is we thoughtful thinkers who cheer consciousness on to a realization it has already had, though not within our observational presence. The *Phenomenology* itself, qua philosophical achievement, results more from our successful efforts than consciousness' own, for what it experiences "must be set forth" (40); and this is "something contributed by *us*, by means of which the succession of experiences through which consciousness passes is raised into a scientific progression—but it is not known to the consciousness that we are observing" (55–56). The science of the *Phenomenology* is the finished knowledge of it, the display of all the stations that preceded the final one of absolute knowing, which was all along implied and determined. It is not observed but observing consciousness, in the form of Hegel and his readers, that accomplishes this. The devout Hegelian may well experience the end of the book as a climactic and mystical merging of three distinct consciousnesses: the book's, Hegel's, and her own—or better, as a lifting of the veil that ever suggested there were really three in the first place.[13]

From the standpoint of spirituality, Hegel's animated monism is not clearly an advance over Spinoza's or even Stoicism's more static ones. Monistic spirituality is relatively uniform. Our charge is to realize our identity with the One, whether that is understood ontologically as substance or epistemologically as consciousness. The holiness of the One is assured by its epistemological distance from us and by its necessity to both our being and well-being. What is new in Hegel is the manner of argument for monism, which proceeds within the Kantian context of an active, determining consciousness which exhausts all of knowing and being. We readers of Hegel come to see ourselves as both posited and reflected by consciousness. Insofar as we are posited, we are independent existents. Insofar as we are reflected, we are reincorporated back into the One, where monistic spirituality would have us be. The process turns on those two intimately intertwined pillars of Hegelian logic, self-reference and expression. Expression underwrites individuality, existence, reality; and self-reference instates those within the confines of the One. Hegel has given us a way of explicating one of the great desiderata of mysticism, a union with the sacred that preserves enough of individuality for the individual to enjoy it.

The unfettered explosions of analogy within the *Phenomenology*, by which progressively enriched content fills a repeating form,[14] transgress all boundaries of distinction between the natural and human sciences. The transgressive analogies testify both to how epistemologically totalizing the work aspires to be and to how much it remains, for the twenty-first century, an anachronism, more so even than the older but more modestly proceeding *Ethics* of Spinoza, or still more recoverable Stoicism of the ancients. But the Hegelian project is rich with spiritually suggestive themes and currents, more or less detachable from the totalizing monism. Amid all the dynamic spiritedness of the *Phenomenology*, Hegel provides for pockets of reposeful spirituality. Once freed of the imperious telos of the binding logic, readers can take up in earnest the invitation implicit in Hegel's claim that "each moment has to be lingered over" (17), to contemplate select themes or passages for spiritual resonance. Surprisingly, one of these Hegel shares with Novalis, the inspiritedness of language. That language follows or is able to follow a self-determined movement is already implied by the speculative proposition, whose subject refuses to hold its place in front of the verb, but collapses into the predicate, which in consequence becomes itself subject. But then Hegel is explicit on the spirituality of language. "Language [functions] as the existence of spirit" (395). The attribution of existence to language allies it with expression, concretion, and reality in their respective and analogous contrasts with essence, abstraction and ideality. But as the existence *of spirit*, language realizes a mediating role between what is already a duo of differentiable poles. If spirit is the mediation between essence and expression, abstraction and concretion, ideality and reality, then language is this too, but in a manner *more* expressed, concretized and real than spirit is, which, with regard to language, is *more* essential, abstract, and ideal. When a relation expresses itself, the expressans embodies relation within itself and, ipso facto, the duo related across the expressed relation. What was differentiable on either side of spirit, which mediated between them, e.g., essence and existence, are coincidental in language, which expresses spirit. And so language acquires a feature traditionally associated with the divine, of essential existence or existing essence, as Hegel does indeed assert for us in the Preface, that language "has the *divine nature* of directly reversing the meaning of what is said" (66) [emphasis ours]. And though it is the inversions of language that here justify its divinity, rather than its inherence of coincidence, the two are not unrelated. Like a switch on a train track that allows a single stretch of track to bear (successively) both north- and southward trains approaching it at once, language, by combining opposites, allows for each of the poles within the opposition it embodies to become the other.

As in the book of Genesis, so in the *Phenomenology*, language is on the scene before it has ever been explained. Consciousness as sense certainty is already using it to try to reach its objects before it or we know whence it came. But unlike Genesis, Hegel does supply a point of origin for it, within the midst of spirit: "Language . . . only emerges as the middle term, mediating between independent and acknowledged self-consciousness" (396); that is, language appears when consciousness, having become one and many, recognizes self-awareness in its own objects. And so the language we find in sense-certainty, of "I" and "this," is really a kind of protolanguage that "we" generously and retrospectively supply to sense-certainty as sympathetic observers of its halting progress. But then, if language is simply signs, and signs as such express "that they mean something else than what they simply are at first sight" (201), then perhaps consciousness has been speaking from the start, with the primordial realization that whatever it took for "this" is really de facto everything. In that case, language pervades the *Phenomenology* not simply as the instrument of its being, but as an implicit and potential object of attention throughout, which Hegel does indeed periodically realize. We already encountered that prefatory instance, in relation to the speculative proposition, which denotes language in motion as it follows the dialectical play of consciousness. But there are others. The Kantian language of the categorical imperative provides a means of realizing that otherwise empty abstraction. Like the Muslim *shahadah*, an instance of the categorical imperative must be proclaimed to be effective, for "the declaration of this assurance [that an act instances a universalizable rule] rids the form [the act itself] of its particularity" (397). This proclamation also doubles as a confession that forgives consciousness "the blemish of determinateness" (392) which Kantian ethics must commit if is to have any reality at all. Or again, having advanced beyond morality to art, consciousness discovers in the self-conscious self-reference of artistic language an advance over the merely referential language of natural observation, or the performative language of Kantian ethics. Artistic language knowingly imitates spirit by giving "utterance to the inner essence" (444) of the speaker, rather than, in expressing "the external aspect of . . . resolves and enterprises, as happens in the language accompanying ordinary actions" (444). The resulting art object, e.g., a poem, is already an incipiently self-conscious externalization of its maker. Artistic language is an advance over ordinary language in subduing the beyond. Religious and philosophical language simply realize the potential self-consciousness of the art object, first into the Christ figure, the perfect picture of absolute self-knowing, and then into the *Phenomenology*, whose sheer conceptuality is more clearly wedded to the consciousness that bears it and the logic it realizes than any mere picture, however perfect, could be. The language of the Hegelian philosopher enacts what it speaks through the proof of what it says embedded in its claim. Philosophy so understood is no longer merely the love of wisdom, i.e., the desire for it, but the possession of it, what Hegel prefers to call Science.[15]

Hegel scholars debate whether language in the form, say, of the speculative proposition, simply follows the dialectical turns of consciousness or actually constitutes them. Given how sporadic Hegel's explicit attentions to language are in the *Phenomenology*, either interpretation might serve. Perhaps language is best identified with the Hegelian Notion, understood as the organization of knowledge within consciousness at any given point on its way. From the standpoint of spirituality, the indeterminateness of language may be a blessing. For the problem of spirituality in Hegel is the problem of distance, to the degree that there is not enough of it to sustain a sense of the sacred. And indeterminacy does impose a distance between our understanding and what it can determine. The elusiveness of language's status, both ontological and epistemological, opens a space for the sacred in Hegel that he never quite closes. As the existence of Spirit, rather than its essence, language is distinct enough from Spirit to warn us away from that term as the chief bearer of Hegelian spirituality, as may well accord with reader suspicions of its so heavily epistemic charge. Language is originary, pervasive and healing, to the extent that opposites in conflict coincide there, which Hegel implies can happen to different degrees. At the highest degree, what a proposition claims contains the proof of it within itself, embedded there; its content descends from a formal chain of reasoning recoverable from beneath its surface. Otherwise put, its form implies its content. Speakers of such a language—Hegelian philosophers—inhabit a space traditionally reserved for God, where essence and existence coincide. Or they do to the extent that circumstances allow them to speak this language.

For those of us who fall short of speaking the language of Hegelian philosophy at its highest, there are lesser languages within the system available to us to speak, for instance, the simple language of "I." This short word, constrained to the space of a single letter, overflows itself with philosophical import. And Hegel captures the simultaneous simplicity and complexity of the word in two sections he devotes to it, within the respective contexts of sense certainty and culture. The "I" of sense certainty has barely appeared before it has vanished in its failure to mean itself—for, like the "this" it inwardly opposes, it lends itself indiscriminately to any one of many, the precise opposite of its intent. The "I" of culture by contrast has learned to incorporate the many into its intent. Culture differs from nature by presupposing not simply a multiplicity of consciousnesses but of self-consciousnesses, each able to return the other's attention to it. This ever-present potency for reciprocal acknowledgment lays the ground for an understanding of the "I" for which a plurality of others is not merely no longer self-underminingly indiscriminate, but actually essential.

> The "I" that utters itself is *heard* or *perceived*. . . . That it is *perceived* or *heard* means that its *real existence dies away*; this its otherness has been taken back into itself; and its real existence is just this: that as a self-conscious Now, as a real existence, it is *not* a real existence, and through this vanishing it *is* a real existence. This vanishing is thus itself at once its abiding. (309)

Language is the medium of self-determination. The self determines itself by being heard. Its definitive action is thus a receipt, or kind of passivity. The "I" spoken within a plurality of self-consciousnesses mediates the speaker into an object of knowledge for others and itself—first for others and, only in virtue of that, for itself. The plurality that is ever dogging the steps of consciousness on its way to its monistic whole of self-knowledge is the simple reality of things, which consciousness already encounters head on in sense certainty. But in the case of "I," plurality converts from undermining the self to constituting it anew as a location of others' acknowledgments of it. This embrace of others into the very meaning of "I" raises it out of its occluded and doomed singularity into a permanent universality. This is what the reversals of the real connote in Hegel's passage quoted above. The self exchanges one understanding of itself, in terms of other-exclusion, for another, in terms of other-embrace. As Hegel puts it more biblically, the self endures in its own vanishing. "The true sacrifice of being-for-itself is solely that in which it surrenders itself as completely as in death, yet in this renunciation no less preserves itself" (308). Could Hegel have come closer to Matt 16:25 ("whoever loses his life ... will find it")?

It is just because the "I" is double that it can simultaneously vanish and endure. Ambiguity supplies the context for the multiple vanishings that haunt the *Phenomenology*. These ambiguities and vanishings are simply turns on the larger themes of self-reference and expression. But they are also openings onto another Hegelian spirituality that stages self-fulfillment over a sequence of self-destructions. That view of ourselves may come as a balm to a twenty-first century consciousness plagued by the imperative to fulfill itself. On the Hegelian view, we are not potentials awaiting fulfillment, a view of ourselves that surfaces and falls with all the others along the dialectical way,[16] but endpoints of a polar opposition awaiting a reversal that comes suddenly, unpremeditatedly. Consciousness is always losing itself in what it reaches for. "The truth vanishes in the expression of it" (104). The beautiful soul that preserves itself within abstraction loses its reality there, until the wicked soul, in partnership with it, by confessing its particularity, obtains recognition and forgiveness from the particularity-disdaining beautiful one. The abstract and beautiful soul thereby attains reality, and the particular and wicked one universality. Both dissolve in the process. All along, they have been twin self-expressions of a single consciousness—an ambiguity—just as were master and slave. It is a logic transcendent to each self-expression that moves them both into the forgiveness the one, to its surprise, seeks, and the other, to its surprise, supplies. But this element of surprise carries a requirement of spirituality, that the sacred shape us, and not we it. The monotheisms exploit it too, in stories of the unexpected, as when David hears from Nathan a parable in which he suddenly recognizes his own wickedness (2 Sam 12:1–23) or when Jesus' disciples wake belatedly to his presence among them at Emmaus (Luke 24:13–35). In those cases, the surprise rests on an unexpected intrusion of the transcendent divine. But in the case of Hegelian consciousness, the conditions of surprise conform to a worldly logic of deception, ambiguity, and vanishing implicit in the process of monistic self-knowing. We experience this surprise only as we identify with consciousness at any point along its way, rather than merely observing it from the standpoint of the privileged "we". We experience it just where Hegel would not place us to savor the climactic union of his, his object's, and his reader's consciousness—stranded at any point *before* the end of the book, forgetful of the privileged "we" we might at any point resume. But many of us may see more of spirituality as we commonly understand it in incomplete spirit than in its absolute perfection. Absolute spirit, in echo of the old Aristotelian ideal, has eliminated all illusions of otherness, all "being burdened with something alien, with what is only for it, and some sort of 'other'" (57). Whereas evolving spirit, still entangled with what appears to exist apart from it and "for" it (rather than "in" it), as "being-for-self . . . is a fragmented being, self-sacrificing and benevolent" (264). Without the ending of the book, this spirit becomes the only one, and its fragmentations, sacrifices, and benevolences, the only reality. If the ending of the book vanishes, then the resolved ambiguities that preceded it remain unresolved and perduring: "the self-repulsion of the self-same" (102), the "dizziness of a perpetually self-engendered disorder" (125), and an "actual world . . . capable of having [a] two-fold meaning" (184). At the same time, a new space for the sacred opens up in these reinstated distances within the self, between selves, and between the self and spirit.

But the book might never have come to its proper end in any case if consciousness had just once woken to its propensity to self-deceive, if, having emerged from any one of its many self-deceptions it had inferred that it would generate yet more, and, in despair, renounced the whole dialectical process. Perhaps it is the greatest surprise of Hegel's book that this never happens. But then, if it had, according to Hegel's own lights, the book could never have been written. As it is, with this train of thought, we risk losing the spirituality of the book to its potential for tragedy, just as before, we risked losing it to an excess of comedy and too simulated a suffering. The privileged "we" would recede before a plurality of distinct subjects whose identity with a polar unity would come under doubt; each would have a separate understanding of its own well-being that likely conflicted with the others'. Suffering would be real and no longer simulation. If from self-suspicion of its own wiliness, consciousness lost its spirit, it and we would have fallen into despair, and we would have had, instead of a phenomenology of spirit, just its opposite, a phenomenology of despair. We would no longer have Hegel, but Kierkegaard.

NOTES

1. Georg Hegel, *Phenomenology of Spirit*, trans. by A. V. Miller (New York: Oxford, 1977), 356. Succeeding references are given parenthetically in the text.
2. Abyssal here has less existential overtones than merely epistemological ones. The abyss is the place of irresponsible claims to unity and wholeness (such as Romantics might make) without any show of the hard logical work it took to get there. With implicit reference to Schelling, Hegel calls it the place where "all cows are black" (9). He cites the abyss again in this sense towards the end of the book, p. 490.
3. Hegel's own words were ". . .erbauen, aber nichts aufbauen." *Phänomenologie des Geistes*, 6th ed. (Hamburg: Verlag Felix Meiner, 1952), 280.
4. See Terry Pinkard, "What is a 'Shape of Spirit'?" in *Hegel's Phenomenology of Spirit: A Critical Guide* (New York: Cambridge University Press, 2008), 112–129.
5. "A self-consciousness, in being an object, is just as much an 'I' as object. With this we already have before us the Notion of Spirit" (110). Spirit is "the absolute

Hegel: The Phenomenology of Spirit   143

Substance which is the unity of the different independent self-consciousnesses which, in their opposition, enjoy perfect freedom and independence" (110).

6. The process of reading Hegel recapitulates the process he describes of processive returns.

7. The language provocatively anticipates Kierkegaard's gallery of pseudonyms.

8. For example, Proust's *Remembrance of Things Past*.

9. Peter Hodgson, introduction to G. W. F. *Hegel: Theologian of the Spirit* (Minneapolis, MN: Fortress, 1997), 7.

10. Hegel also potentizes, for example, "Vanity which knows itself to be such [i.e., vanity which takes itself for vanity] is the double reflection of the real world into itself" (320) [i.e., enacts reality]. Or again, unlikeness unlikened is similarity (97). A "vanishing of vanishing" (245) instates.

11. I borrow this word from the work of Catherine Keller, where it has scientific connotations that would certainly please Hegel. See Keller, "The Entangled Cosmos: An Experiment in Physical Theopoetics," *Journal of Cosmology* 20 (Sept. 2012): 8648–8666.

12. The title of the last chapter.

13. Here is where a monism shows: "Consciousness will arrive at a point at which it gets rid of its semblance of being burdened with something alien, with what is only for it, and some sort of 'other'" (57).

14. It is the logical progression of the enrichments that distinguishes Hegel's idealist monism from, say, Schelling's.

15. Hegel hopes for philosophy to be able to "lay aside the title '*love* of knowing' and be *actual* knowing" (3).

16. See Hegel's comments on "gifts, capacities, powers" (231).

TEN
Kierkegaard

A fragmented Hegelian system opens up any number of new spaces of separation for the holy. If thought no longer generates reality, separations surface wherever it meets its limits, and reopen the possibility of a sacred that lies at the end of a distance no longer merely epistemological, as in the monisms, but also ontological. Thought meets many limits in Kierkegaard; perhaps most famously, "faith begins precisely where thinking leaves off."[1] But thought does not merely leave off at things beyond its ken; it does not even begin before presuppositions that precede it. It is sandwiched between beginnings and endings that transcend it. The beginnings prove in some ways more preoccupying for Kierkegaard than the endings. But that is only natural for any reversal of Hegel, as Kierkegaard is. Presuppositionless Hegelian form generates content; it begins with nothing and ends with everything. Hegelian dialectic reproduces that movement from beginning to end. A simplified précis of Kierkegaard's critique of Hegel is that form does not generate content. Content is present before we even begin to think. This reframes what constitutes understanding in the first place. For Hegel, to understand something is to be able to generate it. For Kierkegaard, to understand something is to uncover its already operative presuppositions. Hegelian understanding prospects for a goal that lures it; Kierkegaardian understanding retrospects for the precedents it stands *on* (rather than *under*). Kierkegaard hints as much, in *Fear and Trembling*, by supplying so much preliminary matter: a preface, a prelude, and a preamble.[2] A reader might wonder where between the preamble and the epilogue the thesis of the book appears, unless the point is less to advance a thesis than to uncover the presuppositions of one (such as: "how momentous a paradox faith is" [FT 82]). The title-paged author of *Fear and Trembling*, Johannes de Silentio, participates with the other pseudonyms in situating Kierkegaard himself as a presupposition, *their* presupposition. Like a dummy come to life, the first pseudonym, Victor Eremita—himself the editor of an editor of another's work[3] —speaks for his master's authorial antics, by which "one author becomes enclosed within the other, like boxes in a Chinese puzzle."[4] Of course, for his readers to understand that he is indeed the presupposition of the pseudonyms, Kierkegaard must identify himself as such, and he does, famously, at the end of *Concluding Unscientific Postscript*. By that act of self-identification, Kierkegaard models for his readers the movement of understanding, which is to uncover, not generate, to probe origins, not ends.

Kierkegaard has his own understanding of his work: "my whole authorship pertains to Christianity, to the issue: becoming a Christian."[5] If Kierkegaard entertains a prospect, it is that. The pseudonyms serve that goal; they are highly engaging but largely unreligious aestheticians who, by the identification they invite from their (Christian) readers, mirror for them how little Christian they really are, the first step towards genuine conversion. From Victor Eremita to the last of them, Anti-Climacus, they advance ever more closely towards and even into Christianity.[6] If Kierkegaard implicitly assigns greater ripeness to the later ones then insofar as we seek a philosophical spirituality from him we must linger with the earlier ones, unripe as they may be, but thereby all the more contiguous with our fabrication of a disintegrative and over-ripe Hegel, who set the stage for them. We will confine ourselves to three, Victor Eremita's aesthetician, whom he names "A," and Judge William, both from *Either/Or*, and Johannes de Silentio, from *Fear and Trembling*.

In that order, the three of them suggest, respectively, another way of reading the whole of Kierkegaard's work, along the lines of his now famous distinction between the three life-stages: the aesthetic, the ethical and the religious. The spaces between them provide another context for thought to founder, for no bridge of mere ideas leads from one to the next. Nor are we ever in a space outside some one of them, from which we might dispassionately compare them. Before we have even begun to think, how and what we think is (passionately) slanted aesthetically, ethically, or religiously. This is another point to the pseudonyms, to show how much personal location precedes thought. Though an abyss to thought separates each life-stage from the next, they can and do cohabit. Judge William, the most serene but also most self-satisfied of our three pseudonyms, suggests this can happen harmoniously: when the aesthetic is "religiously developed" it "is caught up in a higher concentricity" (EO II:47) of the ethical. But then, as Judge William's understanding of the religious unfolds this proves to be tautological. For the religious here is simply the ethical understood, along Kantian lines, as divinely commanded. And a major point for Johannes de Silentio is that the religious, or at least the faithful, cannot be understood that way. Such conflict between the pseudonyms is instructive not simply for reminding us of incommensurability—a favorite Kierkegaardian theme—between the life-stages, but for suggesting that cohabitation among them is not necessarily peaceful, nor the person in whom they cohabit whole.[7]

John Lippitt warns us against the appearance of reliability the pseudonyms make.[8] Their views of the life-stages they consider and/or inhabit are not necessarily Kierkegaard's. But then we are not committed to Kierkegaard's own views of the life-stages either. Indeed, the interpretive lens of philosophical spirituality cuts against the grain of Kierkegaard's understanding of his own program. The open disdain of the pseudonyms for philosophy already suggests as much. Judge William: "I have never passed myself off as a philosopher" (EO II:170); de Silentio: "The present author is no philosopher" (FT 43). We find from "A" no explicit disowning of philosophy, indeed he claims to have one (EO I:40), a disparity among the pseudonyms that may communicate one of Kierkegaard's own beliefs, that there is a natural affinity between aesthetics and philosophy (not a surprising assumption for one reared in *German* philosophy). Certainly Judge William thinks so. "What unites you" with the philosopher, he says to "A," "is that life comes to a halt" (EO II:171). Judge William means that both the reflective aesthete (which "A" is) and the philosopher extract themselves from any forward movement. According to Judge William, this virtually defines the difference between the aesthete, who merely "is what he is," in contrast with the ethicist who, as Kant might have said, too, "becomes what he becomes" (EO II:178); while the (Hegelian) philosopher deems history to have ended in philosophy, an attitude that is as effective as aesthetics in halting any forward movement for himself.

Perhaps the larger problem for both the aesthete and the philosopher is that neither takes account of the location from which they reflect. But reflection is in any case a problem inherited from Hegel; it was the second half of the act of knowing, by which consciousness restored to itself what, in the first half, by positing, it had objectified. Positing and reflecting constitute the dialectic by which consciousness advances. It is not just this pretense of forward movement to thought that Kierkegaard rejects. It is also the license the dialectic grants itself to grasp—*greifen*—what it subjects to knowing. Hegelian knowledge changes its objects in the act of knowing them, a consequence of the mediation it practices between the known and the criterion of knowing, each of which changes to accommodate the other. This is less a problem when the license is simply self-directed; more of one when genuine spaces have intervened between knowing subject and known object. In an extended tribute to the tribulation most of us have suffered on subjecting to thought any long-standing object of love, especially if loved from youth, whether a work of art, an idea, or a person, "A" recalls for us how much "one fears for what one loves, that it will suffer in this change" that thought threatens (EO I:60–61). Part of the discomfort readers may feel with the Seducer whom

"A" edits owes to ease which he allows for reflection on love to sacrifice the engaging beauty of it to the distancing interest of it (EO I:334). And part of the superiority Judge William suggests marriage has over seduction is that it allows for interest to remain in love, "without having this happen by means of a reflection that altered [the beauty of] it" (EO II:57). Reflection obstructs Kierkegaardian understanding by changing rather than uncovering what it claims to register. Not all aesthetes reflect (Don Giovanni does not). But insofar as philosophers do, they are suspect.

Neither "A" nor Judge William need reflect to present the aesthetic and ethical life-stages they respectively represent. Because they live in those stages, they need merely show themselves, as they do via the sheer forms of their self-presentations: "A's" haphazard and far-ranging "diapsalmata," "ventures," and "silhouettes," and Judge William's paradigms of order, his "two long studies and a shorter one," written "on beehive paper with ruled columns such as legal documents and the like are written on" (EO I:7). Only Johannes de Silentio is bound to reflection by his distance from the life he writes about—the faithful life. Johannes is forever thinking, gazing, seeing, beholding, remembering—in short, reflecting. And, for all that he disparages reflection, next to passion—"what we lack today is not reflection but passion" (FT 71)—echoes of a Platonic attitude towards thought surface to fill the breach of what lived experience cannot supply. For by his reflecting, Johannes does experience something, be it mere admiration or, more consequentially, "paralysis" (FT 55), even "annihilation" (FT 62). In reversal of Hegelian reflection, this revived Platonic reflection affects the reflector, who is "blessed to behold the believer" (FT 51). If the hero beheld is changed, it is only by way of expanding in identity to embrace the reflector, who comes to feel "united with the hero" (FT 49), as the Platonic lover was with his ideas. But then, our question to Johannes must be: are these spiritual experiences and, if so, to what extent do his expressions of them move the reader to her own experience of them?

Let us break with Kierkegaard's own presentation of the life-stages, which imply that the spiritual occurs only in the last, religious, or perhaps even Christian stage, and forage for spirituality in these three early, aesthetic pseudonyms. We are looking for evidence of proximity to the sacred, which might be revived for the reader, in the recounted experiences and thoughts of these writers.

Judge William has already evoked for us a Kantian-style moral spirituality, with his sense for "the consciousness of eternity that morality has" (EO II:26). Though Judge William's focus on marriage as the paradigm of ethical life is already twice a break from Kant, who was both unmarried and unforthcoming with content for the moral law, God functions for both as a kind of guarantor: in Kant's case, of the moral law, in Judge William's, of romantic love. Hegelian reflection is once again the foil. Judge William wants a way for married couples to appreciate their love without reflecting on it, which would compromise it in ways that reflection always does. God's blessing upon the union—which is not detached enough from it to constitute reflection, but sufficiently removed from it not to compromise its intimacy—supplies a means by which the couple can vicariously, via God, appreciate their love without reflecting on it. As Judge William puts it, God "is an eyewitness who does not cramp one's style" (EO II:56).

With the use of what the judge himself calls that "frivolous expression" (EO II:56) for God's commitment to the couple, he communicates his awareness that God functions here as a mere means. William is not so unreligious to suggest that this constitutes a spiritual opening to the sacred. The sacred surfaces for William at the heart of his thought, where thought meets yet another of its Kierkegaardian limits, in the fact of freedom. God has already pointed that way, by dislodging reflection from any coercive oversight of marriage, and replacing it with a divine, love-preserving blessing. But now God emerges from out of mere means. As Judge William explains it, what most pointedly distinguishes the ethicist from the aesthete is that he *decides*. The act of deciding is itself a movement, what counts in Hegelian terms for form, not content, and William shows a latent fealty to Kant in his effort to describe, or render contentful for the reader, the all-significance of this sheer form. "The point is not the reality of what is chosen but the reality of choosing" (EO II:176). Content is implicated in any choice, as object of choice, but this can be any one of the many things that fly by consciousness for its delectation. Part of the aesthete's pleasure is in the variety of the presentation, which keeps boredom at bay. In deciding, the ethicist reverses roles with the entertaining panoply of change, himself becomes the mover who subjects it to a center, his object of choice, which acts as a magnet on all the rest, reining it in. Insofar as decision is siding among elements of the panoply, we could say, by a homonymous accident of English, that choosing is really desiding. In consequence, "the consciousness integrates" (EO II:177), "the personality is thereby consolidated" (EO II:167). What was not chosen among the options is not lost, but is changed by its newly subordinate position: "the choice penetrates everything and changes it" (EO II:223).

We hear in this talk of imposed change an echo of that bugbear, reflection. Reflection is indeed implicit in choice, for we must regard before we choose. But as opposed to reflection, within choice it is the subject, not the object, that changes. As William explains, to choose is to acquire a past. This is absent in the aesthetic life, which is always sacrificing time, either to the immediacy in which it lives, subsequently dies, and lives again, or to reflection, which holds the reflector at bay from temporal immersions.

> Now he discovers that the self he chooses has . . . a history. . . . This history contains painful things, and yet he is the person he is only

> through this history.... He is most radically sinking himself into the root by which he is bound up with the whole. This makes him uneasy.... He can give up nothing of all this, not the most painful, not the hardest.... He repents himself back into himself, back into the family, back into the race, until he finds himself in God. (EO II:216)

With this passage, William surpasses a Kantian style moral spirituality. Most noticeably, the choice is not an act of practical reason, or of any other faculty or agency. It is absolutely free in its indeterminacy by any agency outside itself. It is as though, where idealism sacrificed any agent of thought to thinking itself, which generated agency, William has offered up any agent of choice to choosing itself, which generates the self. The self is the consequence of its choosing. I choose myself. Language, which insists on subject and verb, can barely formulate the idea, for the subject in this case presupposes the verb. In the singular case of choice, the space between subject and predicate on which language depends vanishes. In that sense, it is "absolute," as William calls it, in its resistance to analysis into subject and predicate. But now, all contentful identity expressible in terms of subject and predicate follows in its wake, for whatever it selected connects by laws of cause and effect to successions and precedents. William does not argue for an ultimate precedent in God. He need not; because the language of the absolute, where agent and act are one, is already divine. The chooser is not God, but in the moment of choice, which for all its consequence is only a moment, he assimilates to God, to such a degree that we can barely distinguish between them. On the one hand, I "am born through my choosing myself" (EO II:216). On the other, as though to suggest an exchange with God, "I choose the absolute that chooses me" (EO II:213). And I emerge from this encounter a distinct personality I was not before.

Part of what lends to William's language about choice the sense of the sacred are his claims for the hardship of choosing. That hardship—a theme that Johannes de Silentio will underscore for us—registers, psychologically, the distance the sacred must occupy from us to count as holy in the first place. The past I own in choosing myself is so inevitably laden with wrongness, William implies, that no less a religiously freighted term than repentance captures what I do when I identify with it. Or, it may simply be that choosing as siding is inevitably also excluding, the moral burden of which comes down on the chooser with such weight that it can only be repented.[9] Every task I execute in the realization of the self I chose nails the coffin all the more firmly shut on the selves that would have resulted from a different choice. This is the burden the aesthete refuses, but which the ethicist carries. Or, it may simply be that the subordinating change choice imposes on everything that remains besides the chosen carries something of the stain of reflection, which always coerces, after all.

In any case, tasks emerge from my choice that I must muster my energies to realize. For William, these include marriage and work. God remains as a presupposition to all of that, but not otherwise a focus of attention. He need not be, since once we have chosen, a course towards fulfillment lies before us which results in happiness no matter how far we advance on it or what obstacles we encounter. Having chosen the circumstances of the life given him, William enjoys the domestic, professional, and national identity that thus accrues to him and allows that these may sometimes mediate a sense for the sacred (EO II:324). These are not so much self-satisfactions as illustrations of William's larger point that choice once made roots the chooser in subsuming circles of identity whose most outer one, God, sometimes manifests in suffusions of the whole. But to linger in the relation with God that founds me is to become a mystic who neglects his temporal responsibilities for the sake of the eternal (EO II: 246) and in consequence, loses all finite relationship, including that with a spouse (EO II: 245). The God who blesses marriages would thus defeat the blessing. William, himself a weekly church goer, suggests that a brief mystical indulgence is indeed the point of church, which accounts for what might seem the improbable feelings of isolation that congregants experience in gathered worship (EO II:246–7). But prolonged into weekday life, mysticism "becomes a very grave sickness" (EO II: 247). The judge returns to this theme towards the end of his letter, in the context of monasticism, and the appeal a "monastic theory . . . or a quite analogous aesthetic view" (EO II: 328) of moral exceptionality might have in modern times. William can imagine someone who with all due effort cannot choose himself in the way he has described, but remains despite himself cut off from "the root by which he is bound up with the whole," by not marrying, or accepting his history, or affirming his race—who stands apart as "an exception" (EO II:330). But he can accept the integrity of such souls only if they experience more hardship in that detached state than if they had made the effort, like all worldly persons, to choose themselves (EO II:216). Given the effort that self-choice is, William can barely imagine what this even greater struggle would be like. It is "a purgatory, the dreadfulness of which I can at least form an idea" (EO II: 331) but to which no one should aspire.

William has tempted us with his characterizations of the mystic and the monastic. That these lives of religious intensity trouble the ethicist troubles us too, at least to the extent that we take William for a reliable guide to the ethical life. At the same time we must wonder what the other pseudonyms have to say about these more overtly spiritual moral exceptions. William already points to "A" by linking the mystic with immediacy, which focuses the life of at least one kind of aesthete; and the monastic, for his part, conjures the image of Abraham, at least as Johannes de Silentio describes him.

Of course, through William, we have already been trafficking in the aesthetic. Both of his letters elucidate the ethical by way of the contrasts the aesthetic makes with it—a helpful approach given the challenge of writing contentfully about the contentless purity of choice. Though "everyone who lives aesthetically is in despair" (EO II: 192), part of William's point is that an aesthetics subordinated to ethics is not despairing. Within a moral context, the protean variability of aesthetics is calmed and united by the singular choice whose effects ripple through it. William's regard for a properly subordinated aesthetic shows in the compliments and solicitations he extends towards the aesthete, "A," whom he addresses as "my friend." In light of William's theory of friendship, which comes at the end of his second letter, where he explains that what makes for friendship at all is shared world views (EO II: 321), we must wonder how much truth that epistolary salutation carries. Indeed, the very choice of communicative form—the letter—in a relationship that also involves frequent visits (EO II: 333) raises moral doubts, especially since "our relationship by letter remains a secret" (EO II: 333), that veil over openness which aesthetics loves and ethics abhors. William explains his behavior in terms of the allowance a letter makes for a more admonishing tone than conversation does (EO II: 5). But "A," via the Seducer, understands a different use of letters, to create in the recipient a false sense of breathing space from the seduction afoot (EO I: 386). William, viewed from "A's" vantage point is indeed a seducer. And the mystic and monastic function as much as limits on William's seductions, as the justice-preserving Commendatore does within Mozart's *Don Giovanni* on the seductive don.

It would be an irony if "A," who does not write letters, but at most assembles the letters of others (of Johannes the Seducer and Cordelia), turned out, between him and William, to be the more ethically open. But we must be wary of "A" from the start. For the sorrow he expresses in his opening aphorisms, which recall Ecclesiastes, appears also to be a pleasure for him, insofar as he can reflect on it. It is as though "A" is playing with the flip side of reflection, which, for all of its adverse effects on love, may have an improving effect on sorrow. The finite constituents of identity for William, which he weightily repents himself into—"everything temporal and fortuitous" (EO I: 42)—are "booty" for "A's" timeless "eternity of recollection" (EO I: 42). We cannot take seriously a hardship that, by the mere act of reflection, so easily converts to pleasure. And insofar as that is "A's" modus operandi, we may wonder whether any sense of the sacred really registers with him. But it does, only in the unlikely context of seduction.

Seduction serves "A" as a framework for arresting Hegelian coerciveness. Seduction clears another space for the exercise of freedom. This is not so surprising when seduction is contrasted with another more commonly accepted way for freedom to clear space for the sacred, by way of —temptation. The temptation stories of Jesus, Job, and Abraham (as Johannes de Silentio well knows) exercise the freedom of those figures towards the Bible's own end of presenting the sacred. Seduction inverts temptation. Where the lure of temptation is intended ultimately to fail, that of seduction is meant to succeed. Both presuppose freedom to either accept or reject the lure. Johannes the Seducer underscores the importance of freedom to his own seductive arts: "I am a friend of freedom, and I do not care for anything I do not receive freely" (EO I: 409–410). Johannes' pleasure in seducing is in first arousing desire for himself and then the will in the seduced to herself break off the relation. It is not mere puppetry. Judge William, in describing the "summit of the esthetic," perhaps expresses best what Johannes hopes to achieve: "he who feels himself present as a character in a drama the deity is writing . . . in which the individual . . . is not disturbed by the prompter but feels that he himself wants to say what is being whispered to him, so that it almost becomes a question of whether he is putting the words in the prompter's mouth or the prompter in his . . . he alone has brought into actual existence the highest in aesthetics" (EO II:137). Applied to his own case, these words would make of Johannes the deity and Cordelia the summit of his aesthetic creation, except that it is not Cordelia, but Johannes, who savors the sense of her voluntarily speaking words prompted her—against her own self-understanding. To borrow the opening vocabulary of Victor Eremita, the perfect matching of inner to outer that William described as the summit of the aesthetic, and that Cordelia might have realized had she felt herself the actor William describes, becomes in Johannes' hands the precise opposite, a case of "complete contradiction" (EO I: 4) between how the actor sees herself and what is actually happening to her.

Unlike temptation, whose proper ending is happy, successful seduction ends badly for the seduced. "A's" evident distress over the story of Cordelia's seduction—"I . . . can scarcely control the anxiety that grips me every time I think about the affair" (EO I: 310)—reassures the reader of his reliability, but offers no consoling hope for Cordelia, who will be tormented by "multi-tongued reflection" (EO I: 309) as it recollects for her, in variable but vain hopes for peace, her relation with Johannes. Johannes for his part, "A" suggests, will have so perfected his evasions of any commitment to reality as to go effectively mad. The reader seeking here for signs of the spiritual may have stumbled onto its demonic opposite, an impression underscored by a vision "A" raises of another world "behind the world in which we live. . . . a world of gauze, lighter, more ethereal, with a quality different from that of the actual world" (EO I: 306)—a possible evocation of a sacred world, but which turns out to be, instead, the redoubt from the actual in which Johannes loses his sanity; except for a hope "A" holds out fleetingly that this other world can be approached from a "basis either in health or sickness." What would it be like approached from a basis in health?

"A" belongs to an oddly named society called the Symparanekromenoi, or "Fellowship of the Dead,"[10] so-named, we may surmise, because of the extreme detachment its members practice from reality. Dedicated to the "doctrine of the downfall of everything" (EO I: 167), they are less apocalypticists than practitioners of resignation to the "wretchedness of life." They appear to inhabit that otherworld which "A" has already invoked, but with consequences opposite to the seducer's. For instead of breeding sadness, they reflect upon it contemplatively under the moniker "knights of sympathy" (EO I: 177), since they can "step in procession with sorrow." These knights perform a service for just that kind of melancholic as Cordelia becomes. They give voice to the interior sadness of the seduced, which so lacks outward expression it only shows, as it were, in silhouette. Having articulated that suffering, the Symparanekromenoi unite the sufferers in a "harmony of sorrow" (EO I: 214). True, the sufferers treated are all literary characters (from Goethe and the opera librettist, Lorenzo da Ponte), as we might expect from a society of reality-deniers, suggesting that the other-world they inhabit is actually the world of art. Judge William would warn us to expect little in the way of sustenance from that quarter—"as far as poetry and art are concerned, may I remind you . . . that they provide only an imperfect reconciliation with life" (EO II: 273)—but we have learned to not quite trust him on this point.

One of the sufferers, Dona Elivra from Mozart's *Don Giovanni* stands out on two grounds, for having once known the religious life (she had been a nun), though "A" doubts she could know it again—he may not be the best judge of that—and for belonging to two arts at once, literature and music. These two outstanding features of her are not unrelated, for the religious surfaces, as we shall see, in the unity she effects between narrative and music. In his address to the Symparanekromenoi, "A" projects Dona Elvira beyond the opera into her protracted life without the don, whom she alternatively deifies and demonizes, resigns herself to have lost, and expects to return. In her narrative role, Dona Elvira merely illustrates what all the sufferers do, how much reflection on the lie of seduction compounds the secreted sorrow of it. As therapist of her narrated life, "A" can do no more than find words for her self-contradictory sorrow. But in another of his capacities, as music critic, as author of the essay, "The Immediate Erotic Stages," he uncovers for the singer Dona Elvira a religious role she co-creates with Don Giovanni, which simultaneously reunites her with him and directs the listener's attention to the sacred. Here is how that happens.

"A" is sparing with the language of the sacred, but one place it does occur is in his effusive praise for Mozart, who belongs "in that kingdom of the gods" (EO I: 49), whose music is a "sacred joy" (EO I: 48), in the presence of which "I feel myself to be indescribably happy" (EO I: 135). These are not casual ascriptions of transcendence to music. Music shares with freedom and seduction the limit it imposes on thought—"reflection is fatal to music" (EO I: 70). And so, like them, it opens up a space for the sacred to show. That is unexpected, because of the proverbial association of music with the demonic (EO I: 73). But these seemingly opposed tendencies in this singularly "spiritual art" (EO I: 69) derive from the same primal fact about it, that it is the art of pure immediacy (EO I: 70). Music is more purely sensual than any other art because of its more extreme dependence on reception by sense, in this case hearing. It is so immediately sensual as to lack continuity through time. "Music . . . is over as soon as the sound has stopped and comes into existence again only when it sounds once again" (EO I: 102). It is just by way of this pure sensuality, as interpreted by Christianity, that music acquires an affinity with the demonic. For as soon as, thanks to Christianity (according to "A") the spiritual and sensual are opposed, the sensual becomes the medium for manifesting everything opposed to spirit (EO I: 72). But the sheer immediacy of music carries another potential, which links it to the sacred, to be the form for a content that, in its own immediacy, matches music's perfectly.

We may hear an echo of Hegel here, whose *Phenomenology of Spirit* climaxes with the identification, within Consciousness, of form with content; or, otherwise put, of its movements with what its movements yield. For Hegel, Consciousness is finally at rest, and wholly divine, when its awareness of what it generates and of itself as generator coincide. The steps by which it comes to that point follow one another in natural and reasoned necessity. Perfect matchings of form to content are also momentous for "A," but just when they are unnecessitated and simply fortunate (EO I: 57) or, as Novalis might say, casual and magical. This is exactly what happens when music finds its contentful partner in immediacy: unreflective desire, an instantiation of which is the Don Juan legend. Music's pure sensuality partners perfectly with seduction, since "only the sensual . . . is essentially faithless" (EO I: 94). "A" suggests that the Don Juan legend, which had been around for centuries, mistakenly sought expression in literature, which is too reflective a medium to successfully bear it. Only when Mozart set the legend to music did it find its formal mate (EO I: 57). Literature is, by contrast, a suitable medium for the reflective seducer, by whose exquisite planning contradictory desires are awakened and cross-purposed, as Johannes the Seducer illustrates. Perhaps "A" preserves Johannes' diary, even over the moral revulsion it evokes in him, for the aesthetic harmony he discerns between its content and form. Taking the Faust legend for the paradigm of reflective seduction, "A" suggests that each age will find its literary expression of it (EO I: 105); perhaps Johannes' diary is one for "A's" own age. But Don Juan is so identified with desire as to exclude all reflection on it. It is the sheer force of desire in him that seduces in the first place (EO I: 99). What Don Juan embodies is "desire as principle" (85). He is less a desiring individual than desire itself, the conflation (once again) of subject and predicate.

His hoverings between his individuality and the desire that consumes him is "the musical vibration" (EO I: 92). "A's" reflections on desire parallel Judge William's on decision. Both are trying to isolate the pure form of their subject matter apart from any obfuscating content—a self-defeating task for language. "A's" advantage over William is that he can direct his readers to a purely sensual expression of the form he means—music—with injunctions that further undermine the communicative power of his own self-defeatingly reflective words: "hear, hear, hear Mozart's *Don Giovanni*" (EO I:103).

It is a "sacred joy to see united that which belongs together" (EO I: 48), as Mozart accomplishes for music and the Don Juan legend. Compared to the Symparanekromenoi, Mozart heals to perfection. For he really unites Dona Elivra with Don Juan, as "A" describes in words that echo what William called the height of the aesthetic, and which Johannes the Seducer accomplished in reverse, demonically, for Cordelia: when Elvira sings her first aria, as Don Giovanni pursues another seduction in the background, "the unity in the situation is the concordance in which Elvira and Don Giovanni sound simultaneously," so much so that each seems a vehicle for the other's words (EO I: 121,122). This matching, a microcosm of what the whole work accomplishes, opens a place for eternity to sound in time (EO I: 51).

We can imagine Judge William's response. "A" is simply a mystic of art, subject to the fault from which all mystics suffer: the refusal to repent themselves into reality. "A" may inadvertently lend some credence to this when he claims that the effect of the opera is heightened when heard from behind a barrier, making of the music "a world by itself, separated from me" (EO I:120). He seems to identify the opera with that sanity-sapping other-world he critiqued in his introduction to the Seducer's diary. We can imagine William saying that if we must have a Mozart opera, let us have *The Magic Flute*, whose failure from "A's" aesthetic point of view, because of its reflective and unmusical preoccupation with marriage (EO I:83), would be its moral success from Judge William's. But "A" is undaunted in his enthusiasm for the opera,[11] and ranks himself with all who have "glided onward and downward in its music and relished the joy of losing themselves in this way" (EO I: 104). His language is indeed that of mysticism. Leaving aside all dismissive commentary from William, our worry here may derive not so much from the alleged amorality of mysticism, as from its transience. Are we then so dependent on opera houses for our happiness? No, says "A," in this essay's final word, for such understanding as we can claim of the opera, even through the deficient medium of language, but which we can carry with us at all times, is itself transporting, like an overflow of goodness that recalls its source. "I at least feel myself to be indescribably happy in having understood Mozart even remotely" (EO I: 135).

And now comes Johannes de Silentio, the most explicitly religious of these three pseudonyms, with his vocabulary of faith and his preoccupation with the biblical story of Abraham and Isaac. Though Johannes shows no awareness of the other two pseudonyms, he is very aware of their ideas. Problema One and Two, in *Fear and Trembling*, can be read as rejections of Judge William; and Problema Three, of "A." *Fear and Trembling* appears to follow *Either/Or* as a presentation of the religious approach to spirituality, complementing the aesthetic and ethical approaches of its predecessor,[12] and so completing the triadic picture of the life stages. We might well expect Johannes to stake his claims, in part, on the rejection of alternatives. This is already a pattern among the pseudonyms, and is partly what makes Johannes' lyric dialectical, according to the subtitle of his book. Judge William makes his case for ethics over against aesthetics, and even "A" establishes the brilliance of *Don Giovanni* in contrast with less successful literary treatments of the Don Juan theme. It is partly the Hegelian heritage of dialectic that moves Kierkegaard to think in oppositional terms, but also his subject matters, which always border on the apophatic. The spaces Kierkegaard clears for new showings of the sacred occur where thought, once exhaustive in the hands of Stoics, Spinoza, or Hegel, reaches its limits. Where thought fails, language does too, unless it avails itself of apophatic techniques, such as indication by negation. All three pseudonyms strain the most with language when it fails before the numinous limits of thought they respectively encounter: decision, for Judge William; desire, for "A"; paradox, for Johannes de Silentio. But only Johannes indicates by his very name the apophatic tack of last resort: silence.

Johannes appears to have chosen his book's title with care, for his opening and closing point is that common understandings of religious life fail to grasp the hardship of it—the cost in fear and trembling. "Every privilege in the world of spirit can only be purchased in deep pain" (FT 110). (Hegelian) philosophy, with its smug claims for reason to "go further" (FT 42) than faith, is partly responsible for the cheapening of it. For Johannes, faith is already the extremity of human reach; beyond it, the human stops and the sacred begins. Part of what makes faith so hard is that, far from incorporating the individual into the sacred, as "A" suggests happens in his musical mysticism, it establishes the individual all the more starkly in his frightful solitude, and without the comfort of the subsuming and mediating universal, such as marriage and work, so ready at hand for William.[13] More than William or "A," Johannes reflects on the sacred itself, uncolored by either ethics or aesthetics. He even offers a simple argument—a psychological one—for believing in God: without God, we despair; but we do not despair (because there is faith). But there is nothing here to rest in. For the "spiritual distance" (FT 93) that separates us from God is greater than any we have yet encountered among the philosophers.

For Johannes, the sacred is doubly removed from us, first by a difficult act of resignation we must achieve, and then, on top of that, by a contrasting and virtually impossible act of expectation. As though to uncover the heroism implicit in either act, Johannes names the doers of them knights: the knight of infinite resignation, the knight of faith. The infinity of the resignation Johannes intends comprises an investment of all hope in some one thing, presupposed by the conviction that it will never be realized. We encounter preludes to this knight in "A," for whom Mozart is all, and Dona Elivra, whose life is Don Giovanni, though both Mozart and Don Giovanni are (in different ways) beyond reach. In the endless embrace of all that fails to be the hoped-for, this knight experiences, unexpectedly, "the bliss of infinity" (FT 69). As though to underscore the force of this dialectical conversion, from disappointment in the finite, to bliss in the infinite, Johannes suggests it is consistent with the traditional (Christian) view of God as love. For in the infinite resignation, all expectation of harmony between loving God and personal experience is renounced. In a sounding of one of Kierkegaard's key themes, Johannes affirms that "God's love is . . . incommensurable with the whole of reality" (FT 63). It is as though the bliss unexpectedly known in the infinity of all that was not expected is referred to God as source. Johannes knows this bliss, and implies he is himself a knight of infinite resignation. We may wonder whether compatibility between a resignation of this type and the view of God as love implies any necessary connection between them. Might not the sacred known in the infinity of disappointment be quite other to the God of love? But then, the claim that God's love is incommensurable with reality sounds in any case like a positive refashioning of the old apophatic view that whatever we mean by love does not apply to God. As Spinoza taught, we cannot wish God to love. An impersonal sacred seems inescapable for the knight of infinite resignation—which is no criticism of him except of his originality. He sounds like an unusually intense, single-minded sort of Stoic, who knows the inner peace of the Stoic, "enough unto himself" (FT 73).

But it is all to Johannes' purpose if, in search of greater exceptionality in his thought, we want to "go further" than this knight, to his unfathomable, inimitable and truly original counterpart, the knight of faith. The knight of faith evolves from the knight of resignation through an additional renunciation. He renounces the bliss of infinity, which had negated the finite, and so receives the finite back, according to the logic of double negation: a negation negated is a positive. The positivity shows not just in the reassertion of the finite, no longer renounced, but in the character of the sacred, which becomes personal, a "confidant," addressed "in heaven as 'thou'" (FT 105). The two knights differently experience the relation between expectation and fulfillment. The first knight renounces expectation and experiences fulfillment unexpectedly in the renunciation; the second knight revives the lost expectation and experiences fulfillment unexpectedly in the revival—for the second knight, the distance between expectation and fulfillment vanishes. But the happiness in the second fulfillment is much greater than the first. The first compared with the second "is indeed unhappy" (FT 62–63). Johannes is clear that the knight of faith does not simply hope against all odds, but actually experiences the fulfillment of his hope. This "dumbfounds me, my brain reels; for having made the movement of resignation, now on the strength of the absurd, to get everything, to get one's desire, whole, in full, that requires more-than-human powers, it is a marvel" (FT 76). Curiously, Johannes attributes the feat of this to the knight, and not to the reality that absurdly meets his expectations. Johannes is not amazed by a reality that improbably meets expectation with fulfillment, but by the mental habitude of one who successfully inhabits that reality. The success shows in the seamless match between expectation and fulfillment, improbable as it is to the observing eyes of non-knights of faith. Johannes likens the match to the perfectly smooth recovery from impact a gifted ballet dancer makes after landing from a leap. The recovery picks up so smoothly from where the landing leaves off that the two appear to constitute a single, uninterrupted movement (FT 70). The knight's expectation does not compel the fulfillment; reality freely shapes itself to meet the expectation, like, according to another of Johannes' analogies, deep water that buoys a swimmer who has dived into it, or indeed, like the ram that replaces Isaac in sacrifice. Johannes likens himself to the non-swimmer who will not, cannot dive; he is the non-Abraham. The problem is not with his understanding. He knows, precisely from the story of Abraham, that faith receives what it expects. The problem is with his trust—that reality would indeed shape itself to any faith he had. If William had the courage of his decisiveness, Johannes lacks the courage of this trust, which exceeds the courage he does indeed have for every thought (FT 60), but not for the thought-surpassing. This is partly the point: understanding that faith is a double resignation no more realizes the experience of it than knowing the laws of buoyancy secures an ability to swim. Indeed, Kierkegaard may mean for us to suspect that Johannes' understanding of faith blocks his experience of it—if he did not know that faith recovers a renounced expectation that is improbably fulfilled, he would not be blocked from it by his awareness of the improbability.

Of course Johannes, who is no slacker, has chosen one of the most frightful stories of all from the history of literature to explore the implications of faith. What story more compactly combines all the ingredients of faith: the all-investment in some one thing (Isaac), the resignation to its loss, the receipt of it back with no expression of surprise (because expected—superimposed on the resignation—all along)? That Abraham is also the agent of his loss introduces the disturbing moral dimension to the story. It heightens the hardship of faith that it can "suspend" ethics. And it underscores the silence to which his faith commits him; for, just because there is no larger good that the unfaithful listener could understand the sacrifice to serve, there is no language available to Abraham to intelligibly explain it. But the hardship of faith, and the commitment to silence over it, would remain without the exacerbation of them that is always potentially present in their distinction from and indeed incommensurability with ethics. Johannes wants our awed astonishment over the *form* of faith, not the content of this particular story. The Abraham story is simply an extreme pedagogic means towards that end.[14] Abraham himself is for Johannes less the biblical figure revered by monotheists than a personification of the form of faith—the double resignation required to perform it—much as the pseudonyms themselves are of other forms. It is just for this reason that his analysis of faith might be called, over his protests, philosophical—for all the setting of his discussion in a biblical story holy to all three monotheisms, he presumes none of their contentful revelations.

The knight of faith does not so much illustrate a philosophical faith,[15] as a faith-state into which a philosopher might fall without entering any particular religion. That Johannes, in describing the knight of faith, cannot himself illustrate it points up how much the faith intended here is unreflective or better, beyond reflection, much as Johannes himself seems to fail to realize this. Johannes is poised at a self-annihilating culmination of philosophy, but does not take the plunge. That plunge could sport Christian dress, as Abraham does in Christian tradition, beginning with Paul. And Kierkegaard no doubt intends for us to read Johannes as unrealized Christianity, who misses the key to transforming from mere reflector on faith to faith itself: the paradoxical person of Jesus Christ. But we need not read Johannes that way. What Johannes foretells, for us, is a philosophical spirituality that can wear religious dress without requiring it. Such a possibility becomes interesting and viable only after religion has so far ceased to monopolize the spiritual life that philosophy can approach it invitingly. Kierkegaard, after Hegel, who in his estimation (and ours) effectively sidetracked Christianity, fashions in Johannes a philosopher who might wear Christian dress lightly and even disposably. But it will be Simone Weil who realizes this possibility for us.

William and "A" simultaneously personify the forms they describe. Johannes does not. Despite himself, Johannes thereby becomes a model of spiritual life in contrast with the one he describes. The choice resembles what the aesthete has between immediate and reflective forms of aesthetic life; for Abraham, having renounced (reflective) resignation, assumes "not the first immediacy [of aesthetics] but a later one" (FT 109), which actually commits him to the silence that names but does not characterize the reflective Johannes. But Abraham is not really a model at all. "The true knight of faith is a witness, never a teacher" (FT 107). He does not represent an object of choice, for no one who appreciates the fear and trembling of his life would choose it. Johannes implies that faith comes into life unchosen, in defiance of all that William would teach, and more in tune with "A," who has "preferred to let chance prevail" (EO I:10). If we seek a spiritual program, Abraham will not do. Will Johannes himself? We may doubt what Johannes implies, that he is a knight of infinite resignation—he lacks the serenity. It is not so much that he knows too much about the knight of faith to rest content with resignation, but that, in his reflective obsession with faith, he forfeits it and resignation both. But this does not leave him with nothing. As we have seen, Johannes is moved by the mere thought of Abraham, towards admiration, paralysis, annihilation—spiritually evocative terms. He is spiritually moved by his understanding of faith. And this is a philosophical spirituality, too—perhaps for the scholar of faith.

To understand something is to uncover its presuppositions. Faith comprises an expectation presupposing a resignation presupposing an all-investment in some one thing. It is possible to work conceptually backwards from a given reality of faith, such as Abraham's, to its presuppositions, but not the reverse. From the presuppositions of faith, concepts do not culminate in the experience of faith. It is not just that concepts do not, pace Hegel, generate reality, but that they do not necessarily follow in logically necessitated sequence. At least the important concepts do not entail each other but rather meet each other unexpectedly in perfect matchings that provoke less satisfaction than amazement and resemble what Novalis called magic. They less imply each other than nest in each other. Kierkegaard via his pseudonyms has been saying this all along. The amazements he commends to us result from the fortuitous meetings of: romantic love and continuity, in marriage; form and content of desire, in Mozart; fulfillment and expectation, in faith.

The unnecessity of these meetings is partly what makes it so hard to found a life on them. Unlike Novalis, for whom such magical meetings were dependably ubiquitous (for the poet), Kierkegaard's philosophical pseudonyms have identified quite singular holy meeting grounds—Mozart, marriage, faith—that are hardly available to all and that are separated from each other by abysses of thought. Each requires an investment, the cost of which rises with passage over the abysses, from aesthetic to ethical to religious. It is easier to risk a bad night at the opera, than years lived unhappily with a single other, than a whole life lost from the lack of some one thing. Kierkegaard uncovers a false presupposition of philosophy—that it can guarantee. Given results in William's successful marriage, Mozart's *Don Giovanni*, or Abraham's faith, it can uncover the foundations of them. It cannot produce them. Understanding is always retrospective, never generative. A philosophical spirituality that takes its bearings from the early Kierkegaardian pseudonyms must live, without assurances, towards the fortuitous matching of need with supply. It will develop a hypersensitivity to these, which cannot be forced but only registered when they appear. If a philosopher here and there does find herself in Abraham's shoes, she will know a fearsome joy in the most encompassing match of all, which faith enacts, but she will not be able either to communicate her joy or expect it to be seen, even by the reverent Johannes's of the world.

NOTES

1. Kierkegaard, *Fear and Trembling*, tr. Alastair Hannay (NewYork: Penguin, 1985), 82. Page references for subsequent quotations are given parenthetically in the text.
2. Combining chapter titles from the Hannay and older Lowrie translations. Kierkegaard, *Fear and Trembling and The Sickness Unto Death*, trans. Walter Lowrie (Princeton, NJ: Princeton University Press, 1968).
3. Victor Eremita edits *Either/Or*, which includes the work of an unnamed aesthete who in turn has included in his own ramblings the work of an unnamed seducer.
4. Kierkegaard, *Either/Or*, trans. Howard and Edna Hong (Princeton, NJ: Princeton University Press, 1987), 1:9. Page numbers for subsequent quotations are given parenthetically in the text.
5. Kierkegaard, *The Point of View*, trans. Howard and Edna Hong (Princeton, NJ: Princeton University Press, 2009), 23.
6. Clare Carlisle notes a "kind of hierarchy" to the pseudonyms. Carlisle, *Kierkegaard: A Guide for the Perplexed* (New York: Continuum, 2006), 36.
7. Carlisle suggests that on a biographical interpretation of the pseudonyms, they point to conflicting abilities and tendencies within Kierkegaard himself—but so, by extension, in all of us. Ibid.
8. John Lippitt, "How Reliable is Johannes de Silentio?" in *Routledge Philosophy Guidebook to Kierkegaard and* Fear and Trembling (New York: Routledge, 2003), 177–208.
9. An interpretation that Jacques Derrida suggests in "The Gift of Death," in *The Gift of Death and Literature in Secret*, trans. David Wills (Chicago: University of Chicago Press, 2008).
10. In the Hong translation of the Greek.
11. And even insists, against William on its moral integrity: "The aim of the opera is highly moral and the impression it leaves is altogether beneficent" (EO I:115). But then, by "highly moral," "A" means intensely passionate, which does not capture all that William means by ethics.
12. As Mooney also suggests. Edward F. Mooney, *Knights of Faith and Resignation: Reading Kierkegaard's* Fear and Trembling (Albany, NY: State University of New York Press, 1991), 4.
13. This is the point of Problema 2, that there is indeed an "absolute duty to God" (FT 96), which supersedes the universal duties of ethics. The absolute, in its incomparability, stands outside the universal. Johannes works here with a Kantian view of the ethical as the universalizable. William's view of the ethical is more nuanced, involving elements of the absolute (EO II:214–215), the universal (EO II:363) and the particular (EO II:363). But insofar as his ethical contains a universal element, it falls under Johannes' critique.
14. We might compare it with the story of Arjuna's reluctant slaughter, under divine encouragement, of his cousins, in the Bhagavad Gita: the idea is not to encourage murder but to suggest that if even killing lends itself to karmayogic performance, any act does; that is, all of life can be lived without attachment to results.
15. This is a term explicated, above all, by Karl Jaspers. See for example his *Philosophy of Existence*, trans. Richard Grabay (Philadelphia: University of Pennsylvania Press, 1971). But what he has in mind is quite different from the knight of faith.

ELEVEN
Emerson

Emerson, the one-time Unitarian minister, is the only of our philosophers to have once professionally represented institutional religion. But if the Kierkegaardian pseudonyms move towards the church, Emerson, having begun there, moves *from* it. He resigned his pulpit in 1832. His public rejection of received Christology, in his famous address to Harvard Divinity School in 1838 marks his break with the church and reinvention of himself in a new line of work—public lecturing—at which few after have him have been so successful. But Christianity is not so easily discarded. And if it continued to weigh on him, and even to surface indirectly in his thought, this helps explain his obsession with freedom—not as Kierkegaard understood it, as radically uncontextualized (because itself context-creating) choice, but as St. Paul understood it, as freedom *from*. St. Paul's freedom was from sin; Emerson's is from the whole weight of (Christian) tradition, carried to him by generations of ancestral clergy. "How shall a man escape from his ancestors," he laments, in his late essay, "Fate."[1] Towards the end of his life, as what was possibly dementia set in, Emerson edited, with the help of his daughter Edith an anthology of poems, called *Parnassus*. A reader might have thought, given Emerson's claim for the identity of poet and philosopher—"a beauty, which is truth, and a truth, which is beauty, is the aim of both" (*Nature*, 36)—that the ending of Keats' *Ode on a Grecian Urn*—"Beauty is Truth, Truth Beauty"—would have appeared in the anthology,[2] but instead, we find an excerpt from its companion *Ode to a Nightingale*, praised among other reasons for its freedom: "Thou wast not born for death, immortal bird / No hungry generations tread thee down." This picture of a past that hungers for the life of the living, if not to possess it than at least to level it down to its own prone state would be ghoulish if the nightingale did not rise so high above it. If this passage moved Emerson—"an endless seeker with no

Past at my back" (Circles, 412)—even after so many years of distance from his Christian past, and into the last decade of his life, even as an insulating dementia began to obscure the past, then on some level he was still seeking freedom *from*.

But by way of English translation, partly through his friend Coleridge, Emerson had at his disposal the German philosophical tradition, which stood guard for him against the assaults of his Christian past with its own spiritual monism. In a passage reflecting on the ideas that the passing times of day conjure in him—beginning, with a nod to the rising sun of the East, "the dawn is my Assyria"—there is nothing of Christianity brought to mind, but "the night shall be my Germany of mystic philosophy and dreams" (*Nature*, 15). From Kant, Emerson has the idea that what we see is "partly owing to the eye itself"(*Nature*, 14); from Hegel, that "spirit, that is, the Supreme Being does not build up nature around us, but puts it forth through us" (*Nature*, 41); and perhaps most of all, from Schelling, who had this from Spinoza, that the same Universal Spirit which underlies Nature "pervades Thought also"(*Nature*, 30), yielding "the analogy that marries Matter and Mind" (*Nature*, 26). Emerson himself marks his debt to this philosophical tradition by titling one section in his first book, *Nature*: "Idealism." But if only because he does not derive nature from the thought of it—the content from the form—he is not Hegelian. By inverting the Hegelian dependence of content on form, Emerson fashions something new out of Hegel that has more in common with Kierkegaard: a worldview in which content precedes form. Form is derivative, and follows in one Emersonian expression of this view, upon soul (The Poet, 447). But the central content of Emersonian spirituality is: nature.[3] Nature is freedom's ally in the release Emerson sought from the lingering tread of the past. In the idealist tradition, nature and freedom are unlikely partners, cutting against the grain of the opposition in which Kant initially set them. But, in his early essays, Emerson weaves them together as though their bond were natural. Thus, *Nature* begins not with nature, but with a call to reject the "poetry and philosophy . . . of tradition," "the dry bones of the past"—for "our own works and laws and worship" (*Nature*, 7). And the Divinity School address begins not with "divinity," in the 19th century sense of theological learning, which will soon come under attack for its constrictions of spirit, but with, in its very first words, an evocation of "this refulgent summer," a premonition of the freeing role nature will come to play in the speech. "The American Scholar," which stood in less danger of giving its audience offence, calls straight off for an end to "our long apprenticeship to the learning of other lands" (American Scholar, 53), so that Nature can take up its rightful and liberating place as the American scholar's first and foremost teacher.

The missing link connecting Nature and Freedom, and a mark of Emerson's dissent from Kant, is his concept of the Natural. Reflecting on "History" in his essay of that name, Emerson observes of the ancient

Greeks that "our admiration of the antique is not admiration of the old, but of the natural" (History, 248). Out of the storehouse of that very confinement from which Emerson hopes to free us—history—he pulls the linchpin of his thought: the natural. For the natural is precisely the unconstrained, a notion of freedom that takes its bearings from a prior and unnatural constriction. The greater the prior constriction, the more liberating the freedom from it. Emerson had on hand the most notorious constriction on freedom of his own or any day: slavery. And he spoke against it on several occasions—uncharacteristically, by his own admission, since "I do not often speak to public questions."[4] But part of what drew him into the public arena was his recognition, consistent with his larger thought, of an analogy between the institution of slavery and confinements of the human soul, which he cites obliquely at the start of his speech on "The Fugitive Slave Law" (1854), in terms of his "own spirits in prison."[5] And the force of the imperative for release from such extreme constraints, whether outward or inward, is so great that it converts from option to necessity. Lincoln, he observes, in his speech on "The Emancipation Proclamation," "had no choice"[6] but to enact that measure. In this way Emerson honors the Kantian linkage of nature to necessity. But, in extremes of confinement, the very distinction between the natural, the necessary, and the free disappears. The American institution of slavery was such a confinement. But so is much that, by unquestioned custom, holds the human mind in bondage.

Nature not only liberates, it also initiates into spiritual life. Emerson was more than a monist, in the tradition of the Stoics, Spinoza, and Hegel: he was a Pantheist, if the capitalization of that word connotes more than the Greek word for "all," but the Greek god, Pan, god of nature. For none of our philosophers up to now, with the possible exception of Lucretius, had more pleasure in the sheer observation of natural phenomena, whose "every hour and season yields its tribute of delight" (Nature, 10).[7] In his early book, Nature, Emerson states two meanings of that term and implies a third. Philosophically understood, it is everything not my own mind, including my body; commonly understood, it is any materiality that humanity has not reshaped. Emerson suggests, in his pre-environmentalist age, that the difference between these is negligible, since humanly transformed nature is ultimately in analogy with anthills, and no more disruptive than they of commonly understood nature's whole. That whole introduces the third meaning: "the integrity of impression made by manifold natural objects" (Nature, 9). The integrity of nature's manifold carries the spirituality of it, for nature is an integrity because of that "spirit, that is, the Supreme Being" "behind nature, throughout nature" creating it (Nature, 41). If that spirit turns out to be "me," as Emerson implies in his famous passage at the start of Nature about the transparent eyeball I become as I behold nature—"I am nothing, I see all; the currents of Universal Being circulate through me; I am part or parcel of

God" (*Nature*, 10)—then this spiritual understanding of nature, as an integrated product of spirit, circles back to the philosophical understanding of nature with which he began: whatever, by virtue of issuing from my mind, is not my own mind.

Emerson shares with the other philosophical monists a sense that the challenge to spirituality is not metaphysical, but epistemological—to properly *see*: "To speak truly, few adult persons can see nature" (*Nature*, 10). Seeing and sight are central Emerson tropes. "Sight is the last thing to be pitied" (American Scholar, 68); is the organ of mystical union (Over-Soul, 386); is, in an extension of Descartes' famous *cogito*, an expression of who we are: "As I am, so I see" (Experience, 489). It is the one thing he cannot lose in the woods without losing all (*Nature*, 10). My response to the spirit I see through my spiritual sights is "wild delight," "perfect exhilaration," a sense of "perpetual youth" (*Nature*, 10). It is really myself I see, shorn of the vulnerabilities and frailties of finitude. But it is only via nature that I can see my own infinity. This is the mirror image of the Spinozan and Hegelian claim that the sacred sees itself through us. It is monism from the human vantage point, which already signals a fissure within monism itself which in Emerson's case unfolds into a humanism, as we shall see.

What complicates Emerson and heightens his interest is the growing challenge he himself faced in seeing what Nature promised to show. He seems to know that what fuels his holy naturalism is a gift for metaphor—for easy transitions between words for nature and for spirit—that not everyone shares and can even flag in himself. Like the Neo-Platonism they mimic, Emerson's easy transitions from matter to spirit and back mark two directions, up to spirit and down to matter. The question occurs why the down direction exists at all, and Emerson's only reply is the old Neo-Platonic one that "there seems to be a necessity in spirit to manifest in material forms" (*Nature*, 25). Ever since Stephen Whicher's book on Emerson, *Freedom and Fate*,[8] scholars have distinguished between an early Emerson—optimistic, pantheistic, idealistic—and a late Emerson—realistic, humanistic, pragmatic. For Whicher, the contrast between the two Emersons is one between freedom and fate, joy and resignation. The sorrows of Emerson's own life, of loss and aging, effect the change. But on another reading, the two Emersons are not so different. Emerson was always attuned to the sorrows and disturbances of life, from the "noxious work or company" of *Nature* (14) to the "earthquake and volcano" of "Fate" (945). What changes is the framework of consolation (or "compensation," to quote a famous essay title) for these, in terms of an explanatory structure he never abandons, that of antecedent and consequent. At first, nature is a duo of means and ends, whose means naturally, almost instantly, accomplish the ends; then it is a bifurcation of promise and fulfillment, whose fulfillment stretches beyond sight of the promise; and finally, after the fulfillment has disappeared over the horizon of human seeing, nature becomes a dualism of fate and power. The second term of these three relationships—end, fulfillment, power—carries a humanist overtone. For each of these holds the place of consequent at least in part by virtue of its affirmative implications for human well-being. Part of the point of Nature's end, to be a self-integrating whole, is that humanity can merge with it; and of its fulfillment, that humanity can know of it; and of its power, that humanity can embody it.

In his first book, *Nature*, what interests Emerson are what he calls the uses of nature, that is, the means it carries within it towards its own end. The end of nature is the integrated wholeness of it, with which we humans unite in peak moments of vision. Under the headings of Commodity, Beauty, Language, and Discipline, Emerson arrays the various uses or means of nature he discerns. Very little space of effort separates the means from the end. A mere walk in the woods, where Emerson finds most on display the beauty and language of nature, catapults him to mystic union with the whole. The later Emerson—who had experienced the death of a wife and of a son, obliquely and ascetically memorialized in the "Experience" essay[9] —needed more helps. The problem was that Nature could deceive. The "Nature" essay of the Second Series[10] newly uncovers a trickster dimension to nature, "a slight treachery and derision" (Nature, 553) that surfaces for us on our way from nature to spirit, when the promised spirit fails to appear. Those very woods of the book, *Nature*, that bestowed eternal youth, now practice "a certain enticement and flattery, together with a failure to yield a present satisfaction. This disappointment is felt in every landscape" (Nature, 553). The vision of spirit eludes; or, as the Experience essay from the same series tells us, "nature as we know her is no saint" (Experience, 481). From the still later series, *Conduct of Life*, Emerson directly addresses the problem of "Illusions" in an essay of that name. He sets the scene with the recollection of a trip he took to "Mammoth Cave in Kentucky" (Illusions, 1115) where, without so interpreting the episode, he appears to realize the Platonic myth of the cave. For deep within the cave he and his fellow travelers experience, via light refractions on the crystal rock of the ceiling, a simulation of the starry heavens, which was so beautiful that he had to admit, "the best thing which the cave had to offer was an illusion" (Illusions, 1115). But truth-loving Emerson, who had once, with Keats, equated beauty with truth, "did not like the cave so well for eking out its sublimities with this theatrical trick" (Illusions, 1116). But then, "I have had many experiences like it, before and since" (Illusions, 1116)—"'tis all phantasm" and what once seemed a "firmament" now looks to wiser eyes "an eggshell" (Illusions, 1121).

Emerson has at hand two responses to the illusoriness of nature: one is to plumb nature more deeply for resources *within* it to meet the challenges *of* it; the other is to redirect hopes for humanity away from nature and towards humanity itself, towards its own "self-reliance," to quote his famous essay of that name. His early bifurcation of reality into Nature—which can be understood philosophically or commonly—and "Me," surely invites these two responses. Nature philosophically understood, which soon approaches a scientific view of it,[11] may indeed hold ameliorating surprises in store. But then, the early Emerson would not have conceded that humanity itself represents an *alternative* location of resources for human wellbeing. For nature and humanity, or material and conscious reality are so in sync that whatever manifests in one for human benefit has its analog in the other. It is only as the goods, or uses, of nature become more elusive, and the correspondence between material and conscious reality less sure, that hints appear in Emerson's writing of a humanity whose holiness is its own, unparalleled in nature.

Out of the great fecundity of nature two significant forms unfolded that promised to correct for its illusions: language and law. Emerson was not the first to attribute to these a spiritual office: Kant had done so for law, and Novalis for language. Emerson's innovation was to derive these two forms, which, for those earlier thinkers, operated independently of nature (from out of reason or mind) from within nature itself. Nature was itself a language that moved, according to the section named for it, in *Nature*, from words to facts to spirit. Words were simply the half of language; the other half were the very things language indicated, which were themselves "emblematic" of spirit (*Nature*, 20). If nature, in the form of things, suffered from "disagreeable appearances" (*Nature*, 48), which appeared to obstruct the passage to spirit, then nature, in the form of words, the speech of human beings, would eliminate these. But words so effectual are exceptional; only those who see beyond the appearance of nature speak them—only poets. Where nature in the common sense of all untouched by human hands fails, there that distinctive product of human speech—poetry, fills the breach. Emerson differs from his rationalist predecessors, and allies more with Novalis, in the central role he assigns poetic imagination in the transition from blindness to sight. "Imagination is a very high form of seeing" (The Poet, 459). What we see through our imagination is that nature is a symbolic language asking for translation into the spirit it expresses. Poets hear better than most of us the "precantations" (The Poet, 458) of spirit that hover over natural objects, and transcribe them into musical words, so that the rest of us can see through hearing the spirit behind nature. Nature, which now openly suffers from "the accidency and fugacity" of finite material reality, transforms to symbol, to the "independence of the thought on [or better: from] the symbol" (The Poet, 456). "Poets are thus liberating gods.... They are free and they make free" (The Poet, 462). They free from us those very elements of nature in the common sense that threaten us, by connecting us to nature in the spiritual sense, where "the sordor and filths of nature" are no more (*Nature*, 48).

If the spiritual life is no longer secured by walks in the woods, it may now be no less easily accessed by reading and hearing poetry; except that, "I look in vain for the poet whom I describe" (The Poet, 465). For even "the poet finds himself not near enough to his object," (Nature, 553)—an observation that recalls again Keats on the nightingale, whose song is "buried deep in the next valley-glades" before the poet even knows whether the music was real or dream; but it also asks to be paired with a personal lament from "Experience," over what appears to be Emerson's failure to be moved by the death of his beloved son, Waldo: "In the death of my son . . . I seem to have lost a beautiful estate—no more. I cannot get it nearer to me" (Experience, 473). The passage reads, disturbingly, as a tribute to that very integrity of nature that seamlessly absorbs all loss—the monist's inevitable consolation for all sorrows. But, in illustration of Emerson's own observation elsewhere, that "everything may be affirmed and denied with equal reason" (Spiritual Laws, 308), this passage can also be given the exact opposite sense, especially when read in conjunction with the words from "Nature," just quoted: what Waldo's death cannot bring nearer is any passage to a spiritual meaning beyond it.

Natural law picks up where natural language fails. For what the poet revealed, in the pre-cantations he captured, was nothing less than "the laws of the universe."[12] If the discipline that properly monitors those laws is science, then "science was false by being unpoetical."[13] The parallel between poetry and scientific law—"acid and alkali" make between them "real rhymes"[14] —reprises for us once again the harmony between mind and matter. The laws, like the best rhymes, occur unforced and naturally. Conversely, the natural or uncoerced is also lawful—not by merely obeying law, but by *being* "laws which execute themselves" (Spiritual Laws, 307). "What we call nature is a certain self-regulated motion or change" (The Poet, 457). Law unfolds from nature as what it does when uncoerced. Our morality is our natural state, when we "suffer the law to traverse [our] whole being without obstruction" (Spiritual Laws, 321). The work of saving nature from its potentially disturbing aspects now no longer falls to poets, who see beyond the natural surfaces, but to nature itself, which fulfills its own latent promise in the laws it follows. Where nature seems to have gone awry, it simply has not yet fulfilled its promise. Emerson's model of nature's lawfulness comes less from the burgeoning science of his day, and its framework of cause and effect, than from a much older framework, with roots in the Bible, of promise and fulfillment.[15] Only the biblical model is teleological enough to function redemptively, not merely explanatorily, for nature. The relation between promise and fulfillment now supersedes that of means to end, which characterized *Nature*, where natural means so easily accomplished the end.

The consolatory power of the promise-fulfillment model lies in the expansiveness it allows between the times of promise and fulfillment. Already in *Nature*, a passing and parenthetical thought disturbs the fulfillment of the woodland walker—there is "no calamity (leaving me my eyes) which nature cannot repair" (*Nature*, 10). But then, what of the calamity that takes my eyes, understood either literally or metaphorically, as the means of the all-important seeing?[16] That parenthetically dark insertion into the rosy picture of the woods recalls a fairy tale wedding darkened by the curse of the excluded relative, or, for that matter, the Garden of Eden story inflected towards tragedy by the unaccountable serpent. And in the course of Emerson's own writing time, the problem of a potentially darkened seeing returns.

The very title, "Experience," within Emerson's second collection of essays, startles for its incongruity with what had seemed his idealist-monist trajectory. For idealism, mere experience never provides the preferred means of seeing. Within typologies of philosophy, experience belongs to idealism's opposite—empiricism. But if Emerson stops to consider experience it is not because he has succumbed to a "paltry empiricism" (Experience, 492)—words that reaffirm the idealism, but because experience teaches that nature's fulfillments do not follow instantly on her promises after all. The "astronomical interspaces betwixt atom and atom," (Experience, 481) point to a similarly expansive time between promise and fulfillment; to such an extent that experience becomes a catch-phrase for the great extent of our not-knowing. The "perfect calculation of the kingdom of known cause and effect" (Experience, 482), to which we may foolishly aspire, far exceeds our range of vision. "We have not eyes sharp enough to descry the thread that ties cause and effect" (Fate, 963). Nature in the common sense still carries beneath it a lawfully spiritual structure: "Underneath the inharmonious and trivial particulars is a musical perfection; the Ideal journeying always with us" (Experience, 484). We simply cannot see the full extent of its journey, but only that part of it we happen to be near. Just let me be "apprised of my vicinity" (Experience, 484).

And so we lose our power of vision after all, at least partially. Emerson wants us to acknowledge the loss, which he hangs on a traditional theological concept of long Christian standing: "the Fall of Man" (Experience, 487). By this he means our self-conscious awareness, an interpretation that nicely fits the Genesis story, but philosophically inflected towards Descartes, to connote the suspicion that the senses so necessary to our knowing may actually deceive. Nature still fulfills its promises; it is simply less clear to us what these are. For any project any of us may set himself, "it turns out somewhat new and very unlike what he promised himself" (Experience, 484). Worse: "All promise outruns the performance" (Nature, 552). Our vision no longer registers the fulfillment in store, but instead, at such a distance, inevitably introduces wishful distortions. "People forget that is the eye which makes the horizon" (Experience, 487). Emerson concludes that "God delights to . . . hide from us the past and the future. . . . 'You will not remember,' he seems to say, 'and you will not expect'" (Experience, 483). And so "we must set up the strong present tense" (Experience, 481).

Emerson no longer sounds like a monist in the rationalist tradition— the Stoics, Spinoza, Hegel—but more like Ecclesiastes, who advised us to enjoy the moment. But this is not Emerson's message either. For he is still in thrall of the alpha and omega, "the two termini,"[17] which Ecclesiastes resigned any claim to know. It is just that the alphic promise and omegic fulfillment require different names when they are no longer known. And Emerson supplies them. They are Fate and Power, titles of two essays in his last major book, *The Conduct of Life*. This conversion of names conceals a provocative inversion, too, between antecedent and consequent. What was promised becomes the fated, which, though it functions ordinarily as ending or consequent, is here the antecedent; while the fulfillment, which functions ordinarily as end, converted to power, becomes a new beginning or antecedent. Appropriately, "Fate" is the first essay in the collection, and "Power" the second. It is as though when the distance between the Judeo-Christian promise and fulfillment is stretched to its limit they convert to something else and invert their roles. An inversion of alphabetic ordering occurs in the transition from Promise-Fulfillment to Fate-Power, but one Emerson would prefer, since it restores the natural ordering of "f" before "p."[18]

The fated is what unfolds from what is given at the start. Understood as what beginnings promise, the fated is not a negative notion. Indeed, Emerson hints at the positive meaning of the term when, without explicitly citing St. Paul on the love of God, from which "neither death, nor life, nor angels, nor principalities [etc.]" (Rom 8:38) can separate him, he perhaps comically reflects on the "band" of Fate, which "neither brandy, nor nectar, nor sulphuric ether, nor hell-fire, nor ichor, nor poetry, nor genius can get rid of" (Fate, 952). Biblically literate listeners and readers would hear the Pauline echo. With the Stoics and Spinoza, Emerson appreciates the therapeutic import of necessity—"Beautiful Necessity," as he hymns it at the end of "Fate," "which secures that all is made of one piece" (Fate, 967), including even the "rendings from earthquake and volcano" (Fate, 945) that seem so indifferent to human ends. The fateful unfoldings are lawful—they constitute "the laws of the world" (Fate, 943)—and intelligent. Indeed, the "Law . . . is not [simply] intelligent but intelligence" itself (Fate, 968). By virtue of its intelligence, fate outdoes its own limitations and converts to Power. For Power is simply the response of (human) intelligence to fate. Power is "thought, the spirit which composes and decomposed nature" (Fate, 953). Conversely put, "Fate then is a name for facts not yet passed under the fire of thought—for causes which are unpenetrated" (Fate, 958). Power is the human face of fate—a variation on the theme of parallel tracks for nature and mind—which either concedes to the laws of fate, and so rests in them, or else marshals them to further ends, and so extends their unfolding application. Power is to Fate what fulfillment is to promise, as consequent to antecedent. Fate is fulfilled in the human power that channels it towards the future, when it might otherwise hug too close to the past. Power transforms the seeming limitations of fate into advances, as Emerson elaborates with regard to the skepticisms sometimes linked to fatefulness: "For skepticisms are not gratuitous or lawless, but are limitations of the affirmative statement, and the new philosophy [of Power] must take them in and make affirmations outside of them" (Experience, 487). The last word, which is power's word, is also freedom's and the open horizon's, as accords with Emerson's life-long quest for freedom from the past.[19]

But Power is not license or even force. In Emerson's usage of the word, Power gathers to it some unlikely synonyms, which undermine and even reverse its connotations of forcefulness. Renamed potency, as it functioned in the thought of one of Emerson's predecessors, Friedrich Schelling, it recesses back from reality into the world of priors to reality, of potentials—indeed, of promise, the word for which it partially substitutes in Emerson. Power is partly simply the capacity to see potential, to envision "possible houses and farms," (Power, 974), where the weaker eye only discerns forest or field. But in another sense, power simply *is* potential, the "waste abyss of possibility" (Method of Nature, 122). Far from forceful, power in this sense manifests more, if at all, with the tentativeness and exploratory overtones of tendency (Emerson's word). Thus the power humans have to essay a way "out of fate into freedom" (Fate, 960) does not necessarily accomplish its overt aims, but even "where his [our] endeavors do not yet fully avail, they tell as tendency" (Fate, 960). In this way, human power copies what nature teaches out of fateful law, for, in our observations of nature, "we can point nowhere to anything final; but tendency appears on all hands" (Method of Nature, 121). The Fate-Power construct, we must not forget, supersedes, under the sign of not-knowing, what Promise-Fulfillment claimed to offer knowingly. We do not know the end of nature, but only tendencies that point the way to "any number of particular ends" (Method of Nature, 121). As agents of power, we ourselves inform those tendencies, but no less under the reign of law than what otherwise, apart from us, goes by the name of fate. It is only out of fateful law that the most efficacious instances of power emerge, the "Homer, Zoroaster, or Menu," the "Copernicus, Newton, Laplace" (Fate, 951), who so draw Emerson's attention as representative types of humanity that a selection of them make their way into his *Representative Men*. These individuals are not only products of natural law— Emerson speaks hyperbolically when he calls them "the end to which nature works" (Power, 971)—they themselves operate out of a sense that "things went not by luck, but by law" (Power, 971). "A belief in causality, or strict connection between every trifle and the principle of being . . . characterizes all valuable minds" (Power, 971). The principle of being is simply Law itself, which overarches the nexus of Fate and Power.

From our unknowing location within the reign of law, its operations are not necessarily according to our expectation. This partly explains the earthquakes we would never ourselves legislate. But it also draws to the idea of Power two other unlikely synonyms for it—unlikely for their connotations of the uncontrolled and chaotically dispersed, of reckless abandon[20] : excess and ecstasy. "Exaggeration is in the course of things. Nature sends no creature, no man into the world without adding a small excess of his proper quality" (Nature, 54). More: nature pours itself out in "torrents of tendency" (Fate, 951). It is out of the "infinite distribution" of its resources, its "perpetual inchoation (Method of Nature, 118, 119), that nature generates a "wasteful hospitality" (Method of Nature, 120) towards many forms and states of being, only some of which indicate true tendencies in it. Just that infinite waste is the excess of nature, which tells on us who with our power concede to it, as ecstasy.[21] Ecstasy, which is "the law and cause of nature" (Method of Nature, 127) is the translation into subjectivity of the excess that is objectively nature's. As Emerson summarily unites these several terms, "The whole [of nature] is oppressed by one superincumbent tendency, [and] obeys that redundancy or excess of life which in conscious beings we call *ecstasy*" (Method of Nature, 121). If earthquake is excess, then, even in all the tragedy of its consequence, there is room within the psyche of the human response to it for ecstasy.[22]

Emerson never lost his hope in the Spinozan principle of correspondence between nature and mind. The correspondence is so close that the subjectivity of the one converts without notice into the objectivity of the other. Humanity is the cross-over point of the conversion. Humanity's "health and greatness consist in his being the channel through which heaven flows to earth [or mind to matter], in short, in the fullness in which the ecstatical state takes place in him" (Method of Nature, 125). In the act of conversion—the less religious and more naturalistic term, metamorphosis, is what Emerson prefers—subject and object morph. So nature can appropriate the subjectivity of ecstasy, and we humans, the objectivity of excess. We are the master mediators, "betwixt two else unmarriageable facts" (Method of Nature, 123), in imitation of Emerson himself, the poet of wavering boundaries and elided contradictions. For it suddenly seems that we have been walking a tightrope—a "hair's breadth" (Experience, 482)—all along between, on either side of us, law and freedom, predictability and spontaneity, expectation and surprise. Though everything that happens is strictly by law, surprise is one of the "threads on the loom of time" (Experience, 490). Indeed, "life is a series of surprises" (Experience, 483). And one of these may come to Emerson's reader, who is suddenly not sure if transparency, as of the all-seeing eyeball, or illusion, as in the Mammoth Cave, is ultimately setting the spiritual tone. For part of what incorporates surprise into the loom of life is the play of illusion, which seems to lift its veil off our sight, when it does, for the sheer purpose of replacing it with our knowing consent. Perhaps this is yet one more instance of how fate becomes power. The representative men Emerson admires act out of a "good natured admission that there are illusions" (Illusions, 1119), and that without them, whatever power I have could not show: "For no man can . . . do anything well, who does not esteem his work to be of importance. My work may be of none, but I must not think it of none, or I shall not do it with impunity" (Nature, 551).

If Emerson lived knowingly inside an illusion, and commended the same stance to his readers, then his tone would be ironical, like Kierkegaard's in his philosophical work. But Emerson is not ironical here—just the opposite. Caught on the contradiction between transparency and illusion, Emerson tips towards tragedy. He finds in the complaint of a child, who, at the second telling of a bedtime story misses the delight he felt at the first, "the plaint of tragedy" (Experience, 477) which turns on endless variations of this storied theme: "thou wert born to a whole and this story is a particular" (Experience, 477). We were born to a wholesomeness of knowledge we can never have, like the eminent inhabitants of Limbo in Dante's *Inferno*, who longingly know of, without knowing, the Christian truths. By the time of *The Conduct of Life* the best that remains to us, "the great day of the feast of life" (Fate, 955), is the old Stoic and Spinozan conviction that "what is must be" (Fate, 955). Our comfort is our conviction of the "omnipresence of law" (Fate, 955), ignorant as we may be of the law's specifics. Emerson's last picture for us, from that collection of essays, takes up again the image of the tragic child, now a "young mortal," whose life is adrift in "snow-storms of illusions" (Illusions, 1123), for no sooner is one uncovered than another replaces it, until "for an instant, the air clears" (Illusions, 1124). But Emerson has so contrived to leave us in doubt whether this clearing is just another illusion—for already by his designation, the "young mortal" is a character from Greek mythology at the feet of an evocation of Mount Olympus, in sight of gods the reader knows do not exist. The vision of nature's whole recedes into myth.

"Illusions" is an exceptional essay in *Conduct of Life*. Michael Lopez suggests that it is the one essay in that late collection that diverges from what is otherwise its dominant theme: Power.[23] As his own powers faded, and his monism paled, Emerson may indeed have been on a power-quest. And on that path he assuredly indulges an old theodicy claiming that troubles assail us so that we can prove our strength against them.[24] But significantly, and in his bifurcating way, he denies it the final word of the book, which closes on a skeptical note, more in tune with—to contrast two of his "representative men"—Montaigne than Napoleon. Perhaps the import of "Illusions" in *Conduct of Life* is to temporarily lift the veil off the necessary illusions of the earlier essays, whose business, after all, is activity that would not occur unless it (falsely) believed in its own efficacy. It is difficult otherwise to square the endorsements of will occurring in the late work, with the dismissals of it in the earlier,[25] especially when, by the late concept of fate, it is so unnecessary—except as a useful illusion.

Lawrence Buell helpfully suggests that the subsuming contradiction within Emerson's writing is "the tension between monism and individuality."[26] At first, the whole empowers the individual to see clearly and freely and establishes her in her individuality (free of past particularities, inheritances, legacies reaching with a ghoulish deathlessness from past to present). But as the demarcating bounds of the whole recede, so that we register neither beginning nor end, the eyeball loses its transparency and begins to obfuscate; it and the other senses "interfere everywhere" (Illusions, 116) with the reality we thought we knew. Our perverse refusal to see the whole, when it is so open to us, especially in the woods, becomes an inability to see very far at all, from within the woods or anywhere. That transition from willed to imposed separation from the whole changes the spiritual mood. Monism may still be Emerson's metaphysics, but it no longer supplies his psychology. Once it was as though reality was a miraculous circle with one circumference but multiple centers, enough for each us to occupy our own, but from which all of us could see clear through to the common circumference. By the time of Emerson's essay, "Circles," the image has changed. We are still at the center of our own circle. But now no circumference expands to the whole of reality. Instead, "around every circle another can be drawn . . . [and] there is no end in nature" (Circles, 403).[27] That every circumscribing circle can be further circumscribed ultimately eliminates circumference as such: "there is no inclosing wall, no circumference to us" (Circles, 405). Emerson has exploded a classic image of self-containment—the circle—into one of indefinite open-endedness. The separation from the whole that was once a function of correctible illusion is now part of the fabric of reality and our place in it. More: the centered but uncircumferenced human identity now resembles a picture of God Emerson has from Augustine, and which opens the essay: "St. Augustine described the nature of God as a circle whose centre was everywhere, and its circumference nowhere" (Circles, 403). Now humanity fits that image, except that we are multiple circles populating the "everywhere" with our many centers. Divinity is pluralized humanity.

By the parallelism of nature and humanity, any holiness in the one would naturally show in the other. Emerson preaches the divinity of humanity from early on. But predictably, as the character of nature's holiness changes so does humanity's. At first, the divinity in us is the divinity outside us, in nature itself. From *Nature*'s "the currents of the Universal Being circulate through me" (10) to "The Over-Soul"'s "One blood runs uninterruptedly an endless circulation through all men" (399), or "Circle"'s "God is in me" (407), humanity's divinity is monistic. Our sacredness is in our unity with nature itself and one another. It is simply our benighted vision that cannot see that. But as nature pulls away from us, leaving us only the image of its laws, a distance newly informs our interrelationships as well. In fact, the intimacy of shared blood was never secure from the start. The unity with Universal Being could positively mute the sense of connection even with close friends, who become in contrast "a trifle and disturbance" (*Nature*, 10). In *Nature*, Emerson is only interested in the "uses" of Nature's parts towards realizing the peak vision of the whole. Friendship functions there as a "Discipline" (the title of chapter 5 of the book) towards that end. The friend who has come to teach us something about the relation of the parts to the whole soon converts into that teaching and, now our possession in the form of "sweet wisdom," "is commonly withdrawn from our sight in a short time" (*Nature*, 31). The operant psychology there is indeed monistic. On the one hand, friendship "treat[s] its object as a god, that it may deify both" (Friendship, 354). But on the other, friends "descend to meet" (Over-Soul, 391). "We walk alone in the world. Friends . . . are dreams and fables" (Friendship, 352); and there is a "gulf between every me and thee" (Experience, 488) and a "solitude to which every man is always returning" (Experience, 492). If proximity between friends excludes from each the divinity of the other, then Emerson's monism effectively undercuts the very spirituality of friendship he seems to want to promote. For spirituality is only effective as it connects to, not further distances, the divine. It is as though no direct connection exists between human beings, but they can know each other only from afar via the Nature with which they all potentially unite. But in that case, the human connection is merely an incidental and dispensable consequence of union with nature. Humans in themselves are not a spiritual resource for each other, but an obstacle to spiritual life.

Emerson seems an unlikely teacher of any humanistic spirituality, if only because those among his most intimate relations, his friends, appear to distance the holiness they hold in the very act of approaching him—an impression they received from Emerson and lamented.[28] And yet, despite himself, he had his friends and, up to a point, welcomed them as he wished to, as bearers of holiness. "I find them, or rather not I, but the Deity in me and in them derides and cancels the thick walls of individual character" (Friendship, 343). In describing such meetings, Emerson reprises the ecstatic language of the woods. The company of my friend makes "a young world for me again. . . . The earth is metamorphosed; there is no winter and no night; all tragedies, all ennuis, vanish" (Friendship, 342). The language recalls the opening words of *Nature*, which find in the woods "perpetual youth" and joy alone, "from breathless noon to grimmest midnight" (Nature, 10). That the meetings occur over a great distance, never wholly effaced, guarantees the holiness of the encounter.

As Emerson's monism recedes, a space opens up over which the holiness within humans can communicate between humans, without the medium of an all-embracing and all-effacing nature. The goals he advised humanity to have in its intercourse with nature—"your end should always be one inapprehensible to the senses; then will it be a god always approached, never touched, always giving health (Method of Nature, 128)—transfer to his understanding of relationship with the friend, who speaks over a genuine distance, but does indeed communicate.[29] It is as though nature has unexpectedly ceded to friendship the language of redemption it jealously keeps to itself throughout most of Emerson. The essay on Illusions casts doubt on whether we can ever recover even momentary visions of Nature's whole. But it never doubts the possibility of friendship, for "in the worst-sorted connections there is ever some mixture of true marriage" (Illusions, 1119); and, despite all the veils that hide us even from ourselves, there is something we "really are . . . that avails with friends, with strangers and with fate or fortune" (Illusions, 1122)—if not with nature itself. That modest reality of myself, which is not the Whole or Nature, but stands in for all selves, commands the respect even of Fate, the leading idea of *Conduct of Life*. Emerson may merely mean that human friendship is a datum, among others, in the workings of fateful law. But, that what we are *avails* or counts with fate suggests something more, as though, echoing an old Kantian teaching, natural law surrenders its sway at the threshold of human friendship. If, having exhausted the spiritual possibilities of nature, Emerson has left us at door of our friend, then he anticipates those twentieth century religious humanisms that locate the sacred in the human other, such as we find in Buber, Levinas, and possibly Derrida.[30]

Part of Emerson's motive in divinizing humanity was to advance the cause of freedom. A divinized humanity was no longer enslaved to tradition, the past, the ancestors. But a perhaps unintended consequence of this view—illustrating his teaching that what unfolds from our promise is not necessarily what we expect—is a sanctifying distance between humans who, by their very divinity, nonetheless attract each other. The attraction over distance is not necessarily a contradiction, characterize as it may Emerson's own conflicted friendships. Distance works here less in the service of freedom (from the past), than of relation, which needs a distance to bridge. In a humanist spirituality of friendship, freedom (from) is less important than connection (with). If no one thing unites all things, then the means of connection between a plurality of things presses for consideration. "Relation and connection are not somewhere and sometimes, but everywhere and always" (Fate, 958). It is just the absence of monism that heightens the import of relation. Robert Richardson suggests that "friendships were increasingly important to Emerson"[31] in his late life, when he wrote the lecture, "Fate"—more so than in the early days of the conflicted "Friendship" essay, as though the propensity to reflect on friendship were a compensation for its troubled state or even absence, as indeed Kierkegaard might say.

In the context of a humanist response to nature's disappointments, Emerson's veiled mourning for Waldo takes on new meaning. It is not just a case of Yankee reserve, much less the consolations of an omnivorous monism that leaves no sorrow undigested. What Waldo establishes is the holy distance that sanctifies the human soul and moves it beyond reach of all facile consolations. Had Emerson been more attuned to Christianity's roots in Judaism, he might have found comfort in the Jewish prayer for the dead, or Kaddish, which tributes the divine by, among other things, locating God beyond all consolations. That sanctifying transcendence is no longer the monotheistic god's, but the human soul's. Emerson never did break wholly free of his (Judeo)-Christian roots. But perhaps more persuasively than any other of our philosophers, he showed how easily religious categories adapt to philosophical uses. Had he been less burdened by his religious past, he might have written more warmly and affirmatively not just on the uses of nature, but of religion, too, as William James will in fact do.

NOTES

1. Emerson, "Fate," in *Essays and Lectures*, ed. Joel Porte (New York: Library of America, 1983), 946. Succeeding citations from essays in this book are cited parenthetically in the text.

2. "For a writer who equates beauty and truth as closely as Emerson does, it is surprising that he makes no mention . . . of the concluding lines from "Ode on a Grecian Urn." Helen Haworth, "Emerson's Keats," *Harvard Library Bulletin* 19 (1971): 61.

3. "Perhaps no single term in Emerson's lexicon is more important for understanding his multivalent achievement." William Rossi, "Emerson, Nature and Natural Science," in *A Historical Guide to Ralph Waldo Emerson*, ed. Joel Myerson (New York: Oxford University Press, 2000), 102.

4. Emerson, "The Fugitive Slave Law," in *The Selected Writings of Ralph Waldo Emerson*, ed. Brooks Atkinson (New York: Modern Library, 1950), 861.

5. Ibid.

6. Emerson, "The Emancipation Proclamation," in *The Selected Writings of Ralph Waldo Emerson*, 889.

7. Or again, from the later essay, "Nature": "It seems as if the day was not wholly profane in which we have given heed to some natural object" (Nature, 542).

8. Stephen Whicher, *Freedom and Fate: An Inner Life of Ralph Waldo Emerson* (Philadelphia: University of Pennsylvania Press, 1971).

9. For an understanding of the mutely expressed grief in this essay, over his son's death, see Julie Ellison, "Tears for Emerson: *Essays, Second Series*," in *The Cambridge Companion to Ralph Waldo Emerson*, ed. Joel Porte and Saundra Morris (New York: Cambridge University Press, 1999, 140–161.

10. In what follows, the essay, "Nature," is cited in simple Roman type (as Nature), and the book, *Nature*, is cited in italics (as *Nature*).

11. Robert Richardson notes that "Emerson always had a keen interest in the imaginative and creative aspect of scientific discovery." Robert Richardson, *Emerson: The Mind on Fire* (Berkeley: University of California Press, 1995), 563.
12. Emerson, "Poetry and Imagination," in *Emerson's Complete Works* (Boston: Houghton Mifflin, 1894), v. 8, p.41.
13. Ibid., 15.
14. Ibid., 51.
15. More strictly, Emerson reads on top of a scientific mode of explanation he respects, of cause and effect, a teleology of promise and fulfillment, the way a transparency of the human circulatory system is read over a figure of the human body in an anatomy text.
16. In fact, Emerson did suffer from eye disease as a young man, uveitis, as Richardson recounts, *Emerson*, 63.
17. Emerson, "Natural History of the Intellect," in *Emerson's Complete Works*, v. 12, p. 13.
18. As Branka Arsic puts it in her sparkling study of Emerson, he inhabits a "dialectics of departing-arriving, or ending-beginning." Branka Arsic, *On Leaving: A Reading in Emerson* (Cambridge, MA: Harvard University Press, 2010), 9.
19. This inverts the interpretation of Stephen Whicher in *Freedom and Fate*, according to whom freedom, which occupied pride of place in the early Emerson, ceded that status to an oppositional fate, in the late Emerson. Rather, it seems that the early freedom and the late fate were both variations on the theme of promise, which found its complement, in the early writing, in the notion of fulfillment, and in the late writing, in the notion of power.
20. "The way of life is wonderful; it is by abandonment" (Circles, 414).
21. The ecstatic can manifest in physical challenge, as "mythologists" observe about ancient Greece and Rome, where "defects are ascribed to divine natures, as lameness to Vulcan . . . to signify exuberances" (The Poet, 455).
22. Emerson does not shrink from the consequences of this, but asserts that, "the mind that is parallel with the laws of nature will be in the current of events, and strong with their strength," come what may, or "whatever shall happen" (Power, 972). Again: "Every jet of chaos which threatens to exterminate us is convertible by intellect into wholesome force" (Fate, 958).
23. Michael Lopez, "*The Conduct of Life*: Emerson's Anatomy of Power," in *The Cambridge Companion to Ralph Waldo Emerson*, 253–254.
24. After the Holocaust, this is a thoroughly untenable theodicy.
25. For the early Emerson, "will" is one of the antonyms of nature and the natural. He celebrates "the preponderance of nature over will in all practical life" (Spiritual Laws, 306). "Let us draw a lesson from nature. . . . The walking of man and all animals is a falling forward" (Spiritual Laws, 308). Whereas, for the later Emerson, "The one serious and formidable thing in nature is a will," and "the conversion of the man into his will, making him the will and the will him" (Fate, 957).
26. Lawrence Buell, *Emerson* (Cambridge, MA: Harvard University Press, 2003), 207.
27. "Nature is intricate, overlapped, interweaved, and endless." (Fate, 961).
28. See Jeffrey Steele, "Transcendental Friendship: Emerson, Fuller, and Thoreau," in *Cambridge Companion to Ralph Waldo Emerson*.
29. Lawrence Buell suggests that Emerson's gift for letter-writing especially suited his friendship-style, which, at play between the sacred distance and possibly searing closeness of the friend, erred on the side of distance. Buell, *Emerson*, 81
30. According to John Caputo, Derrida generalizes from the otherness of the monotheistic god to otherness as such, however it manifests. "That every other is wholly other, that every other bears the trace of God, would then be the work done by the name of God." John Caputo, *Prayers and Tears of Jacques Derrida: Religion Without Religion*. (Bloomington: Indiana University Press, 1997), 202.

31. Richardson, *Emerson*, 510. This was shortly after one of Emerson's closest friends, Margaret Fuller, had died. Fuller illustrates with regard to Emerson the Emersonian ideal of friendship, as interpreted by Cavell and Arsic: someone who pulls us, even against our will, towards a better version of ourselves. See Christina Zwarg, *Feminist Conversations: Fuller, Emerson, and the Play of Reading* (Ithaca, NY: Cornell University Press, 1995). According to Zwarg, "Fuller enables him to unsettle himself" (Zwarg, 44). John Lysaker suggests that the lecture form itself always pushed Emerson towards the intersubjective, which underlies "the responsive pathos of the Emersonian essay." John Lysaker, "Taking Emerson Personally," in *New Morning: Emerson in the Twenty-First Century*, ed. Arthur Lothstein and Michael Brodrick (Albany: State University of New York Press, 2008), 135.

TWELVE

William James

What William James himself calls "the uses of religion"[1] was a central topic for him. He is the first of our philosophers expressly to plumb religion as a source of philosophical spirituality. One of his own stated interests was "Man's Religious Appetites" and "Their Satisfaction through Philosophy" (xv). If William James, the philosopher, had enough distance from religion to conceive it sympathetically, he has Emerson, in part, to thank for that. For James' father, Henry Sr., who heard, read, and assimilated Emerson, supplied the generation of distance from normative religion that allowed William to return to it with a receptive and appreciative mind. But then, William, who also himself admired and read Emerson, indeed drew comfort from him in depressive moments, followed his own Emersonian lead when he wrote his now classic *Varieties of Religious Experience* (hereafter, *Varieties*)—at least insofar as Emerson's essay on "Experience," marked the older writer's turn from a holy naturalism to a more complex and muted spirituality of the human. And one of William's words for his own pragmatic philosophy was: humanism.

James was circumspect and somewhat conflicted about his own religious life. Though he clearly did not identify as Christian, he gave mixed messages on the extent to which he himself enjoyed religious experience of any kind. Once he confessed to a "state of spiritual alertness," occasioned, as Emerson might prescribe, by a walk in the mountains, when it was "as if the gods of all the nature mythologies were holding an indescribable meeting in my breast."[2] But then, he also denied of himself any living experience of the Divine, which "for my active life is limited to abstract concepts."[3] The second confession follows the first by six years, as though he had either forgotten the nature experience or could not credit it. If he could not credit it, perhaps it was because, on reflection, though he enjoyed nature he was skeptical of it as a spiritual resource[4];

or perhaps, the hypothetical quality of his interpretation—it was "as if" gods were present—counted against it, as it might not have had William had the gifts of literary imagination his brother Henry had. For Henry, who reveled in the subjunctive, did present an Edenic bliss in one of his ghostly tales, "The Great Good Place,"[5] which, inspired by William's experience might have had a natural setting, rather than the architectural one the so much more urban and town-loving Henry supplied for the story.

William's reserve on his own religious life positioned him all the better for the role he saw himself playing, of "mediator between scientific agnosticism and the religious view of the world."[6] That mediating role opened space for a distinctive office, to interpret the extent to which one person's religious experiences could provide evidence or authority for another's religious belief, or even spark in that other a religious experience of her own. For, as James understood what he took for the most paradigmatic and definitive of all religious experience—mysticism, it was self-authenticating for whomever had it; it supplied knowledge of the divine, or was noetic (371–372) but only for the subject of the experience. The experience carried for the subject what James called "immediate luminousness" (19). But no one else, outside the experience, could be expected to be persuaded by accounts of it. All the same, James took it for a project to make the best case possible for the evidence the phenomenon of religious experience supplies—not to those who have it, but to those who philosophically, disinterestedly observe it in others—for actual sacred realms.

So as not to beg the question, James defined religious experience as noncommittally as he could. It was "the feelings, acts, and experiences of individual men in their solitude, so far as they apprehend themselves to stand in relation to whatever they may consider the divine" (31–32). This definition already commits him to *some* things—to a cultivated indifference to doctrine, community or ritual as contexts for religious experience, as has often been noted about James' work; but also to some role for belief, if the experience is to occur at all. James' definition implies that religious experience will not occur except for those who have at hand some believable conception or other of the divine, as he late in the book confirms, though in a complex sentence more of his brother's style: "the spiritual excitement in which the gift [of religious experience] appears a real one will often fail to be aroused in an individual until certain particular beliefs or ideas which, as we say, come home to him, are touched" (504). And this becomes a problem for the philosopher of religion, who, in her analysis of religious experience, must extract the "feelings, acts, and experiences" from the interpretive overlay of "whatever they [who have those feelings, etc.] may consider divine". James' assumption is that the latter, howsoever essential to the religious person, vary too much to be of significant epistemological use to the philosopher of religion, while the former are constant enough already to argue for their veridicality. James' own categories of analysis heighten the look of commonality especially among the *feelings* of religious experience. For as he summarizes it at his most concise, the core of religious experience is a feeling of release from a formerly pervasive uneasiness (498). Out of that core emerges the logical structure of the book, which traces a path from uneasiness (in the chapters on "The Sick Soul" and "The Divided Self") to "Conversion," where the self now unites; to the other-regarding energy that overflows the now united self ("Saintliness"); to "Mysticism," where the inner unity expands to a sense of union with the divine. Much of the book comprises quotations from largely autobiographical narratives, written by others, illustrating these several categories. And that is one of the goals of what James calls the Science of Religions, to enable "impartial classifications and comparisons" (424) among the experiences themselves, or accounts of them.[7]

Part of what favors the look of commonality among the experiences is that, by James' conscious decision, almost all of them are somehow extreme, tending at their most unhappy towards suicide and at their most mystical towards ecstasy. This drew to the book its somewhat dismissive renaming by critics: "Wild Religions I Have Known."[8] James defends his decision on scientific grounds: the intensity of the experiences is in analogy with the microscopic enlargement of scientific specimens that allows them to be more easily studied. But the decision has this additional strategic use for him, that it allies the experiences with pathologies that were understood even in James' day to have their origins in the subconscious. Such an association seems at first to count against the experiences; but in fact it aids them by supplying a scientifically acceptable explanation for why they seem, to those who have them, to be unwilled gifts of grace, conferring knowledge of another world. What comes from beyond our conscious awareness seems to come from beyond us; but the subconscious is by definition beyond our conscious awareness; so whatever is grounded there seems to come from beyond.

The last leg of the argument is the hardest. On what basis does the observer in others of these intense, subconsciously grounded experiences, take them for evidence of the sacred? James admits there is no sure basis for that inference. But he confesses that he is so "impressed by the importance of these phenomena" (513), that is, the religious experiences, that he cannot but "adopt the hypotheses which they so naturally suggest" (513), that they originate beyond the subconscious in a higher consciousness that wishes us well. It is as though what James calls the noetic character of mystical experience is so powerful that it extends its reach beyond the mystic herself to the philosophical observer in others of mystical experiences. The well-wishing of the higher consciousness is evident in the issue of its effect on us, to make us happier, better human beings (saints and mystics). James fills in what he frankly characterizes as "overbelief" (503) on his part, that:

> The world of our present consciousness is only one out of many worlds of consciousness that exist, and that those other worlds must contain experiences which have a full meaning for our life also; and that although in the main their experiences and those of this world are kept separate, yet the two become continuous at certain points, and higher energies filter in (509).

James explains that the evidence of religious experience is only for some form(s) of higher consciousness, which may be either singular or plural. The philosophical problem with religious experience is its open-endedness. The sense of the real it carries is an "enlargement of perception which seems imminent but never completes itself" (375). The universe governed by such a sacred incompletion must be "unfinished."[9] If we name such a sacredness God, we must understand that this "is the name not of the whole of things . . . but only of the ideal tendency in things, believed in as a superhuman person who calls us to cooperate in his purposes."[10] What happens in religious experience is that the ideal tendencies that constitute the higher consciousness(es), normally separate from us, scale the barriers of separation, which for some of us are unusually low to begin with, so that we momentarily become with it (them) "co-conscious."[11] The co-conscious nature of the union accounts for the sense mystics have that they are in touch with something "which in one sense is part of ourselves and in another sense is not ourselves" (513). These mergings of consciousness are ecstatic moments for mystics, but also promises of better times to come for us all, when happy convergences of like kind will saturate reality. Here James reprises the old Emersonian, and still older Judeo-Christian theme of promise-fulfillment. As the old monotheisms taught, the fulfillment is sometime ineluctably future. What is really and finally worthy to be called "the Absolute, God, Spirit or Design"[12] is a possibility not yet realized.

What is startlingly different about this picture of the sacred, from all we have encountered before, is its location in the future, rather than the present or indeed outside time altogether. A definitively temporal sacred bucks the grain of the ancient, Boethian preference for eternity. It is a stress on logic for the sacred to operate out of a realm of possibility. But we already noted, within Emerson's work, how via the mediating notion of potency, the distinction between the potential and the powerful elides. And James presents the over-belief, without pointedly owning it, that "the God with whom . . . we come into . . . [co-conscious] commerce [is] . . . the absolute world-ruler" (508), on grounds that the peace and happiness of the encounter would not otherwise persuade. Also new in this account of the sacred is what almost seems a deliberate fuzziness on the nature of its distinction from us and the world of ordinary experience.

Against a monotheistic inheritance, the notion that the sacred itself is future, and not just its redemption of the world, already implicitly conflates the sacred with the world. And as coworkers towards the full realization of the sacred, "we are indeed internal parts of God and not external creations."[13] Nonetheless, as much as the ontological distinction between us and God may fade in James, the epistemological separation remains. The larger consciousness with which we become co-conscious in religious experience is actually "discontinuous with ordinary consciousness" (379). James underscores the "practical difficulties" (499) of achieving and sustaining co-consciousness. Few of us actually are mystics. That is the underlying motivation for James' book: to wrest from the intense religious experience of others some measure of believability in the otherwise doubtful sacred realms they point to.

James' claims for his achievement are modest. James asks philosophy, when it wants to study and learn from religion, to abandon its inherited pretensions to metaphysics and "transform herself . . . into science of religions" (445). This is what philosophy should become when it sets its sights on religion. But though the philosopher may derive from the study of other persons' religious experiences warrant for her own religious belief, the science of religion cannot itself substitute for religious life, may indeed inhibit it (480). But it seems to be only James the scientist who feels obliged to say this. James the empathic psychologist indirectly admits through the back door a spiritual dimension to the "mere" study of religion. For example, in a letter about the science of religions, he characterizes his work on the *Varieties of Religious Experience* as "*my* religious act,"[14] as though to imply that his very recounting, classifying and philosophizing upon the religious experiences of others constitute perhaps a secondary or derivative religious experience of his own, rather like Johannes de Silentio, who in reflecting on the knight of faith seems to encounter the sacred by proxy. Reflecting within the book on some of the narratives of saintliness James gathered there, he writes that merely to read in them "is to feel encouraged and uplifted and washed in better moral air" (254). This would suggest that the science of religion is itself a spiritual enterprise. At one place in the book, the distinction between James's own spiritual life and his philosophic study of others' spiritual lives breaks down, when he presents a narrative ostensibly from the French about an experience of "horrible dread," stimulated by the writer's memory of an asylum inmate who impressed him as "absolutely non-human"—what utterly unnerves the writer is the sudden realization that nothing in theory separates him from the inmate, "*that shape am I*" (157). The writer implies that what made this a religious experience was the memory of biblical passages that sustained him through it. But the religiosity of the passage does not require any biblical overlay, as it already evokes, in dark parody, the famous pantheistic claim of the Upanishads: that thou art (*tat tvam asi*).[15] James later confessed that this experience was his own.[16] Perhaps from embarrassment, modesty or desire to maintain the appearance of scientific detachment within the framework of the text, James conceals that from the reader.

From another angle, though, it is strange that James does not own his religious experiences in the context of his book. For, in quest of the spiritual import of religion for philosophy, there would seem no more valuable witness than the religious experiences of philosophers themselves, of whom James was certainly one. But philosophers' accounts of their own religious experiences receive remarkably little play in the book. An exemplary candidate for illustration would have been Spinoza, whose lovely autobiographical passage introducing *The Improvement of the Understanding* is not quoted at all. James cites Spinoza, but only to illustrate the worldview of the religiously healthy-minded, that set of souls who lack the deepening sense of suffering and evil, who do indeed receive a chapter of their own at the start of the book, but whose view of the world is rather like a frozen smile, constricted by a blindly shallow optimism.[17] This hardly does justice to Spinoza. James implies, in his discussion of Marcus Aurelius, that the problem with philosophical religious experiences is that they are "so cool and reasonable that we are tempted to call them philosophical rather than religious" (45), as though he had forgotten an aim he stated on the first page of his book, to exhibit, if not here at some later time, the satisfaction of religious impulses through philosophy. For William, one of the problems with philosophical religious experience, especially of the stoic type that both Marcus and Spinoza exhibit, is that it is not *passionate* enough. As opposed to subdued philosophy, James tells us, "we shall see how infinitely passionate a thing religion at its highest flights can be" (47).

This reference to the import of passion, with its dismissive overtones towards philosophy, calls to mind Kierkegaard. That Kierkegaard wrote in Danish and was so relatively unknown to Anglophones until the twentieth century makes for a great missed opportunity, for James to have read and interpreted Kierkegaard. For James, as sympathetic observer of religious experience in others, assumes a pose remarkably close to Johannes de Silentio's, and raises with him the same question of the religious value of *observing* others' religious experience. James even unknowingly echoes Johannes' thought or language in places, for example, about "converted men" that they "as a class are indistinguishable from natural men" (233)—this was one of Johannes' concerns about the knight of faith in comparison with ordinary persons; or about religious feeling generally, in contrast with philosophy, which is meant to suffer in the comparison, that it allows itself to "pass for paradoxical and absurd" (423); or even about "fear and trembling" (450) itself, a phrase James employs though to opposite effect of Johannes' use of it.[18] Kierkegaard's passionate, iconoclastic, church-rejecting Christianity would certainly have appealed to James. His multi-voiced authorship would surely have intrigued James, whose book on religion is, after all, largely an assemblage of other voices.

Only a few decades after James' death, Kierkegaard was known well enough to American readers that Columbia University professor of philosophy, James Randall, could comment about his reception in the United States. In 1948 he wrote that Americans "convert Kierkegaard, if they can take him seriously—few Americans can—into the demand for an adequate psychotherapy and proceed to explore eagerly the appropriate techniques for getting over it."[19] That is to say, Americans take Kierkegaard pragmatically, as perhaps James would have. Existentialism—if this is the movement Kierkegaard foretells—rests uneasily next to pragmatism. Still, for all their differences in tone, style and belief, James and Kierkegaard are partners in protest against their looming idealist predecessors, Hegel and Emerson. James spoke appreciatively of Emerson at the 1903 centennial of his birth, in Concord.[20] But, as Kierkegaard might have said of Hegel, James' critique of Emerson is that he lets "God evaporate into abstract Ideality" (32). Emerson suffers from the same constricted optimism that Spinoza does.[21]

In fact, at several places in his work, James cites a passage from Kierkegaard he had in translation from the European philosophy he read. In *Pragmatism* we read, "We live forwards, a Danish thinker has said, but we understand backwards."[22] The comment captures another side of James who, in addition to the passively received deliverances of the subconscious, took for a major topic of philosophic interest the accomplishments of the conscious will. In some matters, certainty can only be had retrospectively, of past time; within the present and towards the future, we actively and consciously choose without certainty and so inevitably at risk of wrongness. That is the import of Kierkegaard's remark, whose context may be taken for the life ways that array themselves before us without a supervening rationale for choosing one over the other. For Kierkegaard, we have already chosen before we have begun to think, and the role of thought is simply to reveal to us the choice we have made and, perhaps, the alternatives to it. For James, the matter of religious belief is still open. But from a position outside it we cannot expect our understanding to escort us into it. If we will, we can risk the religious life. As James puts it in the closing words of *Varieties of Religious Experience*, "for practical life ... the *chance* of salvation is enough (516).

With this closing comment, James highlights a key distinction between those who have religious experiences, for whom those experiences are authoritative, and those who merely study them for evidence of the sacred. For the former, there is no experience of risk in believing; there is only that for the latter. For powerful as the noetic quality of mystical experience is, even to the mere observer of it, it is still subject to doubt. The evidence of its veridicality can tip either for or against it. But this is just the framework for James' earlier essay, "The Will to Believe," where he argues that where important decisions must be made, as, for example, about the existence of God, but without compelling evidence for either of several choices, we have moral permission to follow our will. Indeed, the participation of our will may be required even for the needed evidence to unfold. We are now outside the passive realm of the subconscious and within the active realm of the conscious. We are also now within bounds of the overarching philosophy James himself espoused—pragmatism.

Pragmatism offers philosophy another channel—alternative to religious experience—for exploring religion's significance to it. For pragmatism, in James' hands, is itself almost by definition a harmonizer, and so already a force for the fuller integration of reality where the future sacred lies. "Believing in philosophy myself devoutly,"[23] James is nonetheless chagrined by the historic division within it between empiricism and rationalism. "The pragmatic method is primarily a method of settling metaphysical disputes."[24] In an itemized contrast between the two, rationalism shows itself to be "tender-minded, intellectualistic, idealistic [and, most importantly here] religious" while empiricism is "tough-minded, sensationalistic, materialistic, irreligious."[25] The modern American temperament wants the religiosity of the rationalist conjoined with respect for what the senses show. And this is just what pragmatism supplies in its orientation towards the consequences of religious belief. The beliefs themselves are tender-minded and idealistic, but the consequences in a more fully integrated reality must show in a visibly more harmonized world. Religion understood pragmatically combines the features of rationalism and empiricism, in furtherance of the very integration that pragmatism takes for hallmark of the future sacred.

Ironically, this integrative work happens at the expense of union in James's own thought. For it has not been lost on interpreters of James that the science of religions and pragmatism are scarcely harmonizable channels for philosophy.[26] In several ways, pragmatism inverts the philosophical orientation of the *Varieties of Religious Experience*, whose investigations are of the origins of religious belief in the subconscious. Pragmatism draws our attention rather "towards last things, fruits, consequences, facts."[27] The pragmatic justification of religious beliefs is in the results of holding them, in lives more fully and harmoniously integrated with their surroundings. The passions which intensify religious experience ally with a notion of passivity—they are "gifts to us from sources . . . always nonlogical and beyond our control" (148); whereas the very root meaning of "pragmatism," as James tells us, is "action."[28] Pragmatically speaking, "true thoughts" are simply "instruments of action."[29] What pragmatism especially activates is the will, for example, the "will to believe."[30] Indeed, the notion of God as "a general cosmological theory of promise," who holds the place of a future realized holiness of harmony, is so connected to the agency of will working towards that end that the two are virtually synonymous.[31] By contrast, for the science of religions, in the presence of God the will falls silent—"no exertion of volition is required" (46), is indeed precluded (206).[32] The very notion of the *presence* of God belongs more to the science of religions than to pragmatism. For though both point to a future realization of the sacred, what the science of religions reveals is a proleptic anticipation of that *now*, in ineffable, passive and transient mystical experience.

It has been said of James that the corpus of his work suggests a personality that "never succeeded in becoming a unified self."[33] Within the framework of the *Varieties of Religious Experience*, this would leave James himself back at the beginning of the book, among the divided souls. It is part of the appeal of William James that he fall, even by his own admission, so much at the beginning of the progression towards saints and mystics he traces in his book, especially when others so readily ranked him, if not among the mystics, at least among the saints.[34] Within the framework of a religious value scheme in which passion ranked so high, James accepted for his own religious life the rather low grade of "pallid" (494). It reads as an act of humility for a pragmatist, for whom the senses in general and seeing in particular are definitive, to devote a whole chapter's worth of tribute to "The Reality of the Unseen," as James does in *Varieties*. But if these implicit self-judgments indicate self-divisions, they also suggest a willingness to hover, if only uncomfortably, between opposites. Hovering is characteristic of neither the scientist of religions nor the pragmatist. The scientist of religion is bent on "general facts which can be defined in formulas upon which everyone may agree" (423). And pragmatism, in its very work of harmonizing, shows as much its intolerance of suspension and abeyance. James doubts the value of any worldview that does not make a "definite difference . . . to you and me, at definite instants of our life."[35] The pragmatist "turns . . . towards concreteness and adequacy, towards facts, towards action and towards power."[36] As Ross Posnock observes, "pragmatism's investment in control is easy to lose sight of amid James' extravagant rhetoric of endless process, vulnerability, risk, and change."[37] But then, to be suspended between two such different philosophical evaluations of religion as the science of religions and pragmatism provide, which nonetheless concur on the importance of resolution, must have been an anxiety for James. And indeed, in his essay on "Reflex Action and Theism," James suggests that to be caught in a prolonged state of "consideration or contemplation of thinking," without resolve in concrete action, "would have to be considered either pathological or abortive."[38]

According to Kim Townsend, at Harvard University in the early 1900s, where James had risen within the academic hierarchy to the rank of professor of both psychology and philosophy, irresolution would indeed have been a problem. For part of the university's mission was to raise up graduates who were "acute and practical," "earnest and courageous," free "from indecision, from despondency and despair."[39] We must picture risk-takers who, at points of indecision, compensate for the want of reason to choose one course over another with the resolve they invest in whichever course they chose. According to Townsend, these values constituted a new concept of manhood, a decidedly gendered view of the ideal male graduate, whose male identity would previously have been subordinated beyond much notice to the obligation on humanity as such to worship God.[40] *The Varieties of Religious Experience* is sprinkled with admiration for actions and traits deemed manly, and disdain for its opposite, effeminacy, which is not the feminine as such, but only its display in the male.[41] For James, it is a question worth several pages of discussion whether saintliness "be an ideal type of manhood" (366).

Anxiety over his own (unmanly?) irresolutions regarding the philosophical understanding of religion may account for one of the singular interests of James' life, which, by some, would certainly have been deemed "pathological or abortive" even in his own day—psychical research. For if the breeding ground for what interested the science of religions was the unseen world of the subconscious, and if the proving ground for whatever mattered to pragmatism was the visible world, then the efforts of psychical research to *see* into "the reality of the unseen" would be a bridge of resolution between them. But James' final evaluation of his work in psychical research, and that of the American Society for Psychical Research he helped found, was inconclusive.[42] And so there was no resolution, as James seems to have implied when in a letter in late life to his brother Henry, he confessed about himself generally that he had been too much "kept in a state of inner tension."[43]

That Henry should have received this confidence testifies to the warmth and closeness between the brothers their whole lives long. But perhaps it is also William's unconscious tribute to Henry's quite different approach to irresolution, which was to observe and narrate it from the multiple perspectives to which it lent itself, without intent, necessarily, of resolution. Ross Posnock suggests that one point of contrast between the brothers was in their responses to the notion of uncertain selfhood: William "'found salvation . . . in self-confidence,'" while Henry "submitted his own selfhood, and the very concept of selfhood, to an extended ordeal of vulnerability."[44] When Posnock further finds in this ordeal an effort to "diffuse traditional gender polarities," so as to clear a way for new aesthetic and social ideals of androgyny, in contrast with "William's muscular pragmatism,"[45] his thoughts interweave provocatively with Townsend's on Harvard manhood. Henry's androgyny reads as an alternative to Harvard manhood, though one William would have had difficulty openly acknowledging, given his own complicity in the idea of that manhood. Complicating the matter is William's disgust for homosexuality, which he obliquely expressed in his then widely influential *Principles of Psychology*.[46] It would be a wonder the brothers were so close, if we did not have readings of Henry James today which suggest he was able to turn the very shame the likes of William would inadvertently have imposed on him, because of his albeit unconfessed sexuality, into narratives and criticism that playfully and even joyfully perform, via the language of extended *double-entendre*, that very sexuality[47] as sometimes happens in sophisticated verbal comedy.

As antidote to William's now dated and suspect manliness, Henry asks to be read in conjunction with his brother. Certainly the two share an interest in consciousness and its border on the subconscious. As though to boldface that border, the imagery of doors and thresholds is frequent in the brothers' writings,[48] foretelling the spiritually resonant notion of liminality, which Victor Turner later introduced more fully into the academic discourse on religion.[49] They also share an interest in the theoretic import and problematic of observation, as opposed to experience—an inheritance, broadly, of modern philosophy. But they pair, too, in other more complementary ways. For Henry found a way to put the irresolution that so haunted his brother to good narrative use, in ghost stories that intensify—turn the screw of—their eerie effects by provoking in the reader that very thing: irresolution. Several of Henry's protagonists in these stories undergo acute moments or periods of irresolute self-division: Morris Gedge, of "The Birthplace," a tour guide to a noted writer's home, was "splitting into halves"[50] over the portrait he was expected publicly to paint of the writer, and his own acquired knowledge of the actual facts about him; John Marcher, of "The Beast in the Jungle," has, during his long travels abroad, "been separated so long from the part of himself that alone he now valued"[51] ; and, most of all, Spencer Brydon, of "The Jolly Corner," cannot assimilate the ghostly other of himself he horrifically encounters when he returns from abroad to his childhood home. If the impact of especially this last irresolution can be read religiously, that is because the reality of the unseen, which the subconscious mediates towards conscious states of harmonious unity, has a kind of *doppelganger*, according to William, which issues instead in "a diabolical mysticism, a sort of religious mysticism turned upside down" (417), whose impact is horror. We know that William anonymously recorded his own experience of this kind, when he found himself identified with a state of blank and mindless stupor. William implied that what inflected the horror religiously was the memory of Bible verses it provoked, but we have already suggested that the experience carried its own religiosity, quite apart from that, because of its dark application of a Hindu monist adage. The religious and the paranormal were, for William, twin outcroppings of the subconscious. William implied as much when he suggested, in the *Principles of Psychology*, that to be religious is "to be haunted by a sense of an ideal spectator."[52] As for Henry, Hazel Hutchison observes that "like many Victorians, [he had] a hazy conception of the modern division between religious and paranormal experience."[53] Here the brothers, who both attended séances, were very much on the same page.

But where William employed the methods of science to describe and classify a religious experience, Henry employed the methods of literature to actually provoke it, or something like it, in his readers.

Henry can be credited with writing at least fifteen ghost stories. Hutchison suggests that "late-Victorian fascination with the ghost-story develop[ed] in the vacuum left by the collapse of religious faith."[54] The observation is apt applied to Henry, who projected less the collapse than the perduring absence of conventional faith. This did not turn Henry necessarily into an atheist. The Jamesian ghost story realizes what more properly characterizes Henry, according to Hutchison, which is restraint from "certainties about unbelief."[55] Certainly some of the stories show, in notable departure from what William would prescribe, a loving attention to religiously evocative rituals, such as lighting candles for the dead ("The Altar of the Dead"), regularly visiting the cemetery ("The Beast in the Jungle"), bowing in deference to the supernaturally other ("The Ghostly Rental"), or simply eating, as in "The Passionate Pilgrim," where dinners at Oxford University are a "religious unction."[56] George Stransom, of "Altar of the Dead," is that story's "little affiliated" protagonist, who nonetheless loves "solemn and splendid ritual," and who believes it "good that there should be churches."[57] But it is not such overt overtones of religiosity that mark the spirituality of the ghost stories, at least from a Jamesian perspective, but rather their conformity to William's understanding of religious experience as both subjectively grounded in the subconscious and objectively noetic or revealing of outward, extraordinary reality. Henry's narration typically connects the ghostly experience of a lead character to her or his (sub)conscious. A friend or supporting character affirms the objective reality of what the other reports, without necessarily sharing in the same experiences, or at least not obviously so or in the same way.[58] In this way, the reader is given both the subjective and objective grounding for the experience. But Henry does not simply describe whatever counts for ghostly in the stories; he shows it emerging in the consciousness of the protagonist, as though from the subconscious, be it from a lingering guilt (as in "Sir Edmund Orme"), a pathological refusal of commitment (as in "The Beast in the Jungle"), or regrets over an unrealized alter-ego ("The Jolly Corner"). The reader is positioned to see the emergence of the ghostly through the consciousness of the protagonist. The support of the trusted confidant or friend, in the story, appeals for the reader's faith in the noetic objectivity of the protagonist's experience, but does not compel or assure it, in part because the very sympathy of the friend compromises her or his credibility. The reader is left poised at the threshold between the paranormal consciousness of the protagonist and the assurance that what registers there is objectively real.

This is the pattern of the most famous Jamesian ghost story, *The Turn of the Screw*, where the governess sees the ghosts of former employees of the Bly estate, the reader sees them through her eyes, and the faithful housekeeper, who does not seem them, nonetheless credits them, at least initially, on the basis of her friendship for the governess. Nothing testifies more to the irresolution in which this leaves the reader, as to the reality of the ghosts, than the critical commentary that has grown up around the story, pleading alternatively for their objective reality or their confinement to the warped (sub)consciousness of the governess, who perhaps fancied dangers to her charges only to cast herself self-importantly with an eye to impressing their distant uncle in the role of savior. James' Victorian readers would have been primed for this second view, more perhaps than we are, by (sexist) impressions they would have been open to of governesses generally as prone to "nervousness, morbidity, hysteria, and insanity."[59] But the same pattern repeats in "The Beast in the Jungle," where the ghostly element is a calamity the protagonist unaccountably anticipates, and the supporting character a friend who credits the calamity, which does indeed arrive, but fails to save him from it; and in "The Jolly Corner," where the protagonist experiences an horrific encounter with his doppelganger—the person he would have become had he made different life choices—from which he only recovers with the help of a sympathetic friend, who intuited from afar the stress of the encounter.

Commenting on his own tales of the supernatural, Henry observed that "good ghosts, speaking by the book, make poor subjects."[60] He meant, primarily, that ghosts as reported in actual apparitional sightings typically *did* nothing, and so could not serve a story line. To have narrative value, they had to be invested with intent towards the characters and this, in his ghost stories, was typically but not always sinister. In "The Third Person," the ghost of a former smuggler works to comic effect by prompting an elderly female character to follow his once living lead, by smuggling into England "a Tauchnitz"—a volume from a series of German editions of English classics forbidden for import to England—which she hid from customs "about my person."[61] In "The Great Good Place," the ghostly element is a monastic paradise the harassed protagonist dreams, or perhaps actually enters, of consummate ease, of "high triumphant clearness,"[62] of gardens, cloisters, and books. But most of the ghosts are after some ill end.

It has been said that Henry's choice to focus more on the menace of the paranormal, than the wholesomeness of it, which absorbed his brother's attention, indicates a "pessimistic sensibility.[63] It is more likely that a secondary meaning inheres in his judgment on "the good ghost," that it does not make for a riveting story. But from the standpoint of the spirituality of these stories, the good or evil import of the ghosts is actually irrelevant. What matters is the effective evocation of the experience of the paranormal. Henry makes of the reader a participant observer in the story, via the protagonist's own consciousness. This "results in a simultaneous sense of detached observation and involved participation in a moment of emergent meaning."[64] In other words, Henry blurs the distinction William works to keep between experience itself and the scientific observation of it.[65] Henry himself is more forthright about his aims, especially as regards the ghost stories, about which he writes in his own preface to them: "The extraordinary is most extraordinary in that it happens to you and me, and it's of value (and of value to others) but so far as visibly brought home to us."[66] Henry positions the reader to experience the paranormal, in what the story visibly brings home to her. This is what makes the stories of the sinister ghosts "among the most terrifying ever written."[67]

The difference of ghostly experience from religious experience is in its emotional impact, towards horror and division, rather than happiness and unity. "Instead of consolations we have desolations; the meanings are dreadful; and the powers are enemies to life" (417), writes William. But the experiences are homologous in that they both "spring from the same mental level, from that great subliminal or transmarginal region . . . of which so little is known" (417) especially its relation to objective reality. Forces inimical to life do indeed manifest in, say, *The Turn of the Screw*, where Miles, the beloved charge of the governess dies; and in "The Jolly Corner," where the protagonist's vision of his alter-ego nearly kills him. But to the extent these stories move the reader to feel the characters' dread, they have brought her into one-half of religious experience—the half that inhabits the normally unseen "transmarginal region." It is by their joint grounding in *that*, as Hutchison implied, that an effective ghost story can seem a substitute for religious experience. It is as though Henry trades in William's full *account* of religious experience for a vivid *evocation*, on the reader's behalf, of *half* the experience, which leaves out the unifying part, as though a fullness of objectivity buys only half of a more precious and so more expensive subjectivity.[68]

Locked within the definitively mediating role of the characters' consciousness, the reader is uncertain whether what she perceives via that consciousness is real within the confines of the story. Henry supplies no equivalent to his brother's over-beliefs, to resolve the suspension. "[Henry] James deliberately opens a field that offers no hope of resolution or explanation," writes Hutchison.[69] The irresolution works two ways: it intensifies, for the reader, the experience of the ghostly, and it lends to the ghostly an additional, mystical aura. The irresolution translates the in-between status of the ghost themselves, between the dead and the living, into a space the reader herself is brought to inhabit. In a sense, the reader becomes a kind of ghost. At the same time, this very suspension of the reader's identity accords with a key feature of mysticism, as William understands it: the effacement of the boundaries of the self, when we become "as nothing in the floods and waterspouts of God" (47). Such ghostly-mystical suspensions characterize Henry's writing as a whole, not just the ghost stories: "hesitation, pause, restraint . . . are also integral to his literary method,"[70] and "enigmatic impalpability, vague imprecision, subtle allusiveness, hovering uncertainty."[71] This aspect of the writing manifests with ironic precision in a favorite Jamesian device, of suddenly reversing perspective. For example, no sooner do we learn, at the start of "Altar of the Dead," that George Stransom "kept each year in his own fashion the date of Mary Antrim's death," than the tables are turned in what is more strictly true, "that this occasion kept *him*."[72] The effect on the reader is of a reversible suspension between subject and object, the blur of a beating wing.

From a spiritual perspective, the most striking application of that device probably lies beyond the ghost stories, in the one purely philosophical essay Henry wrote, towards the end of his life, "Is There a Life After Death?"[73] In its autobiographical sections, the essay recalls the introduction to Spinoza's *Treatise on the Improvement of the Understanding*, in their shared evocation of a good beyond the transience of this world—as though Henry were correcting for William's neglect of that passage, which might paradigmatically have illustrated an intellectualist mysticism in *Varieties*.[74] Henry's essay provides a final point of comparison with William who wrote an essay on the same topic, "Human Immortality." The essays illustrate their contrastive approaches to unanswerable spiritual questions, and the consequent appeal, for the reader, of taking them together.

For Henry, even the question of afterlife is subject to perspectival switch. Our collective record of "brutality and vulgarity, the so easy non-existence of consciousness,"[75] and the piecemeal losses within our own consciousness ("our extinct passions and faculties and interests"[76]) which, having left us, give no sign of being reborn elsewhere, seem to bring home to us the "unmistakable absoluteness of death,"[77] and the emphatic "disconnectedness of those who vanish from our sight"—and now the reversal—"or they perhaps not so much from ours as we from theirs." The effect of the switch, here, is to objectify "us," who had been the subjective activator of this meditation, into the passive object of some others' neglect of us. The impact on the reader is not unlike that on Job when God assumes the speaking voice—a startled silencing of the question, as though a certain self-importance, suddenly undercut, was presupposed in the very putting of the question. Though the reversal appears to presume an afterlife, it does not argue for one, but merely, if there is one, for the indifference to us of its inhabitants. In the end, their silence towards us, when we would have expected some message from them, argues the more for their nonexistence, despite the "evidence" of mediums, whose witness is less to an afterlife than to the fascination of their own personalities. Henry's reversal of perspective on the afterlife question raised the ghost of a realm beyond, only to banish it, but not without leaving behind a sense of our own diminished importance. And this is one quite biblical answer to the question of the afterlife. But Henry has another.

The other enacts what he had been doing all along in the ghost stories when he positioned his reader at the protagonists' eyes; only now it is his own consciousness he offers up for the reader to empathically inhabit. As though chastened by the exposed presumption of the question as first baldly and universally formulated, Henry now repeatedly, in the second part of the essay, scales it to his own experience, so that its inquiry is less into the fate of humanity at large than into his own artistry and any implications towards the afterlife embedded there. Not for a moment does Henry take the temptingly self-aggrandizing line we might expect of the artist, who projects to live in the afterlife of his works. It is rather that the artistic consciousness bears good news for human consciousness at large, that consciousness, by observing the world, as artists do, expands the more of the world and worldly possibility it observes. The expansion of consciousness in this life has the effect of "undermining the conclusion most unfavorable to it"[78] in the next. Rather, the artist carries "the field of consciousness further and further into making it lose itself in the ineffable."[79] The language is redolent of William's understanding of mystical experience, whose first characteristic was its ineffability. Echoes of the second, noetic characteristic sound when Henry adds that "I find myself—I can't express it otherwise—in communication with *sources*"[80] beyond, which ground the experience objectively. Henry will not elaborate, but merely suggests the sources belong to "a possible something that shall be better than what we have known here."[81] The expansions of consciousness towards an afterlife result so naturally from expanding interest in this life that they appear to come in response to the mere desire more fully to know this world; so much so that the consciousness of afterlife "isn't really a question of belief . . . it is on the other hand a question of desire."[82] This explains the strange undercurrent that haunts Henry's essay from the start, of whether we should even *desire* an afterlife. In part, this is Henry's gesture of compassion towards the desperately unhappy, with perhaps his sister Alice in mind, for whom cessation is release. But it also orients the essay towards yet another switch it enacts by the end, away from belief and towards desire as the psychological channel through which the energy of the idea of the afterlife flows to us at all.

This is a departure from William for whom, from the standpoint of cognitive significance, (passive) desire paled in comparison with (active) will, which had the power to summon belief. William's essay takes the form of disarming two supposed arguments against belief in the afterlife—the first, that insofar as consciousness depends on the brain, it cannot survive the latter's clinical death; the second, that the history of life on earth comprises too many individuals to reasonably inhabit any conceivable afterlife. William undermines the first argument by distinguishing two different kinds of dependence: productive and permissive. That which is productively dependent on something else is actually produced by that other and ceases when the production does; but that which is permissively dependent on something else enjoys in the other a mere conduit unessential to its own existence. The smoke a fire produces is functionally dependent on the fire; but the light that passes through a prism is merely conducted by the prism and exists without it. If consciousness is merely permissively dependent on the brain, it could conceivably survive the brain's demise. As for the second argument, William exposes in it a fundamental blindness to the value *other* lives have for the self—"an insensibility to the inner significance of alien lives."[83] There is no reason to suppose that any larger consciousness(es) that might subsume ours within a possible afterlife would suffer from the same deficiency. Indeed, the ghost of Job, which Henry raised without naming, William does name towards the end of his essay, as though in helpful sympathy with his brother's train of thought—like the plaintive Job, we overstate our own importance at the expense of others'.

Like the lives of the brothers themselves, their two essays on immortality intertwine provocatively. Both comprise two parts, a first and second argument. The arguments are analogous but chiliastic in relation. Henry's first argument and William's second reverse perspective from the presumed speaker of the argument to an otherworldly other, from whose vantage point the speaker's presumption of self-importance is exposed. By contrast, Henry's second argument and William's first build on the notion of an elastically expansive consciousness—as though reflection *on* consciousness stretches the experience *of* consciousness towards its own afterlife. This argument is a self-fulfilling prophecy of immortality, a psychological twist on the ontological argument—it illustrates William's idea that some realities depend for their existence on our intentional investment in them, whether by desire, will, or belief. The arguments highlight how important the realm of possibility was for both brothers, as context for understanding the abode of the sacred.

Beyond this structural intertwining the essays also share common themes, which they investigate in analogous ways. For example, the two brothers both draw on their life-long interest in the paranormal, but not, as might be expected, for proof of immortality. For scientific William, mediums are noteworthy not for anything they suggest about an afterlife but, surprisingly and almost ironically, for the application they invite of an old principle of explanation—Ockham's razor—according to which the simplest explanation is best: it is easier to explain the work of mediums on grounds that consciousness depends permissively, and not productively, on the brain. Likewise, for literary Henry, the evidence of mediums is not for an afterlife but for the fascination of their own personalities (which might figure in a story). But William's point implies another both brothers make, that a consciousness that expands beyond the confines of the body coheres with ancient Platonic teachings. When Henry writes that the body is "the mere encasement . . . of a spirit it has no . . . concern in producing" he expresses the old Platonic theory in his brother's language of productive (versus permissive) dependence. This too is not so much an argument for immortality as a happy coherence between theories—unexpectedly, since neither brother especially exhibits a Platonic sensibility. On one theme the brothers do differ, on whether personality continues into the afterlife, or transforms into some impersonal abstraction of it. For Henry, immortality is not interesting unless it preserves personality. He maintains "that conception of immortality as personal which is the only thing that gives it meaning or relevance."[84] William is not so sure. He suspects the loss of some of our personality "would not appear a matter of such absolute regret,"[85] as certainly accords with reports of the more apophatic mystics he studies (one of whom, in an article entitled "The Loss of Personality,"[86] described the rapture attending the "vanishing of the sense of self" (385)). Perhaps this is the difference between a novelist, for whom personality propels the story, and a scientist, for whom it obstructs the experiment. Henry addresses the theme in his ghost story, "The Private Life," which includes a character, Lord Mellifont, who, once out of sight of the other characters, appears simply to disappear, as they discover when they repeatedly cannot find him in places where, based on his known itinerary, he could not help but visibly be. The characters suspect he is periodically "reabsorbed . . . into the immensity of things."[87] As per usual, the reader is not given resolution on this point, but, via Lord's Mellifont's discreet wife, is ushered with her into "the relative grandeur of uncertainty."[88] But Henry, in a letter to his grieving friend, Grace Norton, counsels against the admitted lure of personality loss: "Don't melt too much into the universe, but be as solid and dense and fixed as you can."[89]

But the final impression the two juxtaposed essays leave is of complementarity. Perhaps William could not unite with himself, but he could with his very different brother. For much of what is needed, according to William, to overcome our blindness to "the precious inward personality"[90] —Henry's phrase—of the many alien others, which would admit them all, in their billions, to the next life, is Henry's own particular novelistic gift: imagination. While Henry, for his part, in a rare nod to overt religious belief, notes a coincidence between his own unorthodox theory of consciousness, expanding towards its own immortality, and the "preparations on earth for heaven, of the orthodox theology," or otherwise put, "working out one's salvation."[91] Henry is not daunted by this coincidence, which only shows "how neatly extremes may sometimes meet,"[92] as he and his brother also illustrate. If ghostly phenomena partner with religious experience in manifesting the spiritual, then so do William's science and Henry's stories—a joint venture in commending religion to the experience-oriented philosopher.

NOTES

1. William James, *The Varieties of Religious Experience* (New York: Modern Library, 1902), 448. Pages of subsequent quotations from this text are given parenthetically.
2. William James to Alice Howe Gibbens James, July 9, 1898, in *The Correspondence of William James*, ed. Ignas Skrupskelis and Elizabeth Berkeley (Charlottesville: University Press of Virginia, 2000), 8:390.
3. William James to Henry Leuba, April 17, 1904 in *The Letters of William James*, ed. by his son, Henry James (Boston: Atlantic Monthly Press, 1920), 2:211. James writes of mystical states in particular that "my own constitution shuts me out of their enjoyment almost entirely" (370).
4. "Nature has no one distinguishable ultimate tendency with which it is possible to feel a sympathy" (481).
5. Henry James, "The Great Good Place," in *The Ghostly Tales of Henry James*, ed. Leon Edel (New Brunswick, NJ: Rutgers University Press, 1948).
6. William James to Henry William Rankin, June 21, 1896, in *The Correspondence of William James*, 8:155.
7. James never presumes that these categorizations and comparisons wholly translate for the reader all that happens in religious experience, which is finally *sui generis* and fully known only to those who have it (49).
8. F. O. Matthiessen, *The James Family* (New York: Knopf, 1947), 590.
9. William James, *A Pluralistic Universe* (New York: Longman Green, 1909), 329. "The universe is still in the making." William James, *Pragmatism* (New York: Longmans Green, 1907), 257.
10. Ibid., 124.
11. Ibid., 290.
12. Ibid., 119.
13. James, *Pluralistic Universe*, 318. In earlier works, James insists more on the ontological separateness of the sacred. "In every being that is real there is something external to and sacred from the grasp of every other. God's being is sacred from ours." James, "Reflex Action and Theism," in *The Will to Believe and other Popular Essays in Moral Philosophy* (New York: Dover, 1956), 141.
14. William James to Frances Rollins Morse, April 12, 1900, in *The Correspondence of William James*, 9:186.
15. *Chandogya Upanishad* in *The Upanishads*, trans. Juan Mascaro (New York: Penguin, 1965), 117–118.
16. According to one account, William confessed this many years after the experience to his French translator. See Robert Richardson, *William James* (Boston: Houghton Mifflin, 2006), 543.
17. James' prime illustration of this type are the adherents of mind-cure, a movement popular in his day, whose descendant in our time is, arguably, the literature of self-help. It is a tribute to James' natural modesty that he credits that movement with being America's "only decidedly original contribution to the systematic philosophy of life" (94), when, in fact, that distinction now usually goes to pragmatism, to which James himself so amply contributed.
18. For James the phrase connotes what he considers the mere and outward pomp of ritual.
19. John Randall, "The Spirit of American Philosophy," in *Wellsprings of the American Spirit: A Series of Addresses*, ed. F. Ernest Johnson, Religion and Civilization Series (New York: Institute for Religious and Social Studies, 1948), 128.
20. William James, "Address at the Centenary of Ralph Waldo Emerson, May 25, 1903," in *Writings: 1902–1910* (New York: Library of America, 1987), 1119–1125. James' assessment of Emerson embodies some of the paradox of Emerson himself, who, according to James, preached freedom while carefully respecting the limits of his talents.
21. In *Varieties of Religious Experience*, James appreciates what he takes for the mystical impulses in Hegel, which he thinks must have inspired his philosophy (379). But in

A Pluralistic Universe he judges the Hegelian Absolute an "improbable hypothesis" (111), and suggests reality more likely consists "not of an all but of a set of eaches, just as it seems to" (129). The contrast between the single All and the many Eaches finds a homier, narrative expression in Henry James' story, "The Altar of the Dead," where it explains the different interpretations the two central characters put on the many candles they light to memorialize their dead. Says one character to the other, in explaining the difference, "You had placed a great light for Each—I gathered them together for One!" Henry James, "The Altar of the Dead," in *The Ghostly Tales of Henry James*, ed. Leon Edel (New Brunswick, NJ: Rutgers University Press, 1948), 380. In context of the story, for the one character, each of the many lit candles memorialized a separate soul, while for the other, all of them together fashioned a great light memorializing simply one. In the end, the pluralistic interpretation holds sway, as it did in William's philosophy.

22. James, *Pragmatism*, 223. James cites the same passage, by Kierkegaard's name, in *Essays in Radical Empiricism*, Works of William James, vol. 3 (Cambridge, MA: Harvard University Press, 1976), 121. The passage is from Kierkegaard's *Journals*, where he writes, "It is perfectly true that life must be understood backwards. But they forget the other proposition that it must be lived forwards." Kierkegaard, *Journals of Soren Kierkegaard*, ed. Alexander Dru (New York: Oxford University Press, 1938), 127.

23. James, *Pragmatism*, 6.

24. Ibid., 45.

25. Ibid., 12.

26. Richard Gale refers to the "clashes between James' pragmatic and mystical selves." Gale, *The Divided Self of William James* (New York: Cambridge University Press, 1999), 258.

27. James, *Pragmatism*, 55.

28. Ibid., 46

29. Ibid., 202.

30. A phrase on which James expressly casts doubt in the *Varieties of Religious Experience* (208).

31. James, *Pragmatism*, 119.

32. Quite unpragmatically, James observes in *Varieties*, "we are all such helpless failures in the last resort," inevitably subject to "the vanity and provisionality of our voluntary career" (47).

33. Gale, *The Divided Self of William James*, 18.

34. Reflecting on James' character, Jacques Barzun noted his "broad and quick sympathies" and "evident generosity of spirit." Barzun, *A Stroll with William James* (New York: Harper and Row, 1983), 2. James "cared deeply for others and was loved and admired by almost everyone who knew him. He worked so hard at being virtuous that to many he was something of a saint." Kim Townsend, *Manhood at Harvard: William James and Others* (New York: Norton, 1996), 78.

35. James, *Pragmatism*, 50.

36. Ibid., 51.

37. Ross Posnock, *The Trial of Curiosity: Henry James, William James, and the Challenge of Modernity* (New York: Oxford University Press, 1991), 40–41.

38. James, "Reflex Action and Theism," in *The Will To Believe, and Other Essays in Popular Philosophy* (New York: Dover, 1956), 114. The critique recalls Descartes' of wonder.

39. Kim Townsend, *Manhood at Harvard*, 24, 78.

40. Ibid., 16.

41. For example: "Does not . . . the worship of material luxury and wealth ... make somewhat for effeminacy and unmanliness?" (357).

42. See William James, "Final Impressions of a Psychical Researcher," in *William James on Psychical Research*, ed. Gardner Murphy and Robert O. Ballow (Clifton, NJ: Augustus M. Kelley, 1973), 309–325. James wrote this essay in 1909, a year before his death.

43. William James to Henry James, March 6, 1909, in *The Correspondence of William James*, 3:386.
44. Posnock, 18,19. Posnock's comment on William James here is quoted from James Hoopes, *Consciousness in New England* (Baltimore, MD: Johns Hopkins University Press, 1989), 208.
45. Ibid., 200.
46. Very allusively, James refers to the "fondness of the ancients and of modern Orientals for forms of unnatural vice, of which the notion affects us with horror." William James, *Principles of Psychology* (New York: Henry Holt, 1893), 2:438.
47. See Eve Kosofsky Sedgwick, "Shame and Performativity: Henry James' New York Edition Prefaces," in *Henry James's New York Edition: The Construction of Authorship* (Stanford, CA: Stanford University Press, 1995). Sedgwick's sparkling essay, which uncovers the erotic play in Henry's critical writing on himself, begins by distancing any resort, in so doing, to the methods of self-help literature. The distancing is remarkable for a reference that can be read in it to William James, who is never overtly mentioned in the essay. For William is sometimes taken for one of the founding voices of the modern self-help genre. Sedgwick's distancing of the self-help genre reads as a silencing of William so that Henry can speak
48. For instance, an unaccountably closed door sustains suspense for two pages in "The Jolly Corner," in *Ghostly Tales*, 747–749. William, for his part, writes of the "subliminal door" through which possibly higher powers communicate with us (238). Henry inverts the positive import of that image in his ghostly adaptation of religious experience: a resisting ghost had closed the door, from which the protagonist flees in terror.
49. See especially Victor Turner, *Ritual Process* (Chicago: Aldine, 1969).
50. Henry James, "The Birthplace," in *Complete Stories, 1898–1910* (New York: Library of America, 1996), 460.
51. Henry James, "The Beast in the Jungle," in *Ghostly Tales*, 714.
52. William James, *Principles of Psychology*, 1:316.
53. Hazel Hutchison, *Seeing and Believing: Henry James and the Spiritual World* (New York: Palgrave Macmillan, 2006), xiv.
54. Ibid., 2.
55. Ibid., xx.
56. Henry James, "The Passionate Pilgrim," in *The Passionate Pilgrim and Other Tales* (Boston: Houghton Mifflin, 1917), 108.
57. Henry James, "The Altar of the Dead," in *Ghostly Tales*, 358, 363, 364. The description recalls George Santayana, a pupil and friendly acquaintance of William James who nonetheless recorded that he felt more at ease with Henry, at his first and only meeting with him, than he ever had with William over many years. George Santayana, *Persons and Places*, vol. 2, *The Middle Years* (New York: Scribner's, 1945), 39.
58. On this point, see especially Pericles Lewis, "'The Reality of the Unseen': Shared Fictions and Religious Experience in the Ghost Stories of Henry James," *Arizona Quarterly* 61, no. 2 (Summer 2005): 43–44. For Lewis, the supporting figure works more to establish a shared social world for the characters than to lure the reader's belief.
59. T. J. Lustig, *Henry James and the Ghostly* (New York: Cambridge University Press, 1994), 151. James offers a kinder tribute to the tradition of the governess, already ending in his own day, in "The Speech of American Women," in *Henry James on Culture: Collected Essays on Politics and the American Scene*, ed. Pierre A. Walker (Lincoln: University of Nebraska Press, 1999), 71. Lustig reviews some of the interpretive history of *The Turn of the Screw* in *Henry James and the Ghostly*, 111–115.
60. Henry James, *The Art of the Novel: Critical Prefaces* (New York: Scribner's, 1934), 175
61. Henry James, "The Third Person," in *Ghostly Tales*, 666.
62. Henry James, "The Great Good Place," in *Ghostly Tales*, 586.

63. John Updike refers to "the endlessly productive but resolutely pessimistic sensibility of Henry James." Updike, introduction to Henry James, *Portrait of a Lady* (New York: Oxford, 1999), xii.

64. Lustig, *Henry James and the Ghostly*, 105.

65. Mira Sethi comments on Henry's "free indirect style, the merging of a character's speech with the narrative itself," especially in cases where the narrator is not a character in the novel, but the omniscient author. In fact, William does this too in the *Varieties of Religious Experience*, when he seamlessly transitions from reporting on what mystics say about their experiences, to claiming, in his own voice, the truth about what they say, e.g., that the experience is ineffable, noetic, etc. When a mystic says that his experience "defies expression," does it necessarily follow that "its quality must be directly experienced" (371)?—or simply that the mystic is inarticulate? Perhaps the difference between William and Henry is over how conscious they are of how much they blur the bounds between having an experience and describing it. On Henry, see Mira Sethi, "Henry James' Most Affecting Portrait," *Wall Street Journal* (July 24–25, 2010), W14.

66. Henry James, *Art of the Novel*, 257.

67. Leon Edel, introduction to *Ghostly Tales*, xxvii.

68. Though, of course, the unity may manifest *aesthetically*, in the experience of a story that hangs together. How this relates to *religious* experience is another question. See Ernest Rubinstein, *Religion and the Muse: The Vexed Relation between Religion and Western Literature* (Albany: State University of New York Press, 1999).

69. Hutchison, *Seeing and Believing*, 51.

70. Ibid., 26.

71. Lustig, *Henry James and the Ghostly*, 2. This language evokes the concept of liminality, as employed by Victor Turner, to denote the spiritually charged space experienced at locations between prescribed social stations. See Turner, *Ritual Process* (Chicago: Aldine, 1969).

72. Henry James, "Altar of the Dead," 356.

73. Henry James, "Is There a Life After Death?," in *Henry James on Culture: Collected Essays on Politics and the American Social Scene*, ed. Pierre A. Walker (Lincoln: University of Nebraska Press, 1999), 115–127.

74. Compare Spinoza's opening sentence, "After experience had taught me that all things which frequently take place in ordinary life are vain and futile." (Spinoza, *Treatise on the Correction of the Understanding*, tr. Andrew Boyle, in *Spinoza's Ethics and On the Correction of the Understanding* [New York: Dutton, 1970], 227) with Henry's comment near the beginning of part II of his essay, "I found it long impossible not to succumb . . . to discouragement by the mere pitiless dryness of all the appearance" (Henry James, "Is There a Life After Death?", 122)—and the culmination of both passages in an autobiographical awakening to hopeful conviction of well-being.

75. Ibid., 118.

76. Ibid., 119.

77. Ibid.

78. Ibid., 123.

79. Ibid., 124.

80. Ibid.

81. Ibid., 125.

82. Ibid., 127.

83. William James, "Human Immortality," in *The Will to Believe and Other Essays on Popular Philosophy* (New York: Dover, 1956), 37.

84. Henry James, "Is There a Life After Death?," 120.

85. William James, "Human Immortality," 30.

86. William cites the article: Ethel D. Puffer, "The Loss of Personality," *Atlantic Monthly* 135 (1857): 195–204.

87. Henry James, "The Private Life," in *Ghostly Tales*, 243.

88. Ibid., 235.

89. Henry James, to Grace Norton, July 28, 1883 in *Letters*, ed. Leon Edel (Cambridge, MA: Harvard University Press, 1975), 2:424. Henry's one ghostly exploration of happiness in the loss of personality is "The Great Good Place," where the protagonist, burdened by his earthly life of fame, is briefly transported to a place where he enjoys being "without the complication of an identity." (Henry James, "The Great Good Place," in *Ghostly Tales*, 588). But one reader, Virginia Woolf, judges this story a failure. Virginia Woolf, "The Ghost Stories," in *Henry James: A Collection of Critical Essays*, ed. Leon Edel (Englewood Cliffs, NJ: Prentice-Hall, 1963), 47.
90. Henry James, "Is There a Life After Death?," 123.
91. Ibid., 126,127.
92. Ibid., 126.

THIRTEEN

Bertrand Russell

On February 10, 1901, in Cambridge, England, just a few months before William James would speak in Edinburgh on the topic of conversion, as part of the Gifford lectures he gave there, later incorporated into *The Varieties of Religious Experience*, Bertrand Russell experienced a conversion of his own. Russell's conversion was, according to the stirring account of it he gave in his *Autobiography*, from a life of "flippant cleverness" to one of heightened sensitivity to human loneliness and suffering. He wrote:

> The sense of the solitude of each human soul suddenly overwhelmed me. . . . [and a sense that] nothing can penetrate it except the highest intensity of the sort of love that religious teachers have preached. . . . For a time, a sort of mystic illumination possessed me. . . . Something of what I thought I saw in that moment has remained always with me.[1]

This account belongs as much in James' book, as in Russell's, in part because, in its fullness, it is so well told and would have expanded the relatively meager attention James gave to the religious experience of philosophers. Earlier, on a trip to the United States, in the fall of 1896, with his then wife Alys, Russell had met William James.[2] Forty-five years later, he would devote a chapter to James in his *History of Western Philosophy*. At the start of 1901, James was in Rome struggling with ill health and finishing his Gifford lecture on conversion.[3] Had Russell shared the James brothers' interest in the paranormal, he might from the hindsight of 1931, when he wrote the first volume of what became his three-volume autobiography,[4] have wondered about possible connections between the European proximity of James, writing on conversion, and his own conversion experience.

But James and Russell were never quite on the same page. Russell enjoyed the narratives within the *Varieties of Religious Experience*, which he read shortly after it appeared,[5] but not James' philosophical extrapolations from them; and he had no patience with pragmatism, which he took for epistemological recklessness. As though to underscore their differences, even on the matter of conversion, Russell's experience diverges from what James would have us expect. If for James, conversion was the happy resolution of a prior self-division, for Russell, it was a sorrowful deepening of sensitivity towards the reality of division between human souls. Far from resolving a prior self-division in Russell, his conversion experience intensified a self-division within him over the nature of philosophy itself. For Russell did not by any means abandon his analytical or technical view of philosophy for an aesthetic and mystical view of it, as his account of his conversion implies. He maintained both in tense and unresolved dysphoria.

In 1901, Russell was living between his two great technical achievements, both in the realm of philosophy of mathematics: *The Principles of Mathematics*, finished at the end of 1900, but not published until 1903, and its more famous sequel, written in collaboration with Alfred North Whitehead, *Principia Mathematica* (1910–1913), which deduces arithmetic from logic. The conversion experience occurred while the Russells were living with the Whiteheads, in Cambridge, so that the two philosophers could better collaborate. But what stimulated the experience had nothing to do with that technical work. As Russell explains it, he had just heard a reading of a new translation of Euripides' play, *Hippolytus*, by his friend, Gilbert Murray, and "I was profoundly stirred by the beauty of the poetry."[6] On returning home from the performance, he found Whitehead's wife, Evelyn, in such extreme pain "owing to heart trouble,"[7] that he was overwhelmed, and so begins the conversion experience. Russell implies that the experience was jointly grounded in an experience of literary beauty and of human suffering. And it is out of this dual foundation that Russell moved from writing what is likely his least read work, *The Principles of Mathematics*, to his most read, the short essay, "The Free Man's Worship." The two works, in juxtaposition of time and thought, epitomize Russell's contrasting interpretations of philosophy as the quest for certainty and the enlargement of vision. And it is striking that Russell's most moving testament to philosophical spirituality is framed by his two most technically arcane and seemingly non-spiritual works.

According to his own self-evaluations, unresolved duality was a feature of Russell's life and thought. As he explains in a relatively late essay, from 1956, two distinct motives drew him to philosophy: "the desire to find some knowledge that could be accepted as certainly true . . . [and] the desire to find some satisfaction for religious impulses."[8] These were rarely in sync for him and, under the umbrella of an already long-standing cultural debate that subsumed him, between science and religion, were increasingly in tension. Russell lamented, in the postscript to his *Autobiography*, which he finished in 1952 at age 80, that he never succeeded in synthesizing, as he early on hoped to do, his separately proceeding commitments to abstract thought, in quest of truth, and to concrete action, in quest of goodness.[9] He understood his life to divide, at age 38, between the abstractions that preoccupied him before then and the social and political causes that did so afterwards.[10] But the second was in no significant sense an expression of the first. Philosophy itself was suspended within a "No Man's Land" "between theology and science,"[11] inclining towards science when it reasoned logically, and towards theology when it poeticized feelingly. But philosophy itself less mediated than bifurcated between these, as William James had already typologized, when he contrasted the tender- and tough-minded philosopher and attempted (unsuccessfully, for Russell) with pragmatism to reconcile them.[12]

For a short time, Russell did find spiritual nourishment in mathematics. A conclusion of his 1902 essay, "The Study of Mathematics," is that "in mathematics, more than elsewhere, the love of truth may find encouragement for waning faith."[13] Faith in any distinctly Christian sense had already waned for Russell by his undergraduate days at Cambridge University. What positioned mathematics to supersede faith were certain features it shared with ordinary understandings of religion. It provided access to a world "sublimely pure . . . [and] remote from human passions," a "region of absolute necessity," "stern perfection" and "supreme beauty," yielding up for its devotees "the spirit of delight, the exaltation, the sense of being more than man."[14] Mathematics, as much as art or literature, claimed a place among "the contemplation of great things," howsoever much its "sacred doors"[15] might conceal it from average readers.

This essay constitutes one of the few expanses in Russell's published work that unites his sense for the sacred and his understanding of truth. In general, spirituality and truth are at odds in his work. Truth works against the inner peace that seems the promise of spirituality. Truth was "spectral, insane, ghastly,"[16] and, in the guise of divinity it well deserves, "drives into madness those who cannot bear the full terror of his majestic frown,"[17] according to a section titled, "The Worship of Truth," in his unpublished work from 1902–1903, The Pilgrimage of Life. These words on truth from Russell's young years were eerily prophetic of his later life. According to biographer, Ray Monk, fear of inherited madness was an ongoing worry for Russell that was finally realized most tragically in the life of his first son, John, a talented writer with a doomed penchant for efforts at reconciling the complexly self-divided Russell family.[18] Russell inadvertently illustrates how harrowing the truth can be when, in his Autobiography, rather than confront any part he may have played in his son's mental collapse, he lamely shifts the whole explanatory burden for that onto the fact of his having been "born after 1914."[19] Still, sustaining the metaphor of truth as god, Russell continues in "The Worship of Truth," that "in his service only can the soul grow great."[20]

Part of the appeal, for Russell, of the idea of truth was that it placed an absolute limit on the machinations of human desire—"the tyrannous imposition of our human and temporary demands."[21] This accounts in part for Russell's rejection of pragmatism, which he thought too readily accommodated desire in its theory of truth, to the point of committing "cosmic impiety."[22] In line with Buddhism, Russell's early writings preach that human freedom is fundamentally from desire.[23] By limiting desire, truth liberates. Russell is speaking to this sensibility, which hails as much from the Kantian spirituality of limitation as from any Puritanical leanings his stern grandmother who raised him may have instilled, when he tributes mathematics for its remoteness from human passion and for taking "us still further from what is human, into the region of absolute necessity, to which not only the actual world but every possible world, must conform."[24] As Alan Wood observed of Russell's driving motive, it "was an almost religious passion for some truth that was more than human, independent of the minds of men, and even of the existence of men."[25] In this sense, Russell, in contrast to William James, was not a humanist, but sought the sacred in a variety of locations beyond the human, including, but not exclusively, mathematics.[26] But here is the problem: truth has virtually no light to shed on the sacred. In a letter from 1903, around the same time as the mathematics essay, Russell wrote of his intent "to treat the religious instinct with profound respect, but to insist that there is no shred or particle of truth in any of the metaphysics it has suggested."[27] For one for whom truth was such a defining value, this was a major sacrifice to perform on behalf of the religious instinct. But it also generated a logical bind: for if truthfulness is a condition of respect, how does respect attach to what deflects the light of truth?

A sequence of writings from Russell's early life trace his struggles with this bind and uncover for us a lasting contributing from him to the foundations for philosophical spirituality. For, despite his polemical writings from his later years against religion,[28] which were largely against the institutional church, and the agnosticism he always readily admitted, Russell retained into later life a sense that it was better to have a religious instinct, than not,[29] and a capacity to be religiously moved himself.[30] But it is the essays from his younger years that open up the positive Russellian options for philosophical spirituality: "The Free Man's Worship" (1903), "The Essence of Religion" (1912) and "Religion and the Churches" (1916), and show the evolution of his response to the logical and psychological problem of the religious instinct's respectability.

From a Jamesian vantage point, "The Free Man's Worship" is an exercise in diabolical mysticism. It begins with a story of Mephistophelis, in conversation with Dr. Faustus, explaining the origin of humanity from chaos and return to it at the decree of a cruel god, who indulges the human error to worship him. Russell reprised the theme of world destruction later in his published story, *Satan in the Suburbs*, but it had already surfaced early on, at college, in a test question he would put to acquaintances, to determine if they were pessimists: "'If you had the power to destroy the world, would you do so?'"[31] Russell's fascination with this idea returned to him in late life when the fearsome prospect loomed of nuclear destruction, against which he actively campaigned. But as a young man, such pessimism found a fictional focus in, for example, the character of the darkly disturbing Rogozhin in Dostoevsky's novel, *The Idiot*, with whom he identified.[32] Russell probably did not know that, originally in Dostoevsky's mind, the characters of Rogozhin and his saintly opposite, Prince Myshkin, were united in one complex figure.[33] And that unity gives fictional expression to the Jamesian interpretation of mysticism generally, that it can manifest angelically in heightened states of union with reality, or diabolically in frightful divisions from self and others. From a mystical vantage point, All and Nothing are not so much opposites as mirror images. And from its diabolical beginnings, Russell's essay does indeed move towards an angelic world of worshipped ideals. For in the midst of a world utterly indifferent to human well-being, mankind can indeed fashion ideals that excite reverence and guide action, grounded as they may be in our own imaginations, in much the way an image or figure from a fondly remembered dream may hold our attention, as though a vision from beyond, wholly indebted as on reflection we know it to be to the workings of our own unconscious.

The problem is with where truth lies in this picture. The word itself occurs in this essay only twice, once in connection with what Russell takes for the truth of scientific (and Epicurean) atomism, and its nihilistic implications for human destiny, [34] and the other in context of religion, which pronounces even despite its false leanings "many austere truths."[35] Religion's office here repeats that of the essay itself to segue from deception to truth. But what are the austere truths to which religion guides us?—simply that in the face of an indifferent reality, whatever sustains us must be of our own making. If this truth is austere, it is only because, as Alan Wood taught, Russell himself craves with a "religious passion for some truth that was . . . independent of the minds of men." But the only such truths available are the very ones that undermine religious passion in the first place.

Part of what endears this essay to the reader is how finely it dances on the margins between truth and falsity, refusing the stark choice between them, in contrast to the clear distance it sets between evil and good, darkness and light. The ambiguity already appears in the essay's central theme of resignation: "wisdom . . . is found in the submission of our desires, but not our thoughts."[36] Read through the lens of inverse relation Russell opines between desire and truth, the thoughts that come to us on the submission of desire would be expected to be truthful ones. But truth is not in fact the mark of them, but what Russell evocatively and poetically names "the vision of beauty," which excites our "contemplation."[37]

Tellingly, it is not visions of truth we contemplate and it is not knowledge we gain from the contemplation. For anyone trained in Kantian philosophy, as Russell was, what this brings to mind are the Kantian aesthetic ideas, which, manifested in artworks, hold our attentive gaze while suspending our epistemological judgment entirely. By positioning desireless thought to receive the marks of truth, and then withholding them, Russell suspends himself and the reader in some non-epistemological space between truth and falsity.

His language about the ideals, such as beauty, we contemplate follows suit. For much as the ideals we fashion are unPlatonic, for not inhabiting a sphere beyond us—Russell renounces any wishful identifications of ideals with facts—they nonetheless move us with a claim they make on us, as though originating from beyond ourselves. The original version of this essay, from 1903, included two passages that evoked a world beyond the grim reality it otherwise portrays, "a country of unearthly beauty," reached across "an invisible sea" whose sounds of lapping waves nonetheless move us with a "strange deep music," if only we could follow where it leads.[38] The mood is subjunctive: we only "seem" to hear this music. But the effect is rather like what Keats attains, in *Ode to a Nightingale*, when he imagines the bird's song could charm both

> ... the sad heart of Ruth, when, sick for home,
> She stood in tears amid the alien corn...
> [And] magic casements, opening on the foam
> Of perilous seas in faery lands forlorn.[39]

That is, taking Ruth for an historic person, as Keats likely did, the song could bridge the divide between fiction and reality.

The later Russell had no truck with deliberate ambiguity, and so he omitted those two evocative passages from subsequent printings of the essay. Interpreting the essay from a later vantage point, in 1917, what drew his attention about it was what seemed to him then the too facile presumption that good and evil were objective realities,[40] as though the poetic language of the sacred within it merited no comment at all. Still later on, and into old age, he judged the style excessively "florid and rhetorical,"[41] an implicit critique, perhaps, of the ambiguity attendant on the poetry.

In sync with the analytic style of philosophizing he is credited with helping to found and promote, his next published foray on this topic, "The Essence of Religion," restrains the poetic and intensifies the language of definition and distinction. Here, Russell explicitly seeks a home for the religious instinct outside of epistemology, that is, free of any claims about the actual nature of reality. His goal: "to discover a form of union with the universe which is independent of all beliefs as to the nature of the universe."[42] Such a union cannot be faulted for falseness, since it "involves no [epistemological] judgment whatever."[43] Key distinctions towards realizing the goal are between: existence and being, the finite and infinite life, impartial and selective love.

Desire, identified with finite life, is once again the foil to "self-surrender, when all personal will seems to cease,"[44] in which state we are open to a sense of impartial love for all the exists. In this frame of mind, which constitutes our infinite life, we are "seeking always what is general and open to all men,"[45] a sentiment that Spinoza would endorse. Russell has shifted the inverse relation of the previous essay, between desirelessness and thought, to one between desirelessness and love. And in this way he does indeed skirt the issue of truth. The problem is that not all of reality is indeed lovable, and against a standard of lovability, must, by our own loving efforts, be made so. As though summoned from the Platonic tradition, what rises to hold the place of that standard is "the ideal good,"[46] which does indeed excite our worship. And now it is the ideal good, rather than the vision of beauty, that tantalizes us with its liminal zone between truth and falsity. For it is both an object of knowledge and a product of our creative imagination.[47] This is where the distinction between being and existence applies. The ideal good has being but not existence. It inhabits a space beyond that of actual, individual existents in a "world of universals," which Russell had rescued from its undeserved "oblivion,"[48] in another book roughly cotemporaneous with this essay, entitled *The Problems of Philosophy*. For there, in the chapter, "The World of Universals," he argued for "a world which is neither mental nor physical," which holds the place of such items essential to our thought, but not strictly given in our experience, as the concept of relation.[49] The ideal good resides there too.

In later years, Russell withdrew from so blatant a Platonism, as much as from the poetic richness of the earlier essay. In *My Philosophical Development* (1959), he recalls how similar his earlier outlook was to that "peculiar form of mysticism [that] greatly affected Plato," but notes that "I have no longer the feeling . . . that only Plato's world of ideas gives access to the 'real' world."[50] But that the Platonic universal ideas and the Kantian aesthetic ideas both ultimately failed him in his efforts to account for the respectability of a religious instinct that so resisted the epistemological illumination he sought for it, already points to one of Russell's signal contributions to the notion of philosophical spirituality: that epistemology, significant as it was for Russell to the whole idea of philosophy, is not a useful rubric under which to explicate a spirituality. This marks a turn from the whole Cartesian-Kantian tradition.

That is the implicit message of the last essay in the series considered here, "Religion and the Churches" (1916). The essay forms chapter seven of Russell's *Principles of Social Reconstruction*, which he wrote in response to the outbreak of World War I and which he later considered "the least unsatisfactory" expression of "my own personal religion."[51] The thesis of the book is that, because "impulse has more effect than conscious purpose in moulding men's lives," the institutions of society should nurture impulses towards sharing rather than towards exclusive possession, conflict over which incites war. Notions from the earlier essays carry over, only now desire and the finite life manifest as the impulse towards possession, whereas the infinite life becomes "the life of the spirit." What for Russell was the sheer irrationality of World War I opened him up to more serious consideration of the role of non-rational instinct in human behavior. In consequence, for purposes of the book, epistemology already ceded pride of place in his understanding of philosophy to social and political philosophy. Soon after, Russell's interests would turn towards psychology.[52] Accordingly, "Religion and the Churches," is already primed to free up ample space for values other than truth to show. The distinctions here are between instinct, mind, and spirit. Truth, as the object of knowledge, chiefly determines the life of mind. But this life, of its own, inclines to a "curious inhumanity and lifelessness" and, "because of its detachment, tends to separate a man inwardly from other men."[53] What steers it clear of those ill effects is the warming influence of spirit, which works to universalize such instinctive loves as those towards family and nation, into what Russell calls, "impersonal feeling,"[54] a phrasing that, again, evokes Spinoza.[55] Now, mind and spirit divide between them the impersonal and infinite life Russell celebrated in "Essence of Religion." Thought no longer incites the religious instinct towards claims to know, for universalized or infinite *feeling* is now the exclusive province of spirit. And feeling, Russell following Kant would likely insist, makes no claim to mediate truth.

The very word, "spirit," which we had not much encountered in Russell's earlier work, already invites this essay into the literature of philosophical spirituality. The ambiguity of the term serves him well. For it allows him to sustain the sense of the sacred the preceding essays more poetically capture, without claiming for it any knowledge-conferring status. Thus we read once again of a "sense of . . . a transfiguring vision in which common things lose their solid importance and become a thin veil behind the ultimate truth of the world." But mark: what we are given is not an actual vision of such truth, but merely a "sense" for it. "Contact with this eternal world—even if it be only a world of our imagining—brings . . . strength and . . . peace."[56] Russell is careful to qualify his claims for the life of spirit with suitable subjunctives that restrict it to a world of feeling and imagination which, he stops to consider, is most properly the province of art. And a tiny reflection sounds in passing on the relation between religion and art: they both spiritualize instinct, only from different starting points, art in instinct and religion in spirit.[57]

This constitutes an abdication of philosophy from any constructive heuristic role towards the religious instinct. Insofar as philosophy is essentially epistemology and more essentially still—logic, it fails to speak to the religious instinct, except to police it from erring claims to truth or harmful exercise of power. Much of Russell's writing on religion after World War I was in that vein. But it is possible to read the later writing, and even the earlier, as artistic attempts to approach the sacred, rather than as philosophical fixings of its epistemological status. That Russell won the Nobel Prize for *Literature*, in 1950, already points towards another interpretive lens of his philosophical work. Reviewers of Russell's books commented on the style, which was consistently lucid, engaging, and often witty. He counted among his friends some of the literary luminaries of his day, including Joseph Conrad, D. H. Lawrence, and T. S. Eliot. As an undergraduate, he appreciated how much the great historic systems of philosophy, even where they failed as truth, might succeed as imaginative constructions,[58] and in late life actually published books of philosophical fiction.[59]

But Russell inherited from the rationalist tradition in philosophy, which he critically admired (he kept busts of the philosophers Spinoza and Leibniz[60]), a restraining suspicion of the imagination. In his early thirties, he wrote of himself that "the intellectual habit is too imperious with me" to allow for much writing "of a purely imaginative kind."[61] A mark of that judgment on himself is that he never did finish or publish two longer companion pieces to "The Free Man's Worship," kindred to it in both style and content: *The Pilgrimage of Life* (1902–1903) and *Prisons* (1911), though parts of the latter did surface in his *Problems of Philosophy*.[62] The three works construct from complementary vantage points a spirituality of absence, that is, an approach to the sacred through longing over a distance for it. The distance of the sacred, as noted above, may push it beyond existence, but not necessarily beyond some still remotely accessible being. As Russell put it in a letter to his lover, Ottoline Morel, "Some ghost, from some extra-mundane region, seems always trying to tell me something that I am to repeat to the world, but I cannot understand the message. But it is from listening to the ghost that one comes to feel oneself a ghost."[63] Apart from this evocative language of the paranormal, Russell draws in these works from such literary masters as John Bunyan and Plato. The Platonic tradition, to which Russell subscribed in his early years, supplies the imagery of exile and worldly imprisonment—"We are exiles from the [ideal] land of the heart's desire"[64] and "each human being is born single, separate, enclosed as in a dungeon by strong walls of egotism"[65] —while from Bunyan comes the pilgrimage theme—"We are . . . comrades in this troubled pilgrimage from darkness to darkness."[66] Bunyan, who was very likely childhood reading for Russell, raised by a devout grandmother, lies behind the references in Russell's *Autobiography* to "the dreams of the Golden City" on the "mountain-peak" that beckons us, though "rarely [do we] climb the mountainside."[67] Late in life, remembering his early love of mathematics, Russell drew from Dante when he likened the higher reaches of that discipline to "the last Cantos of Dante's *Paradiso*."[68] In the early writing, echoes of

Milton and Jeremy Taylor also sound.[69] His consolation reading from the Bible was the poetically gifted Ecclesiastes.[70]

Russell dropped his youthful aspirations to write in the poetic tradition of the seventeenth century. In the late essay, "How I Write," he detected "a certain insincerity" in such early efforts as "The Free Man's Worship."[71] But he did not repudiate the comfort he found, while writing that essay, in "the construction of prose rhythms,"[72] or the motive he had "to say something . . . that perhaps by its very nature cannot be said"[73] about the relation between sorrow, solitude and the sacred. In self-critique, he suggested that what he needed was "a more artistic form"[74] than was at his disposal, and so he largely dropped the literary-spiritual enterprise; but not without leaving a philosophic framework for others more artistically gifted than he in different areas for taking it further. This was more than a revival of philosophical romanticism, which also sought the sacred through the artistic. By effectively exhausting the resources of epistemology for philosophical spirituality, Russell freed the religious instinct from the oversight of the ideal of truth, and invited that of beauty to replace it. What was needed was an artist who could picture Russell's "religion of sorrow."[75] And such a one did live within Russell's lifetime but died before Russell published a word. It was Vincent Van Gogh (1853–1890).

Unlikely as the pairing sounds, Van Gogh and Russell shared more than a few years of life on earth. Van Gogh, whose work before painting was preaching, delivered a sermon at the Methodist church in Richmond, England, now part of London, in the fall of 1876. At that time, four year old Russell was living nearby in Richmond Park with his grandparents, who may indeed on the very day of Van Gogh's sermon have taken their young charge to Richmond's Presbyterian Church, their accustomed destination on alternate Sundays.[76] Earlier that year, Van Gogh, writing his brother Theo of a visit he had made to Hampton Court, imagined the presence there of "Lord and Lady Russell."[77] These Russells—William (1639–1683) and Rachel (1636–1723)—were Bertrand's own ancestors, whom he reverenced for helping to found the British Whig tradition. The imagination sparkles at the thought of a conversation between Van Gogh and Russell on English history, or any number of other matters. The early Russell might have been the later Van Gogh's philosopher of sorrow, especially considering the respect Van Gogh had for "English authors . . . their Monday-morning-like soberness . . . and keen analysis."[78] Unpromisingly for our comparison, philosophy was not customary reading for the otherwise well-read Van Gogh, and though Russell would have encountered Van Gogh's work, if nowhere else than at the lavish galleries of the Barnes Foundation outside Philadelphia, where he taught in the early 1940s, he had neither a developed appreciation of art, nor much of a visual sense at all.[79] Nonetheless, several common themes connect their lives: loneliness, depression, mental imbalance,[80] suicidal thoughts, financial troubles, disdain for academic establishments, defiance of social convention, ethic of truthfulness.[81] Both suffered from a sense of imprisonment and were indeed institutionally confined at different points of their lives, Russell for his peace activism, Van Gogh for his self-destructiveness. Even unconfined, the young Van Gogh likened himself to a caged bird.[82] To the extent that, for Russell, "self-interest" was a "prison,"[83] confinement was ubiquitous. Both loved nature: Russell, who wrote that "the sea, the stars, the wind night in waste places mean more to me than even the human being I love best,"[84] would have understood Van Gogh when he wrote that when he felt religious, "I go out at night to paint the stars."[85] Both craved and largely lacked a sense of community, Russell with philosophers,[86] and Van Gogh with artists. Both documented their inner lives in a rich abundance of expressive letters.[87] And of course both, from having been raised in established forms of Christianity, came to channel their religious instincts elsewhere. What mathematics was, spiritually, to the one, art was to the other.[88] Compare Russell's thought on the respect due the religious instinct (see footnote 27 of this chapter) with this from Van Gogh: "One need not agree exactly with the form of that religious sentiment, but if it is sincere it is a feeling one must respect."[89] For them both, the religious sentiment took an impersonal form. Russell, the mathematical theorist of types, surely would have warmed to Van Gogh's way of putting it, that "the highest thing in art" was attained when the artist imaged "the type distilled from many individuals."[90]

Where each seems most to image the other, as though in a mirror reflecting the faces of artists and philosophers back to each other, is across "The Free Man's Worship" and the Richmond sermon, which Van Gogh preached on Psalm 119:19—"I am a stranger on earth, hide not thy commandments from me." If Van Gogh preached his sermon in Russell's childhood environs, Russell began his essay in a setting that would be resonant for Van Gogh, of olive and cypress trees, surrounding the Florentine estate of art connoisseur, Bernard Berenson,[91] married to the sister of Russell's first wife, Alys Smith. For both works, life is a pilgrimage and Bunyan the inspiration.[92] When Russell pictures the pilgrim emerging "out of the cavern . . . [in]to the daylight of wisdom," he unknowingly echoes what Van Gogh wrote to his brother about his feelings on facing from the pulpit the Richmond congregation: "I felt like somebody who, emerging from a dark cave underground, comes back to the friendly daylight."[93] Despite the diabolic beginnings of the essay, both it and the sermon deck the start and conclusion of the pilgrimage in relatively bright colors. For both, the beginning is Mother nature, who having "brought forth at last a child . . . gifted with insight"[94] (Russell), "remembereth no more her sorrow and her anguish for joy that a man is born into the world"[95] (Van Gogh). And though the ultimate destination is, for the theist Van Gogh, "Our Father's house,"[96] and for Russell, simply Death, that death is less a grim finality than a passageway to the "immortality of the past," where all rests peacefully in—as a painter night imagine—"motionless and silent pictures."[97] But then, the very image at all of life as pilgrimage mutes its importance, in favor of some preferable Beyond that is both origin and goal of the passage.

The problem for both is the passage, which is steeped in sorrow, the *leitmotif* of the sermon as it opens—"Sorrow is better than joy"[98] —and for the essay towards its close, after it has seen that sorrow is better than—if not joy, then certainly—desire, defiance, and despair, which are all interlinked. Both lament the loss of youth.[99] Both evoke the image for life of a storm-tossed vessel.[100] What most strikingly connects the sermon and the essay is a vivid sense in each of profound loneliness.[101] A feeling for this was the kernel of Russell's conversion experience. In the sermon, which after all aims to communicate a gospel message, or good news, the loneliness is more a mood than a declaration.[102] Though "we are [all] pilgrims," we appear to walk alone, in contrast to the communal ethos that characterizes religious pilgrimage already from biblical times and Bunyan himself, whose Christian is in continual contact with others. As though in anticipation of his still future vocation, Van Gogh concludes the sermon with his memory of a painting, a "landscape at evening," including a road that winds to a mountaintop city "whereon the setting sun casts a glory."[103] A lone pilgrim walks the road, his only encounter with an angel—no fellow human—in the guise of a woman, who encourages him onward. Van Gogh suggests in a letter to his brother[104] that the painting he had in mind was by one of his favorite artists, an American living in England, George Henry Boughton (1833–1905). Among Boughton's work, the one that comes closest to fitting the description is "God's speed!," which depicts a meeting between what appear to be two male pilgrims and four sympathetic women encountered along the way. The problem is in the plurality of figures. In addition, there is no mountaintop city in the distance, or setting sun. For some interpreters, the discrepancies between this painting and the one Van Gogh remembered count against any identification of the two.[105] But what argues for the identification, despite the differences, is not simply the absence of any suitable alternatives among the known works of Boughton, but what Van Gogh himself reported in late life about how he learned from other artists by copying their work: "[It] is not purely and simply copying. Rather it is translating."[106] The translation might transpose a figure from another artist into a new setting or color scheme, such as Van Gogh did with the figure of the sower from another of his favorite artists, Millet.[107] Synesthetically, Van Gogh transposed in his mind even between art and literature. "There is something of Rembrandt in Shakespeare;" "drawing with words is also an art."[108] What Van Gogh presented at the end of his sermon was a drawing in words translated from Boughton's picture. We should not expect an exact copy. But we may learn from what Van Gogh has changed. The community is reduced to a solitary figure who travels alone and nears the goal of Bunyan's *Pilgrim Progress*, where the Golden City is sighted. Later paintings of Van Gogh featured solitary figures, or even ones wholly absent (from interior settings where they might be expected). "The many solitary figures in van Gogh's work correspond to the lonely outcast—the stranger, the prisoner, the vagabond—he saw himself to be."[109] The images apply equally to Russell, who was indeed imprisoned for his anti-war and anti-nuclear protests, moved many times in his life, was sometimes critically short of finances, and titled an early, unpublished work, *Prisons*. In both cases, the self-image of exile and isolation took a religious turn, in self-identifications with monks.[110] But then, the translation of Boughton's pilgrim(s) into the climactic finish of Bunyan's literary landscape links the isolation and the sorrow to the imminence (though not necessarily the immanence) of the sacred. Van Gogh makes this connection most explicit: "it always strikes me . . . whenever we see the image of . . . loneliness, of poverty and misery . . . the thought of God comes into our minds."[111] This was also, in effect, the message of Russell's conversion experience: "in the endurance of intolerable pain . . . there is a sacredness, an overpowering awe . . . a feeling of . . . the inexhaustible mystery of existence."[112] For both, such sense as we may have "that we are all brethren,"[113] comes from "the tie of a common doom."[114]

Van Gogh explored throughout his artistic life, as both painter and writer, the link between sorrow and the sacred. "I find my serenity in 'worship of sorrow,'" he wrote his brother,[115] as though to anticipate Russell's later "religion of sorrow." His early drawing of *Sorrow*, based on his mistress, Sien, was in his own opinion "the best I've done"[116] up until then. But it is the figure of a seated old man, hiding his face in his hands, entitled *Worn Out: At Eternity's Gate* that best captures Van Gogh's version of this religion. The very title of the work links the sadness of it to the sacred. If life has worn the old man out, it has nonetheless taken him to where the sermon's word picture placed the pilgrim, in sight of the golden city. The title of the painting recalls a memorable metaphor from Van Gogh, alluding to trains, that "we take death to reach a star."[117] The image captures more compactly, less burdened by seventeenth century literary associations, and so more purely, the message of the sermon. Van Gogh first pictured the man, in 1882, as a lithograph, commenting: "In this print I have tried to express . . . the existence of God and eternity, certainly in the infinitely touching expression of a little old man. . . . The poorest little woodcutter or peasant on the hearth or miner can have moments of . . . feeling of an eternal home."[118] Van Gogh reprised the figure in the last year of his own life, as an oil painting in brilliant colors. That the image lasted in significance for him from the start to finish of his artistic life suggests he found in it what Russell sought to perfect and succeed his "Free Man's Worship," but could not find, by the limits on his own medium. If only one of his artistic friends, such as Roger Fry, who promoted the post-impressionists (their work was formally exhibited in London, in 1910) could have shown it to him.[119] But Van Gogh speaks to Russell's own need for an alternative medium to expository prose when he writes, "I never heard a good sermon on resignation, nor can I imagine a good one, except [in] . . . the work of Millet."[120] True to that thought, Van Gogh never names resignation in his own sermon, unlike Russell, who does several times in his essay. In a meeting between the two beyond time[121] we can hear Van Gogh critique Russell's essay for failing in sincerity over the idea of resignation, which only a good picture by Millet (or himself) could effectively image—and we can almost hear Russell agree. What Russell hoped from resignation was "creative idealism" in "the whole world of art and philosophy."[122] And this is just what Van Gogh had—"which is my life, the power to create"[123] —at least in the world of art. And then it is almost as though philosophy resigns to make room for art, as earlier on, reason had in Kant, to make room for faith.

Russell maintained about his conversion experience that "something of what I thought I saw in that moment has remained always with me."[124] It shows less forcefully in his later works. In *What I Believe*, for example, from 1925, the phenomenon of desire, at whose feet Russell's religion of sorrow lay the blame for much of our unhappiness, becomes the chief currency of happiness, if only properly spent. But an unexpected context arose for Russell to revisit the spiritual import of philosophy, by way of a history he was invited to compose of it. In 1940, after Russell had lost his chance to teach logic at the City University of New York, the philanthropist, patron of adult education, and art collector, Albert Barnes, invited him to teach the history of philosophy at his magnificent private gallery of modern paintings outside Philadelphia. Russell had never before been strictly an historian of philosophy, but he had written on the idea of the Past as a sanctum from change and on History as an art. Already in "The Free Man's Worship," Russell had found in the idea of the past another equivalence, besides mathematics, for his sense of sacred, on grounds it shared with mathematics, that it silenced desire. "The Past does not change or strive. . . . [W]hat was eager and grasping . . . has faded away, the things that were beautiful and eternal shine out of it like stars in the night."[125] From the same period as that essay, Russell wrote another, "On History" (1904) that intensified these claims for the sacredness of that "silent temple, which all the ages build," and to which all are finally admitted by "Death's hallowing touch."[126] The Past conforms to the inverse relation Russell saw between truth and desire. As a place of desirelessness, "the past alone is truly real," and "history . . . valuable . . . because it is true."[127] Insofar as the truth always lends itself to science, Russell hoped for a science of history that uncovered from masses of historical data general laws that governed the unfolding of social events, as those of science do of natural events. But in later life, when he wrote again on history, he chose for his title, "History as an Art" (1956) as though to concede the point. Russell may have been driven to this position by his rejection of Marxism, which rewrote history as science. The result was that "history is like poetry" and "must be interesting . . . in the same spirit in which . . . poetry or a good novel" are.[128] If only for the sake of [artistic?] interest, the historian must tell a good story, albeit without distorting the facts, and even apportion praise and blame.

Russell might have been describing his own *History of Western Philosophy*. This book, based on the lectures he gave at the Barnes Foundation, tells the story of philosophy so well that it became a best-seller. Russell is the first of our philosophers to summon the whole history of philosophy for our review, not towards confirming his own philosophy (as in the case of Hegel), but from the conviction he expresses in the last sentence of the book, that "philosophy does not cease to suggest and inspire a way of life."[129] This, too, is a contribution to philosophical spirituality. Precisely as history, and evocation of the past, the book locates itself with other limiters of human desire that Russell valued (mathematics, truth), a point he makes in the book's penultimate chapter, on John Dewey, in protest of Dewey's results- and future-oriented epistemology (826). At the same time, as historical art, the book is notoriously tendentious, and takes no pains to conceal its author's preferences and dislikes among the philosophers. For instance, Russell admires the pre-Socratic philosopher, Anaximenes, who taught that all is air, for the implication of that—that qualitative differences between things are quantifiable (28). Russell favors the first of the following orientations itemized in a series he implicitly generates, over the course of his book, of philosophical typologies, contrasting the empirical and the rationalist, the truthful and soteric, the scientific and religious, the objective and subjective, the credible and the self-consistent. Credible philosophy is typically inconsistent but truth-disclosing, empirical and objective. The paradigm is John Locke, who receives one of the longest expanses of pages in the book, and is the most liberally quoted. Plato may have been an "imaginative writer of great genius and charm," (84) but he was intellectually dishonest (78), "the worst of philosophic sins" (143). How much more truthfully (and humanely) the Middle Ages might have unfolded if its guiding philosophical light had been Democritus, rather than Plato or Aristotle (160). But even the Middle Ages offers up its treasures, such as John the Scot (Johannes Erigena), a "Neo-Platonist [and] . . . a pantheist" (400) who, nonetheless, within the midst of a philosophically dark time, "maintained the equal or even superior authority of a philosophy independent of revelation" (403). Some of Russell's condemnations may startle, for instance, of Aristotle, who might have been supposed to be the empirically minded corrective of the overly rationalist and mendacious Plato. But Aristotle disappoints in part for his baneful influence on the evolution of logic—one of Russell's early and never quite abandoned loves—and also, surprisingly, for omitting from his ethics "the whole sphere of human experience with which religion is concerned" (184). It is perhaps the persistence of Russell's conversion experience, which highlighted despair, speaking there, since the *Nicomachean Ethics* fails chiefly for ignoring those "whom outward misfortune drives to despair" (184).

Sometimes, the tone of neutrality Russell adopts surprises, especially when we would expect a more passionate expression of alignment with a philosopher, or at least livelier appreciation. Isaiah Berlin, in reviewing the book, suggests this is true of Russell's treatment of Hume, which should have been richer, "if only in virtue of his cardinal importance in the genesis of the author's own ideas."[130] But it is perhaps even more true of the account Lucretius receives. For in an essay that preceded the book, Russell announced that "My own view on religion is that of Lucretius."[131] The few pages Russell devotes to that Roman poet-philosopher give little sign of that. It is more than points of view—"denial of Providence, rejection of immortality" (250)—that connect the two thinkers. When Russell writes of Lucretius' "passionate" nature, his proneness to suicide (which he finally committed) and his bouts of "periodic insanity" (248), he might have been writing of his own perduring anxieties. But it is indeed the hatred of institutional religion that most unites the two. Russell had particular cause for that, since it was largely through the efforts of the then Episcopal bishop of New York City, William Manning, that he was barred from teaching logic at the City College of New York, on grounds of views he expressed, outside his writings on logic, on marriage and sex. It was just that public attack on Russell that drew the sympathies of the iconoclastic Albert Barnes and the invitation to teach at his galleries. But Russell somewhat disingenuously observes of Lucretius that it may be difficult to understand "the hatred of religion expressed by [him]"(249), and invokes the very worst of ancient religious excesses to explain it: human sacrifice. Was he hinting at the sacrifice City College made of him under pressure from the seemingly high-civilized Episcopal Church? Perhaps Russell's detachment from Lucretius owes to what by then had become a definite difference from him. Lucretius was a materialist and, as we saw, opened space within his atomism for a spirituality of matter to show. In the last chapter of *History of Western Philosophy*, on logical analysis, Russell explains that under the influence of William James, he no longer acknowledges a dualism between mind and matter, but takes the both for "merely convenient ways of grouping events" that are more elementarily strictly neither (833). But this hardly seems enough difference to trump the similarities. More likely, Russell was simply too close to Lucretius in spirit to display a preference that would reveal more of his inner self than declarations for such obviously different thinkers as John the Scot or Plotinus would do.

But the very admission of preference at all so openly into the book is revealing after all. Russell's pro-science bias, in concert with his faith in the absolute opposition between religion and science, causes him to fixate, disapprovingly, on the religious dimensions of philosophy. In this way, he highlights backhandedly the religious appeal of Plato, for instance, in service of readers seeking the most promising locations of spirituality in the history of philosophy. At the same time, if preference enters the book on grounds of art, to enliven the history, it undercuts any claim the book might make to instance what it most admires—scientific truth-telling. Isaiah Berlin commented astutely on it when he wrote that "its principal value and interest . . . resides in the light which it casts upon the views of its author."[132] As an exercise in subjectivity, the book naturally allies with the philosophies it ostensibly disdains—the soteric, religious, and untruthful ones. In agreement with Russell's earlier views, the book implicitly disowns truth as the optimal standard for measuring the merits of a philosophy and in at least one place (the chapter on Plotinus) admits beauty to that high office (285).

The very origins of the book prepare the way for this. For what Albert Barnes hired Russell to teach at his galleries was the *social* history of philosophy, that is, the impact of an era's social and political conditions on the philosophies that arose during it. Russell attends to this, but not throughout. He notes for example that mystical and Stoical philosophies arise in eras of pervasive worldly unhappiness. To explain the appeal of a philosophy on grounds of the social anxieties it addresses opens a way for other evaluative measures than truthfulness to apply. A measure that surfaces less explicitly in the book than the social-historical one, but more persuasively and engagingly for our purpose, is just the one Russell identified early on as the alternative to truth among the two chief motivators of philosophical reflection: religious longing. How else account for those two among the philosophers who drew Russell's warmest praise: Plotinus and Spinoza, hardly exemplars of scientific empiricism and credibility. What they offer up instead are "systems" of "imaginative delight" that evoke our "hypothetical sympathy" (38–39). The subjunctive mood echoes how Russell had earlier written of the sacred Beyond in "The Free Man's Worship" and accords with what he says at the start of this book, that philosophy's point is "to teach how to live without certainty" (xiv). Remotely mystical as the object of this mood may be, Russell nonetheless acknowledges it in Hegel and even in Kant (206, 230), an echo perhaps of his early training at Cambridge in British idealism. Its antique origin is Orphism, from which "arose the conception of philosophy as a way of life" (24). Improbably, philosophies of the remotely subjunctive apply most continuously to the present indicative—our everyday life. If these unscientific systems are habitable philosophies that answer our religious longing, then Russell in this book counters a claim he made ten years earlier in his *Autobiography* that "philosophy cannot give religion."[133] It can, when it effectively converts to poetry; and all the more when its location is the past, which sanctifies its imaginative structures in eternal stillness. Perhaps this is why Russell devotes, otherwise unaccountably, a whole chapter to Byron, and, citing chapters six and seven of the dishonest *Republic* of Plato, needlessly comments on their "extraordinary literary beauty" (119). Under the rubric of poetic art, philosophy that has bifurcated between science and religion combines features of both in a "fusion of intellect and mysticism" (126), modeled by Plato but imitated by many others, according to this history of philosophy, including several we have already met on our own path: Spinoza, Kant, Hegel, and William James. Russell has produced the photographic negative of a history of philosophical spirituality—the book in hand presumes to be its obviously much lesser development into the positive.

NOTES

1. Bertrand Russell, *The Autobiography of Bertrand Russell* (London: George Allen, 1967), 1:146. Russell biographer, Ray Monk, calls this, "surely the most extraordinary piece of writing in his [Russell's] *Autobiography*." Ray Monk, *Bertrand Russell: The Spirit of Solitude, 1872–1921* (New York: Free Press, 1996), 134. Though not here, later in his *Autobiography*, Russell explicitly characterizes the experience as a "'conversion,'" Russell, 2:191, though admittedly in quotes.
2. Monk, *Bertrand Russell: The Spirit of Solitude*, 113.
3. Robert D. Richardson, *William James: In the Maelstrom of American Modernism* (Boston: Houghton Mifflin, 2006), 401–2.
4. Ray Monk, *Bertrand Russell: The Ghost of Madness, 1921–1970* (New York: Free Press, 2001), 125. Monk calls the part of his *Autobiography* Russell wrote in 1931, "a literary masterpiece."
5. Russell, *Autobiography*, 2:16.
6. Ibid., 1:146.
7. Ibid., 1:145.
8. Russell, "Why I Took to Philosophy," in *Basic Writings of Bertrand Russell*, ed. Robert Egner and Lester E. Denonn (New York: Simon and Schuster, 1967), 56.
9. Russell, *Autobiography*, 3:222.
10. Ibid., 3:220. Russell was 38 in 1910, when he finished the first volume of *Principia Mathematica*. He was actively pacifist through World War I, and involved in many social causes after that, including women's suffrage, world peace, and the anti-nuclear movement
11. Russell, *History of Western Philosophy* (New York: Simon and Schuster, 1945), xiii.
12. Commenting on this distinction in an essay on James, in 1908, Russell identified himself, "with some reserves," with the tough-minded. Russell, *Philosophical Essays* (New York: Routledge, 2009), 105. Surely what kept him partially with the tender-minded were such essays as "The Free Man's Worship." But he never wholly alienated from philosophy those questions "that are of profoundest interest to our spiritual life." Russell, *The Problems of Philosophy* (New York: Henry Holt, [1912]), 241.
13. Russell, "The Study of Mathematics," in *Contemplation and Action: 1902–1914*, ed. Richard A Rempel and others. The Collected Papers of Bertrand Russell, 12 (London: George Allen and Unwin, 1985), 93.
14. Ibid., 86, 91.
15. Ibid., 85.
16. Russell, *Autobiography*, 2:36.
17. Russell, "The Pilgrimage of Life," in *Contemplation and Action*, 43.

18. See Monk, *Bertrand Russell: Ghost of Madness*, 357–372.
19. Russell, *Autobiography*, 3:89.
20. Russell, "Pilgrimage," 43.
21. Russell, "Mysticism and Logic," in *Contemplation and Action*, 177.
22. Russell, *The History of Western Philosophy* (New York: Simon and Schuster, 1945), 828.
23. Russell, *Autobiography*, 1:168.
24. Russell, "Mathematics," 91.
25. Alan Wood, "Russell's Philosophy: A Study of its Development," in *My Philosophical Development*, by Bertrand Russell (New York: Simon and Schuster, 1959), 260.
26. In some ways Russell does ask to be taken for a humanist, as Charles Taylor persuasively does when he suggests that Russell illustrates what he calls "exclusive humanism," i.e., the view that there is no higher goal than human flourishing, which is understood to occur without aid of transcendence. Charles Taylor, *A Secular Age* (Cambridge, MA: Harvard University Press, 2007), 251. Our interpretation of Russell is that transcendence does function for him, but only in the subjunctive, not the indicative, mood.
27. Russell, *Autobiography*, 1:187.
28. "With the years, he [Russell] returned to discuss religion in a less experiential and more anti-Christian fashion. His method became increasingly that of argument used in an anti-theological way as in 'Why I am Not a Christian.'" Richard A. Rempel and Margaret Moran, introduction to *Contemplation and Action*, xxvii.
29. From 1944: "I consider some form of personal religion highly desirable and feel many people unsatisfactory through the lack of it." Russell, "Reply to Criticisms," in *The Philosophy of Bertrand Russell*, ed. Paul Arthur Schilpp, The Library of Living Philosophers, 5 (Evanston, IL: Northwestern University Press, 1944), 726
30. See his account, from 1952, of visiting a church in Greece, when "I realized then that the Christian outlook had a firmer hold upon me than I had imagined." *Autobiography*, 3:68. His daughter Kate took this as part of her evidence that "he was by temperament a profoundly religious man." Kate Tait, *My Father Bertrand Russell* (London: Harcourt Brace, 1975), 184.
31. Russell, *Autobiography*, 1:65.
32. Monk, *Bertrand Russell: The Spirit of Solitude*, 233, 256. Monk takes a passage from *The Idiot* about Rogozhin for the biography's epigraph.
33. Robin Feuer Miller, "The Notebooks for *The Idiot*," in *Dostoevsky's* The Idiot: *A Critical Companion*, ed. Liza Knapp (Evanston, IL: Northwestern University Press, 1998), 76.
34. Russell, "A Free Man's Worship," in *Basic Writings of Bertrand Russell*, 67
35. Ibid., 69.
36. Ibid.
37. Ibid.
38. Russell, "The Free Man's Worship," *Independent Review* 1, no. 3 (Dec. 1903), 420, 422.
39. Though Shelley, not Keats, was Russell's favorite romantic poet.
40. Russell, preface to *Mysticism and Logic and Other Essays* (New York: Longmans, Green, 1918).
41. Russell, *Autobiography*, 3:172.
42. Russell, "Essence of Religion," in *Basic Writings of Bertrand Russell*, 575.
43. Ibid., 570.
44. Ibid., 567.
45. Ibid., 566.
46. Ibid., 569.
47. Ibid.
48. Ibid., 570.
49. Russell, *The Problems of Philosophy*, 140–141.
50. Russell, *My Philosophical Development*, 209, 213.

51. Russell, "Reply to Criticisms," in *Philosophy of Bertrand Russell*, 726.
52. See Ray Monk, *Bertrand Russell: The Spirit of Solitude*, 535–536.
53. Russell, *Principles of Social Reconstruction* (New York: Routledge, 1916, 1997), 144, 149.
54. Ibid., 143.
55. Throughout his writings, Russell expressed admiration for Spinoza, whom he deemed "the noblest and most lovable of the great philosophers." Russell, *History of Western Philosophy*, 569.
56. Russell, *Principles of Social Reconstruction*, 144, 169.
57. Ibid., 143.
58. Monk, *Bertrand Russell: The Spirit of Solitude*, 68–9.
59. For instance, *Satan in the Suburbs and Other Stories* (London: Bodley Head, 1953).
60. Monk, *Bertrand Russell: The Spirit of Solitude*, 234.
61. Russell to Bernard Berenson, Feb. 28, 1903, in *The Selected Letters of Bertrand Russell*, ed. Nicholas Griffin (Boston: Houghton Mifflin, 1992), 1:261.
62. Russell, *Contemplation and Action*, 100.
63. Russell, *Autobiography*, 2:90.
64. Russell, "Pilgrimage," 35.
65. Ibid., 49.
66. Ibid., 41.
67. Ibid., 42, 40. The evidence is that Russell was rereading *The Pilgrim's Progress* in 1902. Ibid., 33.
68. Russell, *Autobiography*, 3:222.
69. Russell, "Pilgrimage," 33.
70. Russell, *Autobiography*, 2:27.
71. Russell, "How I Write," in *The Writings of Bertrand Russell*, 64.
72. Russell, *Autobiography*, 1:150.
73. Ibid., 2:90.
74. Russell to Bernard Berenson, Feb. 10, 1912, quoted in *Contemplation and Action*, 98.
75. Russell's own name for his early efforts to articulate a philosophical spirituality. Monk, *Bertrand Russell: The Spirit of Solitude*, 146
76. Russell, *Autobiography*, 1:40. The church where Van Gogh preached no longer stands. Ms Liz Velluet of the Richmond Local History Society reports: "Unfortunately the Methodist Chapel in Kew Road where Van Gogh preached his first sermon in 1876 was destroyed by fire in 1880. It was replaced by a Methodist Church but that also has disappeared and been replaced with flats. The original Wesleyan Chapel stood at the corner of Kew Road and Evelyn Road and was built in 1871-2—so it would have been new when Van Gogh visited." Email correspondence, Oct. 30, 2011. Sadly, even in history-loving London, no plaque marks the spot of the former church.
77. Van Gogh, *The Complete Letters of Vincent Van Gogh*, [trans. Johanna van Gogh-Bonger and C. de Wood] (Greenwich, CT: New York Graphic Society, [1958]), 1:62. What interested Van Gogh was their marriage, which he had read about in Francois Guizot's biography of Lord and Lady Russell, *L'amour dans le mariage*.
78. Ibid., 1:468. This is not a bad description of Russell's epistemological writing.
79. Russell lacked "visual imagination" and had trouble recalling faces. Monk, *Bertrand Russell: The Spirit of Solitude*, 87. All he reports of the Barnes galleries, whose walls were covered with impressionist and post-impressionist pictures, including several by Van Gogh, was that the French nudes seemed an unlikely backdrop for the philosophy lectures he delivered there. Russell, *Autobiography*, 2:221. In fact, Russell and Van Gogh shared interest in one philosophical writer, the French historian Jules Michelet (1798–1874). A passage from Michelet is the epigraph for Russell's *Principles of Social Reconstruction*, and Van Gogh cites him repeatedly throughout his letters
80. Russell feared insanity in himself, and confronted the proximity of it to his eldest son; he several times considered suicide, and, after his death, his granddaughter, Lucy, actually did so.

81. This manifested for Van Gogh in his practice of painting from landscapes and models, rather than from memory or sheer imagination. He wrote, "I still can find no better definition of the word art than this . . .—nature, reality, truth." *Letters*, 1:189. Albert Lubin comments, "The personal fears that drove him from Christianity made him oppose art that was not consonant with reason." Lubin, *Stranger on the Earth: A Psychological Biography of Vincent Van Gogh* (New York: Henry Holt, 1972), 214.
82. Van Gogh, *Letters*, 1:199.
83. Russell, "Prisons," 102.
84. Russell, *Autobiography*, 2:38.
85. Van Gogh, *Letters*, 3:56.
86. Russell: "There is a 'communion of philosophers' . . . and it is largely that that keeps me from feeling lonely." *Autobiography*, 1:184. Van Gogh: "I had imagined that the painters formed a kind of circle or society in which warmth and cordiality . . . reigned." Van Gogh, *Letters*, 1:519
87. Under the name, "hypergraphia," this has been associated with Van Gogh's psychological troubles. Kathleen Powers Erickson, *At Eternity's Gate: The Spiritual Vision of Vincent Van Gogh* (Grand Rapids, MI: Eerdmans, 1998), 116.
88. Van Gogh: "There is something infinite in painting" *Letters*, 1:441. Higher mathematics offers up "an exact science of the infinite." Russell, "Study of Mathematics," 88.
89. Van Gogh, *Letters*,1:513. Van Gogh is commenting on "the peculiar sentiment of Christmas and the New Year's," which he finds especially religious in "Holland and England."
90. Ibid., 1:520. Van Gogh had in mind the type of the Sower.
91. Russell, *Contemplation and Action*, 62.
92. Kathleen Powers Erickson suggests that Bunyan and Thomas á Kempis were key inspirations for Van Gogh. Erickson, *At Eternity's Gate*. Russell had read Thomas á Kempis, but preferred the work of another Dutchman: Spinoza. Monk, *Bertrand Russell: The Spirit of Solitude*, 68. Calvinism was a backdrop to both Russell's and Van Gogh's childhood upbringings, as it was of course for John Bunyan.
93. Van Gogh, *Letters*, 1:73.
94. Russell, "Free Man's Worship," 67.
95. Van Gogh, "Vincent's Sermon," in *Letters of Vincent Van Gogh*, 1:87.
96. Ibid.
97. Russell, "Free Man's Worship," 72, 71. Death's sting is healed by the Past, "a calm and smiling land, bathed in eternal sunshine." Russell, "The Pilgrimage of Life," 45.
98. Van Gogh, "Sermon,"1:87.
99. Ibid., 1:88. Russell, "Free Man's Worship," 69.
100. Russell, "Free Man's Worship," 71. Van Gogh, "Sermon," 1:88.
101. For Russell, see especially "Free Man's Worship," 71.
102. One interpreter observes that "a sense of passing through life in loneliness and alienation permeates the sermon." Cliff Edwards, *Van Gogh and God: A Creative Spiritual Quest* (Chicago: Loyola Press, 1989), 1.
103. Van Gogh, "Sermon," 1:91.
104. Van Gogh, *Letters*, 1:66.
105. Xander Van Eck, "Van Gogh and George Henry Boughton," *The Burlington Magazine* 132, no. 1049 (Aug. 1990): 539–540.
106. Van Gogh, *Letters*, 3:247.
107. Lubin, *Stranger on the Earth*, 215.
108. Van Gogh, *Letters*, 1:196, 1:395. Van Gogh commented on a work of Victor Hugo that "it is painted—I mean written—like Decamps." Ibid., 1:492. He also transposed between art and music: "Millet is perhaps a stately organ." Ibid., 1:518.
109. Lubin, *Stranger on the Earth*, 5.
110. Russell, *Autobiography*, 1:162; Van Gogh, *Letters*, 3:90, 3:142.
111. Van Gogh, *Letters*, 1:177.

112. Russell, "Free Man's Worship," 71.
113. Van Gogh, *Letters*, 1:91.
114. Russell, "Free Man's Worship," 72.
115. Van Gogh, *Letters*, 2:131.
116. Ibid., 1:419.
117. Ibid., 3:605.
118. Ibid., 1:495.
119. While still a student at Cambridge, Russell was taken to see "Impressionist pictures in the Luxembourg," but dismissed the visit as "an unsuccessful attempt to instill culture into me." *Autobiography* 1:83. He would not likely have seen any paintings by Van Gogh then, since it was only in 1890 that Van Gogh first began to receive critical appreciation from the French art world. Lubin, *Stranger on Earth*, 238.
120. Van Gogh, *Letters*, 1:326.
121. Van Gogh did correspond with an Australian artist friend named John Russell—at the mention of "Russell," in Van Gogh's letters, anyone seeking parallels between Bertrand and Vincent is eerily startled.
122. Russell, "Free Man's Worship," 70, 69.
123. Van Gogh, *Letters*, 3:25.
124. Russell, *Autobiography*, 1:146.
125. Russell, "Free Man's Worship," 71.
126. Russell, "On History," in *Basic Writings*, 527.
127. Ibid., 527, 521.
128. Russell, "History as an Art," 537.
129. Russell, *History of Western Philosophy* (New York: Simon and Schuster, 1945), 836. Page references for further citations are given parenthetically.
130. Isaiah Berlin, review of *History of Western Philosophy*, by Bertrand Russell, *Mind* n.s. 56, no. 222 (April 1947): 162.
131. Russell, "Has Religion Made Useful Contributions to Civilization," in *Russell on Religion: Selections from the Writings of Bertrand Russell*, ed. Louis Greenspan and Stefan Andersson (New York: Routledge, 1999), 169.
132. Isaiah Berlin, review of *History of Western Philosophy*, 152.
133. Russell, *Autobiography*, 1:188.

FOURTEEN
Simone Weil

Between July and November, 1942, while Bertrand Russell was living outside Philadelphia in Malvern, Pennsylvania and still teaching at the Barnes Foundation, Simone Weil was living with her parents in New York City, in flight from Nazi-occupied France and waiting for passage to what would be her final destination, England. At the same time, Weil's brother André had recently moved to Bethlehem, Pennsylvania, fifty miles north of Malvern—to teach mathematics at Lehigh University— where Simone visited him and met her newly born niece, Sylvie. Mathematics is a theme connecting the three of them, Weil through her admiration for it and what she took for its spiritual import, Russell and André Weil through their professional practice of it, which won for each fame in their respective fields. André Weil had been in French prison in 1940, for evading the draft, and Russell was among those who advocated on his behalf.[1] But there is no evidence that Russell and Simone Weil were ever aware of each other's life or work.

A meeting between them would have been odd, but is not unimaginable, as across their different backgrounds and characters they had much in common, for example: pacifism, from which each was only converted by World War II; political activism stemming from heightened social conscience; prison, which Russell knew as an inmate and Weil as a visitor to her brother there, whose forced constraint she envied; a sense for the spiritual significance of the Past; an itinerant life[2] ; a particular appreciation of the story of Hippolytus and Phaedra as dramatized by Euripides (but also, for Weil at least, by Racine, whose version she much admired); a dislike of Aristotle[3] (for different reasons); a regard (approving in Weil, disapproving in the late Russell) for Plato as founding voice in western philosophical spirituality; a distaste for philosophical pragmatism[4] and a wish, in 1942, from their respective American places, to leave for England

(Russell did so in 1944). Weil, though French, had enormous regard for England, which she took for the chief civilized bulwark against Nazism. Across their differences in philosophical culture and descent (from Descartes, for Weil and, arguably, for Russell, from Hume), they shared a suspicion of the philosophical system, whose value each felt lay in its poetry, and understood rigorous philosophical method to inquire first after meaning and only then after truth.[5] Though Russell would have agreed with little in Weil's thinking, he might have admired that she appeared to achieve, on her own terms, what he could not on his, the union of certainty and religious intuition. Neither lacked in their affectional life for presences quite like the other's. Russell's close friend Wittgenstein resembled Weil in some ways,[6] whereas all the kindly figures who looked out for the impractical and self-denying Weil, not least her parents, recall Russell at his most generous and solicitous.

What "Simone Weil" conjures for many readers who recognize the name is an intensely experiential and paradoxical Christianity that nonetheless refuses alliance with the institutional church (rather like Kierkegaard). This impression is so strong that it may occlude how much of a philosopher Weil was. "She was trained as a philosopher . . . [and] essentially remained one."[7] It is not simply that she studied philosophy at the Ecole Normale Superieure, wrote her dissertation on Descartes, and then taught philosophy in the French lycées; her writing evinces several marks of the philosophical temperament, including the concern to: distinguish close but distinct meanings of a single term (like, the good); expose without artificially resolving genuine contradictions (as between goodness and force); subject reasoned inquiry to method (one of her favorite terms), an inheritance from Descartes. Anti-romantic and anti-irrationalist, and so less of a friend to Pascal and Kierkegaard than might be expected, she held herself to standards of truth that it was just the point of rigorous method to guarantee could be met. On those terms, Christianity did not always measure up. Christianity and philosophy intersect, superimpose, and counterpoise in her thought. Her mentors in Christianity, Fr. Joseph-Marie Perrin and Gustave Thibon, suggest that it was just her philosophical commitments that blocked her baptism,[8] and she herself agreed.[9] The interpretation advanced here is that Weil's spirituality is accountable without her Christianity, which serves her as a largely comfortable suit of clothes. In the context of this study she thus represents something new: a philosophical spirituality that inhabits religious dress, perhaps the opposite of Kierkegaard, whose pseudonyms offered up an incipiently Christian spirituality in philosophical dress.

The metaphor of clothing is also an illuminating reality in Weil's case. Weil's biographer, Simone Pétrement reports that from a young age "her way of dressing became more and more that of a poor person or a monk."[10] Others attest to the "vast black cape"[11] that shows in published pictures of her, almost like a religious habit. These images recall a figure from the Greek-speaking antiquity Simone Weil loved, who also communicated a stance towards life through his clothes: Justin Martyr. According to the famous beginning of his *Dialogue with Trypho*, Justin wore what by Hellenistic custom was the philosopher's dress, "a shabby garment which could easily evoke disdain,"[12] comprising a single rectangular cloth that draped the body. Justin's point was that Christianity was the true philosophy superseding its predecessors. Justin's understanding of the relation between Christianity and philosophy sets Weil's understanding of that relation in relief, by the contrast his makes with hers, and underscores how much Christianity was, for her, a kind of well-fitting cloak that draped but did not constitute her spirituality, a topic for the end of this chapter. At that point, too, Justin Martyr opens a path we can only begin to walk into Weil's vexed relation with Judaism and the question residing there of whether Judaism, too, could have been cut to fit the shape of Weil's thought. Justin will be our compass for evaluating Weil's complicated relation with both Christianity and Judaism. But now let us turn to the substance of Weil's philosophical spirituality.

Weil's very understanding of philosophy itself already predisposes it towards the sacred. Philosophy comprises a method, or form of thinking, that uncovers a sacred content. This is the fundamental claim Weil adumbrates in a trio of essays written towards the end of her life, in Marseilles, under the duress of flight from Nazism: "Philosophy" (hereafter P), "A Few Reflections on the Notion of Value" (hereafter V), and "Essay on the Notion of Reading" (hereafter R), only the first of which was published in her lifetime.[13] Here, Weil succinctly links philosophy's method to its content: "thought's noblest function, in this world, is the identification and contemplation of the insoluble contradictions which, as Plato said, draw us upwards" (R298). The contradiction that immediately prompts this claim is epistemological, that the very sign we take of objectivity in our experience—that whatever is objective impress itself upon us independently of our will—depends, in fact, on a "reading" of experience we have already subjectively made of it before it impresses us. This Kantian line of thought communicates with poignancy from the time that Weil wrote it as, prior to this, the exigencies under which she functioned were largely self-imposed. The fall of France was imposed from without. The essay on reading can itself be read as an invitation of Weil, to herself, to rethink the objectivity of France's state in 1941—which she did, later in England, with her book, *The Need for Roots*. But the contradiction that chiefly preoccupied Weil, as we shall see, is between the pitiless force of nature and the beauty of its mathematically lawful operation.

Philosophy does not simply uncover contradictions in the very acts of reading; it is itself embroiled in contradictions at the very start of its exercise. For the readings we make are inflected by the value systems we inexorably inhabit. Having exposed a contradiction in our reading, the philosophical method aims next to detach us, to the extent it can, from the values informing that reading, so as to fashion a space for weighing them in the balance. This is very difficult to do for anyone actually alive, says Weil, because insofar as we live we are in "tension towards a value" (V458) of some kind. We do not escape the difficulty by identifying philosophy's unique methodological value with detachment itself, correct as we would be. We simply resign ourselves to effectively die while we philosophize. But then, what else but philosophy, by hallowed tradition, "aims at life through death" (V460)? And so rightly limits its own exercise: "first philosophize, then live" (V456), in flagrant reversal of the existentialist alternative.

Philosophy effects what Weil, otherwise skeptical of miracles, does not shrink from deeming a miracle (V459) and indeed a grace (V459): detachment from life in the midst of it. But we do not remain there. For the death-void in which philosophy has set us has pared away the expressions of value that have all along concealed their fount and origin, the good itself. For where Descartes and Kant inspire the method of philosophy, Plato supplies the content. Weil was unabashedly Platonic in her view of the sacred. That is most explicit both in style and content in the third of the essays in paraphrase here, itself a tripartite review of two lectures and a dissertation defense Weil heard, and so, by virtue of its moorings in the oral, most like a dialogue. Indeed, this essay can be read as a series of conversations in which Weil, taking a "congenial and supportive" tone, assumes the voice of the speakers, which she sets in dialogue with her own "helpful and friendly addenda" to their work (to borrow the felicitous phrasings of the editors of the English translation).[14] "One could not help thinking of Plato" (P287), writes Weil in review of the dissertation defense of one M. Berger, by virtue of his clearly Socratic method, which inquired after meaning before pronouncing on truths, and so evoked how much philosophies of this kind, which by implication turn up contradictions in the meanings examined, are "oriented towards salvation" (P288). Plato was not far from Weil's thoughts, either, as she listened to the lecture by one M. Marcel Brion, who explored the complementarities between Chinese art and philosophy, for do not the Taoist texts he cited recall for us what "we remember, as Plato used to say . . . on the other side of the sky" (P284)? This, perhaps the loveliest of all Weil's writing on consideration here, concludes, like Plato's Phaedrus, with an appreciative note on idyllic surroundings, in this case the "city of Aix, where the yellow stones, and lovely little squares, and the young people who fill the streets make one think of some Italian University of the Renaissance" (P289).

In 1943, working in London for the French resistance, and under pressure of her assignment, to theorize the post-war reconstruction of France, Weil articulated in as purely secular terms as she could muster the "Profession of Faith" she thought essential to recovering the national rootedness of French society and culture. She wrote:

There is a reality outside the world, that is to say, outside space and time, outside man's mental universe, outside any sphere whatsoever that is accessible to human faculties. Corresponding to this reality, at the center of the human heart, is the longing for an absolute good . . . which is never appeased by any object in this world. Another terrestrial manifestation of this reality lies in the absurd and insoluble contradictions which are always the terminus of human thought when it moves exclusively in this world.[15]

The statement implicitly summarizes the method and content of philosophy, though this time with the addition of the longing for the good, as inalienable from the human heart as contradiction from philosophy, and as essential to the exercise of philosophy as the good itself. Philosophy understood as a passage through death to a vision of the good is certainly life-transforming and not without Christian resonance. A phrasing of faith so noncommittal to Christianity or any other world religion was in part required by her assignment for the Free French, but also fit another aspect of Weil's belief she never tired of repeating, that this very faith has manifested across the centuries and cultures in many guises, a kind of *philosophia perennis*. This was part of the point of the juxtaposition Weil so naturally made between Lao-Tze and Plato. For a westerner ultimately indebted for almost everything of cultural value in her life to Greek antiquity (Weil's self-image), Plato was just the pre-eminent spokesman of the same view also found "in the mysteries and the initiatory sects of Egypt, Thrace, Greece, and Persia."[16] Weil argued that Plato himself was simply passing down an older tradition of spirituality he received from Pythagoras. The point of philosophizing in the west after Plato was merely to restate his thought in whatever idiom the times required (V460).

Russell, though hardly a Platonist in his later thought, would concur that Plato's mystical side descends from Pythagoras. But Russell and Weil take contrasting approaches to the summarizing overview of western philosophical spirituality. Russell incorporates the story in a popular history of western philosophy; Weil replays it in her own thought and life, rehearsing for us in her own vocabulary ideas we have already encountered in the other philosophers considered here. If Plato, Descartes, and Kant[17] are the reigning inspirations, echoes of all our philosophers sound in Weil's work. We might inventory the inheritance, saving these key three for last.

From her overall disdain of Hebrew scripture, Weil excepted the philosophically inclined wisdom books, especially Job, but had surprisingly little to say about Ecclesiastes, whom she scarcely names.[18] Apart from that book's striking performance of contradiction and detachment, and attunement to some of Weil's own critiques—of the "imaginary claim of the past on the future,"[19] of the modern individual who no longer thinks "about his ancestors . . . nor about his descendants,"[20] —and affirmations—of "variations in balance mutually compensated,"[21] of "the infinite in an instant,"[22] and indeed of the "tangible joys, eating, resting, the pleasures of Sunday,"[23] —its theme of work was ripe for harvest from all her beloved texts of the past. How well it might have served what she judged to be the defining goal of her times: "a civilization founded upon the spirituality of work."[24] Weil did not simply identify early on with the French *syndicats*, and their "high regard for the value of work,"[25] and herself join the ranks of the factory and farm laborers, she effectively theorized the very exercise of manual labor into a religious parable. For if a worker consents to a play the part of an instrument of change in the cause-effect nexus of matter, she is crucified on the contradiction between beauty and force inherent to matter, that simultaneously opens onto God (more on this later). And so, as Ecclesiastes opined, what shows through work is the hand of God.

By contrast, neither Marcus Aurelius nor Lucretius escaped her admiring notice, they are virtually the only two figures from Roman antiquity she countenanced. For within the general degradation of Rome, "let it be remarked . . . how extremely mysterious it is that a clear patch should have made it possible for a genuine Stoic, drawing inspiration from Greece and not from Rome, to mount the throne."[26] What distinguished Greek from Roman stoicism, for Weil, was the element of joyful consent to the necessary workings of the natural world, in what was otherwise mere resignation to overweening power. Stoicism is another name for what the manual laborer does who consents to experience via the motions of her body the contradiction in matter between beauty and force. For the Greek-inspired Roman stoic, matter loses its sting by becoming an extension of my own body, "another body to my soul,"[27] rather than a threatening Other to it. In tribute to the Roman emperor, Weil wrote that, prior to her Christian experience, "my only faith had been the Stoic *amor fati* as Marcus Aurelius understood it . . . to love the universe as one's city . . . to cherish it for its beauty, in the total integrity of [its] order and necessity."[28]

Lucretius for his part also qualifies as a "true disciple of the Greeks,"[29] whose verse poeticizes "the purifying effect of the contemplation and experiencing of necessity."[30] But in Weil's judgment he was not enough impressed by the contradictions inherent to natural necessity to "understand that therein lies precisely the principle of its providential design,"[31] and so missed its spiritual import. Still, Weil might have found in the indifference of the Lucretian gods to human well-being a foretelling of the sublime disinterest she admired in Spinoza, and expressed herself in more dramatic terms under her own rubric of detachment, as her consent to drop, blamelessly, to the depths of hell if God so willed.[32]

It was of course Spinoza who denied we could even wish God to love us without negating the very notion of God. Weil appears to disagree when she allows that God's love does descend *ici bas* (here below, a favorite phrase for this world), bringing with it manifestations of beauty[33] —but only to take for its ultimate object God's own self, which appears in the space we, through de-creation, voluntarily cede to it (more on this later). But we must speak more on Spinoza, that thorough-going determinist, whose notion that natural necessity is as rigorously binding (and as aesthetically sublime) as geometric reasoning Weil shares.[34] Spinoza more thoroughly shapes Weil's understanding of the God-world relation, never all that clear in Plato, than any other philosopher,[35] so let us add him to the ranks of the reigning three, and return to him later. Suffice it here to note the provocative claim of Gustave Thibon, that "the case of Simone Weil is somewhat like that of Spinoza."[36]

In the wake of Nazi Germany, Weil distrusted German romanticism[37] and shows no obvious awareness of Novalis, despite the resemblance between that poet's pen name and the anagrammatic one Weil chose for herself during wartime: Emile Novis. In line with Spinoza, she suspected the imagination of lying, and, according to her own unique take on that, of supplying ultimately ineffective consolations for sufferings that should be borne without cushion. But she loved literature and often preferred by its means to teach philosophy. Had she known Novalis, she would have found in him congenial precedent for her own idea that "God is mediation and all mediation is God,"[38] and for her image of the Christian expression of a rooted culture, "in which the light of Christianity would have illuminated the whole of life"[39] —expressed by Novalis subjunctively (just as she had) in *Christendom or Europa*. Novalis would agree with Weil that "the whole of human life can simply be a parable," and that "folk tales contain a spiritual treasure."[40] Weil who, according to Pétrement, "loved above all in nature the purity of mineral things,"[41] would have appreciated Novalis' own work as supervisor of mines. And none of the philosophers treated in this book would respond more warmly than Novalis to the tale Weil repeats in her "Philosophy" essay, of the ancient Chinese artist who entered the image of a cave he had painted "and never reappeared" (P284). Weil was not simply fascinated by how folk and fairy tale conveyed spiritual truths more austerely expressed in philosophy—she was herself by all accounts a master storyteller. One of the most endearing scenes evoked by her niece, Sylvie Weil, in her family memoir, pictures an evening of "magical interlude" during André's prison time, when Simone, seated on the floor with her sister-in-law, "a jarful of cherries in brandy set between them" regaled Sylvie's mother with "fairy tales, as was her custom."[42]

Though Hegel, as paradigmatic systematizer, belonged to the class of philosophers Weil disparaged, she nonetheless found in him some "marvelously penetrating formulas" (P288). Among these are reflections on two relationships that were key for Weil, both in life and thought: master/slave and sister/brother. If Weil was from a young age "always on the side of the slave,"[43] her factory labors converted her into one, at least existentially, and prepared her for what would become her first real experience of Christian identity. Weil had entered the factory hoping to know at firsthand how geometry is realized in manual labor, but she left it with what seemed the different sensation entirely of bearing "forever the mark of a slave."[44] Hegel's account of the master/slave relation, in which each becomes the other through their reciprocal need, paves the way[45] for Weil's understanding of how absolute power of one over another enslaves both in the relation, unless either, through an improbable act of attention, can experience both the power and powerlessness in play as necessary consequences of laws that inexorably govern matter. For beauty (and God) lie on the other side of that experience. The thesis of Weil's perhaps most famous essay, on the Iliad, is that Homer's account of the Trojan War uncovers just such moments of experience for the reader, and so admits it to the canon of the world's great spiritual texts.

Another ancient text, *Antigone*, supplies both Hegel and Weil with matter for reflection on the brother/sister relation, of which Hegel wrote, with Antigone in mind, that "the recognition of herself in him [Polyneices] is pure and unmixed with any natural desire,"[46] even though it crosses the sexes. Already the adjective, "pure," would draw Weil's attention to this comment, which at least partially captures, through the recognition of the sister in the brother, Sylvie Weil's take on the relation between her father and aunt, that they were "a two-headed genius."[47] For Simone Weil, Electra's relation with Orestes balances Antigone's with Polyneices by reversing the direction of helpful agency, from brother towards sister,[48] and, by just that balancing reversal, illustrates Hegel's point that in this relation "a state of rest and equilibrium" is reached.[49] But both brother/sister relations reveal redemptive agency, of healing actor towards suffering recipient, as though to convert to goodness the power that governs the master/slave relation. Weil played the same part herself towards her brother, while he was in prison—visiting, writing, advising, sending books, even attending trials to glean possibly helpful tips for his defense.[50] And sometimes she called herself Antigone.[51]

Though some of Kierkegaard's works were in Weil's library,[52] she rarely cites him. They shared an appreciation of intense states of inwardness that may exhibit outwardly only fine points of difference from their opposites, as, in the case of Kierkegaard, the knight of faith does from the bourgeois, and in Weil, consent to suffering does from resignation to force.[53] But irony was not Weil's philosophical method. Apart from that, they face in opposite directions, Kierkegaard, from philosophy to Christianity, and Weil, from Christianity to philosophy. What speaks from Kierkegaard to Weil is respect for contradiction as portal of entry to spiritual insight.

Unsurprisingly, our two American philosophers are the most removed from Weil. Weil appears to have known William James' work in psychology,[54] but not, regrettably, his *Varieties of Religious Experience* which, of his philosophical work, would have least taxed her with his pragmatism.[55] For Weil would surely have cited James' experience of identification with the mute epileptic, so congruent with her chilling prayer to be "like a total paralytic . . . incapable of receiving any sensation."[56] As to Emerson, his name is difficult to locate anywhere in her writings.[57] They shared a preoccupation with friendship as spiritual venue that, sadly, neither in their own estimation may ever have known. But perhaps of all our philosophers, Emerson most leaves off where Weil begins—appropriating Christian vocabulary to philosophical ends.

Our survey points to an insight about Weil from Dorothy Tuck McFarland and Wilhelmina Van Ness, that, having "received an exceptional education in preeminently nineteenth century French academic and cultural traditions . . . she never broke with . . . pre-twentieth century forms of thought."[58] We might say of Weil what David Tracy said of Iris Murdoch, an English novelist deeply moved by Weil, that "there is something both strange and courageous about [her] decision to develop a form of Platonism in the . . . twentieth century."[59] For Weil, that was neither strange nor courageous but simply the obvious need—which only witnesses further to what Sylvie Weil called her aunt's "artlessness."[60] Plato defines Weil's sense of the sacred; Descartes inspires her method of reaching it, or being reached by it; Spinoza provides a context for that method to actually work; and Kant, the guidance to realize the method in action. Let us take each in turn.

Weil has from Plato, for whom the sacred was both Goodness and God, a heritage of dual and even contradictory vocabulary for naming the sacred. In Weil's work, the two names trade subject and predicate positions in the claims that identify them: God is good, the Good is God. That oscillation captures for Weil her basic belief that God "is personal and impersonal at the same time."[61] Weil's sacred is the God of the apophatic mystics, "which we can neither picture nor define,"[62] and thus impersonal, but also personal by manifesting personally within our (personal) experience. We can only describe the sacred by what it is not—not opposed (unlike worldly good, whose opposite is evil), not coercive (unlike all that acts within nature), not existent, not here, but disclosed to us from "the country beyond the sky that Plato remembered" (P284). Where Weil differs from Plato, and lists towards the Bible, is in identifying "God considered as Absolute Good" with "God considered as creator."[63] And yet she retains from the Gnostics she admired enough of a sense of contradiction between the good and the creator to render their coincidence "impossible"[64] —and thus all the more congenial to the apophatic sensibility.

But it is just the fact of divine creation that opens the path of yet another approach, alongside apophasis, to linguistic indications of God, by way of—analogy. Analogical thinking was of course central to Plato, as Weil agrees when she identifies the "two essential things in Platonic dialectics: contradiction and analogy."[65] Analogies between this world and the other were possible for Plato because some worldly things, though not all, participated in the good. Weil cannot make that claim because of the bar she sets between Absolute Good, which has no opposites, and worldly goods, which do. The two have nothing in common but name. But now, as though to compensate for this departure from Plato, an idea from Kant, who Weil takes for a philosophical descendant of Plato, comes into play. Kant, too, barred the path between the other world of ideas that Reason constructed, and this world of things that the Understanding knows. The world itself, taken as a whole, was one such otherworldly idea. But this is just the idea Weil wants here for her analogy with the Good. It is the world in its wholeness—the totality of necessary relations connecting its parts—that analogizes with God.

Weil bends that image so fruitful for Platonic analogy, of the divided line, back onto itself, to fashion a circle, so that the highest point of goodness juxtaposes with the lowest of base materiality. The two points neighbor but, says Weil, by another route distance each other by the full circumference of the circle, which is infinite, after all, since between every point is another.[66] The juxtaposition of the highest and lowest across an infinite distance draws from Weil this unlikely wish, to herself be like a piece of inert matter[67] that, by mutely consenting to the laws that necessitate its movements, in a world infinitely far from the Good, draws breathlessly close to God.

The juxtaposition of the highest with the lowest, and the consequent analogy of herself to a piece a matter, works because of what creation really is: a divine self-renunciation, a crucifixion before the fact (of Christ's).[68] What fills the space of the divine absence is utterly different from it, a complex of individuals whose acts are determined by necessitating laws. And so we are turned to Plato once again, for one of Weil's favorite quotes from him: "The essence of the necessary is in reality different from the essence of the Good."[69] But then, paradoxically, the very starkness of divine absence within a framework of necessity itself indicates the location of divinity outside it.[70] Worldly suffering intensifies that indication.

This view of the sacred in relation to the world accounts for the otherwise surprising content of Weil's essay on "God in Plato." There she writes that "all Greek civilization is a search for bridges to relate human misery and divine perfection."[71] This, she feels, is as much true of Plato himself as of the tragic poets whom he exiled from his ideal state. In search of Plato's most trenchant image of misery, Weil focuses on his discussion of justice that suffers on account of an outward appearance of injustice it makes. Plato's point is that true justice bears up under anything thrown it, which exposes how much it is truly desired; but Weil's is more that those very things thrown it are its condition of being. Suffering is not a test of goodness, as it appears to be in Plato and Job, but a necessary lens of its indication from a worldly standpoint. This is true even of those indications of divine absence that seem most pleasing—beauty, friendship, even religious rituals. For a necessary distance blocks the desire for union with each of those things that each of them raises.[72]

Analogy is itself a method of reasoning. Conceived as a pairing of proportional ratios, analogical thinking suggests mathematical thinking, which already points us towards Weil's preferred guide to the idea of method—Descartes, who made of method a discourse. Weil's preoccupation with method accounts for such claims as this one, from David Tracy, about Weil's intellect, that it was "logical, rigorous, demanding, speculative,"[73] —a fair assessment of her difficulty to readers. And method was indeed key to her Platonic project: "In quest for the good there can and must be a method."[74] Epistemological method was important because—as Descartes already modeled—rigorously applied, it guaranteed or at least invited a disclosure of truth.

Weil explored the concept early on in her thesis on Descartes for the Ecole Normale Superieure.[75] This thesis is an ingenious recovery of Descartes from the stark mind/body dualism often associated with him, more radical than Plato's. Weil rethinks Cartesian method in the context of two assumptions she implicitly carries over from German idealism, that the mind can only know what it has itself fashioned, and that the mark of something external to us is the obstacle it makes to us. Out of these assumptions Weil draws this principle: knowledge of the external world occurs in the order the mind fashions of the impressions of obstacle made on it. This constitutes a recovery from dualism because knowledge so understood already incorporates the body as the chief locus of impressions of obstacle. It is just because the mind/body nexus can manipulate its impressions of obstacle, to the point of sequencing them as desired in predictable orders, that knowledge can occur. And so Weil rewrites the famous *cogito* this way: "I have power, therefore I am."[76] That is, I have power to order the obstacles that press on me, therefore I know that both I and the world exist.

What the mind/body nexus discovers is that the relations between its own movements and the impressions of obstacle it receives in consequence from the world conform to geometric laws that determine or necessitate all they govern. This opens up two different but related avenues of engagement with the world, towards science, and towards manual labor. Science studies the geometric laws governing matter generally that, in manual labor, apply to specific tasks. The factory machines that generate goods operate according to geometric rules governing gears, levers and pulleys. But, for Weil, what science studies is not essentially different, but simply the universe as "a system of machines."[77] What Weil hoped of her labor in the factory was essentially a scientific experience of applied geometry. But, because of the grueling and restrictive conditions under which she and her co-workers labored, which eliminated the option of so refined an appreciation of their work, what she endured, instead, was an experience akin to slavery. Pétrement says that the factory was "beginning of the second period" of Weil's life.[78]

That second period is, of course, the religious one. But it remains philosophical by its connection to just this methodical way of thinking. The actual content of the method simplified. The experience of obstacle intensified to suffering; the exercise of power reduced to the sheer act of mental attention. This reflects both the factory experience of slavery and what the ideal response to it would have been. The method of knowing the good was simply, in the midst of suffering, to maintain attention on the good, as Weil describes in her well-known essay within *Waiting for God*, "The Love of God and Affliction." Geometric laws govern spiritual experience as much as they do natural experience. They operate on the principle of the lever. As we consent to the suffering that pushes us down, the Good raises us up to itself, like a see-saw. Or again: the response of the good to our attention to it is "strictly and mathematically proportionate to this attention."[79] But what we experience in the good does not admit of any further analysis, as we already know, since it defies description. Weil emphasizes that "the intelligence cannot control mystery itself but it possesses perfectly the power of control over the roads leading to mystery."[80]

If, for Descartes, method reduced to "directing one's reason well,"[81] then for Weil, such well-directed reason was simply sustained attention. When the object of attention was the sacred, there could be no question of manipulating it according to her youthful understanding of epistemological power. Descartes' ontological argument hovered between establishing the reality of God and the human power to establish that reality. Weil retains the argument but absent the incipient hubris. Calling hers an experimental ontological argument—itself an oxymoron—she writes that what sustains her belief in the good is her experience of rising towards it, above whatever previous level of good she had known.[82] But as choice of method, attention expands its scope to include many possible objects— geometry, people, beauty, religious ceremonies, texts. The outward act that expresses inward attention is a kind of non-act—simply waiting. Confronted with an intractable problem in geometry, "we just have to wait for the solution."[83] But the power of attention is that, applied to quandaries, it often exposes a solution.

The chief quandary for Weil is suffering, which, with the Buddhists, she takes to be pervasive. Affliction, her preferred term, shares with the Pali word *dukka* a very broad application, to psychological and physical pain in combination, and to our very subjection to those coercive laws of matter that, from another angle, figure so importantly in our knowledge of the world. For the laws are merciless. They make no exception for instances of beauty or relative goodness, which Weil takes for one teaching of a gospel verse she loves to quote: "He makes his sun rise on the evil and on the good." (Matt 5:45). That is indeed the summation of divine providence which, for Weil, is simply the inviolate mechanism of natural law.[84] Spinoza, whom Weil admired, provides a context for interpreting her understanding of the relation between the good and the world.

The notion of order applies not just to sequentially orchestrated impressions, but to whole realms of impressions. There are chiefly two: "the order of the good and the order of existence."[85] Gustave Thibon's anthology of observations from Weil's notebooks, *Gravity and Grace*, captures the contrast with its title. The order of existence is that of the world, governed by force. Weil attributes to Greece the judgment on force she endorses that it is "an absolutely detestable thing."[86] The contrasting order of the good "has no contact with force," "does not descend into the domain of nature" or "protect the soul against the coldness of force."[87] Weil does not shrink from the consequences of so starkly stated a dualism. "Within the universe there is no good."[88] And, on the other hand, even existence is too confining a concept to apply to the Good. The two orders mutually exclude. But they are not unrelated. But that relationship is paradoxical. The void that the world is from the perspective of goodness is also "the supreme fullness."[89] "The absence of God is the mode of divine presence."[90] "Necessity, in so far as it is absolutely other than the good, is the good itself."[91]

These statements of contradiction should not disturb us. We already know that philosophy's aim is to expose contradictions. And Weil reminds us not to forget (contra Aristotle), "the simultaneous truth of contradictions."[92] But she might have reminded us also how much Spinoza's monism constructs a sustained illustration of that truth. For thought and extension, the twin attributes of God, are identical inverse opposites, infinitely different in kind. The same order of events unfolds in both, oppositely expressed, like the movements of a mirror image in relation to what casts it. The continuation of Weil's claim only partially given above makes the point: "Within the universe there is no good, but the universe is good."[93] Though the orders of necessity and goodness mutually exclude, like Spinoza's thought and extension, they also, like Spinoza's attributes, mutually identify.[94]

Spinoza related the divine attributes as parallel expressions of a single substance. Weil, who is not a monist, cannot take that tack. Instead, she employs two ideas of relationship that, in turn, mutually exclude: superimposition and intersection. By her image of "vertically superimposed levels in the life of the soul,"[95] we can understand the order of the good as a plane in parallel with that of necessity, superimposed on top of it, so that we inhabit both simultaneously. In that coincidence, which is not strictly an identity, necessity can indeed read as the good, much as a Spinozan thought, in coincidence with its material counterpart, could read as extended. But now Weil complicates this image of superimposed parallel planes with an alternative image of intersecting planes. For an even more common assertion in her work is that the orders of the good and of necessity intersect. This is an image she has from Plato, who, in the Timaeus, understands the world to have been created after the image of the Greek letter, *chi*, and so as an intersection of orders—"of the divine substance itself and of the principle of matter," Weil interprets, or of the good and necessity.[96]

Insofar as parallel planes cannot intersect, Spinoza and Plato are in tension here within Weil's thought. Weil herself is undaunted. She simply reminds us that "the point at which parallels meet is infinity."[97] But that is the whole reason to contemplate contradictions: to position ourselves with the sacred, whose infinity transcends our understanding, as both Plato and Spinoza would agree.

In practical terms, the distinction between superimposition and intersection is not important. They both allow enough meeting ground between necessity and the good for the good to reach us even through the nets of necessity. But the intersection cannot be but a place of suffering, since "the union of contradictories . . . is impossible without extreme suffering."[98] We who inhabit that place are effectively crushed in the tension. The good reaches us, in response to our attention to it, the way a rope does that has been thrown to a drowning person—it does not interfere with the operations of force, but changes the impact of the "buffets" of force, to "form a different mechanical whole."[99] Inhabiting that different mechanical whole is the goal of any spiritual life inspired by Simone Weil. And from here out Kant is our guide.

Kant was our tutor in the spirituality of limits. Commentator Miklos Veto observes that "Weil shares with Kant and Plato the sober humility that compels . . . restraint."[100] The mechanical whole that the aspirant to Weilian spirituality inhabits takes restraint to extremes: the self disappears. Kant has already been active in our interpretations of Weil. For the reason the good can identify with necessity is that such wholes of connection as necessity represents are of a logically different order from any of the individuals the whole subsumes, as Kant indicated in his reflections on the World. For Weil insists that no individual thing within the world can be identified with the good—only the world itself can be. One way to read Weil in relation to Kant is as a unifier of what might seem the improbable pairing of themes in the *Critique of Judgment*, of nature and beauty. Nature taken as a whole (as Kant would not), in its rigorous unfoldings of necessitating laws, is beautiful (however much the parts of it may pain us)—in much the way a demonstration in geometry is. Weil's repeated claim about the world, that it lacks "finality,"[101] is simultaneously a rejection of Aristotle and an extension of Kant, by assimilating the world itself to his understanding of an artwork: something whose purpose (or finality) is self-directed and so, really, without purpose.

But Kant is a greater help applied to the actual unfoldings of Weilian spiritual life. If, for Weil, "the word grace . . . [is] the most beautiful word,"[102] then her unlikely compliment to Kant, that he "leads to grace"[103] is high praise indeed. It is by the perhaps paradoxically lawful, even mechanical, operations of grace[104] that desire for the good discloses the good. So close is that relation that merely "in desiring the good my desire is fulfilled to overflowing."[105] And here are the elements of grace: desire, unlike force, is uncoercive and yet the good unfailingly responds to it. It is a case of like responding to like, since neither goodness nor desire coerce. Weil departs here from Kant for whom the undoubtedly coercive will was the locus of goodness in this world. But, for Weil, the will is simply another faculty of mind conditioned by natural forces.[106] Weil is rejecting both Descartes, for whom our will was infinite, and Kant when she writes that "the only thing in us that is unconditioned is desire."[107] But what allies with Kant here is the focus on internal motivations, which is the same in both. Though he would speak more of acts than things, Kant would agree that "the amount of good in the thing itself is the same as the amount of good in the motive behind it."[108]

That is also where the purity, so important to them both, shows. Weil respected the categorical imperative and even applies it.[109] And she fully speaks the language of obedience that the categorical imperative inspires—"I want nothing else but obedience"[110]—only not to law, but to whatever desires emerge within her attention to the good, which "should act by radiance, as an inspiration."[111] Where it is precisely by their indifference to desire that applications of the categorical imperative are pure, what purifies action performed under desire for the good is indifference to the self itself. Under that indifference, the self shrinks to nothing, Weil's goal, which she expresses both prayerfully—"May God grant that I become nothing"[112]—and poetically—"I am the color of dead leaves, like certain unnoticed insects."[113] Our ability to consent to our essential nothingness is the image in us of God, who likewise self-reduces in creation. In that way too we mimic the juxtaposed personality and impersonality of God, though, ultimately, as in the case of God, "what is sacred in a human being is the impersonal in him."[114] And now Spinoza returns. For the justification of Weil's self-assessment is that the space I occupy is primordially God's. Creation is the divine retraction that leaves the space I partially fill. If creation is God's self-separation, really self-crucifixion ("in our being, God is torn"[115]), then I ease the divine affliction by ceding the space I hold back to it. This is what Weil calls decreation.[116] And it makes Spinoza right in the end: "God can only love himself";[117] or, tweaking Plotinus, who characterized spiritual life as a flight from the alone to the Alone, we could say Weilian spiritual life is the love of nothing for the Non-existent.

Suffering in the form of affliction occupies a more central role in Weil's spirituality than in any other philosopher we have yet considered. And this is also the feature of her work that draws to it its Christian dress. If the paradigmatic image of affliction is crucifixion—not just for the protracted physical pain of it, but for the shame and disgrace associated with it in the ancient world—then it is no surprise that in Weil's account of Christianity it absorbs or conditions most other Christian theological concepts. Creation is already the crucifixion of the Good by the relation it now has with necessity. A world of necessity is itself a crucifixion of whatever inhabits it. Prayer is attention to the good in the midst of crucifixion. No wonder Weil can pronounce, with reference to the doctrine of the Resurrection, which succeeds the Crucifixion in Christian theology: "The Cross by itself suffices me."[118]

By most accounts, this is a misreading of Christianity, if only because the Cross does not suffice—to cite only one New Testament authority: "If Christ has not been raised . . . your faith is in vain" (1 Cor 15:14 RSV). Weil herself identified as the chief obstacle to her baptism that she loved so much of what lies outside the church, including some streams of thought explicitly expelled from it, for example, Gnosticism and Catharism. She never acknowledged that her very attitude towards Christian teachings, as "not things to be affirmed . . . [but] to be regarded from a certain distance, with attention, respect and love,"[119] might itself exclude her from the church. So aesthetic an approach to Christian doctrine admits too much and not enough into the church for it to maintain a distinct identity. If "everything which is true is Christian,"[120] and truth appears wherever "one has truly drawn spiritual life from the texts studied,"[121] then, for Weil, the church must identify with Buddhism, Taoism, Greek tragedy, and Egyptian mysteries. But the identification itself, sustained by contemplative appreciation, is not substantively different from what attaches the art lover to a beloved artwork that feeds him. And Weil herself suggests that beauty is indeed the criterion of a text's truth.[122]

Weil missed the possibly illuminating contradiction between her stance towards most Christian doctrine, that it was simply to be contemplated, neither affirmed nor denied, and the one doctrine she isolated as keeping her outside the church—about the untruth of other religious and literary traditions[123]—which she took quite literally, as one to be denied. In the case of this teaching, on salvation outside the church, she asked for the very thing she disparaged with regard to all other Christian teachings—doctrinal certainty. If this teaching deflected loving contemplation from it, it might have taught that (mere) contemplation was not the stance desired for any of the teachings, but rather assent; or perhaps that is the face of the church it must show to potential converts, if not to those raised up in it. In that case, her self-exclusion from the church was not a sacrifice but a faithful witness to what we suggest here, that her Christianity was a well-fitting cloak, but not of her essence.

In a brief fragment in her notebooks, Weil writes: "Justin Martyr, middle of the second century, alliance of Christianity and Greek philosophy."[124] Fr. Perrin wonders if Weil ever really read Justin Martyr,[125] on grounds that that church father would undermine her own understanding of the relation between Christianity and its precedents. And yet, George Panichas points us in the right direction when he suggests that "Simone Weil is the great Christian Hellenist of modern times, occupying a place commensurate with that of Christian Hellenists like Justin Martyr."[126] If Henry Chadwick is right that "of all the early Christian theologians, Justin is the most optimistic about the harmony of Christianity and Greek philosophy,"[127] then a brief comparison of Weil with Justin on a few key points may help us locate her more securely outside of Christianity. For otherwise the two share much. Apart from the death sentence that hung over both, over Justin for being Christian and over Weil for being Jewish, they share: reverence for Plato, adaptation of his *chi*, from the Timaeus, to Christian meaning, a feeling of distress over the plurality of philosophies and intuition that there is really only one,[128] a blurry sense of the distinction between philosophy and religion,[129] appreciation of Stoic ethics, equations of Christ with Greek gods, especially Dionysius, attunement to the notion of *logos* as divine orderer of creation.[130] According to his account of his conversion to Christianity, Justin had previously identified with, in addition to Platonism, two ancient philosophies Weil held dear: Stoicism and Pythagoreanism.[131] But what is key for Weil about Justin is his view that all those outside the visible church "who lived with the logos are Christians . . . among the Greeks, Socrates and Heraclitus,"[132] for this would open the church to the larger compass Weil would like to see.

But if Justin represents as far as Christian apologetics for Hellenism can go, he does not go far enough for Weil. For the point of the philosopher's robe that Justin wears is to indicate that Christianity does not merely share with Plato possession of the truth, but surpasses him in that regard. The Greeks who Justin redeems for Christianity are just those of pre-Christian eras, not any of Justin's own time who followed other teachings Weil held true. Justin allows the equation of Christ with Dionysius but only for apologetic purposes, by way of ingratiating Christianity with the emperor.[133] On reflection, Justin condemns that identification as the inspiration of demons;[134] whereas, for Weil, a host of ancient gods epitomize Christ: Dionysius, Osiris, Prometheus, "Apollo, Artemis, celestial Aphrodite and many others."[135] Weil's writings on Greek culture read less as apologetics on behalf of Christianity, to show its Greek precedents, than as apologetics for Greek culture, to justify a Christian's love for it—the very opposite of Justin's approach. But perhaps most important of all, Weil could show no sympathy for the apologetic ploy Justin and the other Greek church fathers used to rationalize their reverence for Plato, that Plato learned all he did from Moses. For Weil, like Marcion, rejected Hebrew scripture as precedent for the New Testament. On account of that view, and despite her experiences of Christ, post-Holocaust Christianity can never with integrity own Simone Weil. But even in her Christian dress, philosophy can still claim her.

What a reading of Justin against Weilian views of religion provokes is the question of whether Weil's philosophical spirituality might just as easily have donned Judaic dress. Justin would confront Weil with an early Christian emphasis on the supreme import of Hebrew scripture, as predictor of Christianity, for this is largely the theme of the *Dialogue with Trypho*. His emphatic rejection of Marcion (his contemporary) would stand in stark reproof of Weil's bias against Hebrew scripture. This Justinian critique of Weil takes its force from what is otherwise a kinship of spirit between the two. When one of the characters in the *Dialogue with Trypho* rhetorically asks, "'Is this not the task of philosophy, to inquire about the Divine?'" (Dial. 1:3) Weil would sympathize if not exactly agree. The significance for Weil: those words are spoken not by Justin but by his Jewish interlocutor, Trypho, who shows a greater regard for philosophy than Justin allows himself to represent in the dialogue, and even better models the equanimity of temperament the ancient world expected of philosophers[136] — as opposed to the imperious and irritable personality Justin, functioning underneath his philosopher's garb as Christian apologist in the text, assigns himself. Apart from equanimity and regard for philosophy, Trypho exhibits a nonjudgmental curiosity about Christianity, a readiness to let it stand alongside Judaism (Dial. 64:1), and an openness to the *logos* doctrine Justin adumbrates (Dial. 63:1) — all so uncharacteristic of ancient rabbinic Judaism that Timothy Horner, in his innovative interpretation of the *Dialogue*, suggests it represents "a non-rabbinic [Jewish] voice [that] has been preserved in Christian tradition."[137] Here is fertile ground to begin constructing a Weilian Judaism.

In a striking consonance of phrase, that perhaps confirms Sylvie Weil's view of her father and aunt as a single, two-headed person, André Weil wrote of his sister that "her life had unfolded according to its own laws,"[138] echoing what she in turn had much earlier written to one of her pupils, that "every life evolves by its own laws."[139] Both Weils would likely appreciate so methodical a view of life. According to Sylvie Weil, André Weil believed that Simone would have eventually come to positive terms with Judaism, "'because [said André] she was honest, by and large.'"[140] Sympathetic Jewish readers of Weil today — and perhaps not only them — can hardly resist linking Weil's thought to those pockets and streams of Jewish tradition where it would be most at home. Unexpectedly, American Judaism already made place for Weil when one of its premier periodicals, *Commentary*, published an excerpt from her book, *L'Enracinement* (later translated as *Need for Roots*) in its July 1950 issue,[141] before either *Waiting for God* or *Gravity and Grace* were available in English. And some have begun to shape the Judaic garb Weil might have worn, for instance, Thomas Nevin who wrote: "what irony that her own ethics . . . should be so very Jewish."[142] Let us add a few more pieces to this picture.

Justin Martyr starts us off with his attentions to a symbol from Torah also beloved by Weil, the bronze serpent (Num 21:9, cited Dial. 91:4 and several other places in Justin and Weil), which figures the therapeutic import of contemplation. Weil was sensitive to outcroppings of the sacred in otherwise violent texts, such as the Iliad, but also the historical books of Hebrew scripture. She commented on the famous "still small voice" passage of 1 Kings 19:12 that it was "an electrifying touch, a touch of mysticism,"[143] within the text, but there are many more of these in the midst of stories much more violent than Elijah's; for instance, within her least favorite book of the Bible, Joshua, the sun stands still (Josh 10:12–14), an arresting of time that might speak to her intuitions that time is a chief ingredient of human affliction.[144] But of course, Weil's place in Judaism would most naturally be with its own most Hellenized streams: the Septuagint, which she knew,[145] Philo, whose Therapeutae attracted her,[146] and whose interpretation of the name Israel (the one who sees God[147]), could mitigate her discomfort with Jewish (or any kind of) collectivism—and the medievals, not just the kabbalistic mystics (whose views on creation as retraction are in sync with hers) but the philosophers. Weil's term for her approach to Christian doctrine and symbol—adherence (*adhésion*[148]), as opposed to affirmation—recalls a key term from the medieval Jewish philosophers on mystical closeness to God: *hithdavkuth*,[149] from the Hebrew root, to cleave.

But most striking are the affinities specifically with Maimonides, whose ascetic intellectualism would surely have appealed to Weil. Here are three points of congruence: the methodical rule-boundedness of prophecy, which was really contemplative, apophatic mysticism, in Maimonides,[150] and the abandonment of humanity to natural necessity outside the prophetic state;[151] extreme behaviors as a method of attaining desirably moderate ones, especially—in immoderate personalities or cultures—a countervailing intemperance as a means to temperance;[152] pardon for those who abandon national identity under threat (French who collaborate with the Nazis, Jews who convert under duress to Christianity).[153] Those three points of congruence cross mystical, ethical, and social ethical boundaries, inviting a broader exploration of whether a Maimonidean suit of clothes (itself already on Maimonides at his most philosophical only superficially Judaic, by some reckonings) would best fit Weil. Weil remains enough in tension with Judaism (with its self-image, even when carefully nuanced, of chosenness, its vibrant communality, its ritual laws commanding practice, not contemplation, its discomfort with asceticism) as with Christianity, that her philosophical spirituality would simply inhabit it, clothe itself in its vocabulary and texts, but remain as detachable from it as from Christianity. But the point in the case of either religion is the same: Weil illustrates how a philosophical spirituality can reside within a religion and, perhaps by extension (though not for Weil herself), a religious community.

NOTES

1. André Weil, *The Apprenticeship of a Mathematician* (Boston: Birkhauser Verlag, 1992), 138.
2. Thomas Nevin wryly comments that Weil failed in most things but "succeeded brilliantly as an itinerant." Nevin, *Simone Weil: Portrait of a Self-Exiled Jew* (Chapel Hill: University of North Carolina Press, 1991), 305.
3. "Aristotle is the corrupt tree which bears only rotten fruit." Simone Weil, *First and Last Notebooks*, trans. Richard Rees (New York: Oxford University Press, 1970), 355.
4. Weil, *Need for Roots*, trans. Arthur Wills (New York: Putnam's, 1952), 249.
5. Simone Weil, "Philosophy," in *Formative Writings, 1929–1941*, ed. and trans. Dorothy Tuck McFarland and Wilhelmina Van Ness (Amherst: University of Massachusetts Press, 1987), 287–288.
6. See Peter Winch, *Simone Weil: "The Just Balance"* (New York: Cambridge University Press, 1989), who likens Weil to Wittgenstein, and also allies Weil with Russell in their respective critiques of Descartes' *cogito*, p. 9.
7. Dorothy Tuck McFarland and Wilhelmina Van Ness, introduction to *Formative Writings*, 7.
8. J. M. Perrin and G. Thibon, *Simone Weil as We Knew Her* (New York: Routledge, 1953), 29, 132, 149.
9. "I am kept outside the church by philosophical difficulties that I fear are irreducible." Simone Weil, *Seventy Letters*, trans. Richard Rees (New York: Oxford University Press, 1965), 155.
10. Simone Petrement, *Simone Weil: A Life* (New York: Pantheon, 1976), 28. Weil's niece, Sylvie Weil, writes that towards the end of her life, she "dressed like a pauper." Sylvie Weil, *At Home with Andre and Simone Weil* (Evanston, IL: Northwestern University Press, 2010), 128.
11. Dorothy Tuck McFarland, *Simone Weil* (New York: Frederick Ungar, 1983), 2.
12. J. C. M. van Winden, *An Early Christian Philosopher: Justin Martyr's Dialogue with Trypho, Chapters One to Nine* (Leiden: Brill, 1971), 27.
13. For "Philosophy," see note 5. "A Few Reflections on the Notion of Value," trans. E. Jane Doering *Cahiers Simone Weil* 34, no. 4 (Dec. 2011): 455–462. "Essay on Reading," trans. Rebecca Fine Rose and Timothy Tessin, *Philosophical Investigations* 13:4 (Oct. 1990): 297–303.
14. McFarland and Van Ness, introduction to *Formative Writings*, 19.
15. Simone Weil, "Draft for a Statement of Human Obligations," in *Simone Weil*, ed. Eric O. Springsted (Maryknoll, NY: Orbis, 1998), 132.
16. Weil, *Seventy Letters*, trans. Richard Rees (New York: Oxford University Press, 1965), 130.
17. Weil herself singles out Descartes and Kant as noteworthy inheritors of the Platonic tradition. See her essay "A Few Reflections on the Notion of Value," *Cahiers Simone Weil* 34:4 (Dec. 2011): 460.
18. A Latin citing Weil appears to make to Ecclesiastes, perhaps from faulty memory, in *Letter to a Priest*, trans. A. F. Wills (London: Routledge, 1951), p. 65 is actually to Ecclesiasticus 1:10.
19. Weil, *Waiting for God*, trans. Emma Craufurd (New York: Putnam's, 1951), 148.
20. Weil, *Need for Roots*, trans. Arthur Wills (New York: Putnam's, 1952), 100.
21. Ibid., 288.
22. Weil, *Gravity and Grace*, trans. Arthur Wills (New York: Putnam's, 1952), 172.
23. Ibid., 236.
24. Weil, *Need for Roots*, 97.
25. McFarland, *Simone Weil*, 32.
26. Weil, *Need for Roots*, 276.
27. Weil, *Gravity and Grace*, 194. To some extent, Weil regarded her writer's pen this way. See "Science and Perception in Descartes," in *Formative Writings*, 81–82.
28. Weil, *Seventy Letters*, 140–141.

29. Weil, "The Great Beast," in *Selected Essays, 1934–1943*, trans. Richard Rees (New York: Oxford University Press, 1962), 116.
30. Weil, *Science, Necessity and the Love of God*, trans. Richard Rees (New York: Oxford University Press, 1968), 10.
31. Weil, *The Notebooks of Simone Weil*, trans. Arthur Wills (New York: Putnam's, 1956), 442.
32. Weil, *Waiting for God*, 44
33. Weil, *Notebooks*, 440. Weil suggests that the absolute good, which cannot itself manifest in nature, appears to the senses as beauty. *First and Last Notebooks*, 98.
34. Weil, *Intimations of Christianity among the Ancient Greeks*, trans. Elisabeth Chase Geissbuhler (London: Routledge and Kegan Paul, 1957), 184.
35. "Simone Weil had thought deeply about his philosophy and she is at times clearly directly influenced by him." Peter Winch, *Simone Weil*, 4.
36. Perrin and Thibon, *Simone Weil as We Knew Her*, 112.
37. Weil considered that Germany's "romantic tradition" weakened its reason, and opened it to the horrors of Hitlerian conquest. *The Need for Roots*, 146.
38. Weil, *Intimations of Christianity*, 196.
39. Weil, *Need for Roots*, 298.
40. Weil, *First and Last Notebooks*, 268, 273.
41. Petrement, *Simone Weil*, 415.
42. Sylvie Weil, *At Home with Andre and Simone Weil*, 75.
43. Petrement, *Simone Weil*, 25.
44. Weil, *Waiting for God*, 25.
45. Or at least provides precedent for Weil's thought on slavery, as she marks by several times citing Hegel's master/slave relation in her notebooks, e.g., *First and Last Notebooks*, 16.
46. Hegel, *Phenomenology of Spirit*, trans. A. V. Miller (New York: Oxford, 1977), 275.
47. Sylvie Weil, *At Home with Andre and Simone Weil*, 61.
48. See Weil, *Intimations of Christianity*, 11–17.
49. Hegel, *Phenomenology of Spirit*, 274.
50. Petrement, *Simone Weil*, 368–374.
51. Weil, *Seventy Letters*, 161.
52. Petrement, *Simone Weil*, 254.
53. Weil, "A War of Religions," in *Selected Essays, 1934–1943*, 218.
54. Weil, *First and Last Notebooks*, 26.
55. Which, like Russell, she rejected. See *Need for Roots*, 45, 249.
56. Weil, *First and Last Notebooks*, 243
57. Could Nietzsche, whose work Weil knew and abhorred, but who also praised Emerson, have deflected Weil from the American thinker?
58. McFarland and Van Ness, introduction to *Formative Writings*, 6.
59. David Tracy, "Iris Murdoch and the Many Faces of Platonism," in *Iris Murdoch and the Search for Human Goodness*, ed. Maria Antonaccio and William Schweiker (Chicago: University of Chicago Press, 1996), 54.
60. Sylvie Weil, *At Home with Andre and Simone Weil*, 145.
61. Weil, *Gravity and Grace*, 205.
62. Ibid., 58.
63. Weil, *Need for Roots*, 66.
64. Weil, *Notebooks*, 434.
65. Ibid., 46.
66. Weil, *First and Last Notebooks*, 83.
67. Ibid., 236. Another wish is to be like a light-nourished tree. Ibid., 280.
68. Weil, *Intimations of Christianity*, 198.
69. Here, Weil quotes from Rep 493a in *Intimations of Christianity*, 86.
70. Otherwise put, absence is a "way of appearing." Weil, *Gravity and Grace*, 68.
71. Weil, *Intimations of Christianity*, 75.

72. Neither a beautiful object nor a friend can admit of desiring union with it without losing its own self. Likewise, Weil could not join the church (a condition of practicing its rituals) without losing herself.

73. David Tracy, "Simone Weil: The Impossible," in *The Christian Platonism of Simone Weil*, ed. E. Jane Doering and Eric O. Springsted (Notre Dame, IN: University of Notre Dame Press, 2004), 232.

74. Weil, *Science, Necessity and the Love of God*, 45.

75. Weil, "Science and Perception in Descartes," in *Formative Writings*, 23–96.

76. Ibid., 59.

77. Ibid., 86.

78. Petrement, *Simone Weil*, 214. Weil, who subjected herself repeatedly to physically demanding labors, on the assumption that only manual labor could realize practical geometry, seems never to have accepted what Thomas Nevin suggests about her that her real work was what she performed most brilliantly and unselfconsciously: writing (*Simone Weil: Portrait of a Self-Exiled Jew* [Chapel Hill: University of North Carolina Press, 1991], 387). But perhaps her frequent references to the physicality of writing — the pressure of the pen against the paper and the hand as it moves across the page — witness to writing as manual labor. See for example, "Science and Perception in Descartes," 79, 81–82.

79. Weil, *Waiting for God*, 4.

80. Weil, *First and Last Notebooks*, 131. She adds, "If we exercise a sort of compulsion upon God, it can only be a question of a mechanism instituted by God." *Need for Roots*, 264.

81. Weil, "Science and Perception in Descartes," 47.

82. Weil, *Notebooks*, 434; also *First and Last Notebooks*, 309.

83. Weil, *Waiting for God*, 128.

84. Weil, *Need for Roots*, 262–263. She critiques Christianity for personalizing providence.

85. Weil, *First and Last Notebooks*, 297.

86. Weil, *Intimations of Christianity*, 116.

87. Weil, *Gravity and Grace*, 112; *Intimations of Christianity*, 194.

88. Weil, *First and Last Notebooks*, 209.

89. Weil, *Gravity and Grace*, 68.

90. Ibid., 72.

91. Ibid., 162.

92. Weil, *First and Last Notebooks*, 104.

93. Ibid., 209.

94. There is a tension in Weil between Plato's and Spinoza's understanding of the sacred. On the one hand, the good is even above the concept of order (Plato). But on the other, it defines an order that is in identification with necessity (Spinoza). Developing the Platonic position, Weil might say that the order in identification with necessity is really an order of beauty, allied with the good, but that, as in Plato, the good resides somewhere beyond even beauty.

95. Weil, *First and Last Notebooks*, 179.

96. Weil, *Intimations of Christianity*, 93. The image is from Timaeus 36b.

97. Weil, *Waiting for God*, 137.

98. Weil, *Gravity and Grace*, 155.

99. Weil, *Intimations of Christianity*, 194.

100. Miklos Veto, *The Religious Metaphysics of Simone Weil*, trans. Joan Dargan (Albany: State University of New York Press, 1994), 153.

101. Weil, *Intimations of Christianity*, 199.

102. Weil, *First and Last Notebooks*, 19.

103. Weil, *Notebooks*, 202.

104. Weil, *Need for Roots*, 263.

105. Weil, *First and Last Notebooks*, 158.

106. Weil, *Intimations of Christianity*, 181.

107. Weil, *First and Last Notebooks*, 143. Otherwise put, "we have infinity in us only in this central desire" for the good. *Intimations of Christianity*, 121.
108. Weil, *Need for Roots*, 252.
109. To acts of gratitude, of which she says that "he who treats me thus wishes that all who are in my situation may be treated in the same way by all who are in his own." *Gravity and Grace*, 118.
110. Weil, *Waiting for God*, 15.
111. Weil, *Intimations of Christianity*, 121.
112. Weil, *Gravity and Grace*, 80.
113. Weil, *Waiting for God*, 53.
114. Weil, "Human Personality," in *Simone Weil Reader*, ed. George A. Panichas (New York: David McKay, 1977), 317.
115. Weil, *Gravity and Grace*, 141.
116. "God allows man existence so that man may have the possibility of renouncing it out of love for God." *Intimations of Christianity*, 109.
117. Weil, *Gravity and Grace*, 78. "We are a point through which God's divine love for self passes." *Intimations of Christianity*, 197.
118. Weil, *Letter to a Priest*, trans. A. F. Wills (London: Routledge and Kegan Paul, 1953), 55.
119. Ibid., 48.
120. Weil, *First and Last Notebooks*, 80.
121. Weil, *Intimations of Christianity*, 153.
122. For example, "Belief is aroused by the beauty of the texts." *First and Last Notebooks*, 123.
123. In our own day, this position is very much in question among Christian theologians; but in Weil's time, pre-Vatican II, it would have been very bold to deny it. Weil herself anticipates our own time when she writes, "If only the missionaries could say: 'By coming to us, far from losing contact with your ancestors, you will recover the contact you have lost. We have come from afar to bring you their message.'" *Notebooks*, 544.
124. Weil, *First and Last Notebooks*, 109.
125. Perrin and Thibon, *Simone Weil as We Knew Her*, 65.
126. George Panichas, introduction to *The Simone Weil Reader* (New York: David McKay, 1977), xviii.
127. Henry Chadwick, *Early Christian Theology and the Classical Tradition* (New York: Oxford, 1966), 10.
128. One critique of philosophy among the ancient Christian apologists was that there were too many varieties of it. Justin voices this critique at start of his *Dialogue with Trypho* (Dial. 2:1) and Weil addresses it in "A Few Reflections on the Notion of Value," 460–461. The critique allies naturally with what we might call the artless assumption that, if philosophy is true, there can be only one.
129. Weil suggests in one passage that the only difference is the wider and more defined environment a religion infuses. *Seventy Letters*, 130. For Justin, there really was no distinction.
130. "The logos . . . set in order everything." Justin Martyr, *First and Second Apologies*, trans. Leslie William Barnard (New York: Paulist, 1997), 77 [2 Apol. 6]; "The Word is the orderer of the world." Weil, *Intimations*, 185. Weil shares Justin's sense that the impact of the logos extends far beyond visible Christianity (2 Apol. 8). She calls it "the uncreated part of every creature." *First and Last Notebooks*, 103.
131. Justin Martyr, *Dialogue with Trypho*, trans. Thomas B. Falls (Washington, DC: Catholic University Press of America, 2003), 5–6 [Dial. 2:2–4].
132. Justin Martyr, *First and Second Apologies*, 55 [1 Apol. 46]. Weil's trope for how Christianity preceded Christ, though, was less the logos than the crucifixion, which she understood creation to be.
133. Ibid., 37 [1 Apol. 21].
134. Ibid., 62 [1 Apol. 54].

135. Weil, *Intimations of Christianity*, 119. Also *Waiting for God*, 28.
136. As Weil herself knew well: "The connection between humility and true philosophy was known in antiquity. Among the Socratic, Cynic, and Stoic philosophers it was considered part of the professional duty to put up with insults . . . without the slightest instinctive reaction of offended dignity" (*First and Last Notebooks*, 335), which Trypho fairly consistently models against Justin's bellicosity in the *Dialogue*.
137. Timothy Horner, *"Listening to Trypho": Justin Martyr's* Dialogue *Reconsidered* (Leuven: Peeters, 2001), 188
138. Andre Weil, *Apprenticeship of a Mathematician*, 12.
139. Simone Weil, *Seventy Letters*, 13.
140. Sylvie Weil, *At Home with Andre and Simone Weil*, 171.
141. Weil, "Hitler and the Idea of Greatness," *Commentary* (July 1950): 15–22.
142. Thomas Nevin, *Simone Weil: Portrait of a Self-Exiled Jew*, 256.
143. Weil, *First and Last Notebooks*, 272.
144. Ibid., 328; *Seventy Letters*, 139.
145. Weil, *First and Last Notebooks*, 105. The Septuagint especially serves Weil's interest in the beauty of creation, since it translates the Hebrew *tov* (good) that God pronounces on creation with the Greek *kalos* (beautiful).
146. Weil, *First and Last Notebooks*, 179.
147. Philo, *De Abrahamo* 57, and many other places.
148. Comparing adherence to belief, she writes: "Cette adhésion est plutôt amour que croyance." Weil, *Cahiers*, ed. André A. Devaux and Florence de Lussy, Oeuvres Complètes 6 (Paris: Gallimard, 1997), 2:338.
149. Abraham Joshua Heschel, *A Concise Dictionary of Hebrew Philosophical Terms* (Cincinnati, OH: Hebrew Union College, 1941), [28].
150. Maimonides, *Guide for the Perplexed*, trans. Shlomo Pines (Chicago: University of Chicago Press, 1963), 360–412 [2:32–48].
151. Ibid., 625 [3:51].
152. Compare Weil, *First and Last Notebooks*, 30 with Maimonides, *The Book of Knowledge*, trans. H. M. Russell and J. Weinberg (New York: Ktav, 1983), 31. Weil has in mind voluntary self-deprivation as a means to temperance in an excessive society; Maimonides, voluntary public humiliation as a means towards equanimity in a hot-tempered person. The idea is a variation on Weil's theme of the lever.
153. Compare Weil, *Seventy Letters*, 158–159 with Maimonides, "Letter on Apostasy" (Igeret Hashmad) in *Letters of Maimonides*, trans. and ed. Leon Stitskin (New York: Yeshiva University Press, 1977).

FIFTEEN
Conclusion: Philosophical Sensibility as Philosophical Spirituality

By way of introducing his critical assessment of Simone Weil, George Steiner identified four key characteristics of "the philosophic sensibility," that it is: interrogative, disinterested, otherworldly, and ascetic.[1] He notes that by these "harsh lights" Simone Weil more than qualifies as philosopher. But so do most of the other philosophers we have considered here. Steiner is not alone in this itemization of philosophic attributes, extreme as they may seem. Nietzsche famously mocked what he took for the patently ascetic nature of philosophy in a whole chapter devoted to it within *The Genealogy of Morals*.[2] Wilfred Cantwell Smith, according to his own understanding of *philosophia* as religion, implies that a consequence of philosophic rationality is disinterest, which obligates philosophers to "follow wherever the evidence or argument might lead."[3] And journalist Janet Maslin, reviewing Louis Menand's book, *The Metaphysical Club*, about the nineteenth-century circle of philosophers so named, which included William James, observed, in implicit testament to the otherworldly aspect of philosophy, that it is "fitting that a group devoted to exchanging purely philosophical ideas should leave almost no tangible evidence of its existence."[4] Simone Weil, who wished to be nothing herself, would certainly have lauded that.

What is especially striking about Steiner's foursome of qualities is that they apply, for him, to the philosophic sensibility *as such*, even before it inclines towards the sacred—as though spirituality were inherent in it. For what first comes to mind in illustration of Steiner's philosophic sensibility is a Buddhist monk or nun. But then, to invoke an ancient rabbinic mode of reasoning (called *qal v'homer*), if the four qualities characterize philosophy in general, how much the more so philosophic spirituality in particular. Steiner does not give us a set of doctrines but more, as he himself says, a sensibility, that is, an embracing responsiveness, that, in the case of philosophic *spirituality*, we take to be to a family of ideas that include the sacred, its relation to the world, and its impact on human lives that center on it. And so it is with those ideas in mind that we now forage among our fourteen philosophers for marks of Steiner's philosophic character, towards constructing philosophical sensibility as philosophical spirituality.

With his unanswered questions and hanging contradictions, Ecclesiastes already inaugurated for us the interrogative mood. Contradiction is both a method for and a qualifying feature of many of our philosophers' thought. Plato praises dialectical reasoning (which plays off contradiction) but employs its less precise alternative, analogical reasoning, for the final stages of his upward ascent to vision of the good. Descartes, for all his confidence in proper method to skirt error, for him the gravest sin, leaves his readers puzzled over his true stance towards the sacred, and his successors saddled with a brazen dualism between body and mind. Weil's reinterpretation of Descartes gathers steam from the contradictions she finds in his writing and primes him to illustrate her own views on the spiritual uses of contradiction. Hegel marshals contradiction towards a dialectical method but persuades few of us today of its final cogency. James divides indecisively between a pragmatic and "scientific" approach to the sacred. Emerson suspects we escape contradiction only at the price of a "foolish consistency," and Weil would let the contradictions stand because, attentively contemplated, they elevate us towards the good.

Contradictions more specific to the modern age emerge with philosophical reflection on self-consciousness. Self-consciousness may have liberated Ecclesiastes from a biblical tradition too little aware of itself, but modern self-consciousness more popularly understood is a way to lack confidence, especially in public, and hints at the disturbance this idea is even to such solitary philosophical consciousnesses as Descartes fabricated. For the very notion of self-consciousness seems to raise an infinite regress of inabilities of the self ever to fully capture itself since, with each act of self-consciousness, the self so changes as to need yet another act of self-consciousness to wholly encompass itself. The self continually outstrips its own self-knowing. And yet once inaugurated, self-consciousness, like a Frankenstein monster, cannot be stopped. Hegel appeared to solve the problem by reading into acts of self-consciousness a necessary self-deception—a negative—that, itself negated, finally issues in the positive of encompassing self-knowledge. But Kierkegaard doubted that self-consciousness, first cousin to reflection, did much more than painfully distance the self from itself and others and wall it up in a false detachment. More popularly, many of us may wish for release from the ache of self-consciousness, which brings so much that diminishes in its wake, for instance, awareness of where we fall on scales of comparative rating, and of our own approaching deaths. Perhaps this is why we keep pets and visit zoos—the animals, in our brief moments of identification with them, release us from this burden. And so the quandary of self-consciousness— the question of it—remains.

Novalis had an ingenious solution. The error of philosophical idealism was to seek a resolution to self-consciousness in the self, rather than in the other. Novalis suggested that the "potentized" self, or double of itself that self-consciousness connotes, actually finds itself in an other, who magically mirrors the self. These magical mirrorings are available to those who renounce the illusion of self-determination that the self holds out to itself through the very idea of self-consciousness. The popular notion that a self-conscious person is vulnerable to the views of others points to the deeper truth, that it must be another that supplies our self-understanding. Novalis captured this idea most personally by renaming philosophy, philo-Sophie, the love of his particular other, Sophie von Kühn. It is precisely via what or whom we do not control—the other— that we gain our self-control.

But then the very concept of control misleads, for the magical mirrorings do not come as necessary effects of causes. They occur under Novalis' rubric of the casual, the uncaused. And so the interrogative mood returns, now in the guise of uncertainty over whether in fact, in any given case, the magic will occur. Uncertainty is also Russell's theme, when he assigns to philosophy precisely the role of teaching us to live without certainty. Here he agrees with William James, who could not resolutely derive the sacred from the accounts of the experiences of it he gathered and classified and raised an anxiety, likely in himself but certainly in others, over belief that rested so wholly on will. The early Russell had at his disposal what he took for the interstitial world of mathematics, an ideal domain that is also real. And this, for a short time, served him as a model for what could finally satisfy his spiritual longings. Later, it seemed that the very absence of the sacred was its own best witness to its presence elsewhere, as Weil would also attest—it simply needed a more artistic hand than Russell's to show that. But then, this notion of the interstitial is very old with our philosophers. Lucretius located the gods there. Plato's notion of a reality of goodness beyond existence is kindred, as is Kant's of the noumenon and the ideals of Reason. William James' suggestion that the sacred inhabits a domain of future possibility belongs here too, and re-energizes an idea from Spinoza, that the realm of possibilities is in some sense also real, or unfolds onto reality. Our philosophical novelists—Novalis and Henry James—are perhaps best at realizing the sacred interstitial almost experientially for us. Henry James would have us dive "to where, in the dim underworld of fiction, the great glazed tank of art, strange silent objects float."[5] He and Novalis suggest that the world of literature, neighboring philosophy, houses permanent possibilities of experience of the sacred in fictional stories that need only be told to manifest the sacred for us. But for the philosopher, there is something questionable here too—Bertrand Russell questioned it with his signal contribution to logical analysis, the theory of descriptions.[6] And so the spirit of the interrogative sets the final mood.

The interstitial would certainly qualify as an otherworld and a philosophy focused on it, as otherworldly. But our philosophers divide on this point, of whether the sacred they spot is wholly other, wholly here but concealed from us, or somewhere in-between. Our monists—Marcus Aurelius, Spinoza, Hegel, the early Emerson—locate us within the sacred itself, which comprises the whole of things. The problem, as Emerson avers, is that we cannot *see* it. The point of Marcus' meditations are to impress on himself the stoic truths of wholeness that are so hard to see. For Spinoza, the truths of monism hide behind a challenging geometric structure of proofs. But the monists have at hand an attractive method of persuasion: inversion. Two of any kind of thing that seem to be divided, and so apparent evidence of plurality, are actually identical. Like close, competitive siblings, they create an impression of distance and even of quarrel between them. Hegel's masters and slaves are illustrative for seeming to divide humanity between them, when in fact they are dialectically one, as monism would have it. Monistic Emerson practiced inversion too. In the woods, all the seeming opposites of life—youth and age, happiness and mourning, noon and midnight—are mirror images of each other, as Novalis opined even in his non-monistic relationism. Indeed Nature, for the early Emerson, *is* the monistic sacred. And any who have found comfort in walks in the woods might follow him here—even non-monists, like Lucretius, who shows the typically Epicurean delight in such simple pleasures as views onto landscapes. The difficulty of seeing nature in its wholeness, rather than in the disturbance of its violent particulars, keeps the sacred at appropriate bay. But in a post-Holocaust age, this kind of seeing fails to persuade many of us. Monism is a hard sell in a world that has become and remained ripe for Simone Weil's spirituality of affliction. Nature in some of its displays may proffer itself a temporary comfort and reprieve from the troubles of humanity, as it clearly did to Russell, without claiming itself to be sacred.

But then others of our philosophers take the otherworldly sacred at face value and locate it outside the world; for some, such as Plato and Platonic Weil, so far outside as to be indescribable. The question then becomes how it relates to us, and we to it. Weil offered up two methods: contradiction and analogy, which she also took for Plato's methods. Certain fundamental contradictions, as between goodness and necessity, beauty and force, once contemplated over a long period, and especially over against extreme suffering endured, actually catapult towards the sacred. Less painfully, analogies between accessible beauty and inaccessible goodness can also elevate, though beauty carries its own sting. Beauty is an old theme for the philosophers, begun by Plato, continued by

Kant and his German successors, culminated, for us here, by Weil. Within this aesthetic tradition, an ambiguous role falls to art, largely dismissed by Plato, Kant, and Kierkegaard, but celebrated by Novalis, Hegel, and Weil. Metaphor is stock-in-trade for Novalis; it is the perfect method not just for poetry but for a spirituality seeking to shake us loose from our over-reliance, for our understanding, on causal patterns rather than casual but miraculously perfect matchings. And yet even our unaesthetic thinkers "have recourse to metaphor," as Socrates might say. Descartes at least makes way for metaphor even if he does not invite it fully into his picture. Ecclesiastes' metaphors for death beautify it, long before the European romantics, and even Bertrand Russell, who wrote little on this theme is, we hope, helpfully illuminated by that master of verbal, visual and synesthetic metaphor, Vincent Van Gogh.

Where the sacred is ontologically and not just epistemologically other, analogy and metaphor are the natural methodological counterparts to identity—as a relation between things—in the monisms. But they are not the only tack. Kant, perhaps the least metaphorical of our thinkers, employs the notion of limit to good spiritual affect. He creates border regions for us where we can stand—like those protagonists of paintings by Caspar David Friedrich, looking off to the horizon—and view on the other side what is, just as for the apophatic Platonists, indescribably sacred. Kant would not have us linger there, just as Descartes would not let us wonder too long at anything, but we need not follow their advice on this point. Cartesian and Kantian mystics are both possibilities.

Still, metaphor is an effective spiritual tool, as religious teachers know. For some of our philosophers a truly self-conscious metaphor would understand its very linguistic form—language itself—to metaphorically juxtapose the sounded or written with actual things. Language as itself metaphor weans itself from our careless presumption to own it and stands over against us as yet another candidate for the otherworld. Emerson said it most simply, that language is a symbol on the way to the sacred. It was Novalis who taught that, appearances to the contrary, we do not own our languages, not even our native one, which, on the contrary, self-propels through our speech and writing, rather like what Hegel would call a speculative proposition, which, once started, completes itself. For Novalis, what amazes about language is that it mirrors the world precisely by not attending to it, but only to itself. Self-determining language in relation to the world is one of his magical and unnecessitated matchings. Language is "divine" for Hegel precisely because it follows a logic of its own that takes us who follow it to the fully realized sacred. Pseudonymous Kierkegaard, in aesthetic dress, would in pursuit of the sacred compress word and thing so closely together as to fashion something new: music, which emerges from language, perhaps by way of onomatopoeia, as language without words.[7] And now the aesthete has his medium of the otherworldly sacred—or at least as much of it as

Kierkegaard will allow him—experienced best in concert halls and opera houses. Perhaps Russell, taken in hand by Van Gogh, could have found a transposition of language to the wordless visual instead of the wordless auditory, and a home for the sacred in museums. Such self-conscious reflection on language is quite modern and illustrates, perhaps, the upside of this seemingly treacherous practice of self-consciousness—that the distance we uncover from what we are conscious of, even in what appears to be ourselves, may be after all the distance of a sacredness we would like very much to know.

A major philosophical trope for the ideal of disinterest is reason. For Plato, Descartes, Spinoza, Novalis, Russell, and Weil, mathematics, especially geometry, is one channel of reason; law, whether natural or moral, is another, especially for Lucretius, Emerson, and Kant. It is partly the element of necessity understood to guide reason's deliberations, whether mathematical, logical, or lawful, that raises disinterest to its ideal status, resisting the efforts of personality, desire, or will to sway it. Disinterest in humans corresponds to the impersonality most of our philosophers associate with the divine. But the divine too is disinterested. The otherness of the sacred, and the mood of the interrogative surrounding it, count against any definitive attribution of personality to it. And without personality, it seems to lack interests—a major divide from the religions of historic revelation. Conversely, the disinterested human mirrors the impersonality of the sacred. Even Novalis' relationality, though between persons, is impersonal in what it ideally mediates, which is a sense for the wholeness of all inter-relationality. Reason's propensity to subsume particulars under universals also counts against the personal. Impersonality and disinterest are twin interweaving themes among our philosophers, sometimes characterizing the sacred, sometimes the human, sometimes both.

Ecclesiastes, for all his uses of the pronoun, "I," never properly names himself, as though to mirror the impersonality of the divine. Plato marshals reason to effectively detach the higher regions of the soul from the lower, in what seems to modern readers a nearly suicidal disregard for the interests of the self—a virtual mania of disinterest that only the likes of Simone Weil could realize. Marcus Aurelius barely acknowledges within his *Meditations* that he is emperor. Descartes holds our will responsible for all our errors and bids us subordinate it to reason. Spinoza renounces the desire to be divinely loved. Kant excludes personal desires from the exercise of practical reason and any kind of self-interested reference from reason's judgments on beauty. Hegel warns us not to intrude "our own bright ideas" into the unfolding of the divine dialectic. Emerson renounces his confidence that nature serves human need. Bertrand Russell sought in the sacred the silencing of desire, and found it in the frozen Past. Russell recounts with admiration the story of a colleague who so thoroughly followed where logic led that if it foretold a friend's imminent death, what he suffered in sorrow over the loss of life would pale next to the joy he had in such an awesome display of reason's power.[8] Even Weil, for whom desire was important as the first step towards the good, channeled it so utterly into attention towards the good, that the self was swallowed up and relieved of being entirely.

Disinterest is not necessarily grim or without pleasure. It is partly the pleasure in the exercise of reason, Lucretius, Descartes, and Spinoza tell us, that allows us to attain enough detachment from self to be disinterested. Still, this element of pleasure in reason's exercise may undermine its claims to disinterest. When Kant warns pure Reason to beware its propensities to self-deception, he implicitly acknowledges a doomed interest in it to grasp the whole of self, world, and God, which it never really renounces. It is just because of Reason's interests that it must be held within the bounds of critique. Kierkegaard simply pushes the Kantian cautions further when he suggests that the disinterest of reason is finally a fiction of selves without consciousness of their prior commitments to either beauty, ethics, or faith. But then Kierkegaard is our one ironist of this philosophical ideal, which plays out comically in the works of his aesthetic pseudonyms, who live out detachment by feigning commitment, as the seducer does in *Either/Or*. But Kierkegaard also opens the door to counter-ideals, of freedom, imagination, personality, and love. These are not typically associated with disinterest. But their expression among our philosophers is problematic. What mysteriously qualifies Kantian freedom is the radical "propensity to evil in human nature."[9] Freedom that invites reason's inquiry into it presents an abyssal face that frightens. It is the deterministic philosophies of necessity—Marcus Aurelius', Spinoza's, Hegel's, Weil's—that promise serenity. Part of the fracture in philosophical spirituality we find from Emerson on owes to the fall of deterministic reason, or the narrowing of its scope, opening up new spaces of vulnerability. Hegel read incompletely and vulnerably, as we tried to do, is already a foretelling of that. These fractures in reason accord with the interrogative nature of philosophical spirituality. But they can also disturb the peace. Hence Russell's spirituality of resignation and sorrow; Emerson's and Weil's disappointments in friendship; William James' melancholic tentativeness about his own spiritual life.

Henry James, our countervailing lens on William, provides a modern alternative to the philosophical ideal of reasoned disinterest. He does so paradoxically, to the extent that the narrative voice in his novels is, indeed, disinterested. In his dissent from William's sense that our immortal soul, if we have one, will not suffer from loss of personality, Henry insists that the personality remain; and with it, presumably, its distinctive desires and loves. Indeed, for Henry, the desire for life culminates in immortality. If reason does not argue for that—if it did, William would have affirmed it too—at least the imagination can. William recognized that belief in immortality was to some extent dependent on imagination in any case. And imagination was of course Henry's forte. It might also be ours; nor need it lack disinterest in its exercise, if that ideal still holds us. Simone Weil told stories for the benefit of her listeners, like her sister-in-law waiting out the time of her husband's imprisonment. Novalis too models the disinterested exercise of imagination, towards stories in which he hopes every reader will find herself affirmatively mirrored. Socrates hoped for a philosopher who could reasonably readmit poets to his ideal state. The philosophical worry over the imagination, from Plato to Simone Weil, is that it too readily and willingly deceives. Unexpectedly, it is Kant who frees us from that worry. For, unlike pure reason, which reaches unrealistically for ideas it cannot know, and so continually tempts itself with self-deceptions, the imagination directs its aesthetic ideas towards the concrete world of sensed objects, which can in fact be known. If Kant's critiques were of reason, and not the imagination, it was because the imagination does not reach for what it cannot have. But Kant is even more a friend still of the imagination, if we are examining it under the rubric of disinterest, since, within the Kantian tradition of formalist aesthetic theory, no word better characterizes how to appreciate the sensual products of the imagination—which are artworks—than the adverb: disinterestedly. And so this possibly least imagistic of our philosophers clears space for the imagination, just as he did for faith, within a reasoned worldview.

Asceticism is at heart a kind of therapy. It restricts the scope of activity and desire so as to minimize the hurt from them and to funnel within a narrow confine—and so heighten the impact of—what truly does sustain: the sacred. To the extent that marriage marks the anti-ascetic, most of our philosophers are indeed ascetic, as Nietzsche mocked when he almost campily exclaimed of "Plato, Descartes, Spinoza, Leibniz, Kant, Schopenhauer" that "one cannot even *imagine* them married."[10] The only of our philosophers to philosophically affirm marriage is the fictional discovery of a Kierkegaardian pseudonym—Judge William; and that he is among the least attractive voices in Kierkegaard's theater must certainly give us pause. But even the married philosophers—Marcus Aurelius, Hegel, Emerson, James and Russell—exhibit ascetic tendencies of thought, with the possible exception of Hegel, if by this we mean restraint of expectation that the world can supply our wellbeing. Asceticism presumes an ongoing possibility of suffering from excess, and on this all our philosophers agree, some—the ancients, Spinoza, Kierkegaard, Russell and Weil—more emphatically than others. Even Hegel agrees, to the extent that we reenact the sufferings of Spirit as we follow its progress in his book. But not all of our philosophers subsume under their philosophical spirituality a philosophical therapy, ascetic or otherwise. The ancients do. Ecclesiastes, Plato, Lucretius and Marcus Aurelius are all therapists of asceticism. But Descartes, who seemed to take to heart the ancient critique of philosophy, that it inappropriately competed with medicine, looked precisely and explicitly to medicine to cure most human ills. On one interpretation of Cartesianism, it is mainly a philosophy of—or better, for—science. In the wake of Descartes, two of our philosophers appear even anti-therapeutic, in that their spiritualities presuppose some presence or at least ongoing availability of pain: Kant and Weil—though they were surely ascetics themselves.

As Kant and Weil illustrate, asceticism can manifest otherwise than therapeutically. It can show ontologically, when it takes for a goal some diminution of being that approximates or even reaches zero. This is Ecclesiastes' tack when he commends a life lived in the self-contained moment which presumes no connection to nor raises any expectation of another moment. Life is reduced to a succession of time-points, which can end unsurprisingly at any one of them. Spinoza participates in the spirit of that when he locates us as a step in the unfolding of what is analogous to a cosmic geometrical proof, though there we are fixed at the point we occupy. The Kantian noumenon invites diminution as the effect on our sensual being as we increasingly approach it, if degrees of approximation to it are possible. Weil's ontological asceticism, which would rid the world of "I" entirely is the most emphatic.

But asceticism works more commonly among our philosophers as a means of self-determination. Self-containment and self-sufficiency are desiderata that show in varied ways. The self-contained time-points of Ecclesiastes are an instance. Plato's reasoned souls immune to suffering are another. Spinoza's Substance is self-sufficient. And all the monists—Marcus Aurelius, Spinoza, Hegel—guarantee our own self-sufficiencies by our identifications with the cosmic self-sufficiency. Cartesian epistemology presupposes self-sufficiency in the meditator who takes nothing for granted. The measure of Cartesian reality, which comes in degrees, is self-sufficiency. The Kantian moral exemplar exercises complete control over her goodness, which resides in her will. Language in Novalis is independent of the reality it ostensibly intends to copy. Even Novalis' partners in relation are first potentized self-containments, which find their mirror in another self-containment. And Emerson gave us the memorable essay title for this ideal: "Self-Reliance."

As in the case of disinterest, whose hold on us may weaken as we approach the present, so here—for the underside of asceticism is, perhaps paradoxically, a fervent activism which abhors passivity. The activism implicit in Spinoza's asceticism—that by sheer exercise of reason we control our emotions and advance in blessedness—was part of what attracted Nietzsche to that thinker, who might otherwise appear to inhabit another moral and spiritual universe from his. The idealist trajectory in German thought is obsessed with activity, which goes much farther to define what Spirit means in that context than it does to frame what we commonly mean by spirituality now. Spirit is by definition active for the idealists. Spirituality is not exclusively so, but for most of us connotes places and spaces of non-activity differently nuanced, like the non-active action of Hindu karmayoga, or the active non-action of the Confucian ruler.[11] Our more recent philosophers understand this and if we do also, it may be partly because of them. Ludwig Feuerbach already early on in the post-Hegelian traditions chastened idealist activism.[12] But Emerson too follows that line, from his early "Self-Reliance" to his later quandaries over power conditioned by fate. William James' surface machismo masks his own vulnerabilities, which his brother more effectively voiced for them both in his stories. Russell's autobiography is a trail of diminutions in what active reasoning can produce. And Weil personifies a vulnerability that escaped violent death only by the decision she made—against what she believed was her own better judgment—to flee Nazi-occupied France. If, as is generally thought, she later died by her own exercise of will, this only heightens the poignancy of the activist ascetic ideal; for, had she remained in occupied France, as she would have preferred, the life she wished to lose would likely have been taken from her without her having forcefully to will it.

Immortality is the ultimate redoubt of philosophic self-determination. According to Plato, the soul cannot die since the evils distinct to it do not kill it, only disorder it. This is one element of Platonic spirituality that did not wear well over time. Even such an ardent Platonist as Simone Weil hardly acknowledged the doctrine. The immortality our philosophers—Spinoza, Kant, James—hold out for us is too vague or too distant from the embodied identity we now have to much attract, comfort, or persuade. The two essays of the James brothers on the matter are more revealing of their humanity, and the appeal of them taken as a complementary pair, than of immortality itself, which engaged them more as part of their larger interest in the paranormal. Part of the problem is that immortality can hardly be discussed without being desired, in blatant foreclosure on the disinterest the philosophic sensibility also values. On the eternal life of immortal souls, the weight of the western philosophic tradition such as we have examined it here favors the disinterested interrogative over against the ascetic otherworldly, pace George Steiner, who claimed all four qualities for the philosophic temper. From here out, Weil would advise us to contemplate the tensions towards contradiction within the philosophic sensibility itself and see if they draw us upwards. That is for each of us to try.

NOTES

1. George Steiner, "Bad Friday," *The New Yorker* 68, no. 2 (March 2, 1992), 86.
2. Friedrich Nietzsche, "What is the Meaning of Ascetic Ideals," in *The Genealogy of Morals and Ecce Homo*, tr. Walter Kaufmann (New York: Vintage, 1989), 97–163.

3. Wilfred Cantwell Smith, "Philosophia as One of the Religions of Humankind," in *Modern Culture from a Comparative Perspective*, ed. John W. Burbidge (Albany: State University of New York Press, 1997), 40.

4. Janet Maslin, "Big Thinkers in a Nation Transformed by Civil War," *New York Times*, June 4, 2001, Section E, p. 9.

5. Henry James, "The Middle Years," in *Selected Tales*, ed. John Lyon (New York: Penguin Books, 2001), 241.

6. Though we now have from the analytic philosophers proofs from the possibility of God for the actuality of God. Some of these go by way of modal logic. See for instance, Robert E. Maydole, "A Modal Model for Proving the Existence of God," *American Philosophical Quarterly* 17 (April 1980): 135–142. A search of this topic in Philosopher's Index turns up many more such articles.

7. Felix Mendelssohn's *Songs without Words* come to mind.

8. Bertrand Russell, *Collected Papers of Bertrand Russell*, ed. John Slater (New York: Routledge, 1999), 6:xxix.

9. Immanuel Kant, *Religion within the Limits of Reason Alone*, trans. Theodore M. Greene and Hoyt H. Hudson (New York: Harper Torchbooks, 1960), iii.

10. Nietzsche, *Genealogy of Morals*, trans. Walter Kaufmann (New York: Vintage, 1989), 107.

11. The Bhagavad Gita says of the wise person that he "sees inaction in action," so that "he does nothing at all even when he engages in action," that is, he illustrates non-active action. Bhagavad Gita (tr. B. Stoler Miller) 4:18, 20. Conversely, Confucius praises a former ruler "who knew how to govern by inactivity," that is, he illustrates active non-action. Analects (tr. Simon Leys) 15:5.

12. For instance, when he enjoins our transformation "from an 'I' into a 'thou,' where I am passive." Feuerbach, *Principles of the Philosophy of the Future*, trans. Manfred Vogel (Indianapolis, IN: Hackett, 1986), 51.

Bibliography

Allen, Gay Wilson. *William James: A Biography*. New York: Viking, 1967.
Arsic, Branka. *On Leaving: A Reading in Emerson*. Cambridge, MA: Harvard University Press, 2010.
Aristotle. *The Basic Works of Aristotle*. Edited by Richard McKeon. New York: Random House, 1941.
Barth, Karl. *Protestant Thought in the Nineteenth Century: Its Background and History*. Trans. by B. Cozens and J. Bowden. London: SCM Press, 1972.
Barzun, Jacques. *A Stroll with William James*. New York: Harper and Row, 1983.
Behler, Ernst. *German Romantic Literary Theory*. New York: Cambridge University Press, 1993.
Beiser, Frederick C. *The Romantic Imperative: The Concept of Early German Romanticism*. Cambridge, MA: Harvard University Press, 2003.
Benjamin, Walter. "The Task of the Translator." In *Illuminations*, ed. by Hannah Arendt. New York: Schocken Books, 1968.
Berlin, Isaiah. Review of *History of Western Philosophy*, by Bertrand Russell. *Mind* n.s. 56, no. 222 (April 1947): 151–166.
Bhagavad Gita. Trans. by Barbara Stoler Miller. New York: Bantam, 1986.
Bialik, H. N. and Y. H. Ravnitzky. *The Book of Legends*. Trans. by William Braude. New York: Schocken Books, 1992.
Birley, Anthony. *Marcus Aurelius*. Boston: Little Brown, 1966.
Bloom, Alan. *The Closing of the American Mind*. New York: Simon Schuster, 1987.
Bloom, Harold. Review of *Betraying Spinoza: The Renegade Jew Who Gave Us Modernity*, by Rebecca Goldstein. *New York Times Book Review* (June 18, 2006).
Bodeus, Richard. *Aristotle and the Theology of the Living Immortals*. Trans. by Jan Edward Garrett. Albany: State University of New York Press, 2000.
Boethius. *The Consolation of Philosophy*. Trans. by V. E. Watts. New York: Penguin, 1969.
Braun, Lucien. *Iconographie et Philosophie: Essai de Definition d'un Champ de Recherche*. Strasbourg: Presses Universitaires de Strasbourg, 1994.
Brown, F., S. Driver and C. Briggs. *A Hebrew and English Lexicon of the Old Testament*. New York: Oxford University Press, 1953.
Buber, Martin. *I and Thou*. Trans. by Walter Kaufmann. New York: Scribner's, 1970.
Buell, Lawrence. *Emerson*. Cambridge, MA: Harvard University Press, 2003.
Burrus, Virginia. *Saving Shame: Martyrs, Saints, and Other Abject Subjects*. Philadelphia: University of Pennsylvania Press, 2008.
Byrne, James. *Religion and the Enlightenment*. Philadelphia: Westminster, 1997.
Caputo, John. *The Prayers and Tears of Jacques Derrida: Religion without Religion*. Bloomington: Indiana University Press, 1997.
Carlisle, Clare. *Kierkegaard: A Guide for the Perplexed*. New York: Continuum, 2006.
Celsus. *On the True Doctrine: A Discourse against the Christians*. Trans. by R. Joseph Hoffmann. New York: Oxford University Press, 1987.
Chadwick, Henry. *Early Christian Theology and the Classical Tradition*. New York: Oxford University Press, 1966.
Chandogya Upanishad. In *The Upanishads*, trans. by Juan Mascaro. New York: Penguin, 1965.
Chappell, Vere. "The Theory of Ideas." In *Essays on Descartes' Meditations*, ed. by Amelie Oksenberg Rorty. Berkeley: University of California Press, 1986.

Cohen, Hermann. *Religion of Reason within the Sources of Judaism.* Trans. by Simon Kaplan. New York: Frederick Unger, 1972.
Confucius. *The Analects.* Trans. by Arthur Waley. New York: Random House, 1938.
Corrington, Robert. *Nature's Sublime: An Essay in Aesthetic Naturalism.* Lanham, MD: Lexington Books, 2013.
Damian, Peter. *De Divina Omnipotentia.* In *Patrologia Latina,* ed. by J. P. Migne, 145:603. Paris, 1844–1855.
Derrida, Jacques. *The Gift of Death and Literature in Secret.* Trans. by David Wills. Chicago: University of Chicago Press, 2008.
Descartes, Rene. *Discourse on Method and Meditations on First Philosophy.* 4th ed. Trans. by Donald A. Cress. Indianapolis, IN: Hackett, 1998.
———. *The Passions of the Soul.* In *The Philosophical Writings of Descartes,* trans. by John Cottingham, Robert Stoothoff and Dugald Murdoch. New York: Cambridge University Press, 1985.
Descartes, Rene and Elisabeth, of Bohemia. *The Correspondence between Princess Elisabeth of Bohemia and Rene Descartes,* ed. and trans. by Lisa Shapiro. Chicago: University of Chicago Press, 2007.
DeVaux, Andre A. "On the Right Use of Contradiction according to Simone Weil," trans. by J. P. Little. In *Simone Weil's Philosophy of Culture,* ed. by Richard Bell. New York: Cambridge University Press, 1993.
Dreyfus, Hubert and Sean Dorrance Kelly. *All Things Shining: Reading the Western Classics to Find Meaning in a Secular Age.* New York: Free Press, 2011.
Durkheim, Emile. *Elementary Forms of Religious Life.* Trans. by Joseph Ward Swain. New York: Free Press, 1915.
Edwards, Cliff. *Van Gogh and God: A Creative Spiritual Quest.* Chicago: Loyola Press, 1989.
Ellison, Julie. "Tears for Emerson: *Essays, Second Series.*" In *The Cambridge Companion to Ralph Waldo Emerson,* ed. by Joel Porte and Saundra Morris. New York: Cambridge University Press, 1999.
Emerson, Ralph Waldo. *Emerson's Complete Works.* Boston: Houghton Mifflin, 1894.
———. *Essays and Lectures.* Ed. by Joel Porte. New York: Library of America, 1983.
———. *Selected Writings of Ralph Waldo Emerson.* Ed. by Brooks Atkinson. New York: Modern Library, 1950.
Erickson, Kathleen Powers. *At Eternity's Gate: The Spiritual Vision of Vincent Van Gogh.* Grand Rapids, MI: Eerdmans, 1998.
Esolen, Anthony M. Introduction to Lucretius, *On the Nature of the Universe.* Baltimore, MD: Johns Hopkins University Press, 1995.
Fiscella, Joan B. "Embedded Philosophy: A Case for Librarianship as Philosophy in Practice." *International Journal of Applied Philosophy* 4 (Spring 1989): 61–66.
Fitzgerald, Penelope. *The Blue Flower.* New York: Houghton Mifflin, 1995.
Gale, Richard. *The Divided Self of William James.* New York: Cambridge University Press, 1999.
Gilson, Étienne. *The Spirit of Medieval Philosophy.* Trans. by A. H. C. Downes. Notre Dame, IN: University of Notre Dame Press, 1936, 1991.
Gradel, Ittai. *Emperor Worship and Roman Religion.* New York: Clarendon, 2002.
Hadot, Pierre. *The Inner Citadel: The Meditations of Marcus Aurelius.* Trans. by Michael Chase. Cambridge, MA: Harvard University Press, 1998.
———. *Philosophy as a Way of Life.* Trans. by Michael Chase. Malden, MA: Blackwell, 1995.
Hall, Edward Hagaman. *A Guide to the Cathedral of Saint John the Divine in the City of New York.* 17th ed. New York: Dean and Chapter of the Cathedral Church, 1965.
Hatfield. Gary. "The Senses and the Fleshless Eye: The *Meditations* as Cognitive Exercises." In *Essays on Descartes'* Meditations, ed. by Amelie Oksenberg Rorty. Berkeley: University of California Press, 1986.
Hauck, Robert. "Omnes Contra Celsum?" *The Second Century* 5, no. 4 (1985/1986): 211–225.

Bibliography

Haworth, Helen. "Emerson's Keats." *Harvard Library Bulletin* 19 (1971): 51–70.
Haywood, Bruce. *Novalis: The Veil of Imagery*. Cambridge, MA: Harvard University Press, 1959.
Hegel, Georg Wilhelm Friedrich. *Phenomenology of Spirit*. Trans. by A. V. Miller. New York: Oxford University Press, 1977.
Hellman, John. *Simone Weil: An Introduction to Her Thought*. Waterloo, ON: Wilfred Laurier University Press, 1982.
Herman, Arthur. *The Cave and the Light: Plato versus Aristotle and the Struggle for the Soul of Western Civilization*. New York: Random House, 2013.
Heschel, Abraham Joshua. *A Concise Dictionary of Hebrew Philosophical Terms*. Cincinnati, OH: Hebrew Union College Press, 1941.
Hodgson, Peter. *G. W. F. Hegel: Theologian of the Spirit*. Minneapolis, MN: Fortress Press 1997.
Honderich, Ted, ed. *Oxford Companion to Philosophy*. 2nd ed. New York: Oxford University Press, 2005.
Horner, Timothy. *"Listening to Trypho": Justin Martyr's Dialogue Reconsidered*. Leuven: Peeters, 2001.
Hutchison, Hazel. *Seeing and Believing: Henry James and the Spiritual World*. New York: Palgrave Macmillan, 2006.
James, Henry. *The Art of the Novel: Critical Prefaces*. New York: Scribner's, 1934.
———. *The Ghostly Tales of Henry James*. Ed. by Leon Edel. New Brunswick, NJ: Rutgers University Press, 1948.
———. "The Birthplace." In *The Complete Stories, 1898–1910*. New York: Library of America, 1996.
———. "Is There a Life after Death?" In *Henry James on Culture: Collected Essays on Politics and the American Scene*, ed. by Pierre A. Walker. Lincoln: University of Nebraska Press, 1999.
———. "The Lesson of the Master." In *Selected Tales*, ed. by John Lyon. New York: Penguin Books, 2001.
———.*Letters*. Ed. by Leon Edel. Cambridge, MA: Harvard University Press, 1975.
———.*The Passionate Pilgrim*." In *The Passionate Pilgrim and Other Tales*. Boston: Houghton Mifflin, 1917.
———. "The Speech of American Women." In *Henry James on Culture: Collected Essays on Politics and the American Scene*, ed. by Pierre A. Walker. Lincoln: University of Nebraska Press, 1999.
James, William. "Address at the Centenary of Ralph Waldo Emerson, May 25, 1903." In *Writings: 1902–1910*. New York: Library of America, 1987.
———.*The Correspondence of William James*. Ed.by Ignas Skrupkelis and Elizabeth Berkeley. Charlottesville: University Press of Virginia, 2000.
———.*Essays in Radical Empiricism*. Works of William James, 3. Cambridge, MA: Harvard University Press, 1976.
———.*The Letters of William James*. Ed. by his son, Henry James. Boston: Atlantic Monthly Press, 1920.
———.*A Pluralistic Universe*. New York: Longmans Green, 1909.
———.*Pragmatism*. New York: Longmans Green, 1907.
———.*Principles of Psychology*. New York: Henry Holt, 1893.
———.*The Varieties of Religious Experience*. New York: Modern Library, 1902.
———.*The Will to Believe and Other Essays in Popular Philosophy*. New York: Dover, 1956.
———.*William James on Psychical Research*, ed. by Gardner Murphy and Robert O. Ballow. Clifton, NJ: Augustus M. Kelley, 1973.
Jaspers, Karl. *The Great Philosophers: The Disturbers*. New York: Harcourt Brace, 1995.
———. *Philosophy of Existence*. Trans. by Richard Grabay. Philadelphia: University of Pennsylvania Press, 1971.

Jolley, Nicholas. "The Reception of Descartes' Philosophy." In *The Cambridge Companion to Descartes*, ed. by John Cottingham. New York: Cambridge University Press, 1992.
Justin Martyr. *Dialogue with Trypho*. Trans. by Thomas B. Falls. Washington, DC: Catholic University Press of America, 2003.
———. *First and Second Apologies*. Trans. by Leslie William Barnard. New York: Paulist, 1997.
Kafka, P. G. "Reading Spinoza." *New York Times Book Review*, July 2, 2006.
Kant, Immanuel. *Critique of Judgment*. Trans. by Werner Pluhar. Indianapolis, IN: Hackett, 1987.
———. *Critique of Practical Reason*. Trans. by Lewis White Beck. Upper Saddle River, NJ: Prentice Hall, 1993.
———. *Critique of Pure Reason*. Trans. by Norman Kemp Smith. New York: St. Martin's Press, 1965.
———. *Foundation of the Metaphysics of Morals*. In *Critique of Practical Reason and Other Writings in Moral Philosophy*, trans. and ed. by Lewis White Beck. Chicago: University of Chicago Press, 1949.
———. *Religion within the Limits of Reason Alone*. Trans. by Theodore M. Greene. New York: Harper Torchbooks, 1960.
———. "What Is Enlightenment?" In *Critique of Practical Reason and other Writings in Moral Philosophy*, trans. and ed. by Lewis White Beck. Chicago: University of Chicago Press, 1949.
Keller, Catherine. "The Entangled Cosmos: An Experiment in Physical Theopoetics." *Journal of Cosmology* 20 (Sept. 2012): 8648–8666.
Kenny, E. J. *Lucretius*. New York: Oxford University Press, 1977.
Kierkegaard, Soren. *Either/Or*. Trans. by Howard and Edna Hong. Princeton, NJ: Princeton University Press, 1987.
———. *Fear and Trembling*. Trans. by Alastair Hannay. New York: Penguin Books, 1985.
———. *Fear and Trembling and the Sickness Unto Death*. Trans. by Walter Lowrie. Princeton, NJ: Princeton University Press, 1968.
———. *Journals of Soren Kierkegaard*. Ed. by Alexander Dru. New York: Oxford University Press, 1938.
———. *The Point of View*. Trans. by Howard and Edna Hong. Princeton, NJ: Princeton University Press, 2009.
Kosman, L. Aryeh. "The Naïve Narrator: Meditation in Descartes' *Meditations*." In *Essays on Descartes' Meditations*, ed. by Amelie Oksenberg Rorty. Berkeley: University of California Press, 1986.
Lewis, Pericles. "'The Reality of the Unseen:' Shared Fictions and Religious Experience in the Ghost Stories of Henry James." *Arizona Quarterly* 61, no. 2 (Summer 2005): 33–66.
Lippitt, John. *Routledge Philosophy Guidebook to Kierkegaard and* Fear and Trembling. New York: Routledge, 2003.
Littlejohns, Richard. "Everlasting Peace and Medieval Europe: Romantic Myth-Making in Novalis' *Europa*." In *Myths of Europe*, ed. by Richard Littlejohns and Sara Soncini. New York: Rodopi, 2007.
Long, A. A. *Hellenistic Philosophy: Stoics, Epicureans, Sceptics*. London: Duckworth, 1974.
Lopez, Michael. "*The Conduct of Life*: Emerson's Anatomy of Power." In *The Cambridge Companion to Ralph Waldo Emerson*, ed. by Joel Porte and Saundra Morris. New York: Cambridge University Press, 1999.
Lubin, Albert A. *Stranger on the Earth: A Psychological Biography of Vincent Van Gogh*. New York: Henry Holt, 1972.
Lucretius. *On the Nature of the Universe*. Trans. by R. E. Latham. New York: Penguin Books, 1951.
Lustig, T. J. *Henry James and the Ghostly*. New York: Cambridge University Press, 1994.

Lysaker, John. "Taking Emerson Personally." In *New Morning: Emerson in the Twenty-First Century*, ed. by Arthur Lothstein and Michael Brodrick. Albany, NY: State University of New York Press, 2008.
Maimonides. *The Book of Knowledge*. Trans. by H. M. Russell and J. Weinberg. New York: Ktav, 1983.
———. *Guide for the Perplexed*. Trans. by Shlomo Pines. Chicago: University of Chicago Press, 1963.
———. *Letters of Maimonides*. Trans. and ed. by Leon Stitskin. New York: Yeshiva University Press, 1977.
Marcus Aurelius. *The Meditations of Marcus Aurelius*. Trans. by G. M. A. Grube. Indianapolis, IN: Hackett, 1983.
Martianus Capella. *The Marriage of Philology and Mercury*. Trans. by William Harris Stahl and Richard Johnson. New York: Columbia University Press, 1977.
Maslin, Janet. "Big Thinkers in a Nation Transformed by War." *New York Times* (June 4, 2001): E9.
Matthiessen, F. O. *The James Family*. New York: Knopf, 1947.
McFarland, Dorothy Tuck. *Simone Weil*. New York: Frederick Ungar, 1983.
Millner, Samuel L. *The Face of Benedictus Spinoza*. New York: Machmadim Art Editions, 1946.
Molnár, Géza von. *Novalis' "Fichte Studies"*. The Hague: Mouton, 1970.
———. *Romantic Vision, Ethical Context: Novalis and Artistic Autonomy*. Minneapolis: University of Minnesota Press, 1987.
Monk, Ray. *Bertrand Russell: The Spirit of Solitude, 1872–1921*. New York: Free Press, 1996.
———. *Bertrand Russell: The Ghost of Madness, 1921–1970*. New York: Free Press, 2001.
Mooney, Edward F. *Knights of Faith and Resignation: Reading Kierkegaard's* Fear and Trembling. Albany: State University of New York Press, 1991.
Moreau, Pierre-Francois. "Spinoza's Reception and Influence." In *The Cambridge Companion to Spinoza*, ed. by Don Garrett. New York: Cambridge University Press, 1996.
Morgan, Michael. *Platonic Piety: Philosophy and Ritual in Fourth Century Athens*. New Haven, CT: Yale University Press, 1990.
Motschmann, Cornelius. *Die Religionspolitik Marc Aurels*. Stuttgart: F. Steiner Verlag, 2002.
Neubaurer, John. *Novalis*. Boston: Twayne Publishers, 1980.
Nevin, Thomas. *Simone Weil: Portrait of a Self-Exiled Jew*. Chapel Hill: University of Norrh Carolina Press, 1991.
Nietzsche, Friedrich. *Genealogy of Morals and Ecce Homo*. Trans. by Walter Kaufmann. New York: Vintage, 1989.
Novalis. *Briefe und Werke*. Berlin: Verlag Lambert, 1943.
———. *Heinrich von Ofterdingen*. Trans. by Palmer Hilty. Prospect Heights, IL: Waveland Press, 1990.
———. *Notes for a Romantic Encyclopedia*. Trans. and ed. by David Wood. Albany: State University of New York Press, 2007.
———. *Philosophical Writings*. Trans. and ed. by Margaret Mahony Stoljar. Albany: State University of New York Press, 1997.
Nuffelen, Peter van. *Rethinking the Gods: Philosophical Readings of Religion in the Post-Hellenistic Period*. New York: Cambridge University Press, 2011.
Nussbaum, Martha. *The Therapy of Desire: Theory and Practice in Hellenistic Studies*. Princeton, NJ: Princeton University Press, 1994.
O'Brien, William Arctander. *Novalis: Signs of Revolution*. Durham, NC: Duke University Press, 1995.
Pascal, Blaise. "The Memorial." In *Pensées and Other Writings*, trans. by Honor Levi. New York: Oxford University Press, 1995.
Perrin, J. M. and G. Thibon. *Simone Weil as We Knew Her*. New York: Routledge, 1953.
Petrement, Simone. *Simone Weil: A Life*. New York: Pantheon, 1976.

Pfefferkorn, Kristin. *Novalis: A Romantic's Theory of Language and Poetry.* New Haven, CT: Yale University Press, 1988.
Pinkard, Terry. "What Is a 'Shape of Spirit'?" In *Hegel's Phenomenology of Spirit: A Critical Guide.* New York: Cambridge University Press, 2008.
Plato. *The Dialogues of Plato.* Trans. by Benjamin Jowett. New York: Random House, 1937.
Popkin, Richard and Michael Signer. *Spinoza's Earliest Publication? The Hebrew Translation of Margaret Fell's* A Loving Salutation to the Seed of Abraham among the Jews. Wolfeboro, NH: Van Gorcum, 1987.
Posnock, Ross. *The Trial of Curiosity: Henry James, William James, and the Challenge of Modernity.* New York: Oxford University Press, 1991.
Problemata. In *The Works of Aristotle,* vol. 7, trans. by E. S. Forster. Oxford, England: Clarendon, 1927.
Proust, Marcel. *The Captive and the Fugitive.* Trans. by C. K. Scott Moncrieff and Terence Kilmartin, revised by D. J. Enright. New York: Modern Library, 1992.
———. *Sodom and Gemorrah.* Trans. by John Sturrock. New York: Penguin, 2004.
Randall, John. "The Spirit of American Philosophy." In *Wellsprings of the American Spirit: A Series of Addresses,* ed. by F. Ernest Johnson. Religion and Civilization Series. New York: Institute for Religious and Social Studies, 1948.
Richardson, Robert. *Emerson: The Mind on Fire.* Berkeley, CA: University of California Press, 1995.
———. *William James: In the Maelstrom of American Modernism.* Boston: Houghton Mifflin, 2006.
Roberts, J. J. M. "The Hand of Yahweh." *Vetus Testamentum* (1971): 244–251.
Rorty, Amelie Oksenberg. "The Structure of Descartes' *Meditations.*" In *Essays on Descartes' Meditations,* ed. by Amelie Oksenberg Rorty. Berkeley: University of California Press, 1986.
Ross, David. *Plato's Theory of Ideas.* New York: Oxford University Press, 1951.
Rossi, William. "Emerson, Nature, and Natural Science." In *A Historical Guide to Ralph Waldo Emerson,* ed. by Joel Myerson. New York: Oxford University Press, 2000.
Rubidge, Bradley. "Descartes' *Meditations* and Devotional Meditations." *Journal of the History of Ideas* (1990): 24–79.
Rubinstein, Ernest. *Religion and the Muse: The Vexed Relation between Religion and Western Literature.* Albany: State University of New York Press, 1999.
Russell, Bertrand. *The Autobiography of Bertrand Russell.* London: George Allen, 1967.
———. *Basic Writings of Bertrand Russell.* Ed. by Robert Egner and Lester E. Denonn. New York: Simon and Schuster, 1967.
———. *Contemplation and Action: 1902–1914.* Ed. by Richard A. Rempel, and others. The Collected Papers of Bertrand Russell, 12. London: George Allen and Unwin, 1985.
———. "The Free Man's Worship." *Independent Review* 1, no. 3 (Dec. 1903): 415–424.
———. *History of Western Philosophy.* New York: Simon and Schuster, 1945.
———. *My Philosophical Development.* New York: Simon and Schuster, 1959.
———. *Mysticism and Logic and Other Essays.* New York: Longmans, Green, 1918.
———. *Philosophical Essays.* New York: Routledge, 2009.
———. *Principles of Social Reconstruction.* New York: Routledge, 1916, 1997.
———. *Problems of Philosophy.* New York: Henry Holt, 1912.
———. "Reply to Criticisms." In *The Philosophy of Bertrand Russell,* ed. by Paul Arthur Schilpp. The Library of Living Philosophers, 5. Evanston, IL: Northwestern University Press, 1944.
———. *Satan in the Suburbs and Other Stories.* London: Bodley Head, 1953.
———. *Selected Letters of Bertrand Russell.* Ed. by Nicholas Griffin. Boston: Houghton Mifflin, 1992.
Santayana, George. *Persons and Places,* v. 2: *The Middle Years.* New York: Scribner's, 1945.

Saul, Nicholas. *History and Poetry in Novalis and in the Tradition of the German Enlightenment.* London: Institute of Germanic Studies, University of London, 1984.
Schilpp, Paul Arthur, ed. *The Philosophy of Bertrand Russell.* The Library of Living Philosophers, 5. Evanston, IL: Northwestern University Press, 1944.
Schlegel, Friedrich. *Philosophical Fragments.* Trans. by Peter Firchow. Minneapolis: University of Minnesota Press, 1991.
Scott, R. B. Y. *Proverbs, Ecclesiastes.* Anchor Bible. Garden City, NY: Doubleday, 1965.
Sedgwick, Eve Kosofsky. "Shame and Performativity: Henry James' New York Edition Prefaces." In *Henry James' New York Edition: the Construction of Authorship,* ed. by David McWhirter. Stanford, CA: Stanford University Press, 1995.
Sethi, Mira. "Henry James' Most Affecting Portrait." *Wall Street Journal* (July 24–25, 2010): W14.
Sikes, E. E. *Lucretius, Poet and Philosopher.* Cambridge: Cambridge University Press, 1936.
Smith, Wilfred Cantwell. "Philosophia as one of the Religious Traditions of Humankind." In *Modern Culture from a Comparative Perspective,* ed. by John Burbidge. Albany: State University of New York Press, 1997.
Solomon, Robert. *Spirituality for the Skeptic: The Thoughtful Love of Life.* New York: Oxford University Press, 2002.
Spinoza, Benedict. *Ethics, Treatise on the Emendation of the Intellect, and Selected Letters.* Trans. by Samuel Shirley, ed. by Seymour Feldman. Indianapolis, IN: Hackett, 1992.
———. *Tractatus Theologico Politicus.* Trans. by R. H. M. Elwes. London: George Bell, 1891.
Steele, Jeffrey. "Transcendental Friendship: Emerson, Fuller, and Thoreau." In *The Cambridge Companion to Ralph Waldo Emerson,* ed. by Joel Porte and Saundra Morris. New York: Cambridge University Press, 1999.
Steiner, George. "Bad Friday—Portrait of a Self-Exiled Jew, by Thomas Nevin." *The New Yorker* 68, no. 2 (March 2, 1992): 86–91.
Stewart, Robert Bowman. "Some Aspects of Campus Architecture." *The Columbia Varsity* (Dec. 12?, 1924): 10.
Svetasvatara Upanishad. In *The Thirteen Principal Upanishads,* trans. by Robert Ernest Hume. London: Milford, 1934.
Tait, Kate. *My Father Bertrand Russell.* London: Harcourt Brace, 1975.
Taylor, Charles. *A Secular Age.* Cambridge, MA: Harvard University Press, 2007.
Tertullian. *On the Flesh of Christ.* Trans. by Dr. Holmes. The Ante-Nicene Fathers. Grand Rapids, MI: Eerdmans, 1951.
———. *On the Soul.* Trans. by Edwin Quain. In *Tertullian, Apologetical Works and Minucius Felix, Octavius.* New York: Fathers of the Church, 1950.
Thalmann, Marianne. *The Literary Sign Language of German Romanticism.* Detroit: Wayne State University Press, 1972.
Tocqueville, Alexis de. *Democracy in America.* Edited by Phillips Bradley. New York: Vintage, 1945.
Townsend, Kim. *Manhood at Harvard: William James and Others.* New York: Norton, 1996.
Tracy, David. "Simone Weil: The Impossible." In *The Christian Platonism of Simone Weil,* ed. by E. Jane Doering and Eric O. Springsted. Notre Dame, IN: University of Notre Dame Press, 2004.
Turner, Victor. *Ritual Process.* Chicago: Aldine, 1969.
Updike, John. Introduction to Henry James, *Portrait of a Lady.* Oxford World's Classics. New York: Oxford University Press, 1999.
Van Eck, Xander. "Van Gogh and George Henry Boughton." *The Burlington Magazine* 132, no. 1049: 539–540.
Van Gogh, Vincent. *The Complete Letters of Vincent Van Gogh.* Trans. by Johanna Van Gogh-Bonger and C. de Wood. Greenwich, CT: New York Graphic Society, 1958.
Veto, Miklos. *The Religious Metaphysics of Simone Weil.* Trans. by Joan Dargan. Albany: State University of New York Press, 1994.

Walsh, Jerome. "Despair as a Theological Virtue in the Spirituality of Ecclesiastes." *Biblical Theology Bulletin* 12, no.2 (April 1992): 46–49.
Weil, Andre. *The Apprenticeship of a Mathematician.* Boston: Birkhauser Verlag, 1992.
Weil, Simone. *Cahiers.* Ed. by Andre A. Devaux and Florence de Lussy. Oeuvres Complètes, 6. Paris: Gallimard, 1997.
———. "Essay on Reading." Trans. by Rebecca Fine Rose and Timothy Tessin. *Philosophical Investigations* 13, no. 4 (Oct. 1990): 297–303.
———. "A Few Reflections on the Notion of Value." Trans. by E. Jane Doering. *Cahiers Simone Weil* 34, no. 4 (Dec. 2011): 455–462.
———. *First and Last Notebooks.* Trans. by Richard Rees. New York: Oxford University Press, 1970.
———. *Formative Writings, 1929–1941.* Ed. and trans. by Dorothy Tuck McFarland and Wilhelmina Van Ness. Amherst: University of Massachusetts Press, 1987.
———. *Gravity and Grace.* Trans. by Arthur Wills. New York: Putnam's, 1952.
———. "Hitler and the Idea of Greatness." *Commentary* (July 1952): 15–22.
———. *Intimations of Christianity among the Ancient Greeks.* Trans. by Elisabeth Chase Geissbuhler. London: Routledge and Kegan Paul, 1957.
———. *Letter to a Priest.* Trans. by Arthur Wills. London: Routledge and Kegan Paul, 1953.
———. *The Need for Roots.* Trans. by Arthur Wills. New York: Putnam's, 1952.
———. *The Notebooks of Simone Weil.* Trans. by Arthur Wills. New York: Putnam's, 1956.
———. *Science, Necessity, and the Love of God.* Trans. by Richard Rees. New York: Oxford University Press, 1968.
———. *Selected Essays, 1934–1943.* Trans. by Richard Rees. New York: Oxford University Press, 1962.
———. *Seventy Letters.* Trans. by Richard Rees. New York: Oxford University Press, 1965.
———. *Simone Weil.* Ed. by Eric O. Springsted. Modern Spiritual Masters. Maryknoll, NY: Orbis Books, 1998.
———. *The Simone Weil Reader.* Ed. by George A. Panichas. New York: David McKay, 1977.
———. *Waiting for God.* Trans. by Emma Craufurd. New York: Putnam's, 1952.
Weil, Sylvie. *At Home with Andre and Simone Weil.* Evanston, IL: Northwestern University Press, 2010.
Whicher, Stephen. *Freedom and Fate: An Inner Life of Ralph Waldo Emerson.* Philadelphia: University of Pennsylvania Press, 1971.
Winch, Peter. *Simone Weil: "The Just Balance."* New York: Cambridge University Press, 1989.
Winden, J. C. M. van. *An Early Christian Philosopher: Justin Martyr's* Dialogue with Trypho, *Chapters One to Nine.* Leiden: Brill, 1971.
Wolfson, Harry Austryn. *The Philosophy of Spinoza.* New York: World Publishing, 1934.
———. "Spinoza and Religion." *Menorah Journal* (Autumn 1950): 146–167.
Wood, Alan. "Russell's Philosophy: A Study of its Development." In *My Philosophical Development,* by Bertrand Russell. New York: Simon and Schuster, 1959.
Woolf, Virginia. "The Ghost Stories." In *Henry James: A Collection of Critical Essays,* ed. by Leon Edel. Englewood Cliffs, NJ: Prentice-Hall, 1963.
Zwarg, Christina. *Feminist Conversations: Fuller, Emerson and the Play of Reading.* Ithaca, NY: Cornell University Press, 1995.

Index

Abel (biblical figure), 20–21
Abraham (biblical figure), 4, 151–152, 157, 159–162
Activity, 42, 54, 68, 80, 86, 102, 106, 127, 140, 259–260. *See also* power; pragmatism; will
Acts (biblical text), 4
aesthetics, 8; in Hegel, 135, 139; in Kant, 105–106, 112–113, 258; in Kierkegaard, 146, 147–148, 149, 151, 152–157, 160, 161. *See also* artworks; beauty; creativity, artistic
Agamemnon, 45
allegory, 31, 34–35
analogy, 27, 31–32, 34–35, 54, 131, 137, 235–236, 237, 255
Anaximenes, 219
androgyny, 190
Antigone, 234
anxiety, 63, 68, 97, 101, 134, 135, 153, 189, 190, 221
Apollo, 29, 51, 243
Apology (Plato), 29
apophasis, 30, 81, 82–83, 97, 100, 157, 158, 196, 198, 214, 235, 245
Aristotle, 2, 5, 30, 41–43, 60–61, 65, 127, 128, 219–220, 227
artworks, 105–106, 108, 131, 135, 139, 154, 210, 212, 216–218, 233, 240, 255. *See also* creativity, artistic
asceticism, 21, 77, 102, 129, 245, 251, 258–260
atomism, 47, 48–49, 209
attention. *See* contemplation
Augustine, 175
Averroes, 7

Barnes, Albert, 218, 220, 221
Barth, Karl, 126n80
Barzun, Jacques, 200n34

beauty, 254–255; in Emerson, 163, 167; in Lucretius, 56; in Marcus Aurelius, 56; in Plato, 32, 36–37, 38–39; in Bertrand Russell, 206, 207, 209–210, 214, 221, 222; in Simone Weil, 229, 232, 237, 240, 242. *See also* aesthetics
Beck, Lewis White, 100
Behler, Ernst, 126n75
Beiser, Frederick, 113
Benjamin, Walter, 71
Berenson, Bernard, 215
Berlin, Isaiah, 220–221
Bhagavad Gita, 39, 162n14, 261n11
Bible, 121, 169, 243–244, 245
Bloom, Alan, 70
Bloom, Harold, 75
body, 260; in Aristotle, 42; in Descartes, 61, 64, 66, 68; in Emerson, 166, 169; in Lucretius, 43, 43–44, 46–47; in Marcus Aurelius, 53; in Plato, 35–36, 37; in Spinoza, 79–80, 82, 85–87; in Simone Weil, 232, 236, 237
Boethius, xv–xvii, xviiin8, 2, 5, 7, 59, 184
Boughton, George Henry, 216–217
brother-sister relation, 137, 234
Buber, Martin, 110–111, 177
Buddhism, 26, 45, 53, 63, 97, 208, 238, 242, 251
Buell, Lawrence, 175, 179n29
Bunyan, John, 213, 215–217, 225n92
Burrus, Virginia, 124n27
Byron, Lord, 222

Cain (biblical figure), 20–21
Calvinism, 61, 225n92
Carroll, Lewis, 17, 64, 110
Catholic Church, 6, 61, 67, 70, 71, 117
causation, 17, 20, 21, 41, 42, 47, 80, 84, 86, 88, 93, 97, 98, 100, 109, 150, 170,

272 Index

172–173, 232
celibacy, 117–118
Celsus, 3–4, 10n16
Cervantes, Miguel de, 72
Chadwick, Henry, 243
change, 42, 52, 88, 137
chemistry, 104n27
Christendom or Europa (Novalis), 116–119, 121–123, 233
Christianity, 9; and death, 46; and Descartes, 59–61; and Emerson, 163–164, 171; and Hegel, 130, 131; and William James, 181, 184, 186; and Kant, 94, 102, 103; and Kierkegaard, 146, 148, 155, 158, 160, 234; and Novalis, 111, 112, 116–118, 123; and philosophy, 1, 2, 59–61, 229, 234, 235, 243; and Plato, 33; and Bertrand Russell, 207, 208, 215, 223n30; and Spinoza, 75–77; and Simone Weil, 228–229, 231, 233, 241–245
Church of England, 7
Cohen, Hermann, 100, 104n24
Coleridge, Samuel Taylor, 164
Confucius, 260, 261n11
Conrad, Joseph, 213
contemplation: in Descartes, 65, 67, 70; in Ecclesiastes, 23; in William James, 189; in Lucretius, 48, 49; in Marcus Aurelius, 55; in Bertrand Russell, 207, 209–210; in Simone Weil, 232, 238, 240, 242, 245, 260
contradiction: in Descartes, 70–71, 73, 252; in Ecclesiastes, 16, 23, 71, 252; in Emerson, 173, 175, 252; in Hegel, 70, 131, 132, 134–135, 138–139, 141, 252; in William James, 189, 252; in Kierkegaard, 153; in Plato, 252; in Simone Weil, 228–230, 231, 231–232, 234, 235–236, 239–240, 242, 252, 254, 260
creation, 3, 15, 18, 23, 29, 65, 84, 104n21, 235, 236, 241–242
creativity, artistic, 105, 113, 127, 196, 218. *See also* artworks; aesthetics; literature; Mozart; music; poetry

Dante, 63, 78–79, 101, 103, 174, 213

David (biblical figure), 141
death: in Ecclesiastes, 15, 16, 17, 22; in Emerson, 169, 178; in Hegel, 135, 141; in Lucretius, 44, 45–46, 47; in Marcus Aurelius, 52–53; in Novalis, 109, 122; in Plato, 39–40; in Bertrand Russell, 216, 218; in Simone Weil, 230. *See also* immortality
Democritus, 47, 219
Derrida, Jacques, 177, 179n30
Descartes, Rene, 6, 7, 8, 9, 59–74n23, 255, 256, 257, 258–259, 259; and Aristotle, 60, 65; and Christianity, 59–61, 63; and Ecclesiastes, 62; and Emerson, 166, 170; and Ignatius of Loyola, 67, 73; and Kant, 101; and Lucretius, 62, 68; and Marcus Aurelius, 59, 62, 67, 68; and Novalis, 119; and Pascal, 70; and Plato, 62, 64, 65, 66, 72; and Spinoza, 61, 70, 75, 77–79, 81, 83, 84–85, 87–88; and Stoicism, 69; and Simone Weil, 70, 228, 230, 231, 235, 237–238, 241
desire: in Descartes, 68; in Henry James, 196; in Kant, 93, 94, 95, 95–96 98, 99, 102; in Kierkegaard, 155–156, 159, 161; in Lucretius, 44; in Plato, 32, 40; in Bertrand Russell, 208, 209, 211, 216, 218; in Spinoza, 77, 85–86; in Simone Weil, 231, 241
despair, 79, 135, 142, 152, 157, 189, 216, 219
detachment, 40, 50, 53, 55, 230, 231, 232, 251, 256–258, 260
Deuteronomy (biblical text), 13–16
Dewey, John, 219
dialectic: in Emerson, 179n18; in Hegel, 102, 132, 138–139, 141, 145, 252; in Kierkegaard, 157, 158, 252; in Plato, 32–35, 38, 39. *See also* inversion
Dionysius, 243
disinterest. *See* detachment
dreams, 48, 64, 72, 108, 109, 119–120, 121, 209
Dreyfus, Hubert, 9
dualism, 64, 73, 95, 107, 220, 237, 239, 252
Durkheim, Emile, 6

Ecclesiastes (Biblical text), 8, 9, 13–24n8, 252, 255, 256, 258, 259; and Descartes, 62; and Emerson, 171; and Kant, 92, 93; and Kierkegaard, 152; and Lucretius, 44; and Marcus Aurelius, 51–52; and Plato, 23, 26–27, 29; and Bertrand Russell, 214; and Spinoza, 77, 78; and Simone Weil, 231–232
ecstasy, 33, 173, 176–177, 183, 184
Either/Or (Kierkegaard), 146–156, 160–162
Electra, 234
Elijah (biblical figure), 245
Eliot, T. S., 213
Elisha ben Abuyya, 3, 13
Emerson, Ralph Waldo, 7, 8, 9, 163–180n31, 255, 256, 257, 258, 259, 260; and Christianity, 163–164, 170, 171; and Descartes, 166, 170; and Ecclesiastes, 171; and Hegel, 164, 165, 166; and William James, 181, 187; and Judaism, 178; and Kant, 164–165, 168, 177; and Kierkegaard, 163, 164, 174, 178; and Lucretius, 165; and Novalis, 168; and Plato, 167; and Spinoza, 164, 165, 166, 171, 174; and Stoicism, 171, 174; and Simone Weil, 235
emotion: in Descartes, 61, 63, 67–69; in William James, 182–183, 186, 188, 189; in Lucretius, 43, 47; in Novalis, 122; in Bertrand Russell, 207, 208, 211–212; in Spinoza, 77, 79–81, 85–87
empiricism, 7, 170, 188, 219
Epicureanism, 2, 8, 18–19, 41, 43, 45, 47–49, 52, 54–56, 209
epistemology, 6, 8, 255; in Descartes, 61–62, 259; in Emerson, 166; in Hegel, 130, 137; in William James, 185; in Kant, 91, 94–95, 101, 105, 106; in Marcus Aurelius, 55; in Novalis, 110; in Plato, 28, 30, 31, 35; in Bertrand Russell, 210, 211, 212; in Spinoza, 83; in Simone Weil, 229, 237. *See also* ideas; knowledge; truth
Er (Platonic figure), 36

error, 55, 62, 88, 94–95, 97, 101, 167, 170, 173–174, 208. *See also* self-deception
eternity, 48, 78–79, 83–84, 87, 88, 156
ethics: in Descartes, 62–64, 66, 69; in Emerson, 169; in Hegel, 129, 131, 135, 139, 141; in Kant, 8, 91–93, 94–95, 96, 98–99, 101–102, 105, 106; in Kierkegaard, 146, 147, 148, 148–152, 156, 157, 159–160, 161, 162n13; in Marcus Aurelius, 54, 55; in Novalis, 107; and philosophy, 2; in Plato, 26, 28; and religion, 1, 2, 146–147; in Bertrand Russell, 207, 212, 219; in Simone Weil, 241, 244, 245, 250n153. *See also* Good
Eucharist, 61
Euripides, 206, 227
evil(s): and Descartes, 62; and Ecclesiastes, 14; and William James, 194; and Judaism, 3; and Kant, 94–95, 99; and Lucretius, 44–45; and Marcus Aurelius, 52–53; and Plato, 3, 26–27, 31, 35–36, 38; and Spinoza, 88. *See also* suffering
existentialism, 96, 187, 230
Exodus (biblical text), 14, 19
experience, religious, 1, 2; in Hegel, 137; in William James, 181–189, 191–192, 194, 197–198; in Kierkegaard, 148, 159; in Plato, 26; in Bertrand Russell, 205–206, 207, 218; in Simone Weil, 235, 238. *See also* mysticism; sacred

faith, 91, 130, 145, 157–162
fate, 166–167, 171–173, 177
Faust legend, 155, 208
fear, 44, 47, 68, 69, 135
Fear and Trembling (Kierkegaard), 145–147, 157–162
Feuerbach, Ludwig, 102, 260
Fichte, J. G., 107, 109, 112
Fitzgerald, Penelope, 106
force, 131, 137, 232, 239, 240. *See also* power
Frederick II, King of Prussia, 91–92
"Free Man's Worship" (Russell), 206, 208–210, 213, 215–218, 221

freedom: in Ecclesiastes, 22; in Emerson, 163–164, 166, 168, 172, 173, 177; in Kant, 94, 98, 99, 100, 102, 103, 105, 257; in Kierkegaard, 149, 150, 152–153, 154; in Marcus Aurelius, 56; in Bertrand Russell, 208; in Spinoza, 88
Friedrich, Caspar David, 255
friendship, 45, 57n14, 152, 176–178, 235, 237
Fry, Roger, 218
Fuller, Margaret, 180n31
future, 184–185, 188, 231. *See also* past

Galileo, 70
Gamaliel, Rabbi, 4
Genesis (biblical text), 3, 13, 15–16, 22–23, 84, 114, 127, 138, 170
geometry, 75, 87, 103, 237–238, 240, 259
ghost stories, 182, 191–196, 198, 200n22, 201n48, 203n89
ghosts, 213
Gilson, Étienne, 60
Gnosticism, 235, 242
God: in Aristotle, 41–42; in the Bible, 2, 127; in Descartes, 60–61, 62, 64–67, 69–70, 81; in Ecclesiastes, 15, 17–21, 23; in Emerson, 165–166, 171, 175–176; and the Good, 3, 235; in Hegel, 79, 130, 140; in William James, 181, 188, 188–189; and Judaism, 3; in Kant, 92–93, 96–97, 98, 99, 100, 101, 102; in Kierkegaard, 149, 150, 151, 157, 158; knowability, 4; in Novalis, 111; and philosophy, 1, 2, 4, 6, 8; in Plato, 29; and religion, 2; in Bertrand Russell, 208; in Spinoza, 79, 81–88; in Simone Weil, 232–233, 235–237, 239, 241. *See also* apophasis; sacred
gods, Greek, 25, 29, 41, 174, 243
gods, Roman, 44, 47–48, 50, 51, 54, 232
Good: in Kant, 92–93, 95, 96, 98, 102; in Plato, 3, 4, 25, 29–31, 32, 33, 34–37, 38, 42, 65, 82, 253; in Bertrand Russell, 206, 211; In Simone Weil, 229, 230, 231, 235–237, 238–241, 242. *See also* ethics; sacred

Gospels, 21. *See also* John; Luke; Matthew
Gradel, Ittai, 50
Greek religion, 25–26

Hadot, Pierre, 2, 6, 47, 50, 56
happiness, 257; in Aristotle, 42; in Descartes, 64, 69; in Emerson, 166, 176–177; in William James, 183, 184; in Kant, 92, 95, 96, 97, 99, 102–103; in Kierkegaard, 151, 156, 158, 158–159, 162; in Lucretius, 45, 48, 49; in Novalis, 112; in Plato, 27–29, 31, 35, 38; in Bertrand Russell, 207, 212, 218; in Spinoza, 78, 79, 81
Haywood, Bruce, 117
Hegel, Georg Wilhelm Friedrich, 8, 9, 127–143n16, 255, 256, 257, 258, 259; and Christianity, 130, 131; and Emerson, 164, 165, 166; and William James, 199n21; and Kant, 102, 106, 127, 129, 130, 133, 134–135, 139; and Kierkegaard, 142, 145, 146, 148, 149, 155, 157, 160; and Lucretius, 49; and Novalis, 128, 132, 135, 137; and Plato, 128, 129; and Bertrand Russell, 221; and Spinoza, 127, 137; and Stoicism, 137; and Simone Weil, 233–234
Heinrich von Ofterdingen (Novalis), 113, 116–117, 118–123
Hesiod, 25–27
Hinduism, 39, 47–48, 191, 260
history, 118, 120–121, 131, 147, 164–165, 218–219. *See also* past
History of Western Philosophy (Russell), 205, 218–222
Homer, xvi, 25–26, 172, 234
homophobia, 190–191, 201n46
Horner, Timothy, 244
humanism, 6, 167–168, 175–178, 181, 223n26
Hume, David, 106, 220, 228
Hutchison, Hazel, 191–192, 194
hypocrisy, 94

idealism, 7, 8, 41, 85, 101, 102, 103, 106, 107, 108, 115, 131, 150, 164, 170, 187, 188, 237, 259

ideas, xv; in Aristotle, 42–43; in Descartes, 63, 64–65, 66–67; in Hegel, 131; in Kant, 97, 105–106, 210; in Kierkegaard, 161; in Novalis, 113; in Plato, 29–30, 35–36, 37, 39, 40; in Bertrand Russell, 209–210, 211; in Spinoza, 83, 84–85, 86–87. *See also* reason
The Idiot (Dostoevsky), 209
Ignatius Loyola, 67, 73
The Illiad, 234, 245
illusion, 49, 173–175. *See also* error; self-deception
imagination, 257–258; in Descartes, 71–72; in Emerson, 168; in Hegel, 132; in William James, 198; in Kant, 105–106; in Lucretius, 49; in Marcus Aurelius, 55; in Novalis, 122; in Bertrand Russell, 209, 211, 212, 213; in Spinoza, 77, 82; in Simone Weil, 233
immortality, 260; in Aristotle, 43; in William James, 195–198; in Kant, 99, 100; in Plato, 36, 37; in Bertrand Russell, 216; in Spinoza, 87
impersonality, 18, 198, 208, 212, 215, 235, 241, 256. *See also* detachment
Index Librorum Prohibitorum, 61
infinity: in Emerson, 166, 173; in Hegel, 130; in Kant, 97; in Kierkegaard, 158; in Lucretius, 48; in Novalis, 108, 109, 110, 111; in Bertrand Russell, 211, 212, 225n88; in Spinoza, 78–79, 82, 83–84, 85, 86, 88; in Simone Weil, 236
intentionality, 23, 114
interrogative mood, 2, 16, 189, 192, 194, 195, 198, 221, 251–254, 256, 260
interstitial. *See* liminality
inversion, 17, 52, 138, 152, 171, 194, 195–196, 201n48, 254
Iphigenia, 45
irony, 50, 56, 174, 257
Isaac (biblical figure), 4, 157, 159
Isaiah (biblical text), 16

James, Alice, 196
James, Henry, 8, 9, 20, 182, 190–198, 200n22, 253, 257–258, 260

James, Henry, Sr., 181
James, William, 5, 7, 8, 9, 181–203n92, 251, 253, 257, 257–258, 260; and Christianity, 181, 184, 186; and Emerson, 181, 187; and Hegel, 199n21; and Kierkegaard, 185, 186–187, 200n22; and Marcus Aurelius, 186; and Plato, 198; and Bertrand Russell, 205–206, 207, 208, 220; and Spinoza, 186, 187, 195; and Simone Weil, 234–235
Jaspers, Karl, 11n28, 70, 162n15
Jeremiah (biblical text), 16
Jesuits, 59, 67
Jesus Christ, 3–4, 33, 39, 43, 75–77, 139, 141, 152, 160. *See also* Christianity
Job (biblical text), 18, 21, 92, 101, 152, 195, 197, 231, 236
Johannes Erigena, 219
John, Gospel of, 33, 43
Johnson, Samuel, 43
Joshua (biblical text), 245
Judaism: and Emerson, 178; and Kant, 98, 102, 103; and Novalis, 111; and philosophy, 1, 2–3, 4, 244–245; and Plato, 3, 33; and Spinoza, 75–77, 78; and Simone Weil, 229, 244–245
Justin Martyr, 5, 229, 242–245, 249n128, 250n136

Kabbalah, 89n14, 245
Kaddish, 178
Kant, Immanuel, 8, 9, 91–104n29, 253, 255, 256, 257, 258, 259, 260; and Descartes, 101; and Ecclesiastes, 92, 93; and Emerson, 164–165, 168, 177; and Hegel, 102, 106, 127, 129, 130, 133, 134–135, 137, 139; and Kierkegaard, 93–94, 146, 147, 148, 149, 150; and Novalis, 107–110, 111, 112, 123; and Plato, 94, 95, 103, 106; and religion, 91, 102–103; and Bertrand Russell, 210, 211, 221; and Spinoza, 81, 91, 92, 96, 98, 99, 100, 101, 103, 104n8; and Stoicism, 96, 99; and Simone Weil, 229, 230, 231, 235, 236, 240–241
Karmayoga, 260
Keats, John, 163, 167, 169, 210, 223n39

Keller, Catherine, 143n11
Kelly, Sean Dorrance, 9
Kierkegaard, Soren, 5, 8, 9, 145–162n15, 255, 257, 260; and Christianity, 146, 148, 155, 158, 160, 234; and Ecclesiastes, 152; and Emerson, 163, 164, 174, 178; and Hegel, 142, 145, 146, 148, 149, 155, 157, 160; and William James, 185, 186–187, 200n22; and Kant, 93–94, 146, 147, 148, 149, 150; and Novalis, 155, 161; and Plato, 148; and Spinoza, 79, 157, 158; and Stoicism, 157, 158; and Simone Weil, 228, 234
Kings, 1st (biblical text), 245
knowledge: in Descartes, 62; in Emerson, 172, 174; in Hegel, 128–130, 133–137, 141, 143n15, 147; in William James, 182, 183–184, 187–188, 192, 202n65; in Kant, 91, 97, 101, 103; in Kierkegaard, 145–146, 159, 160–161; in Lucretius, 49; in Novalis, 108, 110; in Plato, 31–32, 33, 34–36, 37, 37–38; in Bertrand Russell, 211, 212; in Spinoza, 79; in Simone Weil, 237, 238. *See also* epistemology; truth
Kundera, Milan, 21

Lady Philosophy, xvi–xvii, xviiin8, 2, 5, 7, 9, 59
language, 255; in Descartes, 71; in Emerson, 168–169; in Hegel, 132, 137–142; in Kierkegaard, 150, 156, 157, 160; in Lucretius, 48; in Novalis, 113–114, 116, 120; in Plato, 30, 38, 39; in Spinoza, 82–83, 87
Lao-Tze, 231
law: in Emerson, 168, 169, 171–174, 256; in Kant, 93, 94, 96, 98–99, 101–102, 106, 148, 256; in Lucretius, 44, 256; in Novalis, 123; in Spinoza, 77; in Simone Weil, 229, 236, 237–238, 241, 244. *See also* causation
Lawrence, D. H., 213
The Laws (Plato), 25
Leibniz, Gottfried Wilhelm, 213, 258
Levinas, Emmanuel, 177
Leviticus (biblical text), 22

Lewis, Pericles, 201n58
liminality, 191, 202n71, 253–254
Lippitt, John, 147
literature, 9, 106, 114–116, 118, 154, 155, 191–195, 213–214, 216, 233. *See also* aesthetics; metaphor; poetry
Locke, John, 219
logic, 206, 212, 219, 220. *See also* law; mathematics
logos, 3, 243, 244, 249n130. *See also* reason
Lopez, Michael, 174
love: in Aristotle, 42; and Christianity, 1; in Descartes, 68, 70; and Judaism, 1; in Kierkegaard, 147–148, 148, 158, 161; in Novalis, 109–110, 111–112; and philosophy, 1; in Plato, 32, 33, 36–38, 39; in Bertrand Russell, 205, 211, 212; in Spinoza, 78, 79, 81, 84
Lucretius, 8, 9, 43–50, 52, 55–56, 253, 254, 257, 258; and Descartes, 68; and Ecclesiastes, 18, 43–44; and Emerson, 165; and Marcus Aurelius, 51, 52, 54, 55–56; and Plato, 43, 44; and Bertrand Russell, 220; and Simone Weil, 232
Luke, Gospel of, 9, 141
Lutheranism, 94, 121
Lysaker, John, 180n31

Maimonides, 75, 245, 250n153
Manning, William, 220
Marcion, 243–244
Marcus Aurelius, xvii, 8, 50–56, 256, 257, 258, 259; and Aristotle, 51; and Descartes, 59, 67, 68; and Ecclesiastes, 51–52; And William James, 186; and Lucretius, 51, 52, 54, 55–56; and Plato, 50, 52, 53, 54, 55, 56; and Simone Weil, 232
marriage, 116, 148, 148–149, 151, 156, 161, 220, 258
Martianus Capella, xvi
Mary, Virgin, 9
Maslin, Janet, 251
materialism, 41, 42, 43, 47, 56, 220
mathematics, 99, 108, 111, 114, 206, 207, 208, 213, 215, 218, 227, 253, 256. *See also* geometry

matter. *See* body
Matthew, Gospel of, 141
McFarland, Dorothy Tuck, 235
mediation: in Emerson, 173; in Hegel, 128–129, 138, 140; in William James, 182; in Novalis, 109, 111–112, 117, 122, 123, 128; in Simone Weil, 233
medicine, 5, 61
meditation. *See* contemplation
melancholy, 5, 68, 154
memory, 72–73
Menand, Louis, 251
Mendelssohn, Moses, 75–77
metaphor, 17, 20, 22, 34, 38, 45, 47, 56, 70–73, 109, 115, 117, 166, 217, 255
metaphysics, 6, 8, 28, 30, 31, 35, 65, 66, 188, 255, 259
Metaphysics (Aristotle), 41
Methodism, 214, 224n76
Michelet, Jules, 224n79
Middle Ages, 7, 59, 91, 116–120, 123, 219
Midrash, 3–4
Miller, A. V., 129
Millet, Jean François, 216, 218, 225n108
Milton, John, 214
mind: in Aristotle, 43; in Descartes, 61, 64, 66, 68; in Emerson, 164–166, 169, 171–172, 173; in Kant, 91, 95; in Kierkegaard, 145, 146, 159; in Lucretius, 43, 46–47; in Marcus Aurelius, 53; in Novalis, 113; in Bertrand Russell, 212; in Spinoza, 79–81, 82, 85–87. *See also* body
Molnár, Géza von, 109, 112, 117, 122
momentariness, 20–22, 23
monism, 254, 255, 259; in Emerson, 164, 165, 166, 169, 175–176, 178; in Hegel, 128, 129, 130, 131, 137, 143n13; in Marcus Aurelius, 55; in Spinoza, 8, 75. *See also* pantheism
Monk, Ray, 207
Montaigne, Michel de, 174
Moravians, 111
Morel, Ottoline, 213
Moses, 14, 243
Mozart, Wolfgang Amadeus, 152, 154–156, 158, 161
Murdoch, Iris, 235

Murray, Gilbert, 206
Muses, 33
music, 154–156, 255–256
mysteries, 25, 26, 36, 238, 242
mysticism: in Descartes, 255; in Emerson, 164, 165, 167; in Hegel, 137; in William James, 182, 183–185, 187, 188, 191, 194, 196, 197; in Kant, 255; in Kierkegaard, 151, 156, 157; in Bertrand Russell, 205, 208, 211, 221; in Simone Weil, 235, 245. *See also* experience, religious
myth, 26, 36, 41, 44–45, 174, 179n21, 181

nature: in Descartes, 65–67; in Ecclesiastes, 19, 21–22, 44; in Emerson, 164–173, 175–177, 254; in Epicureanism, 18; in Hegel, 131, 135; in William James, 181; in Kant, 95, 96, 97, 99, 101, 102, 105–106; in Lucretius, 44, 45, 46, 49, 56, 254; in Marcus Aurelius, 51, 53–56; in Novalis, 107, 111, 113, 116, 119; in Plato, 27–28; in Bertrand Russell, 215, 254; in Spinoza, 81, 83; in Simone Weil, 229, 232, 239–240
necessity. *See* law; nature
Neo-Platonism, 7, 26, 85, 166, 219
Nevin, Thomas, 244, 246n2, 248n78
Nietzsche, Friedrich, 48, 86, 93, 247n57, 251, 258–259
Nothing, 20, 21, 22, 23, 79, 96, 111, 124n36, 208, 241, 259
noumena, 97–99, 101–103, 104n21, 106, 108, 253, 259
Novalis, 8, 9, 105–126n81, 253, 254, 255, 256, 258, 259; and Christianity, 111, 112, 116–118, 123; and Descartes, 119; and Emerson, 168; and Hegel, 128, 132, 135, 137; and Kant, 107–110, 111, 112, 123; and Kierkegaard, 155, 161; and Plato, 113, 120, 123; and Spinoza, 108, 111; and Simone Weil, 233
Nussbaum, Martha, 2, 57n14, 57n29

observation. *See* reflection
Oedipus (Sophocles), 46

ontological argument, 65, 81, 83, 197, 238
ontology. *See* metaphysics
Orestes, 234
Osiris, 243
the other, 109–110, 111, 140, 196. *See also* relationality
otherworldliness, 251, 254–256. *See also* Sacred

Panichas, George, 243
pantheism, 83, 165, 219. *See also* monism
paranormal, 190, 191, 192, 197–198, 205, 213. *See also* ghost stories
Pascal, Blaise, 4, 61, 66, 69–70, 104n9, 228
passion(s). *See* emotions
Passover, 13
past, the, 15, 118, 149–150, 163–164, 177, 216, 218–219, 222, 227. *See also* future
Paul, Saint, xvii, 5, 46, 121, 160, 163, 171, 242
perfection, 65–66, 93, 207
Perrin, Joseph-Marie, 228, 242
Petrement, Simone, 228, 233, 238
Pfefferkorn, Kristin, 109, 114, 118, 126n74
Phaedrus (Plato), 25, 32–33, 36–39, 230
Pharisees, 3
Phenomenology of Spirit (Hegel), 127–142
Philo of Alexandria, 245
Plato, 9, 25–39, 253, 256, 258, 259, 260; and Aristotle, 41–42; and Descartes, 62, 64, 65, 66, 72; and Ecclesiastes, 23, 29; and Emerson, 167; and Hegel, 128, 129; and William James, 198; and Kant, 94, 95, 103, 106; and Kierkegaard, 148; and Lucretius, 43, 44; and Marcus Aurelius, 50, 52, 53, 54, 55, 56; and Novalis, 112, 120, 123; and religion, 8; and Bertrand Russell, 211, 213, 219, 221, 222; and Spinoza, 78, 82, 85; and Simone Weil, 227, 229, 230, 231, 235–237, 240, 243; and western philosophy, 8

pleasure, 19–20, 21, 46, 77, 79, 91, 149, 232
Plotinus, 220–221, 241
poetry: in Descartes, 72; in Emerson, 163, 168–169; in Kierkegaard, 154; in Lucretius, 47, 50; in Novalis, 109, 110, 113–116, 119–123; in Plato, 28–29, 30, 33, 34, 35, 39, 258; in romanticism, 107; in Bertrand Russell, 206, 213–214, 218, 222; in Spinoza, 77; in Simone Weil, 228, 241
Posnock, Ross, 189–190
power, 167, 171–166, 171–173, 174, 189, 212, 233, 237, 238. *See also* force
pragmatism, 7, 166, 181, 187, 188–190, 199n17, 206, 207, 208, 227
prayer, 33, 37, 67, 178, 241, 242
Prometheus, 45, 243
promise and fulfillment, 13–15, 23, 166–167, 169–172, 184
prophets, Biblical, 16, 19, 77, 79, 87, 114, 245
Proust, Marcel, 72–73, 75, 87
Proverbs (biblical text), 16, 17, 49, 77
Psalms (biblical text), 17, 95, 124n36, 215
psychical research. *See* paranormal
Pythagoras, 231, 243

Quakers, 77

Randall, James, 187
rationalism. *See* reason
reason, 256, 257–258; in Celsus, 4; in Descartes, 62–63, 65, 67; in Ecclesiastes, 22, 23; in Hegel, 133, 134; in Kant, 91–94, 96, 97, 99–100, 101–103, 218; in Lucretius, 46, 49; in Marcus Aurelius, 51, 54–55; in Plato, 31, 34, 36, 38; and rationalism, 7, 188, 213, 219; in Spinoza, 77; in Stoicism, 49; in Simone Weil, 238. *See also* ideas
reflection, 23, 116, 128–129, 147–148, 148–149, 150, 152, 155, 160, 191, 197. *See also* self-consciousness
Reines, Alvin, 10n22

relationality, 109–112, 120, 123, 130, 140–142, 177, 254, 256, 261n12. *See also* friendship
religion: definition of, 30; in Emerson, 178; and fear, 44; in William James, 181, 182–183, 185–190, 198; in Kant, 91, 102–103; in Kierkegaard, 146, 157–162; origins of, 1; and philosophy, 1–6, 8–9, 160, 178, 243, 245, 249n129, 251; in Bertrand Russell, 206, 208, 209, 210–211, 220–222. *See also* Christianity; Experience, Religious; Judaism
Republic (Plato), 25, 27–29, 29, 30, 31, 31–35, 37–39
resignation, 158–159, 161, 166, 209, 218, 230
Revelation, 1, 3, 4–5, 18
Richardson, Robert, 177, 179n11
ritual, 2, 3, 44, 50, 77, 102, 124n36, 182, 192, 237, 245
Roman religion, 50–51. *See also* gods, Roman
Romanticism, 50, 106, 107, 108, 115, 117, 124n12, 233
Rorty, Amelie, 61
Russell, Bertrand, 5, 7, 8, 8–9, 9, 205–226n133, 253, 254, 255, 256, 256–257, 258, 260; and Christianity, 207, 208, 215, 223n30; and Ecclesiastes, 214; and Hegel, 221; and David Hume, 228; and William James, 205–206, 207, 208, 220; and Kant, 210, 211, 221; and Lucretius, 220; and Plato, 211, 213, 219, 221, 222; and Spinoza, 78, 81, 211, 212, 213, 221; and Simone Weil, 227–228, 231

the sacred, 6, 8, 252, 254–256; in Aristotle, 41, 42; in Descartes, 61, 71, 255; in Ecclesiastes, 23; in Emerson, 166, 168, 175–178, 254; in Hegel, 129, 130, 132, 138–139, 142, 145, 155, 254; in William James, 182, 183–185, 197, 253; in Kant, 91, 95, 97, 98–99, 102–103, 253, 255; in Kierkegaard, 148, 149, 150, 151, 152–153, 154–155, 157–158; in Lucretius, 48, 49; in

Marcus Aurelius, 50, 51, 54, 254; in Novalis, 110–111, 112, 123, 253; in Plato, 29, 30, 31, 254; in Bertrand Russell, 207–208, 210, 211, 213–214, 217, 218, 221, 253; in Spinoza, 83, 84, 254; in Simone Weil, 229–231, 238, 241, 248n94, 253, 254. *See also* God; Good
sacrifice, 44, 56, 134, 142, 148, 158, 159–160, 220, 233
Samkhya philosophy, 47–49
Samuel, 2nd (biblical text), 141
Santayana, George, 201n57
Schelling, Friedrich Wilhelm, 164, 172
Schlegel, Friedrich, 113–116, 125n62
Schleiermacher, Friedrich, 123
science, 9, 41, 49–50, 61, 66, 100, 104n27, 111, 137, 139, 169, 182, 198, 206–207, 218, 219, 237, 259. *See also* mathematics
Sedgwick, Eve Kosofsky, 201n47
self-consciousness, 256; in Descartes, 63–64, 68, 252; in Ecclesiastes, 22–23, 252; in Emerson, 166, 170; in Hegel, 127–130, 131–137, 138–142, 148, 252; in Idealism, 108; in Kant, 107–108; in Kierkegaard, 147–148, 148, 252; in Novalis, 107–108, 110, 114, 121, 253; in Spinoza, 79, 85–86. *See also* reflection; self-division
self-containment, 259; in Aristotle, 42; in Descartes, 64–65, 66, 68–69, 70; in Ecclesiastes, 23; in Emerson, 175; in Kant, 91, 98, 101, 109; in Lucretius, 48; in Marcus Aurelius, 51, 56; in Novalis, 108–109, 114, 115–116, 120; in Plato, 30, 36; in Spinoza, 80, 83–84, 85, 88
self-deception, 93–94, 128, 131, 141–142, 170
self-division: in Descartes, 59, 63–64; in Hegel, 128–129, 133, 134–135, 141; in Henry James, 191; in William James, 183, 185–186, 189, 190; in Kant, 95, 98–99; in Kierkegaard, 147; in Marcus Aurelius, 53; in Novalis, 123; in Bertrand Russell, 206–207; in Simone Weil, 241

sensation, 37, 134, 137, 138, 140, 155–156, 170, 232
Septuagint, 245, 250n145
Sethi, Mira, 202n65
sexism, 189–191, 193, 200n41
Silber, John, 98
silence, 157, 159, 160
Simchat Torah, 13
sin, 22
sister-brother relation, 137, 234
Sisyphus, 45
skepticism, 60, 61, 63, 172, 174
Smith, Alys, 215
Smith, Wilfred Cantwell, 5, 10n20, 251
Socrates. *See* Plato
solitude, 157, 175, 182, 205, 214, 216, 217
Solomon (biblical figure), 16, 77
Song of Songs (biblical text), 1, 49
soul: in Aristotle, 42–43; in Descartes, 61, 67; in Emerson, 164; in Lucretius, 43, 47; in Marcus Aurelius, 50, 53, 56; in Plato, 26, 28–29, 30–31, 33–34, 35–37, 38, 256; in Samkhya philosophy, 49; in Simone Weil, 239
Spinoza, xv, 75–88, 256, 257, 259, 260; and Christianity, 75–77; and Descartes, 61, 70, 75, 77–79, 81, 83, 84–85, 87–88; and Ecclesiastes, 77, 78; and Emerson, 164, 166, 171, 174; and Hegel, 127, 137; and Judaism, 75–77, 78, 89n15; and William James, 186, 187, 195; and Kant, 81, 91, 92, 96, 98, 99, 100, 101, 103, 104n8; and Kierkegaard, 79, 157, 158; and Lucretius, 81; and Marcus Aurelius, 81; and metaphysics, 8; and Novalis, 108, 111; and Plato, 78, 82, 85; portraits of, xvi; and religion, 8; and Bertrand Russell, 78, 81, 211, 212, 221; and science, 9; and Simone Weil, 86, 232–233, 235, 239–240, 241
spirit: in Emerson, 165–166, 167, 168, 171; in Hegel, 127, 129–130, 131, 132–133, 134, 138–139, 141–142; in Kant, 106, 114, 127; in Lucretius, 43; in Novalis, 121; in Bertrand Russell, 212
spirituality, meaning of, 6

Steiner, George, 251–252, 260
Stoicism, 40, 41, 43, 49, 51, 52, 54, 55, 56, 96, 137, 165, 171, 174, 221, 232, 243
story-telling, 258; in Novalis, 109, 115–116, 118–119, 121; in Plato, 26; and religion, 1–2, 44; in Bertrand Russell, 208, 213, 219; in Spinoza, 77; in Simone Weil, 233. *See also* ghost stories; myth
subconscious, 183, 190, 191–192, 193–194, 209
suffering, 2, 8, 257, 258; in Descartes, 61, 68; in Ecclesiastes, 14, 19, 21, 22; in Emerson, 166–167, 170, 174, 178; in Hegel, 130, 133–135, 141–142; in Henry James, 190–191, 193, 195, 196; in William James, 181, 183, 185–186, 191; in Judaism, 13; in Kant, 93–94, 95; in Kierkegaard, 147, 150, 151, 152, 153–154, 157; in Lucretius, 43–47; in Marcus Aurelius, 50, 51–52, 55–56; in Novalis, 109, 115, 119; in Plato, 26; in Bertrand Russell, 205–206, 213–217; in Spinoza, 77, 86, 202n74; in Simone Weil, 233–235, 236, 238, 240, 241–242. *See also* therapy
suicide, 46, 183, 214, 220, 224n80
Sukkot, 13
surprise. *See* wonder
symbol, 168. *See also* metaphor
Symposium (Plato), 1

Taoism, 230, 231, 242
Taylor, Charles, 6, 223n26
Taylor, Jeremy, 214
Tertullian, 4–5, 10n16
Thalmann, Marianne, 113
therapy, xv, 5, 8, 258–260; in Aristotle, 42; in Descartes, 61, 62–64, 67–70; in Ecclesiastes, 19, 22, 23; in Emerson, 166–167, 168, 171; in Hegel, 131; in William James, 183; in Kant, 95, 99, 101; in Kierkegaard, 154, 156; in Lucretius, 44, 46–47; in Marcus Aurelius, 52–54, 55; in Plato, 29, 30–31; in Spinoza, 78–81, 86–87
Thibon, Gustave, 228, 233, 239
Thomas à Kempis, 225n92

Thomas Aquinas, 60
thought. *See* mind
Tieck, Ludwig, 116
Timaeus (Plato), 28–29, 54, 240, 243
Tocqueville, Alexis de, 9
Tolstoy, Leo, 46
Townsend, Kim, 189–190
Tracy, David, 235, 237
truth: in Descartes, 63–64, 66; in Emerson, 163; in William James, 188; in Lucretius, 49; in Plato, 30, 35; in Bertrand Russell, 206–208, 209–212, 214, 218, 219, 221; in Spinoza, 87; in Simone Weil, 228
Turner, Victor, 191

uncertainty. *See* interrogative mood
Unitarianism, 163
Upanishads, 49, 185, 191
Updike, John, 202n63

Van Gogh, Vincent, 8, 214–218, 255
Van Ness, Wilhelmina, 235
Venus, 48–49
Veto, Miklos, 240
vision: in Descartes, 65–66; in Emerson, 166, 167, 168, 170, 176, 177; in Lucretius, 43; in Marcus Aurelius, 55; in Plato, 34–37; in Bertrand Russell, 206, 209–210, 212

Weil, Andre, 227, 233, 234, 244
Weil, Simone, xvii, 5, 7, 8, 9, 227–250n153, 251, 254, 256, 257, 258, 259, 260; and Christianity, 228–229, 231, 233, 241–245; and Descartes, 70, 228, 230, 231, 235, 237–238, 241; and Ecclesiastes, 231–232; and Emerson, 235; and Hegel, 233–234; and William James, 234–235; and Judaism, 229, 243–245; and Kant, 229, 230, 231, 235, 240–241; and Kierkegaard, 160, 228, 234; and Lucretius, 232; and Marcus Aurelius, 232; and Novalis, 233; and Plato, 227, 229, 230, 231, 235–237, 240, 243; and Bertrand Russell, 227–228, 231; and Spinoza, 86, 232–233, 235, 239–240, 241
Weil, Sylvie, 227, 233, 234, 235, 244
Whicher, Stephen, 166, 179n19
Whitehead, Alfred North, 206
Whitehead, Evelyn, 206
will: in Descartes, 62, 63, 68, 69; in Emerson, 175; in William James, 187, 188–189, 196; in Kant, 93, 95, 98, 99–100, 101; in Bertrand Russell, 211; in Simone Weil, 241; in Spinoza, 83. *See also* power
wisdom: in Ecclesiastes, 14–15, 16, 22; in Hegel, 139; and philosophy, 1; in Plato, 28, 30, 32, 36; in Proverbs, 49; in Bertrand Russell, 209; and Virgin Mary, 9
Wittgenstein, Ludwig, 228
Wolfson, Harry Austryn, 91
Wood, Alan, 208, 209
Woolf, Virginia, 203n89
wonder, 2, 68, 69–70, 96, 97, 121, 141, 159–160, 161, 173, 255
work, 19, 151, 232, 234, 237, 248n78
world. *See* nature

Yeats, William Butler, 88

Zeus, 25, 51, 54
Zwarg, Christina, 180n31

About the Author

Ernest Rubinstein is adjunct assistant professor of humanities at the New York University School of Continuing and Professional Studies and an associate librarian emeritus at Drew University. He has taught also at Drew University, the New School University, and in synagogue settings. He has written two previous books, *An Episode of Jewish Romanticism: Franz Rosenzweig's* Star of Redemption, and *Religion and the Muse: The Vexed Relation between Religion and Western Literature*. His scholarly interest is most broadly in areas of intersection between philosophical, religious, and aesthetic sensibility.

CPSIA information can be obtained at www.ICGtesting.com
Printed in the USA
BVOW03*2350270714

360501BV00003B/3/P

9 781611 477245